EU Law in Ireland

EU Law in Ireland

By
Dr Elaine Fahey

CLARUS
PRESS

Published by
Clarus Press Ltd,
Griffith Campus,
South Circular Road,
Dublin 8.

Typeset by
Datapage International Limited,
157 Rathmines Road Upper,
Rathmines,
Dublin 6.

Printed by
CPI Anthony Rowe,
Chippenham,
Wiltshire,
UK.

ISBN
978-1-905536-30-6

FOREWORD

As Ireland faces into the fortieth year of membership of the European Union, Dr Fahey's book is to be welcomed. The book contains an examination of many fundamental concepts of EU law and its impact on the Irish legal system. The manner in which the relevant law is approached by the author, intertwined with an analysis of the political landscape in which it was framed, is a novel approach on which she should be commended.

Dr Fahey has provided a comprehensive review of contemporary issues in EU law as it applies in this country. The study, in Chapter 9, of the law relating to the European Arrest Warrant is particularly welcome. This new EU procedure introduced significant changes to the prior law and practice relating to extradition has been the subject of many decisions of the Courts in this Jurisdiction since its introduction. The clarity with which Dr Fahey deals with this complicated matter will be appreciated by both practitioners and students of the law alike.

While this book together with the wealth of legal authority it contains will be beneficial to lawyers and those in academic circles, Dr Fahey's scholarship and obvious command of her subject will allow the book to be accessible to people without a legal background who might be interested in EU law in Ireland. I congratulate Dr Fahey on the production of this worthy addition to Irish legal writing.

MARY FINLAY GEOGHEGAN
The High Court
6th October 2010

PREFACE

A rather critical eye may be cast on various Irish institutional actors in EU law and it is with this prism or perspective that the text herein adopts. While the Supreme Court alone may be an isolated place of expertise and careful case management in the main, a not insignificant number of litigants have been denied their rightful remedies as a matter of EU law in various courts and by virtue of poor legislative drafting or mis-implemented provisions. This might seem veering towards an overstatement but one need only consider the shameful drafting of the original European arrest warrant Act 2003 which alone has spawned a startling number of Supreme Court appeals and taken a huge workload allowance from the highest Court. Also, the haphazard means by which the Oireachtas has accepted its new responsibilities pursuant to the Treaty of Lisbon leaves a lot to be desired. There are certainly many litigants who ought to have been able to avail of the doctrines of direct effect, indirect effect and supremacy, but were thwarted by interpretations thereof in the national courts. All of the foregoing is explored in the text which follows, but after nearly forty years of membership of the European Union, this remains a quite curious state of affairs to be exploring at this point.

Readers are advised that specialist texts on EU law should be consulted at first instance and that the text herein purports to be only a modest contribution at national level and no more. The voluminous core texts of Craig and De Burca and Chalmers *et al* remain core companion texts for students and readers of EU law generally.

An effort is made throughout this work to set out the operation of certain key legal doctrines of EU law in the national context and recent Irish developments. On account of the reasonably straightforward acceptance of the doctrines of direct effect and indirect effect in Irish law, the text here focuses upon the Emanation of the State doctrine in Irish law, where controversy is centred and a briefer account of the aforementioned doctrine then takes place, briefer than the reader might have anticipated.

The peaceful surroundings of the Tuscan Hills of Florence provided a very sympathetic backdrop for what has been a far from peaceful labour! I am grateful to the library staff of the European University Institute, Florence, Dublin Institute of Technology, Aungier Street, Christopher Fretwell of the Court of Justice, Luxembourg and the Irish Supreme Court office staff for their help. I am grateful also to participants at seminars, workshops and conferences in the EUI Florence, the University of Salford, Greater Manchester, Trinity College Dublin, the Irish Society for Comparative Law and the University of Birmingham, where various parts of the text or ideas therein were developed and reflected upon. I am grateful for the support and multi-faceted infrastructure of the EUI Max Weber Programme which assisted me in completing this project. Thanks to Ian Kavanagh, Declan Walsh, Bruno de Witte for their help. Thanks also to John Bruton. I am grateful to David McCartney of Clarus Press for his assistance with this project. A special thanks to Gergo for all his support!

All errors and omissions are solely those of the author.

Elaine Fahey
September 2010

CONTENTS

TABLE OF CASES

TABLE OF LEGISLATION

Acts of the Oireachtas

Secondary Irish Legislation

EU Treaties

European Union

International Treaties and Conventions

Other Jurisdictions

CHAPTER 1
Overview of EU Law in the Irish State 1973–2010

Background

[1–01] The diverse cycles of historical, economic and political changes occurring over almost four decades of Irish membership of the European Union (EU) do not form a linear account. The legal dimension of this evolving relationship of "Ireland within the European Union" is to similar effect. The experience of the Irish legal order and the European project over thirty-seven years, i.e. 1973–2010, should be particularly distinctive in view of the timing of Irish accession to the (then) European Economic Community (EEC). Politically and legally, the consequences of membership were well known, with their implications for domestic constitutionalism.[1] Membership for Ireland began at a time of economic and constitutional stagnation at domestic and European level, yet eventually Ireland would become, temporarily at least, a major economic success story in an enlarged Europe of immense regulatory powers and increasing geographical landmass.[2] The Irish judiciary, over time, would become more *communautaire*, European law would increasingly penetrate all public and private spheres of life and pro-European sentiment would, in the main, be domestically widespread.[3] Ireland would join the Euro-zone, admit new "enlargement citizens" as

---

[1] See, for an early account, Robinson, "The Irish European Communities Act, 1972" (1973) 10 CMLR 352 and 467.

[2] See, as to the initial experience and recent "boom years and aftermath", Laffan and O'Mahony, *Ireland and the European Union* (Palgrove, Basingstoke, 2008); O'Donnell ed., *Europe: The Irish Experience* (IIEA, 2000); Coombes ed., *Ireland and the European Communities: Ten years of membership* (Gill and Macmillan, Dublin, 1983); Laffan and O'Mahony, "Managing Europe from an Irish Perspective: Critical Junctures and the Increasing Formalisation of the Core Executive in Ireland" (2007) 85 *Public Administration* 167; Sweeney *The Celtic Tiger: Ireland's Continuing Economic Miracle* (2nd ed., Oak Tree Press, Cork, 1999); Geary, *An Inconvenient Wait- Ireland's Quest for Membership of the EEC 1957–1973* (IPA, 2010); Kelly, "The Irish Credit Bubble" UCD Centre For Economic Research *Working Paper Series* WP09/32 (2009); O' Mahony, "Ireland's EU Referendum Experience" (2009) 24 *Irish Political Studies* 429.

[3] See *Campus Oil v Minister for Industry and Energy* [1983] IR 82; *ICMSA v Government of Ireland* (Unreported, High Court, Barrington J, 25 October 1979); *Doyle v An Taoiseach* [1986] ILRM 693.

workers after 2004 (unlike many other States), but would also be part of a "separatist" group, opting-out of the Schengen Acquis and availing of the complicated provisions of constitutional differentiation as well as obtaining the infamous Abortion Protocol in the Treaty of Maastricht. Several referenda on Treaties ranging from the Single European Act to the Treaty of Lisbon would see the Irish voters often as the singular "legitimation" of European Treaty developments. Two negative referendum results would be reversed by later successful polls to alter the earlier result. The relationship between Ireland and Europe throughout this thirty-seven year period is thus dramatic, controversial and constant, as well as, paradoxically, one of change.

[1–02] While the relationship of the Irish Supreme Court with European Convention of Human Rights (ECHR) law in 2010 may now be an issue of major controversy,[4] the Irish judiciary is overwhelmingly pro-*communautaire* in matters of EU law. Key legal doctrines of EU law regarding, for example, supremacy and direct effect, well-established from the outset of Irish membership of the EEC (as it then was), were embraced earlier and much more readily and consistently than amongst its closest common law counterpart, the British judiciary.[5] Almost half of the Irish Supreme Court bench, including the Chief Justice, have served on of the Court of Justice in Luxembourg.[6]

---

[4] See the strangely defensive landmark Supreme Court decision on the particulars of the incorporation of the European Convention on Human Rights into Irish law, *McD v L* [2009] IESC 81, a fuller discussion of which is outside the scope of the current work, suffice to say that the decision could ultimately permit Irish courts to act in defiance of the jurisprudence of the European Court of Human Rights. Although see the recent preliminary reference from the Supreme Court on the question of the impact of the Charter of Fundamental Rights on Council Regulation (EC) 2201/2003 now legally binding after the ratification of the Treaty of Lisbon in relation to the custody rights of an unmarried father: *McB v E* [2010] IESC 48, pursuant to the urgent preliminary reference procedure (Art 104b Rules of Procedure of the Court of Justice). There are still those who reflect on a legal order where the Supreme Court would adopt a position analogous to the German Constitutional Court, for example see Phelan, "Can Ireland legislate contrary to European Community law?" (2010) 33 ELR 530, considered above.

[5] For a superb account on the evolution of EU law in the UK courts and the relatively mild reception given by the Law Lords to EU law since accession, in anticipation of the actions of the new UK Supreme Court, see Arnull, "The Law Lords and the European Union: swimming with the tide" (2010) 35 ELR 57. But *cf.* Lord Mance (writing extra-judicially) emphasising the effectiveness of UK institutional actors in EU affairs: "Opting into Community law and interpreting Convention rights: is the United Kingdom more or less committed?" (2009) July (3) PL 544, and also writing in a judicial capacity, when referring questions to the Court of Justice in *Office of Communications (Respondent) v The Information Commission (Appellant)* (UK Supreme Court, 27 January 2010), where he cited the "duty" on the court to refer such questions, i.e. taking careful cognisance of the EU law-obligations of last instance courts. I am grateful to Declan Walsh for drawing my attention to the latter.

[6] See above. As to the relatively unproblematic acceptance of supremacy and direct effect in Ireland, where judicial review is a constitutional mechanism enshrined in the Irish Constitution since 1937, see Hogan and Whelan, *Ireland and the European Union: Constitutional and Statutory Texts and Commentary* (Butterworths, Dublin, 1995). But see also Phelan, *Revolt or Revolution: The Constitutional Boundaries of the European Community* (Round Hall, Dublin, 1997). See the relative ease with which the Supreme Court dealt with, for example, interim relief as to the operation of a statute in *Pesca Valentia Ltd v Minister for Fisheries* [1985] IR 193, which contrasts markedly with the constitutional crisis generated in the UK by Case C-213/89 *R. v Secretary of State for Transport, ex parte Factortame* [1990] ECR I-2433.

By way of background to the ensuing text, an effort is made here to outline the operation and genesis of EU law in Ireland over nearly forty years, employing four general headings (rather loosely), those being: (1) Irish politics within the EU; (2) Irish litigation at EU level; (3) domestic constitutional questions and EU law; and (4) the Irish Supreme Court and EU law. **[1–03]**

Irish Politics Within the European Union

As to Irish politics within the EU, the relationship of the UK with the EU is often depicted as awkward or troubled, earning the UK a reputation as the "European Union's trickiest customer".[7] This label is not, however, used by commentators referring to Ireland when describing its EU credentials. As to policy, similar to the UK and throughout many decades of EU membership since accession, Irish concerns expressed in the lead in to the adoption of the Constitutional Treaty (and to a lesser extent the Treaty of Lisbon) related to tax harmonisation, foreign policy and some aspects of Justice and Home Affairs and they continue now to be areas of sensitivity. Ireland maintains the need for unanimity in these areas, although this position is rarely antagonistic and is usually rooted in the UK policy position.[8] The failures of the Nice I and Lisbon I referenda have been portrayed in a variety of ways.[9] Such portrayals, however, do not posit Euro-scepticism on the part of Ireland or its people or relate it to **[1–04]**

---

[7] Fletcher, "Schengen, the European Court of Justice and Flexibility under the Lisbon Treaty: Balancing the United Kingdom's 'Ins' and 'Outs'" (2009) 5 ECLR 71, 76, who cites George, *An Awkward Partner: Britain in the European Union* (Oxford, Oxford University Press, 1998) and Wall, *Stranger in Europe: Britain and the European Union from Thatcher to Blair* (Oxford University Press, Oxford, 2008). See also Fahey, "Swimming in a sea of law: Reflections on water borders, Irish (British)-Euro Relations and opting-out and opting-in after the Treaty of Lisbon" (2010) 47(3) CMLR 645.

[8] See Brown, *The Debate on the Future of the European Union in Ireland* (Institute of European Affairs, Dublin, 2003), quoting an address give by the then Minister for Foreign Affairs and current Taoiseach, Mr Brian Cowen TD, prior to the signing of the Constitutional Treaty. See the results also of the research commissioned after the first negative referendum result on the Treaty of Lisbon- *Post-LisbonTreaty Research Findings* (Millward Brown IMS, Dublin, September 2008), http://www.imsl.ie/ conducted on 2,101 adults.

[9] The European Commission has produced a report documenting how the Irish media has become more Eurosceptic and tabloid in recent years. The "changing media landscape" between 2002 and 2008 is identified as an important determinant of changes in public opinion which influenced the Lisbon referendum: see "Irish media more Eurosceptic, warns EC report", *The Irish Times*, (2 September 2008). Equally, extensive efforts were made to quell Commission discussion of a common corporate tax base in the lead-in to the Lisbon II referendum in Ireland, on the basis that the harmonisation of corporate tax rates might have induced the Irish business lobby to turn against the Lisbon Treaty after, for a number of years, enjoying one of the lowest corporate tax rates in the European Union ("EU corporate tax plan delayed to at least end-2009" (Reuters, 30 January 2009) http://www.reuters.com/article/rbssBanks/idUSLU68494320090130. Equally, the Commission expended considerable resources in Ireland on explaining the Lisbon Treaty to citizens, facing down accusations that the Commission was circumventing a difficult legal position subsisting in Ireland that the Government of the day was not constitutionally empowered to fund a "Yes" vote in a constitutional referendum, even in European affairs, a criticism that the Commission rejected: "Commission rebuffs Irish pro-Lisbon 'propaganda" (EurActiv, 5 February 2009) http://www.euractiv.com/en/eu-elections/commission-rebuffs-irish-pro-lisbon-propaganda/article-179164.

Irish-British relations, indicating the paradox or ambiguity that surrounds Ireland as an actor within the EU.

[1–05] There are some who suggest that the continued Irish support for British policies in European affairs during the UK Blair government years was to the detriment of Ireland and at the expense of developing ongoing links and strategic alliances in policy and practices with continental countries.[10] Moreover, it has been asserted that there has been a continual "drift" by the main Irish government party, Fianna Fáil, in power continuously for over a decade to the present day[11] towards closer association with Britain, entailing that it is now necessary to avoid feeding renewed continental suspicions that Ireland is a veritable "British satellite".[12] However, there appears to be an increasing tendency for Ireland to adopt "Euro-sceptic" strategies in its dealings at European level, whereby it frequently follows the lead of the UK in European affairs, perhaps more so than in its initial years of membership of the Communities. Fianna Fáil has only recently joined the Liberals Group (ALDE: Alliance of Liberals and Democrats for Europe Group) in the European Parliament and has come under some degree of criticism for the manner in which it has begun to operate within this political dynamic for abstaining from critical votes, for example.[13] Irish-European politics is manifestly not at the heart of mainstream European Union politics in Europe.

The Irish State and EU Litigation

[1–06] As to the actions of the Irish State as to EU litigation, in the context of the former Third Pillar (prior to its abolition by the Treaty of Lisbon), Ireland had not accepted the jurisdiction of the Court of Justice pursuant to ex Article 35 EU[14] and voluminous judgments, for example, have been delivered by the Irish Supreme Court as to the

[10] See Fitzgerald, "Irish Support for Blair was damaging to our interests" *The Irish Times* (31 October 2009). Fitzgerald, a former (Fine Gael) Taoiseach (Prime Minister of Ireland), cites a more recent practical example of the Irish support for Blair (former UK Prime Minister) for the position of President of the European Council, in lieu of supporting the policies of other small size states or even States of similar political character, a stance which was ultimately not successful.

[11] Along with the Green Party since the General Election in 2007.

[12] See Fitzgerald *ibid.* Arguably, he fails to consider the importance of post-Belfast Agreement Good Friday (Good Friday Agreement) Peace Deal developments in 1998 and their resulting influence on British-Irish relations. Strand III of the Good Friday Agreement provided for the establishment of a British-Irish Intergovernmental Conference to promote bilateral co-operation between the Irish and British Governments. The Conference was established in December 1999, replacing the Anglo-Irish Conference established under the Anglo-Irish Agreement of 1985. It brings the two Governments together to promote bilateral co-operation at all levels on matters of mutual interest. The Irish Constitution was also amended in the wake of the Good Friday Agreement in respect of Irish Citizenship law and a controversial Supreme Court decision and immigration boom into the Celtic Tiger economy: now see Arts 2 and 9 of the Irish Constitution and the Irish Nationality and Immigration Act 2001 and the Twenty-Seventh Amendment of the Constitution Act 2004. Prior to these changes, the entitlement of persons born on the island to citizenship was statutory in origin and not everyone born on the island of Ireland was entitled to citizenship.

[13] Fianna Fáil were, until recently, part of a now defunct anti-federalist grouping within the European Parliament, demonstrating that finding a European political family has not been an easy task for the centre-right main coalition government party.

[14] And has not at the time of writing.

European arrest warrant, often raising serious substantive and procedural issues, in the absence of supervision from the Court of Justice.[15] In more recent times, serious reservations expressed over Irish participation, for example in the European arrest warrant, are well-documented, on account of national sovereignty and its common law criminal justice legal order.[16] However, the need to respond effectively to terrorism in the wake of the attacks of 11 September 2001 ("9/11") was prioritised by Ireland. Litigation trends before the Court of Justice indicate that Ireland frequently supports the UK in direct actions and preliminary references.[17] Recently, during the Treaty of Lisbon negotiations, the Irish Minister for Foreign Affairs came under pressure domestically not to opt-out of the Charter of Fundamental Rights and not to position Ireland strategically alongside the UK and Poland, who took a more hard-line negotiating stance.[18] Ireland was notably outvoted in recent times in the Council of Ministers during the adoption of the controversial Data Retention Directive[19] and litigated this isolation unsuccessfully in 2006.[20] This legal challenge, on account of being outvoted, represented an unusual move for Ireland on its own accord, traditionally not initiating such challenges at European Union level.[21] The case of *Ireland v Council and*

[15] This area is discussed above in Ch 9. A similar position prevails for the UK and Denmark. The level of acceptance of this jurisdiction has proven to be rather uneven across the Member States and some conflicting notices have been published also: see OJ 2005 L 327 p 19; 1999 OJ C 120 p 24; OJ 2005 L 327 p 16.

[16] O'Mahony and Payne, *Negotiating European Issues: National Strategies and Priorities* (OEUE Phase I Occasional Paper 1.2-11.03), who provide a fascinating account of the political negotiation of the European arrest warrant from an Irish perspective. See Cowen, "The European Constitution" (2005) 12 IJEL 169.

[17] Discussed below in Ch 6.

[18] Witness, for example, the furore at national level as to the decision of the Government on whether to opt-out of the Charter of Fundamental Rights, ultimately not taken on account of the reaction of Trade Unions in Ireland: *The Irish Times* (5 October 2007); see also "Ireland and Poland get 'opt-out' option on EU rights charter" *EU Observer* (26 June 2007). Limiting the scope of the Charter represented one of the red lines of the UK negotiating teams.

[19] Directive 2006/24/EC of the European Parliament and of the Council of 15 March 2006 on the retention of data generated or processed in connection with the provision of publicly available electronic communications services or of public communications networks and amending Directive 2002/58/EC p 5.

[20] In 2004, France, Ireland, Sweden and the UK introduced a proposal for a draft framework decision under Title IV EU which would have harmonised data retention obligations of service providers. Directive 2006/24/EC, which purported to harmonise the laws of the Member States with respect to data retention so as to ensure the data is available to investigate serious crime, was later adopted pursuant to Art 95 EC (now Art 114 TFEU) in response to terrorism concerns arising within the European Union, with its preamble specifically and explicitly referencing the London terrorist attacks of July 2005. However, in the adoption of the instrument, both Ireland and Slovakia were both outvoted in the Council of Ministers and notably, the Directive benefited from an unusually speedy conception and publication (Ireland litigated its "out voting"- Case C-301/06, *Ireland v Parliament and Council* [2009] ECR 1-0593). The actions may be attributable to the out-spoken stance of a recent Minister for Justice: see Fahey "The Irish Challenge to the Data Retention Directive: Reflecting on Irish litigation in the European Legal Order" (Paper delivered at Society of Legal Scholars Annual Conference, September 2008 (available from the author)).

[21] Litigation trends before the Court of Justice indicate that Ireland frequently supports the UK in direct actions and preliminary references: See Fahey *ibid.*

European Parliament,[22] however, involves Ireland acting as antagonistic litigator, challenging legal norms within the EU legal order and indicated a new dynamic in Irish-European litigation, although this litigation could be attributable to the outspoken stance of a recent Minister for Justice.[23] Once more, there is conflicting evidence of Ireland participating haphazardly but also strategically in European litigation.

[1–07] Low rates of preliminary references from the Irish courts (and there were zero references in 2009),[24] low participation rates as interveners in litigation before the Court of Justice by the Irish State and a relatively poor compliance rate by the State with implementation of internal market legislation, until recently, have cumulatively characterised Ireland as litigator at European level.[25] Ireland recently mounted a campaign against an unfavourable decision to the State of the Court of Justice (Grand Chamber). The State lobbied extensively for the amendment of the related Directive, engaging in an unsuccessful battle of unparalleled proportions.[26] It seems difficult, however, to suggest that Ireland could ever be a "repeat player" at European level, like Ryanair or the European Commission, for example, a concept derived from US political science theory, denoting corporate bodies or associations who litigate frequently or the converse of a "once-off" litigator. The Irish initiation of litigation as to European issues has in reality been both exceptional and remarkable.[27] While it is possible for small Member States in the EU to "punch above their weight" politically, as a matter of policy, Ireland has excluded itself from key EU policies on account of Irish-British relations, for example, as to the Schengen Agreement and the Area of Freedom, Security and Justice (AFSJ).[28] The failure of the State to employ litigation so as to gain influence or to contribute to policy areas from which it is excluded is then remarkable. Ultimately, Ireland does not sit well in theoretical terms as regards its exercise of policy

---

[22] Case C-301/06 *Ireland v Council and European Parliament* [2009] ECR I-0593.

[23] *ibid.*

[24] Although in *Goshawk Dedicated Ltd v Life Receivables Irl. Ltd* [2009] IESC 7, the Supreme Court expressly indicated that it would refer questions to the Court of Justice but no order for reference was made in 2009 and the proceedings were still before the Supreme Court in 2010. See above Ch 6. A major shift seems apparent in 2010, however, with three references pending at the time of writing, as well as two others to be lodged, three from the High Court and two from the Supreme Court.

[25] See above Ch 6.

[26] Case C-127/08 *Metock and Others v Minister for Justice, Equality and Law Reform* [2008] 3 CMLR 39, where the Irish legislation implementing the Citizen Rights Directive and the controversial decision of the Court in Case C-109/01 *Secretary of State for the Home Department v Akrich* [2003] ECR I-9607 were successfully challenged. See the reaction of the State in *The Irish Times,* (22 September 2008) and its unsuccessful campaign in Smyth "How do we close information gap between Dublin and Brussels?" *The Irish Times* (29 September 2009). However, the European Communities (Free Movement of Persons) (Amendment) Regulations 2008 (SI No. 310/2008) were passed swiftly to give effect to the decision.

[27] Discussed below further in Ch 6. As to the conceptual point, see Galanter, "Why the 'Haves' Come Out Ahead: Speculations of the limits of legal change" (1974) 9 *Law & Society* 95.

[28] See generally, Panke, *Small States in the European Union: Coping with Structural Disadvantages* (Routledge, Ashgate, London, 2010).

preferences in a multi-speed Europe, saying "yes" to Euro-membership and Charter of Fundamental Rights and "no" (to a degree) to Schengen and the AFSJ.[29]

Domestic Constitutional Questions and EU Law

The new constitutional provisions introduced by way of referendum in order to facilitate the Irish State's participation in the "variable geometry"[30] provisions of the Treaties of Amsterdam and Nice and now Lisbon respectively,[31] have entailed that there are aspects of membership of the EU that are mediated through "flexible constitutionalism". This permits the Oireachtas acting alone, i.e. without a referendum, to sanction participation in diverse areas of the "variable geometry" that is currently two-tier Europe. No further constitutional referenda are necessary in order for the State to so participate in certain areas. Thus, a *pragmatic* approach is adopted as to constitutionalism, providing for an alternative means of protecting sovereignty. **[1–08]**

The decision of the Supreme Court in *Crotty v An Taoiseach*[32] has entailed that a referendum has been held consistently since that decision on European Treaty ratification. The decision there prescribed that a Treaty had to be submitted by referendum to the people where a proposed Treaty altered the scope and objectives of the Communities (now Union) such that the initial popular consent to EU membership had been exceeded and has led to many protracted, controversial and expensive ratification referenda. It would seem that certain referenda have been held to satisfy political, as opposed to constitutional, expectations (for example, the referenda as to Amsterdam and Nice). The defeated Nice I and Lisbon I referenda aside, the Irish electorate has been broadly in favour of the European Union, unlike the British electorate.[33] The Third Amendment to the Constitution Bill, 1971, put to the people so as to accede to the European Economic Community, as it then was, was passed by plebiscite in 1972 by 1,041,890 votes in favour of the amendment, 211,891 **[1–09]**

---

[29] Jensen and Slapin, "Institutional Hokey-Pokey: The Politics of Multispeed Integration in the European Union" (UCD Dublin European Institute Working Paper 10/01).

[30] As to which see Hogan and Whyte, *Kelly: The Irish Constitution*, (Butterworths, Dublin, 2003) para 5.3.86 *et seq*; Brown, *Enhanced Cooperation: A Two Tier Europe* (Institute of European Affairs, 2002); see Travers, "The Reception of Community Legislation into Irish law and Related Issues Revisited" (2003) 37 *Irish Jurist* 58; Usher "European Union Variable geometry or concentric circles: patterns for the European Union" (1997) 46 ICLQ 243; Harmsen "European Union: A European Union of variable geometry: problems and perspectives" (1994) 45 NILQ 109.

[31] See the Eighteenth, Twenty-Sixth and Twenty-Eighth Amendments to the Constitution respectively.

[32] *Crotty v An Taoiseach* [1987] IR 713. It has forced difficult referenda campaigns for each new European treaty upon the hapless electorate, a point made by Fanning, "Lisbon Vote is not Democracy but an Exercise in Buck-Passing" *The Irish Times* (22 April 2008).

[33] See http://ec.europa.eu/public_opinion/index_en.htm for the latest Irish results but in particular see Flash "Eurobarometer Attitudes towards the European Union in the UK" (Flash EB No 274 — Gallup, July, 2009). Hogan and Whyte, *Kelly: The Irish Constitution* (4th ed., Lexis-Nexis, 2003) para 5.3.45 *et seq*; Sinnott, and Quinlan "Soft Supporters of the EU need to be inspired to vote Yes to Lisbon Treaty" *The Irish Times* (30 January, 2008). See Hogan, "The Nice Treaty and the Irish Constitution" (2001) 7 EPL 565, Hourihane ed., *Ireland and the European Union: The First Thirty Years 1973–2002* (Lilliput Press, Dublin, 2003) and Costello, "Peoples' Vengeances: Ireland's Nice Referenda" (2005) 1 ECLR 357.

against.[34] The Treaty of Maastricht was passed by 68.7% of the electorate in 1993, the Treaty of Amsterdam was passed by 61.7% of the voting electorate in 1998, the Treaty of Nice was passed on a second successful attempt (the first referendum being unsuccessful) by 63% of the voting electorate.[35] The first Treaty of Lisbon referendum was rejected by 53.4% of the population (862,415) where the turnout was 53.1% (1,614,866), thereby precipitating a constitutional crisis of sorts at national and European level. In the second referendum, the people voted in favour of the Treaty by a final margin of 67.1% to 32.9% (1,816,098 turnout or a 58% turnout). A high turnout in European-related referenda had been equated with the success thereof until the first failed Treaty of Lisbon referendum.[36] Thus, the most recent referenda have challenged commonly held beliefs and perceptions as to Irish-European relations, demonstrating the fluctuating dynamic of this narrative, that being national sentiment or national policy preferences.

The Irish Supreme Court and EU Law

[1–10] There has been a dramatic shift in the last decade in EU law in Ireland so far as the Irish Supreme Court is concerned. Since the composition of the Keane and then Murray Supreme Courts in the early years of the twenty-first century, the Supreme Court has made considerably more preliminary references than the High Court. This alters a trend developing over several decades, whereby the High Court was largely the main referral body in the Irish legal order, discussed above.[37] This much can be explained by the presence of three former members of the Court of Justice on the Supreme Court and thereby bringing a wealth of experience to the Supreme Court.[38] This might also, however, be a reason for a reduction in the number of references, on the basis of an adequacy of knowledge within the Court to determine the outcome of proceedings, which was not the case for the first decade of the twenty-first century. A number of the preliminary references made to the Court of Justice in this period are disposed of by small chambers of the Court of Justice and with brief judgments,[39] perhaps diminishing in that process the dynamic of the relationship that might be otherwise garnered from such activity. Mr Justice Fennelly, a former Advocate General

[34] See Referendum Results 1937–2009 (Department of Environment, Heritage and Local Government, 2009), available on www.environ.ie (detailed referendum results for Ireland since 1937).

[35] See also Hourihane, ed., *Ireland and the European Union: The First Thirty Years 1973–2002* (Lilliput Press, Dublin, 2003) and O'Mahony, "The Irish Referendum Experience" (1998) 35 *Representation* 225; Coakley and Gallagher, eds., *Politics in the Republic of Ireland* (5th ed., Routledge, London, 2010).

[36] See http://ec.europa.eu/public_opinion/index_en.htm and Sinnott, Richard and Stephen Quinlan, "Soft Supporters of the EU need to be inspired to vote Yes to Lisbon Treaty", *The Irish Times,* (30 January 2008).

[37] See above Ch 6.

[38] Murray CJ, Fennelly and Macken JJ are the respective judges. See generally, Fahey, *Practice and Procedure in Preliminary References to Europe: 30 years of Article 234 EC Caselaw from the Irish Courts* (Firstlaw, Dublin, 2007).

[39] For example, Case C-221/05 *McCauley Chemists v Pharmaceutical Society of Ireland* [2006] ECR I-6869; C-209/07 *Competition Authority v Beef Industry Development Society Ltd & Barry Brothers (Carrigmore) Meats Ltd* [2008] ECR I-8637; C-372/07 *Hassett v South Western Health Board* [2008] ECR I-7403.

on the Court of Justice,[40] has delivered a sizeable majority of decisions relating to EU law questions in Supreme Court decisions since his appointment to the Court and has contributed to a highly analytical and well-reasoned jurisprudence of EU law related matters considered by the Supreme Court.[41] On the other hand, the Supreme Court, historically, has not had a positive influence on EU affairs in Ireland, prior to the Supreme Courts under the stewardship of Chief Justices Keane and Murray, at least. The legacy of the decision of the Supreme Court in *Crotty v An Taoiseach* from the late 1980s remains a legal and political noose on the nation as regards EU Treaty ratification, which has yet to receive a re-examination by way of challenge to its precedential status. Then, in the mid-1990s, the Supreme Court authorised the legislature to implement European Union law by means of secondary or delegated legislation[42] and, since then, the legislature has used secondary legislation frequently to implement important EU legislation, such as the Unfair Consumer Contract Terms Directive[43] or, more recently, the Citizens Rights Directive.[44] Also, the legislature has given unto itself sweeping, indeed swingeing, powers to implement EU law by way of delegated legislation in the European Communities Act 2007, while only adopting a minimalist role to its new far-reaching obligations in the Treaty of Lisbon.[45] Moreover, the legislature has mis-implemented EU law frequently since accession, the most recent and high-profile example of this being the European arrest warrant, while other notable examples include the Commercial Agents Directive.[46] The national courts have

---

[40] From 1995–2000.

[41] See, for example, *Leo Laboratories Ltd v Crompton BV* [2005] 2 IR 225; *Kennedy v AG* [2005] IESC 36; *Short v Ireland* [2006] IESC 46; *Albatros Feeds v Minister for Agriculture* [2006] IESC 51; *In the Matter of Eurofoods Ltd & In the Matter of the Companies Acts 1963–2001* [2006] IESC 41 & [2004] 4 IR 370; *Maher v Minister for Agriculture* [2001] 2 IR 139 (although not the only opinion delivered here) and *SIAC Construction Ltd v Mayo Co. Co.* [2002] 3 IR 148. More recently, many of the significant European arrest warrant decisions have been delivered by Fennelly J, Murray CJ and Denham J, indicating perhaps, a broader spread of the Court in EU law matters, but less so Macken J. See the analysis of Ryall and Walsh, "Article 234 EC and the Pursuit of Legal Certainty: Environmental Impact Assessment Law in Ireland" (UACES conference paper, Angers, 2009).

[42] *Meagher v Minister for Agriculture* [1994] 1 IR 329.

[43] Council Directive 93/13/EEC of 5 April 1993 on unfair terms in consumer contracts was implemented into Irish law by way of secondary legislation, European Communities (Unfair Terms In Consumer Contracts) Regulations, 1995 (SI No 27 1995).

[44] Directive 2004/38/EC on the right of citizens of the Union and their family members to move and reside freely within the territory of the Member States amending Regulation (EEC) No 1612/68 and repealing Directives 64/221/EEC, 68/360/EEC, 72/194/EEC, 73/148/EEC, 75/34/EEC, 75/35/EEC, 90/364/EEC, 90/365/EEC and 93/96/EEC. The (Irish) European Communities (Freedom of Movement of Person) Regulations 2006 purported to transpose Citizens Rights Directive (SI No 226 of 2006).

[45] See below Ch 8.

[46] See Council Directive No. 86/653/EEC of 18 December 1986, on the co-ordination of the laws of the Member States relating to self-employed commercial agents was implemented by firstly, the European Communities (Commercial Agents) Regulations, 1994 (SI No 33/1994) and then later, the European Communities (Commercial Agents) Regulations, 1997 (SI No. 31/1997). For another finding of mal-implementation of the European Arrest Warrant Act 2003, as amended, see most recently *Rimsa v Governor of Cloverhill* [2010] IESC 47 and see below Ch 9.

responded patchily to such derelictions of duty by the legislature.[47] As a result, litigants and society at large are adversely affected by such actions (or inaction) of the legislature. The manner in which the legislature fulfils its role in EU affairs appears to be in the realm of carte blanche, having been so authorised by the Supreme Court since the 1990's. This has a major bearing upon the operation of EU law in Ireland today.[48]

Conclusion

[1–11] The genesis of EU law in the Irish courts from 1973 to 2010 is a far from linear account, similar to the relationship of Ireland with the EU and arguably reflects the hazy equivocation that the Irish State employs as to EU policies and activities. As a matter of politics, the relationship of the State with the EU has a particularly curious link to the UK. The policy preferences exercised by the Irish State as a small-sized and geographically peripheral State are often difficult to place in theoretical terms. The challenges posed by a written constitution and the sovereign values protected therein form a small, but not necessarily significant, factor in the account of Irish-European relations over a thirty-seven year period. This is allied to the fact that institutional actors in Ireland have played a disappointing role in EU affairs generally, which has an impact on any cumulative assessment conducted.

[1–12] In many respects, a description of EU law in the Irish legal order over a period of thirty-seven years contains many surprising elements. For a jurisdiction joining the EEC in the midst of economic depression worldwide as well as "EU-sclerosis" and at a time *after* the enunciation of landmark legal doctrines, it is particularly remarkable that Ireland joined the Community simultaneously with the UK and Denmark, both of which would become the "trickiest" members of the Union, arguably unlike Ireland, yet with which Ireland would exercise certain common policy preferences and would stand away from European integration in its fullest sense. Moreover, Ireland would become a major net beneficiary of EU funds and would then proceed to experience temporarily extraordinary economic growth, followed by a need for significant EU financial assistance and/ or "comfort" in the midst of a very serious domestic economic downturn. The experience of two fractious referenda on the Treaty of Lisbon more recently, the most serious and challenging of all the referenda campaigns held as to European treaties since 1987 in Ireland, affords further reason for reflection at this point in time and the position that EU affairs reached in Irish society during this

[47] Contrast *Eircom Limited v Commission for Communications Regulations* [2007] 1 IR 1 and *Minister for Justice, Equality and Law Reform v Ferenca* [2008] IESC 52 as well as the proactive nature of the engagement of the Supreme Court with the Court of Justice (discussed in Ch 6) with, for example, *Minister for Justice, Equality and Law Reform and Commissioner of An Garda Siochana v. Director of Equality Tribunal* [2009] IEHC 72 and the "MIBI saga" discussed above in relation to the Emanation of the State doctrine in Irish law. And see the discussion on the adequacy of the implementation of Council Directive 97/80/EC of 15 December 1997 on the Burden of Proof in cases of discrimination based on sex and how the Equal Status Act 2000 was affected by the Directive in *Kelly v National University of Ireland* [2008] IEHC 464, which led to a preliminary reference, pending at the time of writing. See, by contrast, *Hosey v Minister for Environment* [2010] IEHC 61, for a recent finding of adequate transposition into Irish law of the Bird Directives (Council Directive 79/409/EEC on the Conservation of Wild Birds).

[48] See above.

particular period is worthy of critical assessment. Frequently, the metaphor of the "incoming tide" is employed in the UK to describe the reception of EU law in that jurisdiction, the metaphor having its origins in a colourful judgment of the late Lord Denning.[49] There is no similar metaphor that one can employ to describe the reception and operation of EU law in Ireland, itself a telling indication of the comfortable zone in which matters European have travelled in this jurisdiction.

[49] *Bulmer v Bollinger* [1974] Ch. 401, 418 per Lord Denning, to the effect that then EEC Treaty was like "an incoming tide. It flows into the estuaries and up the rivers. It cannot be held back."

CHAPTER 2
The Supremacy or Primacy of EU Law in Ireland

Overview

The supremacy or primacy[1] of EC law is mostly but not uncritically accepted in world-wide scholarship, since *Costa v ENEL*.[2] As is well-known, primacy or supremacy of EC law exists where a divergence exists between national and Community law and the conditions for direct effect are satisfied such that Community law ought to prevail.[3] In Ireland, supremacy of Community law is not provided for explicitly, but rather indirectly in legislation and not in the Constitution, in the form of s 2 of the European Communities Act 1972, prior to the ratification of the Treaty of Lisbon. This provided that: **[2–01]**

> "From the 1st day of January, 1973, the treaties governing the European Communities and the existing and future acts adopted by the institutions of those Communities shall be binding on the State and shall be part of the domestic law thereof under the conditions laid down in those treaties."

Section 2 of the Act of 1972 has now been amended by s 3 European Union Act 2009, which provides that: **[2–02]**

---

[1] The origins of the terminology are discussed above and both are used here for ease of reference.

[2] See C-6/64 *Costa v ENEL* [1964] ECR 585; Dougan "When worlds collide! Competing visions of the relationship between direct effect and supremacy" (2007) CMLR 931 (Distinction between a "primacy" and "trigger" model and considers "exclusionary effects" and "substitutionary effects"); Alter *Establishing the Supremacy of EC Law* (OUP, Oxford, 2001) (Inter-court competition as basis for acceptance of supremacy); Kumm and Comella, "The Primacy Clause of the Constitutional Treaty and the Future of Constitutional Conflict in the European Union" (2006) 3 IJCL 473.

[3] An even more nuanced view distances itself from direct effect and sees indirect effect and State liability as manifestations of supremacy: Case C-106/89 *Marleasing SA v La Comercial Internacional de Alimentacion SA* [1990] ECR I-4135 (mode of consistent interpretation or "indirect effect"); Joined cases C-6/90 and C-9/90 *Francovich v Italian Republic* [1991] ECR I-5057 (State liability resulting in damages for breach thereof).

"(1) The following shall be binding on the State and shall be part of the domestic law thereof under the conditions laid down in the treaties governing the European Union:

a. the treaties governing the European Union;
b. acts adopted by the institutions of the European Union (other than acts to which the first paragraph of Article 275 of the Treaty on the Functioning of the European Union applies);
c. acts adopted by the institutions of the European Communities in force immediately before the entry into force of the Lisbon Treaty; and
d. acts adopted by bodies competent under those treaties (other than acts to which the first paragraph of the said Article 275 applies)."

[2–03] Thus, the scope of supremacy has been widened as to the bodies whose acts are binding on the State. However, supremacy is still provided for in legislative and not constitutional format and the enumeration of circumstances where supremacy applies is more of an exercise to prevent unnecessary constitutional disputes. This discussion also has a related counterpart in the Irish context, namely Article 29.4.6° prior to the Treaty of Lisbon, the constitutional immunity attaching to legislation immunising EU law obligations, which is considered above in more detail on account of developments in the relevant case-law and in scholarship, which has not raised directly the question of supremacy and is particularly *sui generis* as a result.[4] The consequences of supremacy have been accepted largely unquestioningly by the Irish courts, with only one threat to this state of affairs on the thorny question of abortion that never came to fruition.[5] The Irish courts are overwhelmingly pro-*communautaire* and three former members of the Court of Justice sit on the Irish Supreme Court, arguably eliminating many potential supremacy debacles. It is common case that the doctrines of supremacy and direct effect were well known at the outset of Ireland's Community membership, by virtue of the Third Amendment to the Constitution and the European Communities Act 1972. They have been endorsed directly or indirectly across a vast cross-section of time, both in the High Court and the Supreme Court,[6] and a wide variety of European-emanating legal instruments have been applied without conflict or difficulty.[7]

---

[4] See generally Phelan, *Revolt or Revolution: The Constitutional Boundaries of the European Community* (Round Hall, Dublin, 1997) and the discussion above.

[5] See *Pesca Valentia v Minister for Fisheries (No. 2)* [1990] 2 IR 305 (Interim relief granted as to Act of the Oireachtas); *Tate v Minister for Social Welfare* 1995] 1 ILRM 507 (Doctrine of State Liability accepted); *Coppinger v Waterford County Council* [1998] 4 IR 220 (Doctrine of State Liability accepted); *Eircom Limited v Commission for Communications Regulations* [2006] IEHC 138 (Doctrine of indirect effect accepted).

[6] Also in the District and Circuit Court, from the limited amount of written decisions and reports that can be ascertained, for example, *Dublin Bus v The MIBI* (Unreported, Circuit Court, 29 October 1999) and see the discussion above as to a reference from the District Court.

[7] As to the High Court: Case 177/78 *Pigs and Bacon Commission v McCarren and Co. Ltd* [1982] IR 451; [1979] ECR 2161; *McDermott and Cotter v Minister for Social Welfare* (High Court, Hamilton P, 10 June 1988); [1990] CMLR 94, *Murphy v An Bord Telecom* [1989] ILRM 63; *Lawlor v Minster for Agriculture* [1990] 1 IR 356; *Eircom Limited v Commission for Communications Regulations* [2007] 1 IR 1. As to the Supreme Court: see *Campus Oil v Minister for Industry and Energy* [1983] IR 82;

The courts have also emphasised their entitlement to ensure that Community law is fully applied and respected.[8] The only dissent from this much being in relation to fundamental rights in an isolated decision as an *obiter* comment in *SPUC v Grogan*[9] and the vast body of jurisprudence on the European arrest warrant had the potential to become mired in *kompetenz* conflict and fundamental rights issues, none of which has materialised and the Supreme Court, in particular, has undertaken its obligations faithfully. Thus, in *SPUC v Grogan*, the Supreme Court effectively rebuked a High Court judge for her decision to refer interlocutory proceedings relating to the right to life of the unborn and the provision of services to the Court of Justice. There, the Court of Justice diffused any controversy by deciding that financial consideration for services did not exist so to bring the EC Treaty into play as to the facts of the dispute involving the provision of abortion information by student unions, although the decision resulted in a Protocol being attached to the Treaty of Maastricht for the benefit of Ireland.[10] When the case returned to the Irish Supreme Court, Walsh J notably suggested with some force, *obiter*, that the question of the primacy of EU did not rest with the Court of Justice in the event of conflict between national and European law. The isolated nature of such an instance (singular), however, is particularly remarkable and the absence of intervention of the Supreme Court in EU affairs generally is perhaps curious in comparative terms.[11] **[2–04]**

Meagher v Minister for Agriculture and Food [1994] 2 IR 329; *Nathan v Bailey Gibson Ltd* [1998] 2 IR 162; *Emerald Meats Limited v The Minister for Agriculture and Others (No 2)* [1997] 3 IR 1; *Lancefort Limited v An Bord Pleanala (No 2)* [1999] 2 IR 270; *Maher v Minister for Agriculture* [2001] 2 IR 139. Generally, see the important sentiments as to EEC membership expressed in *ICMSA v Government of Ireland* (Unreported, High Court, Barrington J, 25 October 1979); *Doyle v An Taoiseach* [1986] ILRM 693.

[8] See, for example, the eloquent and detailed decision of McKechnie J in *Eircom Limited v Commission for Communications Regulations* [2007] 1 IR 1, outlining how national courts have extensive powers to ensure that Community law is applied and fully respected within Member States, involving the Court going to extensive length to ensure that Community law would prevail where it conflicted with domestic law, depriving litigants of the remedies of Community law. See also the *obiter* comments of Denham J in the Supreme Court in *Lancefort Limited v An Bord Pleanala (No 2)* [1999] 2 IR 270:

> "There is thus no question of the application by the national court of its rules as to standing resulting in a failure by the court to ensure that the relevant principles of European Union law are applied in the State, as happened, for example, in the United Kingdom when it was sought to rely on the doctrine of parliamentary sovereignty as precluding the enforcement of community law in that jurisdiction: see Case C-213/89 *Factortame* [1990] ECR I-2433".

[9] C-159/90 *SPUC v Grogan* [1989] IR 753; [1990] ILRM 350; [1991] ECR I-4685: Phelan, *Revolt or Revolution: The Constitutional Boundaries of the European Community* (Round Hall, Dublin, 1997). See also Phelan, "Right to Life of the Unborn v Promotion of Trade in Services: The European Court of Justice and the Normative Shaping of the European Union (1992) 55 MLR 670.

[10] Now (post Lisbon) Protocol (No. 35) on Art 40.3.3. of the Constitution of Ireland.

[11] See Phelan, "Can Ireland legislate contrary to European Community law" (2010) 33 ELR 530; Phelan, "Political Self-control and European Constitution: The Assumption of National Political Loyalty to European Obligations as the Solution to the Lex Posterior Problem of EC Law in the National Legal Orders" (2010) 16 ELJ 253. See also Cahill, "Ireland's Constitutional Amendability and Europe's Constitutional Ambition" (2008) 9 (10) GLJ.

[2–05] However, recently, a political scientist in Ireland, considering the terms of the European Communities Act 1972 as well as the terms of Article 29.4.6° (ex Article 29.4.10° prior to the Treaty of Lisbon amendments) has contended that there is no Irish (constitutional) law obligation to apply EU treaty obligations in place of contrary Irish law and that Irish courts do not recognise a direct Community law obligation to apply Community law in place of contrary Irish law.[12] It is suggested here that the thrust of this analysis overlooks a large body of case-law in the Irish Superior courts over thirty-seven years across a range of subject areas applying EU law faithfully, as well as the force of directly effective EU treaty obligations, the duty of co-operation for example, incumbent on Member State courts, pursuant to Article 4(3) TFEU (ex Article 10 EC) and the duty to dis-apply conflict national law in favour of EU law emanating from the treaties. This analysis also overlooks the manner in which the Supreme Court has emptied Article 29.4.6° of its value so as to downgrade its respective importance, discussed here later, as well as managing to downplay the importance of the timing of Irish accession, such that the doctrines of direct effect and supremacy had already been enunciated by the Court of Justice by this time.[13]

[2–06] Returning, then, to the place of supremacy or primacy in EU law, Article I-6 of the ill-fated *Treaty Establishing A Constitution for Europe*,[14] provided that "[t]he Constitution and law adopted by the institutions of the Union in exercising competences conferred on it shall have primacy over the law of the Member States". Much controversy was generated by the manner of this formulation and the explicit statement of constitutional supremacy in the text of the treaties.[15] "Primacy" is not now provided for in the text of the Treaty of Lisbon,[16] but rather in a Declaration, with a legal opinion of the Council attached thereto, which is not binding as a matter of law and recites the *Costa v ENEL* decision.[17] The German Constitutional Court, in its decision on the Treaty of Lisbon, dismissed the clause as essentially insignificant on account of its guardianship of constitutional supremacy, although the Court of Justice in January 2010, shortly after the entry into force of the Treaty of Lisbon, has begun to refer to the employ the new terminology of the "primacy of European Union law," a phrase not previously

[12] Phelan, "Can Ireland legislate contrary to European Community law?" (2010) 33 ELR 530.

[13] See the endorsement made by Denham J extra-judicially as to national courts and the Treaty of Lisbon (Annual Brian Walsh Lecture, Irish Society for European Law, November 2010 (see www.isel.ie).

[14] OJ 2004 C310, p 1.

[15] See Kumm and Comella, "The Primacy Clause of the Constitutional Treaty and the Future of Constitutional Conflict in the European Union" (2006) 3 IJCL 473; Kumm, "The Jurisprudence of Constitutional Conflict: Constitutional Supremacy in Europe before and after the Constitutional Treaty" (2005) 11 ELJ 262; Reestman, "Primacy of Union Law" (2005) 1 ECLR 104.

[16] OJ 2007 C306, p 1.

[17] Declaration 17, Annexed to the Final Act. See Dougan, "The Treaty of Lisbon 2007: Winning Minds, Not Hearts" (2008) 45 CMLR 617 at 700.

part of its lexicon or case-law.[18] Primacy or supremacy nonetheless remains the cornerstone of EC law, both in theory and practice.

The Duty to Disapply and the Doctrine of Supremacy or Primacy

As regards the practical consequences of primacy, it is now trite to recount that the Court of Justice held in the infamous decision in *Costa v ENEL*[19] that the new legal order of the European Economic Community, autonomous as it was from international law, resulted in the supremacy of Community law in the event of conflict arising before national courts between national law and European law. This entailed that: [2–07]

> "law stemming from the treaty, an independent source of law, could not, because of its special and original nature, be overridden by domestic legal provisions, however framed, without being deprived of its character as Community law and without the legal basis of the Community itself being called into question…".

The rationale for such supremacy was enunciated to be "that the Executive force of community law cannot vary from one state to another …without jeopardising the attainment of the objectives of the treaty." The practical operation of the doctrine of supremacy was then established in *Amministrazione del Finanze dello Stato v Simmenthal*,[20] where the Court held that in case of conflict that supremacy resulted in: [2–08]

> "a national court …[being] under a duty to give full effect to those provisions, if necessary refusing of its own motion to apply any conflicting provision of national legislation, even if adopted subsequently, and it is not necessary for the court to request or await the prior setting aside of such provision by legislative or other constitutional means".[21]

In fact, as the Court has clarified in *Ministero delle Finanze v IN.CO.GE.'90 Srl*,[22] *Simmenthal* did not entail that a national law rule in such a case of conflict was non-existent but rather that the national court was obliged to "dis-apply" conflicting national law. More recently, it its decision in *Kucukdeveci*,[23] the Court of Justice has held that a principle enunciated by the German Constitutional Court, entailing that a national court could not dis-apply conflicting national law in the absence of a preliminary reference to the Court of Justice, did not necessarily have the consequences that it intended and that the national court still had a discretion or option to refer questions to the Court of Justice irrespective, meanwhile expressly referencing the [2–09]

---

[18] Judgment of 30 June 2009 of the Federal Constitutional Court, 2 *B v E* 2/08, 2 *B v E* 5/08, 2 *B v R* 1010/08, 2 *B v R* 1022/08, 2 *B v R* 1259/08 and 2 *B v R* 182/09, available at www.bundesverfassungs gericht.de/pressemitteilungen/bvg09-072en.html. See Doukas, "The verdict of the German Federal Constitutional Court on the Lisbon Treaty: not guilty, but don't do it again!" (2009) 34 ELR 866; See Case C-555/07 *Kücükdeveci v Swedex GmbH & Co KG.* [2010] IRLR 346, para. 54.

[19] Case 6/64 *Costa* v *ENEL* [1965] ECR 505.

[20] in Case 106/77 *Amministrazione del Finanze dello Stato v Simmenthal* [1978] ECR 629.

[21] At para 24.

[22] C-10/97 to C-22/97 *Ministero delle Finanze v IN.CO.GE.'90 Srl* [1998] ECR I-6307.

[23] See Case C-555/07 *Kücükdeveci v Swedex GmbH & Co KG.* [2010] IRLR 346, para 54.
The decision of the Court of Justice (Grand Chamber) was delivered in January 2010 after the Treaty of Lisbon judgment of the Court of Justice and the sensitive manner in which the Court answers the referred questions and controversial German law at issue is perhaps understandable.

newly visible primacy of EU law.[24] While Phelan has recently suggested that there is no *constitutional* bar to a national judge in Ireland refusing to dis-apply Irish law in favour of EU law, it is argued here that this much overlooks the duty on national courts to dis-apply conflicting national law in favour of EU law, as provided for in the Treaties, the case-law of the Court of Justice, considered further below. Moreover, there are many examples of the judiciary faithfully dis-applying conflicting Irish legislation in favour of EU law.[25] In fact, one of the very first Irish preliminary references to the Court of Justice in the 1970s concerned a District Court and the question of compatibility of criminal prosecutions taken under Irish secondary legislation (Sea Fishing (Sea Fisheries (Conservation and Rational Exploitation) Orders 1977) with the Treaty of Rome, where the Court of Justice held that a conviction under the Irish secondary law was incompatible with EC law. The net result, almost forty years ago, was that Irish law would be "dis-applied" by the District Court in favour of EC law.[26] While not impossible, it seems most unlikely that the current Supreme Court would make an intervention into European constitutionalism in the same way as the German Constitutional Court. This much can be deduced from, firstly, the largely *communautaire* nature of the existing case-law; secondly, the tendency of the Court to cooperate with the Court of Justice, to avoid conflict with its responsibilities as a matter of EU law[27] and to seek its assistance regularly pursuant to Article 267 TFEU; and, thirdly, its tendency to readily apply the duty of co-operation incumbent upon national courts.

Recent Case-Law in the Irish Courts on the Doctrine of Supremacy

[2–10] The recent decision of the Irish High Court in *Minister for Justice, Equality and Law Reform & Commissioner of An Garda Siochana v Director of Equality Tribunal*[28] might, at first glance, appear as the unlikely source of a *kompetenz-kompetenz* constitutional crisis. In fact, however, the decision may represent the most recent instance of a threat to the supremacy of European Community (EC) law in Ireland or, at the least, a decision of extraordinary incongruity to litigants seeking to rely upon EC law and is considered here to demonstrate difficulties with existing Irish case-law. The decision of Charleton J concerned a "Henry VIII" clause, whereby secondary legislation had the effect of amending primary legislation, similar to the famous "Metric Martyrs" case in the UK.[29] In proceedings before the Irish Equality Tribunal, the subject of judicial review

---

[24] At para 54 of the decision of the Court. The context of this decision is surely of great significance, as is the absence of detail in the decision of the Court as to the German rule or decision at issue which the referring court was questioning.

[25] See above.

[26] C-88/77 *Minister for Fisheries v Schonenberg* [1978] ECR 473. Although, no explicit question was put to the Court on this basis and the Court was in fact applying a ruling it had delivered that day. However, a District Court would not normally possess the constitutional powers to deem a conviction to be invalid or to declare secondary legislation unconstitutional.

[27] i.e. that the Supreme Court has never refused to apply the case-law of the Court of Justice or has never refused to abide by a preliminary reference sought, the *Grogan* debacle aside.

[28] *Minister for Justice, Equality and Law Reform & Commissioner of An Garda Siochana v Director of Equality Tribunal* [2009] IEHC 72.

[29] *Thoburn v Sunderland City Council* [2003] QB 151 ("Metric Martyrs"), discussed above. See Gwynn Morgan, *The Separation of Powers in the Irish Constitution* (Round Hall, Dublin, 1997) pp 246–250 (Henry VIII clauses).

proceedings before Charleton J, a conflict arose between primary and secondary legislation, raising the question as to whether the Tribunal was entitled in effect to set aside a statutory instrument, by virtue of the operation of EC law. A complicating factor in the case is the interpretation by Charleton J of a recent decision of the Court of Justice[30] on the powers of quasi-judicial bodies to apply the doctrine of direct effect, but not supremacy, resulting in what is suggested here to be a most incongruous outcome.

The notice parties in *Minister for Justice, Equality and Law Reform & Commissioner of An Garda Siochana v Director of Equality Tribunal* applied to train as members of Garda Siochána (Irish police) but were deemed ineligible by virtue of their age, which was governed, *inter alia*, by secondary legislation (the Garda Siochána (Admission and Appointments) (Amendments) Regulations 2004).[31] However, the (Irish) Equality Act 2004 sought to give effect to Council Directive 2000/78/EC,[32] which prohibited discrimination, *inter alia*, on the basis of age. Temporally, the secondary legislation was passed *subsequent* to the primary legislation so as to implement the Directive and, thus, Irish law conflicted with EC law.[33] The procedural history of the case resulting before Charleton J in the High Court from the Equality Tribunal is unfortunately not outlined and whether these proceedings arose prior to the enactment of the secondary legislation is not clear.[34] However, Charleton J framed the issue before the Court as being: **[2–11]**

> "whether the Equality Tribunal, as a body whose powers are defined by statute, is entitled to commence a hearing that has the result that it assumes a legal entitlement to overrule a statutory instrument made by the first applicant where by law it is not entitled so to do. My view is that it is not...".

Charleton J held that it was beyond the scope of any decision that he was required to make to assess whether national legislation correctly implemented the Directive and stated that the obligation to construe national legislation, in light of the obligation under EC law, did not extend to "re-writing" the legislation. [35] In support of this much, Charleton J cited the recent decision of the Court of Justice in *Impact v Minister for Agriculture and Food*,[36] meriting closer analysis. *Impact* concerned a claim by Irish civil servants challenging their pay and pension entitlements as fixed-term contract workers **[2–12]**

[30] Case C-268/06 *Impact v Minister for Agriculture and Food* [2008] 2 CMLR 47.
[31] Which entailed that they had to be at least 18 years of age and under 35 years of age in the year that they applied.
[32] Council Directive 2000/78/EC of 27 November 2000 establishing a general framework for equal treatment in employment and occupation.
[33] The secondary legislation was passed in November 2004 and the primary legislation came into effect in July 2004.
[34] The High Court noted *en passant* correspondence from the Equality Authority that had previously expressed the view that the admission criteria discriminating on the basis of age were not consistent such legislative provisions. The nature of this correspondence or its relevance to the actual proceedings was not specified by the Court.
[35] Without citing or discussing any relevant case-law, but ostensibly meaning the case-law resulting from Case C-106/89 *Marleasing SA v La Comercial Internacional de Alimentacion SA* [1990] ECR I-4135 (doctrine of "indirect effect," obliging national judge to read conflicting national law in light of European legislation).
[36] Case C-268/06 *Impact v Minister for Agriculture and Food* [2008] 2 CMLR 47, a referral from the Irish Labour Court.

and the manner and effect of the renewal thereof. The issue arose, *inter alia*, as to the direct effect of a Directive implementing a Framework Agreement[37] and the jurisdiction of the Irish Rights Commissioner or Labour Court to consider the claim of a fixed-term worker as to direct effect in respect of a period after the due date for implementation and prior to the date of transposition of the Directive.

[2–13] No express jurisdiction had been conferred on these bodies as to European law matters under Irish law, although generally they had, what was argued by the Irish State, to be "an optional jurisdiction" over claims arising and so a High Court challenge could have been initiated by the claimants in the alternative. The Court of Justice held that to compel the applicants to have to bring a separate action before the High Court to assert their rights would have resulted in procedural disadvantages to them, including cost and time disincentives, which the national referring court would have to consider. The Court of Justice in *Impact* reasoned that the:

> "principle of effectiveness requires that those individuals should also be able to seek before the same courts the protection of the rights which they can derive directly from the directive itself ... the obligation to divide their action into two separate claims and to bring the claim based directly on the directive before an ordinary court leads to procedural complications liable to render excessively difficult the exercise of those rights conferred on the parties by Community law.
>
> If the referring court were to find such an infringement of the principle of effectiveness, it would be for that court to interpret the domestic jurisdictional rules in such a way that, wherever possible, they contribute to the attainment of the objective of ensuring effective judicial protection of an individual's rights under Community law".[38]

[2–14] Only part of the above quotation was referred to by Charleton J which, it is suggested here, supports the contrary proposition, that is, that the Equality Tribunal *should* have been able to consider the direct effect of the Directive at issue and that to compel parties to re-litigate in another forum was, in fact, precluded by the decision in *Impact*.[39] Instead, Charleton J held that:

> "[t]here is no principle of European law which allows an administrative body or a court of limited jurisdiction to exceed its own authority in order to achieve a result, whereby it is of the view that European legislation has not been properly implemented ...".[40]

[2–15] Strictly speaking, this statement is incorrect in that the transposition of the Directive was not ostensibly challenged (albeit by deduction we must draw this conclusion) but rather that subsequent Irish secondary legislation enacted after the transposition of the Directive by primary law was simply inconsistent with the aims and provisions of the Directive. Charleton J then held that the Equality Tribunal should have held that no

---

[37] Council Directive 1999/70/EC of 28 June 1999 concerning the framework agreement on fixed-term work concluded by ETUC, UNICE and CEEP. The doctrine of supremacy was not a feature of *Impact*.

[38] At paras. 53–54. Only para 54 is cited by Charleton J.

[39] The failure of Charleton J to discuss the facts of *Impact* is most unsatisfactory, especially where it is unclear as to the date of the commencement of the proceedings here and whether the jurisdiction of the Equality Tribunal to invoke the doctrine of direct effect was at issue.

[40] At para 8.

remedy was forthcoming from that Tribunal and that the complainants should have subsequently sought a declaration from the High Court that the secondary legislation had purported to, in his words, "over-rule" European law. It is submitted that Charleton J fundamentally misinterpreted the decision of the Court of Justice in *Impact*, particularly given the interpretation that the Irish Labour Court itself, practitioners and scholars have been attributing to that decision.[41] The absence of any reference by Charleton J to the question of supremacy and the duties incumbent upon national courts flowing therefrom is also most striking indeed. Many clear decisions, thus, were available on the question before Charleton J in 2009 and the failure of the Court to correctly resolve the issue before the Court leaves Irish jurisprudence in a most unsatisfactory state. In any event, the Equality Tribunal is most certainly captured by the duties envisaged by the *Simmenthal* or *IN.CO.GE.'90 Srl* decisions and should have been instructed by the High Court simply to "dis-apply" the conflicting Irish statutory instrument. Some of the most important decisions in EU and EC law have been generated by lower courts from all over the EU lacking any powers of judicial review as a matter of domestic constitutional law and thereby benefiting from supremacy and direct effect.[42]

A major difficulty with the reasoning of Charleton J is that it invented procedural obstacles to the resolution of a relatively elementary point of EC law. The effectiveness of EC law is substantially diminished if the litigation of EC law rights becomes mired in claims before multiple fora and is rendered costly and inefficient. [43] The proceedings in the instant case of course were generated by the Equality Tribunal and the ability of such a quasi-judicial body to constitute a Court or Tribunal for the purposes of Article 267 TFEU is capable of little dispute.[44] **[2–16]**

---

41 *Kildare County Council v Halton* (FTC/05/15, 21 November 2008 (Labour Court)); O' Mara, "European Developments" (2008) 5(2) IELJ 80: "The importance of this judgment for Ireland is really to be found in the findings that the Rights Commissioners and the Labour Court (and implicitly, where relevant, the Employment Appeals Tribunal) are 'national courts' for the purpose of Community law. Even though the Oireachtas has not conferred retrospective jurisdiction on them to interpret and enforce Community law, they are now confirmed to have this capacity".

42 Alter, *Establishing the Supremacy of EC Law* (OUP, Oxford, 2001); Fahey, *Practice and Procedure in Preliminary References to Europe: 30 Years of Article 234 EC Caselaw from the Irish Courts* (Firstlaw, Dublin, 2007).

43 *Impact,* para. 46. See Case 33/76 *Rewe-Zentralfinanz and Rewe-Zentral* [1976] ECR 1989; Case 45/76 *Comet* [1976] ECR 2043; Case C-312/93 *Peterbroeck* [1995] ECR I-4599 and Joined Cases C-222/05 to C-225/05 *van der Weerd and Others* [2007] ECR I-4233.

44 Case C-178/99 *Doris Saltzmann* [2001] ECR I-4421, para 13: the Court held that in order to determine whether a referring body was a court or tribunal the Court had to take into account a number of factors, such as whether the body is established by law, whether it is permanent, whether its jurisdiction is compulsory, whether its procedure is *inter partes*, whether it applies rules of law and whether it is independent. The Equality Tribunal on this basis is a suitable referring body, satisfying a majority of these factors, given that it is, *inter alia*, established by law, a permanent body, an independent body and applies rules of law. See Employment Equality Act 1998–2008, Equal Status Act 2000–2008 and the Pensions Act 1990–2004. See also www.equalitytribunal.ie, which states that: "[t]he Equality Tribunal is the impartial forum to hear or mediate complaints of alleged discrimination under equality legislation. It is independent and quasi-judicial and its decisions and mediated settlements are legally binding".

[2–17] Perhaps the litigants would have been best advised to have sought a preliminary reference to the Court of Justice, although presumably the judicial review proceedings initiated were intended to have a speedier outcome than a preliminary reference might have offered, given the unlikelihood that the accelerated procedure could have been availed of.[45] No constitutional crisis need necessarily follow from an Irish case considering such an elementary question as that before the Court in this particular case and the Irish courts have previously accepted the consequences of supremacy almost unquestioningly in the Irish legal order, none of which received any analysis here by Charleton J. Nonetheless, the operation of the doctrines of direct effect and the supremacy of EC law in Ireland is significantly affected by such an erroneous interpretation of EC law, as are litigants, in light of the *communautaire* nature of the Irish judiciary.

More recently, yet another disappointing decision has been delivered by the Superior Courts as to the application of primacy to decisions of quasi-judicial bodies and lower courts in *An Taoiseach v Commissioner for Environmental Information*[46] There, the notice party had sought by way of freedom of information a Cabinet discussion from 2002-2007 on greenhouse emissions. The Ombudsman, acting as Commissioner for Environmental Information, had ordered disclosure of the document. She found that Directive 2003/4/EC on Public Access to Environmental Information, implemented into Irish law by EC (Access to Information on the Environment) Regulations 2007, was specifically framed to exclude the refusal of a request on confidentiality-based grounds, if that request related to information on emissions. The Regulations specifically excluded Cabinet Confidentiality from the ambit of the legislation, deriving this from Article 28 of the Constitution, while the Directive provided for a narrower range of discretionary grounds to refuse access to information on the basis of confidentiality of the proceedings of public authorities.

The Irish Regulations instead were found by her to make provision for a blanket prohibition. She thus found that the Directive was directly effective but that it had not been correctly transposed into Irish law. On appeal to the High Court where the jurisdiction of the Commissioner to disapply Irish law was at issue, it is of interest then that the decision of Charleton J discussed above was argued by the Commissioner to have been delivered *per incuriam* the decision of Keane J in *Murphy v An Bord Telecom*.[47] However, O'Neill J, in a landmark decision, chose to accord primacy to Cabinet Confidentiality enshrined in Irish law pursuant to Article 28.4.3° of the Constitution when it came into conflict with a Directive, implemented into Irish law by the Regulations. Ultimately, the proceedings were treated by the High Court as involving a jurisdictional question. O'Neill J held that the particular problem in the case was not securing supremacy or primacy of Community law over domestic law but discerning the correct procedural means for doing this. The judicial architecture of the State could not permit a vast array of administrative bodies to determine all questions of law and fact as to the application and enforcement of EC law rights. National systems of law would be undermined otherwise and the principle

[45] See Art 104a of the Rules of Procedure of the Court of Justice.
[46] Unreported, High Court, 4 June 2010, O'Neill J.
[47] *Murphy v An Bord Telecom (No. 2)* [1988] ILRM 53.

of equivalent would be "turned on its head". He held that the Commissioner had no jurisdiction to decide the effect of regulations in national law. He thus held that disclosure of the constitutionally protected communications would undermine the discharge of collective responsibility by the government and he refused a preliminary reference to the Court of Justice to decide the question arising in the proceedings.[48]

What is remarkable about this decision is the alarmist tone adopted by O'Neill J about an elementary application of EC law by a quasi-judicial body. There is no doubt but that the Irish regulations went considerably further that the parent Directive, by reason of its particularity. The correctness of this Irish specific "exclusion" ought to have been the basis for a preliminary reference, it is suggested here. However, it is likely that the Court of Justice would not have sought to engender a constitutional supremacy challenge of the nature arising on the facts and perhaps the question of the conflict between the Regulations and the Constitution, i.e. the domestic question, would have been tactfully remitted to the Irish courts. Nonetheless, the broader point at issue in the decision, i.e. the jurisdiction of lower courts below the Superior Courts to disapply conflicting national law, even where they lack judicial review powers, remains also the critical one. The alarmist language of O'Neill J as to rudimentary operation of EU law in this regard goes well beyond the "incoming tide" envisaged by Lord Denning, describing the impact of EC law then on the British legal order several decades ago. There is scant analysis of the primacy of Union law in case-law or in the Treaty of Lisbon or scholarly analysis thereof in the judgment of O'Neill J and once more, a particularly disappointing decision of the Superior Courts is delivered on the primacy of EC law in domestic law, post-Lisbon. Moreover, again the jurisdiction of such bodies is misinterpreted by O'Neill J, forcing litigants to initiate expensive and unnecessary proceedings so as to obtain their due entitlements.

Conclusion

The decisions of Charleton J and O'Neill J are largely exceptional but, nonetheless, **[2–18]** demonstrate the practical difficulties that may stand in the way of litigants seeking to avail of the doctrine of supremacy or primacy in Irish law and has been discussed here at length to demonstrate the very serious predicament that results from a failure to identify a supremacy or primacy dispute. In the main, however, supremacy has been accepted unquestioningly in the Irish courts, both expressly and by implication, in the case-law. It seems unlikely that the Irish Supreme Court could engender a constitutional crisis or a *kompetenz-kompetenz* debacle, on the basis of existing case-law and practices to date. The Charter of Fundamental Rights, now legally binding after the Treaty of Lisbon, may generate particular types of competence dispute in the future but, for the moment at least, it does not seem likely that supremacy or primacy will pose any specific difficulty for the Irish courts in their daily application of EU law.

[48] On a request from the Commissioner, the appellant opposed a preliminary reference and the notice party was neutral on the question: para. 3.17 of the decision. The author is not aware at the time of writing whether any appeal is currently pending to the Supreme Court, which would possible result in a preliminary reference, arising from the operation of Art. 267 TFEU.

CHAPTER 3
The Emanation of the State Doctrine in Ireland

Direct and Indirect Effect in Irish Law

The doctrines of direct effect[1] and indirect effect[2] as outlined by the Court of Justice in its jurisprudence have resulted in a significant body of rights-based law for the benefit of EU citizens.[3] The substantive law on this topic is not considered here in detail for reasons of space: the discussion here is limited to relevant issues in Irish law. The Motor Insurers Bureau of Ireland and Motor Insurance Directives have generated a vast body of case-law in this jurisdiction and comprise a strange series of cases, where key doctrines of EU law were misapplied or applied mostly restrictively, generating several preliminary references to the Court of Justice from the Irish courts and various [3–01]

---

[1] Case 26/62 *Van Gend en Loos* [1963] ECR 1; Case 43/75 *Defrenne v Sabena* [1976] ECR 455; Case 41/74 *Van Duyn v Home Office* [1974] ECR 1337; Case 152/84 *Marshall v Southampton and SW Hampshire Area Health Authority* [1986] ECR 723; Case 148/78 *Criminal Proceedings against Ratti* [1979] ECR 1629; and now the controversial case of Case C-144/04 *Mangold v Helm* [2005] I-ECR 9981. There is some disagreement as to the precise meaning of the term and its relationship to direct applicability but it is used in a general sense here, as to vertical direct effect. At its most rudimentary level, a provision must be clear, precise, unconditional and confer specific rights on individuals in order for it to have direct effect.

[2] Case 14/83 *Von Colon v Land Nordrhein-Westfalen* [1984] ECR 1891; C-106/89 *Marleasing SA v CIA* [1990] ECR I-4135; C-105/03 *Criminal Proceedings against Pupino* [2005] ECR I-5283; C-168/95 *Criminal Proceedings against Luciano Arcaro* [1996] ECR I-4705; Case C-456/98 *Centrosteel* [2000] ECR I-6007.

[3] See generally, Prechal, "Direct effect, indirect effect, supremacy and the Evolving Constitution of the European Union" in Barnard, ed., *The Fundamentals of EU Law Revisited* (OUP, Oxford, 2007); Prechal, "Does direct effect still matter?" (2000) 37 CMLR 1047; Dougan "When worlds collide! Competing visions of the relationship between direct effect and supremacy" (2007) 44 CMLR 931; Dashwood, "Viking and Laval: Issues of Horizontal Direct Effect" (2007–2008) 10, CYELS 525; Craig, "The legal effect of Directives: policy, rules and exceptions" (2009) 34 ELR 349; Hinarejos, "On the Legal Effects of Framework Decisions and Decisions: Directly Applicable, Directly Effective, Self-Executing, Supreme?" (2008) 14 ELJ 620; Arnull, *The European Union and its Court of Justice* (2nd ed) (OUP, Oxford, 2006) p 185. As to Ireland, see Curtin and O'Keefe, eds, *Constitutional adjudication in European Community and National Law: Essays for the Hon. Mr. Justice T.F. O'Higgins* (Butterworths, Dublin, 1992); Hogan and Whelan, *Ireland and the European Union: Constitutional and Statutory Texts and Commentary* (Butterworths, Dublin, 1995); Keville and Lucey,

written decisions of the Circuit and High Court. Moreover, the Motor Insurers Bureau of Ireland and Motor Insurance Directives comprise a disproportionate amount of the litigation, as do environmental and planning law decisions featuring lay litigants. Fewer cases, again, feature from lower courts and quasi-judicial bodies as to the application of the doctrine of direct effect, aside from a small number of written Circuit Court decisions on the status of the Motor Insurers Bureau of Ireland (MIBI),[4] bodies that do not usually provide written judgments and that may state a case to a higher court for such questions, although not strictly necessitated as a matter of EU law.[5]

[3–02] The first major application of direct effect as to a Directive in the jurisdiction was in *Tate v Minister for Social Welfare*[6] following on from the litigation in *Cotter and McDermott v Minister for Social Welfare (No 1)*[7] and *Cotter and McDermott v Minister for Social Welfare (No 2)*[8] where the Court of Justice held that Directive 79/7/EEC on the progressive implementation of the principle of equal treatment for men

---

Irish Perspectives on EC Law (Round Hall, Dublin, 2003); McMahon and Murphy, *European Community Law in Ireland* (Butterworths, Dublin, 1989); Phelan, *Revolt or Revolution: The Constitutional Boundaries of the European Community* (Round Hall, Dublin, 1997); Scannell, "The influence of the general principles of Community Law on rules of procedure and rules of substance in Ireland" (2001) 1(1) JSIJ 64; Gaffney, "Pleading EC Law in Irish Litigation: A Case Study" (2005) 5 JSIJ 153. See also O' Reilly, "The Private Enforcement of European Community Law in the Irish Superior Courts" (2009) 31 DULJ 324; Tomkin, "Implementing Community Legislation Into National Law: The Demands of a New Legal Order" (2004) 4(2) JSIJ 130.

4 See above.

5 Although such bodies often do provide written judgments when considering EU law matters, albeit that this is exceptional: *Dublin Bus v MIBI* (Unreported, Circuit Court, 29 October 1999). It has not been common in the last thirty five years for such bodies to state a case to the High Court or Supreme Court for the resolution of EU law matter. Recent high profile exceptions to this are *Minister for Justice, Equality and Law Reform & Commissioner of An Garda Siochána v Director of Equality Tribunal* [2009] IEHC 72, and *An Taoiseach v Comms for Environmental Information* (Unreported, O'Neill J, High Court, 4 June 2010) discussed above.

6 *Tate v Minister for Social Welfare* [1995] 1 IR 418. See the account of the impact and background of the case in the Law Reform Commission Report, *Report — Multi-Party Litigation* (LRC 76-2005) (at para. 1.35–1.37):

> "…. the aftermath of the failure to implement the 1978 Directive on Equal Treatment In Social Welfare, only 11,200 married women, out of a total of 69,000 instituted proceedings claiming to be entitled to benefits which, prior to December 1984, had only been payable to married men. The cases of *Cotter and McDermott v Minister for Social Welfare (No. 1)* and *Cotter and McDermott v Minister for Social Welfare* (No. 2) were test cases for those 11,200 women. The State settled these two cases without admission of liability as well as a further 2,700. However this still left approximately 8,500 claims to be dealt, with as well as the potential claims of the remaining 58,000 married women who had not yet initiated proceedings. In the later test case of *Tate v The Minister for Social Welfare* involving 70 of these women, Judge Carroll in the High Court held that they too were entitled to the relief sought. As a result of the decision in *Tate*, the Government announced that all relevant payments, totalling approximately £265m, would be made to the entire group of 69,000 women. The 70 plaintiffs in *Tate* did not seek to prove the extent of each individual plaintiff's entitlement, and it was agreed for the purposes of the proceedings that this would be dealt with by the Department of Social Welfare in the light of the Court's decision".

7 *Cotter and McDermott v Minister for Social Welfare (No 1)* [1987] ECR 1453.

8 *ibid.*

and women in matters of social security had direct effect. Thus, in *Tate v Minister for Social Welfare*[9] Carroll J, in a landmark decision, held that the Irish State had been in breach of its obligations to fully, or properly, implement the Directive and held that the plaintiffs were entitled to receive the same benefits and rules as applied to married men and held that they were entitled to damages. The High Court applied the case-law as to State liability without difficulty.[10]

Indirect effect has largely arisen in Ireland only in the specific context of the European arrest warrant, which is considered separately here, although there are several important applications of the doctrine in recent case-law.[11] Notable, then, is the successful invocation of indirect effect in *Eircom Limited v Commission for Communications Regulations*[12] by Eircom to ameliorate an incorrect transposition of Regulations in Irish law so as to afford Eircom a right of appeal in respect of the Council Directive 2002/21/EC ("The Framework Directive"), which was implemented in Irish law by the European Communities (Electronic Communications Networks and Services) (Framework) Regulations 2003[13] ("The Framework Regulations") and the Council Directive 2002/19/EC (The Access Directive), which was implemented into Irish law by the European Communities (Electronic Communications Networks and Services) (Access) Regulations 2003[14] ("The Access Regulations"). Thus, McKechnie J held that the secondary law had to be favourably construed as to its objective in light of EU law, expressly invoking the jurisprudence of the Court of Justice: **[3–03]**

> "In any event a problem remains as to how (if at all) this Regulation 17 of the Access Regulations can be harmoniously integrated in the overall Regulatory Framework and in particular as to how it can operate in conformity with the demands of Article 4 (1) of the Framework Directive and with Part II of the 2003 Framework Regulations.

---

9 *Tate v Minister for Social Welfare* [1995] 1 IR 418.

10 See the discussions on the doctrine of direct effect is discussed and/or applied, mostly but not exclusively without controversy: *Abbeydrive Development Ltd v Kildare County Council* [2010] IESC 8; *Tate v Minister for Social Welfare* [1995] IR 418; *Coppinger v Waterford County Council* [1998] 4 IR 220; *Friends of the Curragh Environment Limited v An Bord Pleanála* [2006] IEHC 243; *Browne v An Bord Pleanála.* [1989] ILRM 865; *Short v Ireland,* [1996] 2 IR 188; *McBride v Galway Corporation* [1998] 1 IR 485; *De Burca v Wicklow County Council,* [2002] 2 IR 196; *Delargy v Minister for the Environment* [2005] IEHC 94; *Dublin Bus v MIBI* (Circuit Court, His Honour Judge McMahon, 29 October 1999); *Gogolova v Minister for Justice, Equality and Law Reform* [2008] IEHC 131; *I v Minister for Justice, Equality and Law Reform* [2008] IEHC 388; *Farrell v Whitty & Ors* [2008] IEHC 124; *Smith v Meade* [2009] IEHC 99; *Competition Authority v O'Regan* [2007] IESC 22; *Khashaba v Medical Council* [2009] IEHC 12; *B. v Minister for Justice, Equality and Law Reform* [2009] IEHC 447; *Cairde Chill an Disirt Teoranta v An Bord Pleanála* [2009] IEHC 76; *Sweetman v An Bord Pleanala* [2007] IEHC 153; *D.T v F.L* [2006] IEHC 98; [2008] IESC 48; *Albatros Feeds v Minister for Agriculture and Food* [2006] IESC 52; *Shell E & P Ireland Limited v McGrath* [2006] IEHC 99.

11 See Colneric, "Interpretation of Community law and Interpretation in conformity with Community law" (2005) 12 IJEL 142. See *Nathan v Bailey Gibson Limited* [1998] 2 IR 162; *Albatros Feeds v Minister for Agriculture* [2006] IESC 52; *B. v Minister for Justice, Equality and Law Reform* [2009] IEHC 447; *Kelly v UCD.* [2008] IEHC 464; *Smith v Meade* [2009] IEHC 99; *In the Matter of Bell Lines (In Liquidation)* [2010] IESC 15; *Izevbethau v Minister for Justice, Equality and Law Reform* [2010] IESC 303, paras 82 and 83.

12 *Eircom Limited v Commission for Communications Regulations* [2007] 1 IR 1.

13 SI No 307 of 2003.

14 SI No 305 of 2003.

> In attempting to resolve this matter, the court is obliged to interpret both the Framework Regulations and the Access Regulations, which as previously noted were passed in order to incorporate the aforesaid Directives into national law, in a manner, so far as is possible, in conformity with the Directives and in particular in this case with the Framework Directive. This is a well established principle and is set out with clarity in the case of … *von Colson…*
> *In conclusion the court will issue a declaration that decision D1/05 and the follow on enforcement procedures cannot be operated in such a manner as would impair or curtail the right of Eircom to appeal to the Appeal Panel in accordance with Part II of the 2003 Framework Regulations*".[15]
>
> (Emphasis supplied)

[3–04] This represents a bold reading of the doctrine of indirect effect in Irish law by way of interpretation only and the beneficiaries were institutional or legal persons and not natural persons. As a footnote to the above, contrast this decision with that of Laffoy J in *Tesco Ireland Ltd v Dunnes Stores,*[16] discussed below,[17] who refused to fashion a remedy (an interlocutory order) in proceedings taken by a leading retailer to "stamp out" misleading comparative advertising by a rival retailer. Nonetheless, Laffoy J was construing Irish legislation and Regulations which implemented EU law and did not expressly provide for the form of order sought, although the objective of the legislation may have suggested otherwise. Instead, Laffoy J ordered the reconstitution of the proceedings, adding considerable procedural obstacles to the path of the plaintiff. Clearly, Laffoy J could have adopted a similar approach to McKechnie J so as to fashion a remedy for the plaintiff by operation of EU law, although the merits of this are considered further above.

[3–05] As to the doctrine of State Liability[18] for a breach of EU law, this doctrine has been successfully invoked against the State in Ireland in a number of instances and the most thorough applications of the relevant tests are to be found in the decision of

[15] At paras. 34–35, 46.

[16] *Tesco Ireland Ltd v Dunnes Stores* [2009] IEHC 569.

[17] See Ch 7.

[18] As to its origins and evolution in the extensive case-law that it has generated (for a selection): Joined Cases C-6/90 and C-9/90 *Francovich and Others* [1991] ECR I-5357; Joined Cases C-46/93 and C-48/93 *Brasserie du Pêcheur and Factortame* [1996] ECR I-1029; Case C-392/93 *R v HM Treasury, ex parte British Telecommunications* [1996] ECR I-1631; Case C-5/94 *Hedley Lomas* [1996] ECR I-2553; Joined Cases C-178, 179 and 188–190/94 *Dillenkofer and Others* [1996] ECR I-4845; Joined Cases C-283/94, C-291 and C-292/94 *Denkavit Internationaal and Others v Bundesamt für Finanzen* [1996] ECR I-5063; Joined Cases C-192/95 to C-218/95 *Comateb and Others* [1997] ECR I-165; Joined Cases C-94 and C-95/95 *Bonifaci and Others* [1997] ECR I-3969; Case C-127/95 *Norbrook Laboratories v MAFF* [1998] ECR I-1531; Case C-319/96 *Brinkmann Tabakfabriken v Skatteministeriet* [1998] ECR I-5255; Case C-118/00 *Larsy* [2001] ECR I-5063; Case C-224/01 in *Köbler v Republic of Austria* [2003] ECR I-10239; Case C-63/01 *Evans v Secretary of State for the Environment, Transport and the Regions, Motor Insurers' Bureau* [2003] ECR I-4447 and more recently, Case C-118/08 *Transportes Urbanos y Servicios Generales SAL v Administración del Estado* [2010] ECR-0000 (at para 30–31):

> "the Court has held that individuals harmed have a right to reparation where three conditions are met: the rule of European Union law infringed must be intended to confer

Laffoy J in *Tate v Minister for Social Welfare* and in the decision of the Circuit Court in *Dublin Bus v MIBI.*[19] Applicants to date have been successful in finding a County Council, the MIBI and Government Ministers liable for breaches of Community law, including failing to properly implement Directives as well as failing to carry out obligations under a Regulation.

The Emanation of the State Doctrine in Irish Law

The "Emanation of the State" doctrine in Community law is one that has been developed by the Court of Justice as a measure to expand the concept of vertical "direct effect" of Directives. [20] The doctrine entails that the concept of the State is broadened and liberally defined, so that enforcement of Directives is permissible against State organs and domestic administrations that play no formal role in the implementation of the European legislation, albeit that they are bound to apply the provisions of European Directives in practice. While there are several decisions that apply the doctrine and a series of MIBI cases and references that eventually result in a favourable outcome for the litigants after considerable delays in reaching this point, it has received some substantive analysis in Irish law and the jurisprudence of the Court of Justice appears not to have been followed on many occasions by the Irish courts in this area. There are many instances, it is submitted, where the guidance of the Court of Justice should have been sought via Article 276 TFEU (ex Article 234 EC) but where this possibility was not discussed. The issue is one of immense importance as it is **[3–06]**

rights on them; the breach of that rule must be sufficiently serious; and there must be a direct causal link between the breach and the loss or damage sustained by the individuals ...".

The literature is extensive — see, for a comprehensive survey, Craig and De Burca, *EU Law: Texts, Cases and Materials* (4th ed) (OUP, Oxford, 2007) p 328, *et seq*; Tridimas, "Liability for Breaches of Community Law: Growing Up and Mellowing Down" (2001) 38 CMLR 301.

[19] *Tate v Minister for Social Welfare* [1995] 1 IR 418; *Coppinger v Waterford County Council* [1998] 4 IR 220; *Dublin Bus v The Motor Insurance Bureau of Ireland (MIBI)* (Circuit Court, 29 October 1999); *Emerald Meats Limited v The Minister for Agriculture and Others (No 2)* [1997] 3 IR 1; *Maxwell v Minister for Agriculture, Food and Forestry* [1999] 2 IR 474; *Farrell v Whitty* [2008] IEHC 124, but was unsuccessfully invoked in *Rooney v Minister for Agriculture, Food and Forestry* [2004] IEHC 305, *Dekra Erin Teoranta v Minister for the Environment and Local Government* (Unreported, High Court, 2 November 2001), *Glencar Explorations plc and Andaman Resources plc v The County Council of the County of Mayo* (No 2) [2002] 1 IR 84, *Short v Ireland* [2004] IEHC 64, *An Blascaod Mor Teoranta v The Commissioners of Public Works In Ireland (No4)* [2000] 3 IR 565.

[20] The Court itself has long foreclosed the possibility of Directives having horizontal direct effect albeit that on another level, the Court continuously veers towards such a position. For a discussion of the substantive concept, see Craig and De Búrca, *EU Law: Texts, Cases & Materials* (4th ed) (OUP, Oxford, 2007) Ch 8. It has resulted in a broad and liberal definition being accorded by the Court to an organ of the State so as to afford relief to applicants: See Case 103/88 *Fratelli Constanzo SpA v Commune di Milano* [1989] ECR 1839, where the Court of Justice held that "decentralised authorities such as municipalities" would be regarded as the State for the purposes of liability under the doctrine and thus afford relief to an applicant. See Case C-188/89 *Foster v British Gas plc* [1990] ECR I-3313 and Case 152/84 *Marshall v Southampton* [1986] ECR 723. However, local or regional governmental authorities are not regarded as a "Member State" for the purposes of Art 263 TFEU (ex Art 230 EC): see C-417/04P *Regione Siciliano v Commission of the European Communities* [2006] ECR I-388.

fundamental to a litigant's ability to invoke Community law that this doctrine be liberally construed. The doctrine might also be said to be key to an effective system of remedies at national and Community law level, of major constitutional importance. Thus, the treatment by the Irish courts of this subject is not insignificant.

[3–07] One of the first occasions when the Irish High Court had to consider this question of "an Emanation of the State" was in *Browne v An Bord Pleanála.*[21] There, Barron J examined the question as to whether an application for planning permission had complied with the provisions of Council Directive 85/337/EEC on the assessment of the effects of certain public and private projects on the environment. The status of the respondent (An Bord Pleanála) arose for consideration there. Upon examining the leading authorities of the Court of Justice as to the "Emanation of the State" doctrine *Foster v British Gas*[22] and *Marshall v Southampton Health Authority,*[23] Barron J concluded that although the respondent had replaced a government Minister as the appellate tribunal in planning matters,[24] neither the Minister, when so acting, nor the respondent has or had any powers wider than an appellate tribunal.[25] Under no circumstances, he held, could the respondent be held liable for the failure of the State to implement the Directive, if they had so failed. The remaining issues for decision in *Browne* will not be discussed here, suffice to say that this represents a particularly narrow reading of the doctrine of State liability, given the functions and special powers of the respondent were established pursuant to statute which could be argued to fall squarely within the *Foster* test.

[3–08] This stands in marked contrast to the subsequent High Court decision of Geoghegan J in *Coppinger v Waterford County Council.*[26] There, Geoghegan J relying upon the settled jurisprudence of the Court of Justice, found no difficulty in concluding that the County Council in question fulfilled the criteria he found "neatly summarised" in *Foster v British Gas.* Thus, the County Council was to be treated as though it were the State. However, despite the obvious correctness of the decision, there is no searching

---

[21] *Browne v An Bord Pleanála* [1989] ILRM 865.

[22] *Foster v British Gas* [1990] ECR I-3313, which held, in reference to British Gas which was at the time of the proceedings a nationalised industry and a monopoly, that a body would be an "Emanation of the State" for the purposes of Community law if (at paras. 18–20):

> "whatever its legal form, which had been made responsible pursuant to a measure adopted by the State, for providing a public service under the control of the State and has for that purpose special powers beyond those which result from the normal rules applicable in relations between individuals…".

[23] *Marshall v Southampton Health Authority* [1986] ECR 723, where the Court of Justice held that a Health Authority would be regarded as an organ of the State for the purposes of Community law.

[24] An Bord Pleanála was established in 1977 under the Local Government (Planning and Development) Act 1976 and is responsible for the determination of appeals and certain other matters under the Planning and Development Acts 2000 to 2002, and with appeals under the Building Control Act 1990, the Local Government (Water Pollution) Acts 1977 and 1990 and the Air Pollution Act 1987.

[25] *Browne v An Bord Pleanála* [1989] ILRM 865, 873.

[26] *Coppinger v Waterford County Council* [1998] 4 IR 220. See Travers, "The Liability of Local Authorities for Breaches of Community Directives by Member State" (1997) 22 ELR 173.

analysis of the powers and functions of the County Council here which accordingly affects its precedential value.[27]

In *Short v Ireland*,[28] the issue arose for consideration as to whether British Nuclear Fuels plc was an "Emanation of the State" for the purposes of Community law. There, the plaintiff had been granted leave to serve on the third party defendant (British Nuclear Fuels plc) notice of a summons for injuries allegedly arising from the operation of the publicly funded nuclear processing plant of British Nuclear Fuels plc. The plaintiffs served the summons on the third defendant rather than notice thereof which the defendant sought to set aside. The plaintiffs argued before Barrington J in the Supreme Court that they would invoke alleged non-compliance by British Nuclear Fuels with the Directives[29] to attack any administrative authorisations which they may have received for the THORP project in question.[30] In the Supreme Court, Barrington J for the Court noted that British Nuclear Fuels plc was a company incorporated under English company law and had shares held in it, by or on behalf of the UK through Secretaries of State. However, it denied that it constituted, for the purposes of Community law, an "Emanation of the State". Barrington J held that this was an issue to be determined at trial. Nonetheless he commented, *obiter*, that it would have far-reaching consequences to find that the doctrine of direct effect could be invoked against such a body. However, once again, the *Foster v British Gas* test appears not to have received any analysis and it is highly likely that British Gas and British Nuclear Fuels could be found to be reasonably similarly constituted, which is of great relevance to the future stages of the proceedings here, the former having being found to be an organ of the State by the Court of Justice,[31] at least for the purposes of the doctrine of the largely construed "State". **[3–09]**

The Irish Supreme Court has recently had to consider the concept of the "Emanation of the State" and its consequent liability but refused a preliminary reference to determine the issue. Thus, in *McBride v Galway Corporation*[32] the applicant had sought to quash the decision of the respondent to invite tenders for the construction of a waster water treatment plant on Mutton Island. It was argued that Council Directive 85/337/EEC[33] was directly applicable as to the result to be achieved and that the respondent as an "Emanation of the State" was obliged to ensure that the objectives of the Directive were met. The Supreme Court held, *per* Keane J, that the defendant Corporation, although undoubtedly an organ of administration, could not be regarded as in breach of the **[3–10]**

[27] See the decision of the Court of Justice in Case 103/88 *Fratelli Constanzo SpA v Commune di Milano* [1989] ECR 1839, where the Court of Justice held that decentralised authorities such as municipalities would be regarded as the State for the purposes of liability under the doctrine and thus afford relief to an applicant.

[28] *Short v Ireland* [1996] 2 IR 188.

[29] Council Directive 85/337/EEC on the assessment of effects of certain public and private projects on the environment and Council Directive 80/836/Euratom on informing the general public about health measures to be applied and steps to be taken in the event of a radiological emergency.

[30] That is, a Thermal Nuclear Reprocessing Plant, a nuclear fuel reprocessing plant, located at Sellafield in Cumbria, operated by British Nuclear Group (GNP), a subsidiary of BNFL.

[31] See *Foster v British Gas, supra.*

[32] *McBride v Galway Corporation* [1998] 1 IR 485.

[33] Council Directive 85/337/EEC on the assessment of the effects of certain public and private projects on the environment.

requirements of "the Environment Directive", as it was the Member States who were required to ensure that environment impact assessments were prepared.[34] Keane J held that it would have been within the competence of the relevant ministers to provide that an EIS should, in all cases, be prepared by the competent authority authorised to give such consent, such as the Minister for the Marine. An application for a preliminary reference was refused by the Court. This conclusion was reached despite the examination by the Supreme Court of the principles of law as set out by the Court of Justice in *Fratelli* and *Marshall*: the latter being a principle of broad application to "decentralised authorities". This, however, appears to be an unduly restrictive view of the City Council (Corporation) in question and bucks the trend towards a large and liberal conception of the State in Community law. The City Council in question possessed extensive powers indeed. In fact, City Councils would consider themselves to have all of the functional powers of a County Council[35] and a conclusion against finding it to be an Emanation of the State appears at odds with the construction mandated by the Court of Justice.

[3–11] Finally, (and not in chronological order) in the case of *De Búrca v Wicklow County Council,*[36] an equally narrow view of the State was expressed by Ó Caoimh J in the High Court. There, the applicant sought to judicially review the defendant's waste management policy as being in breach of the requirements of Article 7 of Council Directive 91/156/EEC.[37] The applicant member of the respondent alleged, *inter alia*, that the Directive had direct effect against the respondent as an Emanation of the State. Whilst the remainder of the applicant's claim will not be discussed here further, Ó Caoimh J concluded that the applicant was not entitled to the relief sought. As regards the implementation of the Directive, however, he held that the only respondent here was a local authority which was not responsible for the making of regulations under the Act of 1996 and that no order, accordingly, could be made in relation to the alleged failure of the Minister or the State generally as to the implementation, transposition or application of the provisions of the Directive. This represents yet another restrictive interpretation of the doctrine of the "Emanation of the State" and again it is notable that there is no examination whatsoever of the relevant case-law here which would indicate a conclusion to the contrary. [38]

---

[34] *McBride v Galway Corporation* [1998] 1 IR 485, 528.

[35] I am grateful to officials of Galway Corporation for their discussion of the matter with me. See generally Butler, ed., *Keane on Local Government* (2nd ed) (Firstlaw, Dublin, 2003).

[36] *De Burca v Wicklow County Council* [2002] 2 IR 196.

[37] Council Directive 91/156/EEC on waste. The Directive was transposed in to Irish law by the Waste Management Act 1996, which required local authorities to make waste management plans.

[38] To similar effect, for a reasonably strict but correct application of the case-law to a less than substantive argument, see *Friends of the Curragh Environment Limited v An Bord Pleanála* [2006] IEHC 243, where Kelly J held that, *inter alia,* Art 3 Directive 2003/35/EC (providing for public participation in respect of the drawing up of certain plans and programmes relating to the environment and amending with regard to public participation and access to justice Council Directives 85/337/EEC and 96/61/EC) did not have direct effect and that the Turf Club could not be an Emanation of the State:

> "... I am satisfied that that Directive does not meet the criteria which would render it capable of being given direct effect in this jurisdiction. Even if it did, it could not be utilised as a vehicle for granting a PCO in respect of the Turf Club since that is not an emanation of the State".

The Motor Insurers Bureau of Ireland Litigation and the Motor Insurance Directives

A series of cases was generated by the Irish courts on the status of the Motor Insurers Bureau of Ireland and the Motor Insurance Directives, as to the rights and obligations flowing from the Directives. Somewhat disappointingly, this series of litigation has only recently resulted in a favourable outcome for the individual litigants. Three Motor Insurance Directives are of relevance to the case-law here: the First, Second and Third Directives (Council Directive 72/166/EC, Council Directive 84/5/EEC and Council Directive 90/232/EEC). The Second Directive deemed void insurance exemption clauses in certain instances and the Third Directive covered liability for personal injures to all passengers and sought to protect injured persons from gaps in insurance. The Third Directive had not been timely transposed into Irish law. An initial decision of a series of cases as to the status in EU law of the MIBI which follows this particularly restrictive trend is *Delargy v Minister for the Environment*.[39] There, Murphy J in the High Court was asked to determine whether Council Directive 72/166 EEC, as amended, in respect of compulsory motor insurance, had direct effect in order to indemnify the plaintiff who had been unable to enforce an award to her from the Motor Insurance Bureau of Ireland ("MIBI") for injuries suffered as a pillion passenger in a motor accident. Murphy J held that at the relevant time, the Directive lacked direct effect in Ireland. **[3–12]**

However, *obiter*, he determined that, having considered the unreported Circuit Court decision of *Dublin Bus v MIBI*[40] which had found the MIBI to be an Emanation of the State and, *inter alia*, the decision of the House of Lords in *White v White*,[41] where the English MIB was held not to constitute an emanation of the State, without any further reasoned analysis or consideration, Murphy J held that he found the latter to be more persuasive than the Circuit Court authority and thus concluded that the MIBI did not constitute an "Emanation of the State" for the purposes of EU law. With respect, this conclusion is difficult to accept given that the issue was not necessary for determination and appears to lack the form of analysis required for such a significant **[3–13]**

---

39 *Delargy v Minister for the Environment* [2005] IEHC 94.

40 The decision of His Honour Judge McMahon (as he then was), Circuit Court, 29 October 1999. See the criticism of this decision by Keville, "The Principle of Effectiveness and the Development of a System of Remedies at European Community Law" in Lucey and Keville, eds, *Irish Perspectives on EC Law* (Round Hall, Dublin, 2003) and Costello and Drake, "Enforcing EC Motor Insurance Directives: Navigating the Maze" (2003) 9 EPL 371. However, it would have appeared from a cursory reading of the case-law that surely the MIBI must be found to be an Emanation of the State, given the constitution, powers, legislative relationship and governmental relationship that is possesses. To similar effect, see Quigley, "EC law and the MIB Agreements" (2001) 4 JPIL 422. The House of Lords in *White v White* [2001] 2 All ER 43, without much discussion, held that the MIB agreement was not legislation, rather it was a private contractual agreement. The Motor Insurance Directives did not specify a particular body to provide compensation, thus Member State governments could accord this task to a range of bodies. However, the *Foster v British Gas* test, for example, is not considered in this analysis and it is eminently plausible to contend that the MIBI, established *by* the State, with special powers and distinctive features, operating pursuant to legislation, could be held to be an "Emanation of the State".

41 *White v White* [2001] 2 All ER 43.

finding, in addition to arguably constituting a misinterpretation of the case-law of the Court of Justice.

[3–14] Subsequent to *Delargy*, Birmingham J in the High Court in *Farrell v Whitty*[42] referred a question to the Court of Justice as to whether the Third Directive had direct effect.[43] The Court of Justice had held in *Farrell v Whitty,*[44] a decision arising from a referral from the Irish High Court in the proceedings in 2005, that Article 1 of the Third Directive had direct effect and resulted in Birmingham J in *Farrell v Whitty* concluding that the MIBI was an Emanation of the State when the case returned to the Irish courts after the reference entailing a favorable outcome for the litigant. Thus, after an extensive consideration of the case-law, including *Delargy*, Birmingham J held in his final decision in 2008 that the MIBI was an Emanation of the State and set out his reasoning with much clarity and jurisprudential support, emphasising the need for a liberal view of the *Foster* tests:

> "...All these factors lead me to the view that the MIBI, in substance, if not in form operates as a quasi-State claims agency giving effect to an important aspect of public social policy. As such it falls to be identified with the State and is to be regarded as an emanation of the State. In seeking to determine whether the MIBI is as a matter of European Law an emanation of the State I have been conscious that European Law in this area is not static... I have stated my view that it is not appropriate to apply rigorously the *Foster* tripartite test to establish the status of the MIBI. However, I should, before concluding state briefly that even had I been minded to apply that test more rigidly I believe I would have reached the same conclusion.
>
> For reasons that will already be apparent I would have had no hesitation in concluding that the Bureau performs a public service. The position in relation to State control and special powers is less clear cut. Nonetheless I am of the view that aspects such as the operation of a veto on the alteration on the memorandum and articles as well as the entitlement of the Minister to give a binding direction in the event of a disagreement between a claimant and the bureau are indicative of a significant level of State control. This is hardly surprising given that it is the State that ultimately controls the scope of the obligations of the Bureau as it is the State that determines the extent of the requirements for compulsory insurance.
>
> The third test, that of "special powers", is obviously the most difficult but here too I would have been prepared to identify special powers particularly in the area of the requirement for membership of the Bureau on the part of those bodies seeking to conduct insurance business.
>
> In summary, I am of the view that the Motor Insurance Bureau of Ireland is to be regarded as an emanation of the State ...".[45]

[42] C-356/05 *Farrell v Whitty* [2007] ECR I-3067; [2008] IEHC 124.

[43] See also the referral from the Supreme Court in Case C-221/05 *Sam McCauley Chemists (Blackpool) Ltd. v Pharmaceutical Society of Ireland* [2006] ECR I-6869 and in Case C-268/06 *Impact v Minister for Agriculture and Food* [2008] 2 CMLR 47 from the Labour Court.

[44] C-356/05 *Farrell v Whitty* [2007] ECR I-3067; [2008] IEHC 124, where Birmingham J noted the conclusions of the Circuit Court on the status of the MIBI in *Dublin Bus v The MIBI*, (Unreported, Circuit Court, 29 October 1999) and *Withers v Delaney and MIBI* (Unreported, Circuit Court, 9 March 2001).

[45] At paras 13.4 onwards.

While the outcome of this decision is to be commended, that the decision took over three years to obtain is to be deplored and demonstrates the difficulty with the preliminary reference procedure and its usefulness for individual litigants. Of note then is *Smith v Meade and Others,*[46] a final installment of the saga. The plaintiff there was injured in 1999 when the car in which he was a passenger owned by the second defendant and driven by the first defendant, was in collision with another vehicle. The plaintiff was in the part of a vehicle not designed and constructed with seating accommodation and FDB, the insurer, sought to refuse to indemnify the defendants pursuant to s 65 Road Traffic Act 1961, as amended. Section 65 of the 1961 Act provided for a definition of excepted persons who were not required to be covered in a policy of insurance. The issue arose as to whether the High Court was under an obligation to read Irish law in light of the Motor Insurance Directives pursuant to the obligation as set out in the decision of the Court of Justice in *Marleasing.*[47] Peart J in the High Court held that there was no dispute but that at the date of the accident in 1999 the Third Directive had not been transposed into Irish law. The objectives therefore were very clear that an exclusion of liability as here was *prima facie* void. The amendment in s 65 of the Road Traffic Act 1961 was in conflict with these objectives and so Peart J held that he was required to read s 65 of the Act of 1961, as amended, in light of the Third Directive. Thus, he held that the clause contained in the policy of insurance was void disentitling the insurer from relying thereon to refuse to indemnify the first and second defendants for the loss of the plaintiff. Thus, Peart J stated that: [3–15]

> "The amendment to s.65 of the Road Traffic Act, 1961 which I have set forth above is clearly in conflict with these objectives, and the failure to transpose the Third Directive by the date required has meant that on the date of the accident in which the plaintiff received his injuries, the law of this State was out of line with what was required by community law.
>
> I have set out the relevant passage from the Court of Justice's judgment in *Marleasing*. It requires a national court, when applying national law, to do so as far as possible in the light of the wording and purpose of the directive in order to pursue the result sought to be pursued by the directive. It seems inescapable that in the present case this Court is required to read s.65 of the Act as amended by S.I. 346 and 347 of 1992 by overlooking or ignoring the exclusion permitted therein in respect of liability for injuries caused to persons such as the plaintiff in this case. It seems to follow inevitably from this that the Court must conclude that the clause to that effect contained in the policy of insurance by the second named defendant must be regarded as void, therefore disentitling FBD from relying upon it in order to refuse to indemnify the first and second named defendants in respect of the plaintiff's claim for damages for his injuries and loss, in the event that he is found at hearing to have so suffered as a result of the negligence of the first named defendant. I so find".[48]

An interesting feature of this case would appear that the doctrine of State Liability was not in issue in the proceedings and that no claim for damages was being pursued by the plaintiff under this particular heading, albeit that the plaintiff was pursuing a claim for damages as against the first and second defendants generally and that the dispute was [3–16]

---

[46] *Smith v Meade* [2009] IEHC 99.

[47] Case C-106/89 *Marleasing SA v La Comercial Internationale de Alimentacion SA* [1990] ECR I-4135.

[48] *Smith v Meade* [2009] IEHC 99.

determined solely in relation to the indemnifications refusal on the part of the insurer. In substance, perhaps a claim for damages arising from State Liability may have been perceived as double compensation.[49]

Conclusion

[3–17] Thus, in summary, there appears to be a significant difficulties with the correctness of the strict construction of the State in the Irish case law, the MIBI litigation aside, particularly since most of the cases appear not to follow the general tenor of the *Foster v British Gas* or *Fratelli Constanzo SpA v Commune di Milano* tests. Arguably then, the case for a preliminary reference as to the interpretation of the "Emanation of the State" doctrine beyond the MIBI litigation has become all the more compelling. However, the probability of this occurring in the near future seems less than likely, with the Irish courts content to resolve the issue themselves. It is particularly important that the Supreme Court should overrule decisions such as *Delargy* and its own decision in *McBride v Galway Corporation*, in order that the case-law becomes more effective for ordinary litigants.

[49] See also *Minister for Justice, Equality and Law Reform & Commissioner of An Garda Siochana v Director of Equality Tribunal* [2009] IEHC 72, a decision of the Irish High Court concerning the doctrine of direct effect in an age discrimination case and the powers of quasi-judicial bodies and tribunals and *An Taoiseach v Comms for Environmental Information* (Unreported, Neill J, High Court, 4 June 2010) on the ability of the Ombudsman to apply the doctrine of primacy.

CHAPTER 4
The Duty of Sincere Co-Operation on National Courts in Ireland

Overview

National courts are under a duty of co-operation with the Court of Justice, pursuant to the general principle of EU law of sincere co-operation between the States and European institutions, as expressed in Article 4 TEU (ex Article 10 EC) and the related jurisprudence considering this duty.[1] A small but not insignificant body of case-law is developing in Ireland as to the consequences of this obligation in recent times. Moreover, this case-law has a bearing upon the practical operation of the doctrine of supremacy or primacy and direct effect in the domestic legal order. This duty encompasses a wide range of actions and principles, as well as adherence to case-law and the implementation of the doctrines of direct effect, supremacy, State liability and the duty to dis-apply conflicting national law contrary to EU law obligations. The Court of Justice held in *Kühne and Heitz NV v Produktschap voor Pluimvee en Eieren*[2] that the duty of co-operation imposed on national courts pursuant to Article 4 TEU encompassed an obligation to take into account the interpretation of the law by the Court of Justice. Moreover, the extension of the principle of State liability to the national judiciary for breaches of Community law in the controversial case of *Köbler v Republik Osterreich*,[3] [4–01]

[1] See generally Craig and De Burca, *EU Law: Texts, Cases and Materials* (4th ed) (OUP, Oxford, 2007), in particular Ch 9.

[2] Case C-453/00 *Kühne and Heitz NV v Produktschap voor Pluimvee en Eieren* [2004] ECR I-837. See Caranta "Casenote" (2005) 42 CMLR 179. See also Jans, "State Liability and Infringments Attributable to National Courts: A Dutch Perspective on the *Köbler* Case" in Zwaan, Jans and Nelissen, eds., *The European Union: An Ongoing Process of Integration Liber Amicorum Alfred Kellerman* (TMC Asser, 2004).

[3] Case C-224/01 *Köbler v Republik Österreich* [2003] ECR I-10239. In *Köbler*, the possibility of *Francovich* damages for State liability resulting from the refusal of a national court to apply an answer of the Court of Justice in response to a preliminary reference was addressed by the Court of Justice, which sanctioned such damages in the event a party could show loss and damage as a result of non-compliance. See C-118/08 *Transportes Urbanos y Servicios Generales* [2009] ECR I-000; C-173/03 *Traghetti del Mediterraneo* [2006] ECR I- 5177. See Buttimore, "State Liability for Judicial Error: A Bridge Too Far?" (2004) 11 IJEL 446; Nassimpian, "... And we keep on meeting: (de)fragmenting state liability" (2007) 32 ELR 819. See as to changes to the rules of

relates also to the duty of co-operation, although the force of this decision has now substantially diminished.[4]

Case-Law in Ireland

[4–02] In the Irish Courts, the duty of co-operation has manifested itself mostly in one particular area, as to the domestic litigation of matters the subject of proceedings before the Court of First Instance and the Court of Justice or, alternatively, the subject of investigation by the Commission pursuant to Article 258 TFEU (ex Article 226 EC).[5] In *Masterfoods Ltd v HB Ice Cream Ltd*,[6] the Supreme Court was considering an agreement or practice pursuant to Articles 101 and 102 TFEU (ex Articles 81(1) EC and 82 EC), on which a Commission decision had been taken and then a preliminary reference was sought as to the advices of the Court of Justice. Masterfoods Ltd, brought proceedings in Ireland against HB Ice Cream Ltd, a subsidiary of Unilever, for a declaration that its agreements to provide retailers with freezer cabinets on terms that they stocked only HB ice cream contravened Articles 101 and 102 TFEU. The High Court dismissed the action and granted an injunction to restrain Masterfoods from inducing retailers to break their agreements by stocking Masterfoods ice cream. Masterfoods made a complaint to the Commission and gave notice of appeal to the Supreme Court. In the course of discussions with the Commission, HB offered to make some changes in its agreements and the Commission issued a notice saying that it proposed to grant exemption under Article 102 TFEU. However, as in this case, the Commission changed its mind and issued a decision (98/531) stating that HB's agreements infringed Articles 101 and 102 TFEU.

[4–03] HB then applied to the Court of First Instance to annul the decision of the Commission. That was the state of affairs when the appeal came before the Supreme Court in June 1998. The Court then made a reference to the Court of Justice seeking guidance as to how it should proceed. It asked whether it should stay the Irish proceedings pending the decision of the Court of First Instance and whether the decision of the Commission on the HB agreements prevented HB from seeking to uphold the contrary decision of the national court. The Advocate General sounded a note of caution as to the actions of the national court in its decision to refer, given the existence of a Commission decision as to the matter at hand and the consequences of the reference as interpreted when received by the national court. He stated:

> "there is not merely a potential, but a clear and imminent conflict between the decision of the first instance Irish court and a decision of the Commission that has already been adopted. That conflict would have occurred already had the Court of First Instance not suspended the operation of the Commission's decision. Furthermore, there will be a

---

the UK Supreme Court as to certain EU Law obligations and refusing to make preliminary references: Arnull "The Law Lords and the European Union: swimming with the incoming tide" (2010) 35 ELR 57, 61.

[4] See Case C-234/04 *Kapferer v Schlank* [2006] ECR I-2585.

[5] But see also, for example, its invocation as to a failure to implement a Directive in *Dublin Bus v MIBI* (Unreported, Circuit Court, 29 October 1999).

[6] Case C-344/98 *Masterfoods Ltd v HB Ice Cream Ltd* [2000] ECR I-11369.

> contradictory decision of the Commission and the Irish Court if, in the context of the main proceedings, the Supreme Court adopts views contrary to those formulated in Commission Decision 98/531. That is likely to happen if the Supreme Court holds, first, that the grounds and operative part of the High Court's decision are correct, or secondly, that although the grounds of the first instance decision are wrong, nevertheless the operative part is correct, on the basis of other evidence".[7]

The Court of Justice held that the risk of conflict arose out of the possibility of the Supreme Court continuing an injunction to enforce agreements which the Commission had held to be unlawful and so the Irish courts had to give priority to the decisions of the European institutions on the validity of the agreements which they were being asked to enforce. The operative part of the decision of the Court of Justice is particularly significant. The Court held that: **[4–04]**

> "[w]here a national court is ruling on an agreement or practice the compatibility of which with Article 85(1) and 86 of the EC Treaty is already the subject of a Commission decision, it cannot take a decision running counter to that of the Commission, even if the latter's decision conflicts with a decision given by a national court of first instance...".[8]

The duty of co-operation was the subject of consideration in the recent decision of *O'Leary v An Bord Pleanála*[9] where the appellants challenged a decision of the first respondent to grant planning permission for a waste incinerator. It was alleged that the grant of planning permission was invalid on the basis that the Board had failed to carry out an integrated assessment of the project as required by the Environmental Impact Assessment (EIA) Directive, Council Directive 85/337/EEC. In the second set of proceedings, the appellants sought to set aside a decision to grant a waste licence, also in respect of the EIA Directive assessment. Both sets of proceedings had been adjourned pending a Supreme Court decision on the validity of the transposition of the Directive, which it upheld.[10] The appellants sought a further adjournment of the proceedings since the Commission had elected to institute proceedings against Ireland pursuant to ex Article 258 TFEU in 2007, following a reasoned opinion in respect of the transposition of the EIA Directive but no proceedings had in fact been commenced. The issue arose as to whether the proceedings should have been further adjourned so as to avoid conflict between a decision of the Irish court and the Court of Justice or Commission if the Commission proceedings were to be upheld, in light of the decision of the Court of Justice in *Masterfoods Ltd v HB Ice Cream Ltd.*[11] Also, the reasoned opinions were not before the Supreme Court *O' Leary*, rendering the decision all the more abstract. **[4–05]**

The Supreme Court, per Murray CJ[12] in dismissing the appeal, held that to adjourn the proceedings pending the outcome of, as yet, non-existent proceedings could deprive **[4–06]**

[7] Para 25.

[8] *cf.* C-453/00 *Kühne and Heitz NV v Produktschap voor Pluimvee en Eieren* [2004] ECR I-837 and Case C-224/01 *Köbler v Republik Österreich* [2003] ECR I-10239.

[9] *O'Leary v An Bord Pleanála* [2008] IESC 55.

[10] *Martin v An Bord Pleanála* [2007] 2 ILRM 401.

[11] Case C-344/98 *Masterfoods Ltd v HB Ice Cream Ltd* [2000] ECR I-11369.

[12] Denham, Hardiman, Geoghegan and Fennelly JJ concurring.

the respondents and/ or notice parties of any effective protection of their rights. Murray CJ held that:

> "Given that no proceedings have been commenced by the Commission and that it is not known when, assuming that they will eventually, be commenced there is a risk of a denial of justice to the respondents and the notice parties if this case were adjourned without any knowledge or even perception as to when the proceedings might eventually commence and, consequently, when they might conclude".

[4–07] The Court held that it had a "general discretion" under national law to grant an adjournment of proceedings for any reason. Here, however, the interests of justice would not be served by the adjournment of the proceedings. The fundamental difference between *Masterfoods* and *O'Leary*, however, remained the fact that a particular action had been taken in *Masterfoods* that entailed that the ultimate decision making process would be upset or interfered with.

See *Phonographic Performance (Ireland) Ltd v Ireland*[13] where the argument was made that the maintenance in force of s 97 of the Copyright Act 2000, as amended, was in breach of the obligations of the State pursuant to Article 4 TFEU as to its implementation of Council Directive 92/100/EC of 19th November, 1992 on rental right and lending right and on certain rights related to copyright in the field of intellectual property, as codified by Directive 2006/115/EC of the European Parliament and the Council of 12 December, 2006. There, the Court had to decide whether a hotel or guesthouse which provides TV or radio sets in guest bedrooms, and distributes to those TV and radio sets a signal received centrally, is a "user" making a "communication to the public" of phonograms which may be played on TV or radio broadcasts for the purposes of Article 8(2) of the Directives. The proceedings are pending before the Court of Justice by way of a preliminary reference at the time of writing.

[4–08] Also of note, finally, is the decision of the High Court in *Kingdom of Belgium v Ryanair*,[14] where there O' Neill J refused an application for a stay in proceedings pending the determination of annulment proceedings pending before the Court of First Instance[15] as to a Commission decision of 2005 on the compatibility of transactions deemed to be illegal State aids from the Walloon region. The plaintiff there issued proceedings to recover the sums paid, invoking Council Regulation (EC) No. 659/1999. The defendants intimated that a preliminary reference would be sought as to the validity of the Commission decision. O' Neill J held that:

---

[13] [2010] IEHC 79.

[14] *Kingdom of Belgium v Ryanair* [2006] IEHC 213. See also as to a conflict between the potential use of Art 267 TFEU and Art 258 TFEU proceedings in *Friends of the Irish Environment Limited v The Minister for the Environment, Heritage and Local Government* [2007] 3 IR 459 where Murphy J granted a stay to the defendants in proceedings initiated in 2004 challenging the validity of s 33(2)(c) of the Planning and Development Act 2000. The Commission had indicated that it intended to issue proceedings against the State as to the implementation of Directive 85/337/EEC on the assessment of the effects of certain public and private projects on the environment and a reasoned opinion had been given in 2003. There is little discussion of much relevant case-law in the judgment, although the outcome appears correct.

[15] T-196/04 *Ryanair Ltd v Commission* [2009] 2 CMLR 7.

> "... the *Zuckerfabrik* case and the *Masterfoods* case form part of a cohesive jurisprudence ... The obligation of sincere co-operation enjoined on member States by Article 10 of the Treaty ... implies that National Courts ... must apply the general jurisprudence of the Community Courts...".

The High Court held that no risk of conflict occurred with judgments of the Court of First Instance, as the Court was not questioning the validity of the decision at issue and that an Article 267 TFEU request would not be successful and the Court refused the stay sought. The decision of the High Court is notably reasoned with more careful analysis of the principles at issue than the Supreme Court decision in *O'Leary*. **[4–09]**

Conclusion

The small handful of decisions considered here collectively represent rare instances where the duty of co-operation arises in the Irish courts and are significant in light of their constitutional consequences and the manner in which the application of the doctrines of direct effect and supremacy are potentially affected as a result. *Masterfoods* is a clear warning to national courts to respect the parameters of their role, while also constituting importance assistance for a national judge weighing the competing and conflicting claims of such a fact matrix. **[4–10]**

CHAPTER 5
Implementing EU Law in Ireland: The Constitutional Dimension

Overview

[5–01] The powers of the State to implement EU law have an important constitutional dimension in Ireland, pursuant to both Articles 15.2.1° and the Article 29.4.6° of the constitution after the Treaty of Lisbon, The former provides for the parameters of the ability of the Oireachtas to delegate legislative powers and the latter provides for a constitutional immunisation of laws implementing European Acts. The focus of the discussion here is intended to be on the former but the latter is an omnipresent feature of that discussion and must be considered accordingly by way of background. A discussion of the recently enacted European Communities Act 2007 follows, which concludes with an analysis of more recent case-law on the topic.

[5–02] Thus, Article 15.2.1° provides that "[t]he sole and exclusive power of making laws for the State is hereby vested in the Oireachtas: no other legislative authority has power to make laws for the State." Article 29.4.6° (ex Article 29.4.10°) prior to the changes effectuated by the Treaty of Lisbon provided that:

> "No provision of this Constitution invalidates laws enacted, acts done or measures adopted by the State which are necessitated by the obligations of membership of the European Union

> or of the Communities, or prevents laws enacted, acts done or measures adopted by the European Union or by the Communities or by institutions thereof, or by bodies competent under the Treaties establishing the Communities, from having the force of law in the State".

[5–03] The revised Article 29.4.6° after the Twenty-Eighth Amendment to the Constitution Act 2009, which repeals and replaces this former provision to take account changes made to the pillar structure by the Treaty of Lisbon and to the role of agencies in legislating, now provides that:

> "No provision of this Constitution invalidates laws enacted, acts done or measures adopted by the State, before, on or after the entry into force of the Treaty of Lisbon, that are necessitated by the obligations of membership of the European Union referred to in subsection 5° of this section or of the European Atomic Energy Community, or prevents laws enacted, acts done or measures adopted by—
>
> i. the said European Union or the European Atomic Energy Community, or institutions thereof,
> ii. the European Communities or European Union existing immediately before the entry into force of the Treaty of Lisbon, or institutions thereof, or
> iii. bodies competent under the treaties referred to in this section, from having the force of law in the State".

Firstly, the background to this clause, its history and early case-law interpreting the provision are assessed here now.

Background and Purpose of Article 29.4.6° — Immunising EU-Related Legislation from Attack

[5–04] The content of Article 29.4.6°[1] could be described as amounting to a domestic immunity for national laws from constitutional challenge, provided under the terms of the Constitution, as to "necessitated" measures implementing aspects of the State's membership of the European Union. Remarkably, Article 29.4.6° represents a particularly narrow basis for integrating the European legal order, when compared and contrasted against other Member State constitutions. Writing in the early 1970s Temple Lang observed that:

> "... [Article 29.4.6°] in comparison with the provisions in the constitutions of the Netherlands, West Germany, Italy, Luxembourg and Norway, it is narrow. This is because it is limited to the three existing Communities, and does not authorise the transfer of any executive, legislative or judicial powers to any future Community whether a new economic community or some future political or military community. If say such new community was set up, the amendment would have no application at all ...".[2]

Over time, however, Article 29.4.6° has become a quagmire of complexity.[3]

---

[1] Hereinafter referred to interchangeably as Art 29.4.6° or the "necessitated" clause".
[2] "Legal and Constitutional Implications for Ireland of Adhesion to the EEC Treaty" (1972) 9 CMLR 167.
[3] On the peculiar and narrow interpretation of the term "necessitated", see the *obiter* comments of Cooke J in *T & Others v Minister for Justice, Equality and Law Reform* [2009] IEHC 529.

Debate within academic circles raged for almost twenty-five years as to the question of jurisdictional and constitutional "*kompetenz-kompetenz*"— as to who would judge just what was "necessitated" and accordingly as to the laws of which legal order?[4] For example, Phelan contended over a decade ago that: **[5–05]**

> "Overall, the provision constitutes a bar to constitutional challenges to European Community law rules and Irish implementing measures. It is not enabling. It does not make European Community law rules part of domestic law . . . European Community law has a similar status in the Irish hierarchy of norms as a statue, the status being conferred by a statute which benefits from a jurisdictional immunity of debated extent. European Community law does not have a status superior to constitutional law, rather the interaction of the 1972 Act and Article 29.4 generally preserves its application".[5]

Phelan has contended that European Communities Act 1972 in tandem with Article 29.4.6°, entails that there is no obligation in Irish law to apply EU treaty obligations in place of contrary Irish law and that Irish courts do not recognise a direct Community law obligation to apply Community law in place of contrary Irish law.[6] This analysis is argued here to overlook a large body of case-law in the Irish Superior courts over thirty-seven years across a range of subject areas applying EU law faithfully, as well as the force of directly effective EU treaty obligations, the duty of co-operation for example, incumbent on Member State courts, pursuant to Article 4 TFEU and the duty to dis-apply conflict national law in favour of EU law.[7] The sweeping immunity afforded to measures implemented or enacted into Irish law via Article 29.4.6° is an important reminder of what supremacy entails for sovereignty in Ireland and how pragmatism may prevail over principle. The particularly unprincipled stance adopted by the Superior Courts in recent years, clearly keen to uphold the constitutionality of laws the subject of a presumption as to their constitutionality, and meanwhile sacrificing the substance of the putative constitutional immunity, has led to state of affairs where Article 29.4.6° is largely redundant. The Constitution Review Group, when reviewing the substantive and operational workings of the Constitution in 1996 decided against any wholesale amendments being made to the "necessitated" clause then.[8] However, the review undertaken by the Group was, it is submitted, a particularly narrow one without much discussion or deliberation and temporally was a review that was to take place prior to many changes of major constitutional significance, domestically and at European level, discussed above, that would impact with major significance upon the "necessitated" clause, which surely tempers its conclusions. **[5–06]**

---

[4] See generally the discussion in Phelan, *Revolt or Revolution: The Constitutional Boundaries of the European Community* (Round Hall, Dublin 1997).

[5] Phelan, *Revolt or Revolution: The Constitutional Boundaries of the European Community* (Round Hall, Dublin,1997) pp. 333 *et seq*.

[6] Phelan, "Can Ireland legislate contrary to European Community law?" (2010) 33 ELR 530. See also Cahill, "Ireland's Constitutional Amendability and Europe's Constitutional Ambition" (2008) 9 GLJ 1191.

[7] See above generally in Ch 2.

[8] *Report of the Constitution Review Group* (Constitution Review Group, 1996) p 113 *et seq*.

Legislative History to Article 29.4.6°

[5–07] The legislative history to the Third Amendment of the Constitution Bill 1971, now Article 29.4.6°, is particularly revealing. In particular, the discussions of the politicians of the day as to the constitutional immunity afforded through the "necessitated" clause are as relevant today as ever. Despite this fact, it still is most remarkable that no subsequent Superior Court decision has adopted a historical interpretation of the "necessitated" clause to date and so a historical analysis of the clause or any clues as to its objectives is potentially of use in the future.

[5–08] The eminent Dr Browne TD had argued in the Dáil at the time of the discussion of the Bill that:

> "This Bill is a blank cheque. We will do anything to remain a member of the British Commonwealth of Nations, which we have never left from an economic point of view".[9]

[5–09] Unfortunately, most of the focus of the interpretation of the "necessitated" clause has been on that itself, i.e., its interpretation and not the *existence* of the clause, itself a notable phenomenon given the absence of same in other jurisdictions. In a passage that is most frequently cited by academia and many judicial decisions, the words of Mr Cosgrave TD, have become of immense importance, explaining the opposition amendment to the wording of the Bill from "consequent upon" to "necessitated" to decrease constitutional immunity to secondary legislation and enhance any remnants of constitutional sovereignty possible. He stated that, in proposing the amendment, it was imperative:

> "In Part II, page 6, line 9, to delete "consequent upon" and substitute "necessitated" by "the obligations of"... The reason for the amendment ... is that the words "consequent upon" are too wide. The proposed amendment will limit the changes which may become necessary as a result of the accession of this country to the EEC in the event of this referendum being accepted by the people-that the changes, which will have the force of law, will only be those that are "necessitated" by the obligation of membership, those which are strictly necessary rather than any changes involving actions done or measures adopted consequent upon membership ... It is designed to ensure that the proposed amendment in no sense exceeds the necessary changes which must be made in order to conform with the Treaty of Rome".[10]

[5–10] However, there were those who believed the merits of such an amendment to be futile, sentiments that were to be borne out in later judicial constructions of the clause. Mr Keating TD opined that:

> "... even dropping the words "consequent upon" in line 10 and substituting the words ""necessitated" by the obligations of", the imprecision of the phrase "acts done or measures adopted" is not removed".[11]

---

[9] Vol. 258 *Dáil Debates*, 26 January 1972, 588.

[10] Vol. 258 *Dáil Debates*, 25 January 1972, 394.

[11] Vol. 258 *Dáil Debates*, 25 January 1972, 426.

In response, Dr Browne TD, stated that:

> "[t]he simple substitution by Fine Gael of "necessitated" for "consequential on" is really whistling past the graveyard".[12]

It seems clear from subsequent judicial decisions that the only interpretation of the clause that would assume real importance would be that of Mr Cosgrave TD. However, it seems also apparent that the change of wording as adopted does little to clarify the murkiness of the wording of the clause. Arguably, the legislative history of the clause serves one immensely important purpose: that of demonstrating the profound differences of opinion as to European integration that still manifest themselves in the Irish Supreme Court[13] as to the type of immunity or shield that is desirable for two competing legal orders to co-exist. **[5–11]**

The judicial construction of Article 29.4.6° on the part of the Superior Courts has not proved to be linear. In fact, the interpretation of the clause by the Irish courts never quite reached for consideration the matters that had preoccupied the scholarship for several decades, particularly as to the question of *kompetenz-kompetenz.*[14] The substantive operation of Article 29.4.6° was not to be considered in any great detail by the Supreme Court until some twenty years after its initial inception, a most considerable time indeed and testament to the ostensible difficulties involved in surmounting the operation of the clause; that is proving that a measure was not "necessitated" by membership obligations. **[5–12]**

Early Case-Law on Article 29.4.6°

The first major High Court decision to consider the full constitutional effects of Article 29.4.6° occurred in the decision of *Lawlor v Minister for Agriculture*[15] and has long been regarded as somewhat controversial, in so far as its construction of the "necessitated" clause goes, although it has never been the subject of reconsideration on the part of the Supreme Court to date. The facts of *Lawlor* concerned the European Communities (Milk Levy) Regulations 1985, which had purported to give retrospective effect to Commission Regulation (EEC) No 1371/84. The plaintiffs challenged the retrospective application of the Regulations as being, *inter alia*, an interference with **[5–13]**

[12] Vol. 258 *Dáil Debates,* 25 January 1972, 429.

[13] *Meagher v Minister for Agriculture* [1994] 1 IR 329.

[14] See generally Hogan and Whyte, eds, *Kelly: The Irish Constitution* (4th ed) (Lexis-Nexis, Dublin, 2003); Casey, *Constitutional Law in Ireland* (3rd ed) (Round Hall, Dublin, 2000); Gwynn Morgan, *The Separation of Powers in the Irish Constitution* (Round Hall, Dublin, 1997); O' Higgins, "The Constitution and the Community— Scope for Stress" in O'Reilly, ed, *Human Rights and Constitutional Law: Essays in Honour of Brian Walsh* (Round Hall, Dublin, 1992); Gallagher, "The Constitution and the Community" (1993) 2 IJEL 129. *Cf.* Phelan, *Revolt or Revolution: The Constitutional Boundaries of the European Community* (Round Hall, Dublin, 1997). See also Temple Lang, "Legal and Constitutional Implications for Ireland of Adhesion to the EEC Treaty" (1974) 11 CMLR 167 and Robinson, "The Irish European Communities Act, 1972" (1973) 10 CMLR 352 and 467. See Fahey, "*Mccauley Chemists: The Supreme Court invokes Article 234 EC to Resolve the "Necessitated" Question*" (2006) 28 DULJ 401.

[15] *Lawlor v Minister for Agriculture* [1990] 1 IR 356.

constitutional property rights, arguing that they were not "necessitated" by the provisions of Article 29.4.6°. In rejecting the plaintiffs claim, Murphy J held that he was satisfied that:

> "the apparent infringement would fall within the exception provided by Article 29, s. 4, sub-s. 3 of the Constitution [now Article 29.4.10°]. It seems to me that the word "necessitated" in that sub-section could not be limited in its construction to laws, acts or measures all of which required in all of their parts to be enacted, done or adopted by the obligations of membership of the Community. *It seems to me that the word "necessitated" in this context must extend to and include acts or measures which are consequent upon membership of the Community* and in general fulfilment of the obligations of such membership, and even where there may be a choice or degree of discretion vested in the State as to the particular manner in which it would meet the general spirit of its obligations of membership." (Emphasis supplied).[16]

[5–14] It is felt by many that this interpretation, including measures "consequent upon" membership within the ambit of Article 29.4.6°, was both inconsistent with the earlier decision of the Supreme Court *Crotty v An Taoiseach*,[17] wherein a particularly narrow view was adopted of constitutional authority to act in foreign affairs on the part of the State,[18] and also with regard to the legislative history to the Third Amendment to the Constitution Bill 1971.[19] Moreover, as Costello suggests, it is an exceptionally wide view of what is "necessitated" by Community law.[20]

[5–15] The subsequent decision of Murphy J in *Greene v Minister for Agriculture*[21] operated to temper his earlier approach and involved a challenge to the exclusion of farmers in a disadvantaged area from an administrative scheme awarding compensation payments

---

16 At p 377.

17 *Crotty v An Taoiseach* [1987] IR 713. In *Crotty*, the Supreme Court had to address the full implications of the first sentence of Art 29.4.3 [now Art 29.4.6°], as to Membership of the Communities and Title III of the Single European Act. The Supreme Court declared the State's purported ratification thereof to be unconstitutional and outside the purpose and scope of the licence granted by the people in the joining the Communities. Thus, their assent by way of referendum was required in order to permit Ireland to adopt foreign policy decisions within the framework of European Political Cooperation, as provided therein. Thus, while strictly speaking the Supreme Court was not concerned with the latter part of Art 29.4.6° as to the "necessitated" clause, the narrow and formalistic view of the licence granted by Art 29.4.6° and the rigid view taken there as to the State and foreign policy as being subject at all times to the provisions of the Constitution, was surely a matter of some relevance to be considered in *Lawlor*.

18 See Hogan, "The Supreme Court and the Single European Act" (1987) 16 *Irish Jurist* 55 and Temple Lang, "The Irish Case Which delayed the Single European Act: *Crotty v An Taoiseach*" (1987) 24 CMLR 709. See also Casey, *Constitutional Law in Ireland* (3rd ed) (Round Hall, Dublin, 2000) p 214 *et seq.*

19 See also Hogan and Whyte, eds, *Kelly: The Irish Constitution* (4th ed) (Lexis Nexis, Dublin, 2003) para. 5.3.65.

20 Costello, "European Community Judicial Review in the Irish Courts-Scope, Standards and the Separation of Powers" in Lucey and Keville, eds, *Irish Perspectives on EC Law* (Round Hall, Dublin, 2003).

21 *Greene v Minister for Agriculture* [1990] 2 IR 17.

pursuant to Council Directive 75/268/EEC. Article 6.2 of the scheme provided that "Member State may lay down additional or restrictive conditions for granting the compensatory allowance". The schemes, which the Minister implemented by way of a means test were challenged as *ultra vires* the Minister and not "necessitated" by the obligations of membership pursuant to Article 29.4.6°. Murphy J held that whilst undoubtedly membership of the Communities required Ireland to implement a scheme complying with the Directive at issue, it did not follow that every scheme drafted pursuant to the Directive was "necessitated". Referring to his judgment in *Lawlor*, Murphy J stated in an important passage that:

> "I have no doubt but that laws enacted, acts done and measures adopted by the State are necessitated within the meaning of the Third Amendment aforesaid by obligations of membership of the Communities *even where the particular actions of the State involve a measure of choice, selection or discretion*. If there were no such flexibility it would hardly be necessary to say that the particular actions were adopted by the State at all. Presumably they would have operated as a Community Regulation rather than as a Directive by it.
>
> On the other hand there must be a point at which the discretion exercised by the State or the national authority is so far-reaching or so detached from the result to be achieved by the Directive that it cannot be said to have been "necessitated" by it".[22] (Emphasis supplied)

Thus, it appeared to Murphy J that the phrase "necessitated" involved some degrees of necessity or limits as to discretion. In the instant case, the particular provisions introduced by the Minister as to income of a farmer could not be said to have been "necessitated" by the obligations of membership of the Community. Murphy J, thus, proceeded to invalidate the scheme. Professor Casey has suggested that the later decision of the Supreme Court in *Meagher v Minister for Agriculture*[23] considered *infra*, would in fact appear to subsequently confirm the correctness of the findings of Murphy J in *Greene v Minister for Agriculture.*[24] However, this seems difficult to accept in view of the low and pragmatic threshold set by the *Meagher* Court for delegated legislation to be constitutional and immunised from review, whereas the *Greene* decision suggests some more formal limits to implementation without specifying those limits. **[5–16]**

Of note, further, is the decision of *Condon v Minister for Agriculture*,[25] which concerned a challenge to the Ministerial scheme that sought to implement Community Regulations as to milk quotas. Without any analysis of existing case-law or the legislative history to Article 29.4.6°, Lynch J in the High Court held that where the details, as therein, of the implementing Community Regulations were reasonable, it was "necessitated" by Community obligations. If the details of implementation were unreasonable or unfair,[26] he held they could hardly then be said to be "necessitated" by the obligations of Community membership and would thus be open to Community **[5–17]**

22 At p 25.

23 *Meagher v Minister for Agriculture* [1994] 1 IR 329.

24 Casey, *Constitutional Law in Ireland* (3rd ed) (Round Hall, Dublin, 2000) p 212.

25 *Condon v Minister for Agriculture*, Unreported, High Court, 12 October 1990; [1993] IJEL 151.

26 At p 9.

challenge. Clearly, this test set the threshold for validity excessively low, to an administrative law test level and appeared to bypass somehow the test of "necessity" for immunity contained in Article 29.4.6°, contrary to its own legislative history.[27] Yet again, however, *Condon* has yet to be judicially disapproved of.

[5–18] Chronologically, at least, the position had been reached at High Court level of a particularly pragmatic and wide ranging view of the "necessitated" clause. Thus, the constitutional immunity therein intended was being upheld both in spirit and in purpose. However, no definitive Supreme Court decision had been delivered as to the implications of the immunity shield contained in Article 29.4.6° and two key judgments were shortly to be delivered that would critically impact upon this jurisprudence. The judgments also relate to the other key constitutional clause, 15.2.1,° which is briefly considered here first prior to a substantive analysis of the cases.

Delegated Legislation and EU Law

[5–19] As to Article 15.2.1,° the Irish Courts have, in the past twenty years, taken to espousing a particularly strict view of the powers of the Oireachtas to delegate legislation pursuant to Article 15.2.1° of the Constitution.[28] It appears particularly difficult in more recent times to invalidate delegated legislation, both in the High Court and Supreme Court generally.[29] The test enunciated by the Supreme Court as to the validity of Executive delegated legislation was most famously set out in the decision of *Cityview Press Ltd v An Chomhairle Oiliuna,*[30] which in turn has unfortunately governed the European dimension to delegated legislation. The test in *Cityview* remains to this day the definitive one as to the validity of delegated subordinate legislation pursuant to a parent statute, to be tested by whether delegated legislation is giving effect to principles and policies in a parent act. The Supreme Court there held that:

---

[27] See Hogan and Whyte, *op.cit.* para. 5.3.66.

[28] As to which, see the analysis of the Hogan and Whyte, eds, *Kelly: The Irish Constitution op.cit.,* 4.2.09 *et seq.* See also Carolan, "Democratic Control Or "High-sounding Hocus-pocus"?—A Public Choice Analysis Of The Non-delegation Doctrine"(2007) 14(1) DULJ 111; Carolan, *A New Separation of Powers: A Theory for the Modern State* (OUP, Oxford 2009); Doherty, "Land, Milk and Freedom— Implementing Community Law in Ireland" (2004) 11 IJEL 141; Costello "European Community Judicial Review in the Irish Courts" in Lucey and Keville, eds, *Irish Perspectives on EC Law* (Round Hall, Dublin, 2003); Travers, "The Constitutionality of the Implementation of EC Directives into Irish Law Revisited" (1994) 88 GLSI 99; Gwynn Morgan, *The Separation of Powers in Irish Constitution* (Round Hall, Dublin, 1997) p 245 *et seq*; Fanning, "Reflections on the Legislative Process following *Leontjava v Director of Public Prosecutions*" (2004) 39 *Irish Jurist* 286.

[29] *Dunnes Stores v Central Statistics Office* [2009] IEHC 561; *English v H. S. E.* [2008] IEHC 398; *Bupa Ireland Ltd v Health Insurance Authority* [2006] IEHC 431; *Clarke v South Dublin County Council* [2008] IEHC 84 (HC); *Article 26 and the Health (Amendment) Bill 2004* [2005] 1 IR 105 (SC). But see on appeal in the Supreme Court, where the delegated legislation was concluded to be *ultra vires,* albeit on different grounds to the High Court: *Bupa Ireland Ltd v Health Insurance Authority* [2008] IESC 431.

[30] *Cityview Press Ltd v An Chomhairle Oiliuna* [1980] IR 381, 399.

> "In the view of this Court, the test is whether that which is challenged as an unauthorised delegation of parliamentary power is more than a mere giving effect to "principles and policies" which are contained in the statute itself. If it be, then it is not authorised; for such would constitute a purported exercise of legislative power by an authority which is not permitted to do so under the Constitution. On the other hand, if it be within the permitted limits — if the law is laid down in the statute and details only are filled in or completed by the designated Minister or subordinate body — there is no unauthorised delegation of legislative power".

Indeed, it has been fairly suggested that the application of the *Cityview* principles to the European dimension of the Article 15.2.1° case-law has operated to muddy the waters and failed to address the level of discretion possessed by Member States.[31] Thus, a consideration of the case-law outside of the European context is of immense importance. The decision of the Supreme Court in *Meagher v Minister for Agriculture*[32] is surely the seminal decision to be considered as to this EU dimension. *Meagher* was to be the first major consideration by the Supreme Court of Article 29.4.6°. **[5–20]**

The Landmark Case of *Meagher v Minister for Agriculture*

The facts of *Meagher v Minister for Agriculture* concerned legislation that Member States were obliged to implement as to a Directive relating to prohibited substances in animals.[33] Ireland amended the ordinary Statute of Limitations time limit applying to summary offences of 6 months, under s 10(4) of the Petty Sessions Ireland Act 1851, extending this time limit to two years. The applicant farmer was charged with offences under the legislation implementing the Directive[34] and sought to challenge the validity of s 3(2) of the European Communities Act 1972 as pursuant to Article 15.2.1° in so far as it purported to allow the Minister to amend primary legislation. Section 3 of the European Communities Act 1972 prior to its later amendment provided that: **[5–21]**

> "1. A Minister of State may make Regulations for enabling section 2 of this Act to have full effect.
> 2. Regulations under this section may contain such incidental, supplementary and consequential provisions as appear to the Minister making the Regulations to be necessary for the purposes of the Regulations (including provisions repealing, amending or applying, with or without modification, other law, exclusive of this Act).
> 3. Regulations under this section shall not create an indictable offence.
> 4. Regulations under this section may be made before the 1st day of January, 1973, but Regulations so made shall not come into operation before that day."

The respondents conceded that a statute authorising the Minister to amend law by way of delegated legislation was invalid. However, it was contended that the impugned measures were acts done or measures "necessitated" by the obligations of membership, pursuant to Article 29.4.6°, thus shielding the measures from scrutiny. In the High Court, Johnson J, (as he they was) in a bold act of constitutional construction, declared **[5–22]**

---

31 See *Maher v Minister for Agriculture and Food* [2001] 2 IR 139. Hogan and Whyte, *Kelly: The Irish Constitution* (4th ed) (Lexis-Nexis, Dublin, 2003) 5.3.71 *et seq.*

32 *Meagher v Minister for Agriculture* [1994] 1 IR 329.

33 Council Directive 85/358/ EEC.

34 European Communities (Control of Oestrogenic, Androgenic, Gestagenic and Thryrostatic Substances) Regulations, 1988.

s 3(2) of the Act of 1972 to be unconstitutional insofar as it entitled the Minister to, *inter alia*, repeal or amend legislation, thereby potentially invalidating thousands of statutory instruments enacted pursuant to the section. He held that the Regulations had not been validated by the procedure set out in s 3(4) of the Act of 1972 and so thus were invalid.[35]

[5–23] On appeal to the Supreme Court, however, the Court allowed the appeal. Two judgments were delivered for the Court, by Blayney and Denham JJ respectively, Blayney J[36] rejected the submission that the Directive did not expressly require a two year time limit and held that the Directive clearly required the offences to be created and effectively prosecuted. It was not necessary that the Directive itself should fix a time but rather it was for the State to so do. There was no need to make the amendment to the Act of 1851 by Statute as the State was, in his view:

> "*not free. It was obliged* to implement the Directive and is so obliged to choose a method of implementation...".[37] (Emphasis supplied)

[5–24] Thus, he held that although Article 29.4.6° left the choice and form of the implementation of the Directive to the State, it was nonetheless "necessitated" by the obligations of membership, clearly adopting a strong practical stance in this regard.

[5–25] Denham J, by contrast, adopted both a legal and practical stance.[38] For Denham J, it was necessary to read the "necessitated" clause along with Article 15.2.1°.[39] Membership of the Community did not require a special form or method of implementation to be adopted but, as the Regulations were made pursuant to s 3 of the Act of 1972, the Directive was binding as to the result to be achieved. She held that:

> "If the Directive left to the national authority matters of principle or policy to be determined then the "choice" of the Minister would require legislation by the Oireachtas. But where there is no case made that principles and policies were determined in the Directive, then legislation by a delegated form, by Regulation, is a valid choice".[40]

---

[35] In the wake of the decision, the European Communities (Amendment) Act, 1993 was enacted to assuage fears that all statutory instruments enacted pursuant to the Act of 1972 might be invalid and, in the words of one TD, to "make everything legal that the High Court had declared to be illegal, while at the same time insisting in its own legislation that this effort was unnecessary because in the Government's view everything the High Court found to be illegal is in fact, legal." (Mr Phil Hogan TD, 44 *Dáil Debates*, 1709).

[36] At pp 351-360.

[37] At p 360.

[38] See Travers, "The Constitutionality of the Implementation of EC Directives into Irish Law Revisited" (1994) 88 GLSI 99, 100, who suggests that Denham J's judgment accords more with democratic principles, where by contrast, Blayney J's emphasis on appropriateness and effectiveness is more accommodating to Government Ministers. It is argued here that this perhaps is an unduly far-fetched interpretation of the judgments and that, in reality, both are deeply rooted in pragmatism, with Denham J giving more of a constitutional gloss to the matter. See also Carney, "*Meagher v Minister for Agriculture*: An Opportunity to Angel Dust Article 29.4.5" (1995) 13 ILT 187.

[39] At p 365.

[40] At p 365.

Hence, the Regulations pursuant to s 3 of the Act of 1972 amounted to a mere giving effect to the "principles and policies" of the Directive. Rather, Denham J held that to require the Oireachtas to legislate would be *sterile and artificial*[41] and to say that the Regulations breached Article 15.2.1° in fact was based on a false premise that the Minister was determining policy. **[5–26]**

The test here adopted by Denham J of a legal standard, that of reading the "necessitated" clause with Article 15.2.1° and Article 29.4.6°, is classically a *harmonious* construction of constitutional questions.[42] However, this will always be a subjective analysis and it is difficult to discern from such a harmonious test what "principles and policies" are evident. To suggest that requiring the Oireachtas to legislate would be *sterile* has been refuted by numerous commentators- an "omnibus Statute" could have been used to incorporate many Directives, for example.[43] Overtly, the analysis reached is a practical and result-orientated one, to save the constitutional validity of potentially thousands of statutory instruments. Moreover, the level at which Denham J discerns a policy is particularly curious. Moreover, as Hogan states, **[5–27]**

> "[h]ow could it seriously be argued that the decision taken to extend the time limit to two years was not a policy choice which had been taken by the national authorities?"[44]

Arguably, what is most curious about the decision in *Meagher v Minister for Agriculture* is the manner in which the "necessitated" clause is sidestepped so radically and that the "principles and policies" test appears to be the primary focus of the decision in order to overcome the former. The analysis of "principles and policies" and what is "necessitated" by the obligations of membership does not evolve and the finding of the former seems to entail the finding of the latter, because *of it*. **[5–28]**

A powerful critique is leveled by Whelan at the decision in *Meagher v Minister for Agriculture* as follows: if the Court of Justice says that a measure must be legally effective to be *appropriate* as a means of implementing EU law, and the Supreme Court (as in *Meagher v Minister for Agriculture*) says that a measure need only be appropriate to be legally effective, a vicious circle is created.[45] Whelan's solution is to abandon the Supreme Court test in favour of a strict test of necessity by reference to EC law requirements.[46] If so, a measure satisfies Article 29.4.6°. The difficulty with this otherwise compelling analysis is that the Supreme Court does not in fact require a measure to be appropriate **[5–29]**

---

[41] At p 367.

[42] See Hogan and Whyte, *op.cit.* para. 1.1.12 *et seq.*

[43] See generally Travers, "The Constitutionality of the Implementation of EC Directives into Irish law Revisited" (1994) GLSI 99.

[44] Hogan, "The Implementation of European Union Law in Ireland: The *Meagher* Case and the Democratic Deficit" (1994) 2 IJEL 190, 197.

[45] Whelan, "Constitutional Law— *Meagher v. Minister for Agriculture*" (1994) 15 DULJ 152.

[46] Temple Lang also favoured such a test of "legal necessity under Community law": "Legal and Constitutional Implications for Ireland of Adhesion to the EEC Treaty" (1974) 11 CMLR 167, 170.

to be legally effective, it merely requires it to be doing something legally effective because of the pragmatist tone of the decision. Further, if we are to adopt a strict test of necessity along the lines of what Whelan suggests, we clearly would open up a vast array of measures to scrutiny.[47] Whether or not one thinks that is a good idea, is an autonomous domestic test that relies upon objective standards ever going to be the paradigm solution?[48] Moreover, another danger is run with the adoption of the Whelan test, of further unnecessary preliminary references being made to the Court of Justice similar to that in the *McCauley Chemists (Blackpool) Ltd v Pharmaceutical Society of Ireland* for guidance as to the interpretation of domestic rules, thereby overburdening the Court of Justice with domestic constitutional concerns, discussed above.[49] Perhaps the most satisfactory way of summarising the manner in which the Irish Supreme Court dealt with Article 29.4.6° in *Meagher v Minister for Agriculture* is to describe it as perhaps an unfortunate case of the Irish judiciary demonstrating yet again that they are excessively pragmatic in this area of law.

Case-Law After *Meagher v Minister for Agriculture*

[5–30] The decision of the Supreme Court in *Maher v Minister for Agriculture*[50] is also one of immense importance as to the tangled relationship between Articles 15.2.1° and 29.4.6°. However, instead of the Ministerial implementation of a Directive, as was the case in *Meagher v Minister for Agriculture*, this time the Court had to address the finer question of the implementation of a *Regulation* by means of secondary legislation.[51] Robinson, writing in 1973 as to the newly enacted Irish European Communities Act

[47] After all, legal doubt would be generated as to many pieces of legislation for the opinion of the Court of Justice as to the level of discretion possessed by Member States as to each piece of legislation is mostly neither a known nor tested fact.

[48] Hogan and Whelan, *Ireland and the European Union* (Butterworths, London, 1995) suggest that *Meagher* is open to criticism in that is overrides fundamental constitutional values in a manner that is unnecessary so far as the separation of powers is concerned. An interesting suggestion is made by them as to how to reconcile *Meagher* and *Crotty v An Taoiseach* [1987] IR 713— they suggest that while *Crotty* set out a test of strict legal obligation as to European matters, the Supreme Court in *Meagher* adopted a more teleological stance. See also Gwynn Morgan, *The Separation of Powers in Irish Constitution* (Round Hall, Dublin, 1997) p 245 in this regard, per Gwynn Morgan, the *Meagher* reasoning is in error in that it proceeds from the perspective that the Minister has no choice, consequently Article 15.2.1° is violated. To him, the proper focus of the provision is not the Minister— it does not say that the Minister must not determine questions of policy. It is rather a positive provision- that the Oireachtas is the body that ought to so act. This is the central precept then that is suspended as is necessitated by the obligations of membership. However, as Gwynn Morgan notes, it is far from every EU Directive that violates Art 15.2.1° and in fact an omnibus statute could be used by the Oireachtas to incorporate such Directives, etc. This, it is submitted, constitutes the most appropriate view of the governmental discretion at play.

[49] See Case C-221/05 *Sam McCauley Chemists (Blackpool) Ltd v Pharmaceutical Society of Ireland* [2006] ECR I-6869.

[50] *Maher v Minister for Agriculture* [2001] 2 IR 139.

[51] Although Member State action may be required to implement a Regulation on occasion, Case 34/73 *Variola v Amministrazione delle Finanze* [1973] ECR 981.

1972,[52] noted the criticism the Act had been subjected to in the Oireachtas by virtue of the failure of the Act to distinguish between Directives and Regulation.[53] Robinson argued that the Act required amendment to allow for the Oireachtas to play a greater role as to the implementation of European Regulations. It would appear that it was not for almost 30 years before this prescient critique would be laid bare in *Maher v Minister for Agriculture,* It is a fundamental principle of Community law that Regulations are said by Article 288 TFEU (ex Article 249 EC) to be "directly applicable" unlike the legal effect of Directives.

In *Maher v Minister for Agriculture,* the Minister had enacted the European Communities (Milk Quota) Regulations 2000 pursuant to a Council Regulation.[54] The Council Regulations provided in Article 7(1)(b) that "Member States may decide not to apply the provisions on transfer of reference quantities in Article 7(1)". The domestic implementing Regulations had in fact provided for, *inter alia,* detailed provisions relating to family transactions that were not contained in the Council Regulation and thus constituted an exercise of some discretion on the part of the Oireachtas. The applicants in *Maher v Minister for Agriculture* were the holders of lands with a milk quota in which they alleged they possessed property rights that were infringed upon by the provisions of the Regulations and that the Regulations were not "necessitated" by the provisions of Article 29.4.6°, being *ultra vires* Article 15.2.1°. In the High Court, Carroll J held that the discretion which had been left to the Member States was within the "principles and policies" of the Council Regulation and was, thus, *intra vires.*[55] Hence, she held, the Regulations were "necessitated" by the obligations of membership of the Community.[56] On appeal, the judgments of the Supreme Court diverged considerably in substance on the issue. **[5–31]**

Keane CJ proceeded from the basis that membership of the Communities was dynamic in nature. Had s 3 of the Act of 1972 not been enacted, he held that it would have been necessary for Directives and Regulations to be implemented by way of an Act of the Oireachtas.[57] Considering the decisions of Denham and Blayney JJ in *Meagher,* Keane CJ concluded, perhaps somewhat unsatisfactorily, that neither decision lent support to the interpretation contended for by counsel, to the effect that where it was convenient **[5–32]**

---

[52] s 3 of the European Communities Act 1972 provided that (prior to its amendment, discussed above):

> "(1) A Minister of State may make Regulations for enabling section 2 of this Act to have full effect.
>
> (2) Regulations under this section may contain such incidental, supplementary and consequential provisions as appear to the Minister making the Regulations to be necessary for the purposes of the Regulations (including provisions repealing, amending or applying, with or without modification, other law, exclusive of this Act).
>
> (3) Regulations under this section shall not create an indictable offence.
>
> (4) Regulations under this section may be made before the 1st day of January, 1973, but Regulations so made shall not come into operation before that day."

[53] Robinson, "The Irish European Communities Act, 1972" (1973) 10 CMLR 352.

[54] Council Regulation (EC) No. 1256/99.

[55] *Maher v Minister for Agriculture* [2001] 2 IR 139, 157.

[56] Despite extensive submissions on the point, Carroll J refused to consider the legislative history of Art 29.4.6°: see pp 145-146.

[57] At p 176.

or necessary for a Community measure to be implemented in the form of a Regulation rather than an Act, that the making of the Regulation could be said to be "necessitated" by the obligations of membership. However, he also held that:

> "Doubtless, where no policy choices are left to the Member State, expedition *is one of the facts which may legitimately be taken into account* in deciding to opt for the making of a Regulation rather than the enactment of primary legislation, but it would be a serious overstatement to say that it justifies the making of Regulations rather than the enactment of an Act in the case of every Directive or...Regulation...".[58] (Emphasis supplied).

[5–33] That conclusion, he stated, was reached by him without any consideration of the change of wording of the Third Amendment of the Constitution Bill 1971 from "consequent on" to "necessitated". The discretion that Ireland possessed in this regard had been reduced to almost vanishing point and he held that the relevant "principles and policies" were to be found in the Council Regulation and that the secondary legislation was *intra vires* without more.

[5–34] Denham J did not examine the issue as to whether the implementing Regulations were "necessitated" *per se* and instead cited from her own decision in *Meagher* as to the role of the Oireachtas becoming "sterile," if an Act of the Oireachtas was employed so as to implement the Council Regulations. She thus concluded that the relevant "principles and policies" were to be found in the European Regulation and that it was open to the Minister to proceed by way of statutory instrument.[59] The case was not, she held, about any putative democratic deficit.[60] However, the difficulty with this much is to underline how diverse the basis of the decisions of Keane CJ and Denham J remains.[61] Murray J considered exclusively the right to property and thus did not address any point as to whether the Regulations were "necessitated" by membership of the Communities or Union.[62]

[5–35] For Fennelly J, the substantive issues for consideration were to be more logically addressed. Thus, the first question arising was as to whether the Regulations represented a valid exercise of the powers delegated to the Minister. If that was the case, this entailed that they were valid; whereas if not, the question of whether they were "necessitated" did not arise. On that basis, it was not necessary for Fennelly J to consider the issue of whether they were "necessitated" and he upheld the Regulations as a valid method of transposition. However, a number of interesting observations as to the "necessitated" question were made by Fennelly J. He refuted any suggestion that the implementation of Community law might necessarily be carried out by Regulation. Rather, the issue of "necessity" was more appropriately considered by reference to the content and not the form of the instrument.[63] He further took issue with the argument

[58] At p 182.
[59] At p 209.
[60] At p 222.
[61] Murphy J did not deliver a judgment and instead concurred with Denham J.
[62] At p 223 *et seq*.
[63] At p 252.

that in *Meagher* the court had upheld implementing measures to be "necessitated," notwithstanding the discretion possessed by Ireland as to implementation generally.[64] Rather, he held this was to confuse the interpretation of the question of being "necessitated" with the interpretation of Community law.

However, there are many who contend that the decision in *Maher* is incorrect as a matter of domestic law and, that while a national implementation measure must comply with general Community law principles, that to apply the *Cityview Press* test here as to delegated legislation is "to muddy the waters".[65] For Costello, Ireland had a policy choice to make in the act of implementation. However, in general, *Maher* is regarded as a reconsideration of *Meagher* and its less lenient stance on any general immunity attaching to implementing measures.[66] The essential difficulty with *Maher* is that we are left without doubt that pragmatism can prevail, but that the range of precise factors to decide *when* pragmatism must prevail remains undefined. Arguably, the change in wording in the European Communities Bill 1971, immunising measures necessitated by membership and not those merely "consequent upon" membership is greatly significant still, even over thirty years later and yet this critical difference is not considered much judicially. Moreover, the tenor of *Meagher* remains without a convincing rebuttal from the collegiate court in *Maher* and there appears to have been little effort to disapprove of the result-orientated view prevailing in the *Meagher* Court.[67] **[5–36]**

It is submitted what is clearly an issue here, that was dismissed without much analysis by the Supreme Court, was surely that the proceedings concerned Regulations which are, as a result of Article 288 TFEU, directly applicable and binding in their entirety. That no Member State action is, *per se*, legally objectively required is itself an important issue to consider, that the Court in *Maher* did not. The fact that Member **[5–37]**

[64] It was argued (p 253) that on a true analysis of the Community Directives at issue in *Meagher* that Ireland as a Member State had discretion and was not bound to adopt the particular implementing measures and that the Court in *Meagher* had nonetheless still found them to be necessitated.

[65] Costello, "European Community Judicial Review in the Irish Courts-Scope, Standards and the Separation of Powers" in Lucey and Keville, eds, *Irish Perspectives on EC Law* (Round Hall, Dublin, 2003) p 38. Costello has suggested that the policy choice of the Member States was not as constrained there as the Supreme Court analysis would suggest, such that the implementation could not be regarded as a matter of policy.

[66] *ibid.* See also Hogan and Whyte *op.cit.* 5.3.71, where it is stated that as a result of *Maher v Minister for Agriculture*:

> "it can never be said that the transposition of a Community legislation by means of a statutory instrument is itself 'necessitated' for the purposes of Article 29.4.10…[and that]… it is clear that the critical test in this area is whether the Directive which is sought to be transposed by way of primary legislation … would be superfluous [to transpose in such fashion]".

This appears to be an unduly optimistic interpretation of *Maher v Minister for Agriculture* and given the divergences between the opinions of the collegiate court. Perhaps they might best be more narrowly construed as to implementing European Regulations where *some* discretion is possessed at national level.

[67] However, see Doherty, "Land, Milk and Freedom— Implementing Community Law in Ireland" (2004) 11 IJEL 141.

State discretion has become much more common in Regulations, resulting in a greater need for implementing measures, does not alter the strict legal position that a Regulation is directly applicable. Thus, it is submitted that in *Maher* the Court, in fact, misinterpreted the Council Regulation at issue with respect to Member State discretion.[68] Whilst the Court is interpreted here to have clarified that no immunity attaches *per se* to domestic implementing measures, the *Meagher* interpretation of the "necessitated" clause and the factors that must be considered as to the operation of the clause have yet to receive a thorough consideration. It is of great significance that a mere Ministerial declaration in the Dáil chamber that a measure is putatively "necessitated" by the obligations of membership[69] is insufficient now in law because of the decision in *Maher* and that a searching analysis as to "principles and policies" must be conducted first.

[5–38] The Supreme Court has recently had to revisit the *Meagher* and *Maher* jurisprudence in two subsequent decisions *Browne v Ireland*[70] and *Kennedy v Attorney General*.[71] The latter pair of cases, that bear striking similarities when considered together, are a particularly good barometer of the current difficulties in Irish constitutional law as regards the implementation of European law over thirty years after membership of the European Union, with which the Supreme Court continues to grapple. In *Browne v Ireland*, the applicant was a master of a fishing vessel that was charged for being in breach of drift net Regulations. The applicant had challenged, by way of judicial review, the *vires* of an Order[72] made pursuant to s 223A of the Fisheries (Consolidation) Act 1959, as amended, as being *ultra vires* and in violation of s 3(1) of the European Communities Act 1972 or, if *intra vires*, that the delegation was in breach of Article 15.2.1° of the Constitution.[73] In the High Court, Kearns J he noted that both sides had agreed that the use of a statutory instrument rather than an Act of the Oireachtas was the most appropriate vehicle for transposition, as the detailed rules were not "necessitated" by the obligations of membership. The key question remained whether Community law set out the relevant principles so as to obviate the need for domestic primary legislation. Kearns J held that a choice between different enforcement measures did not represent a significant reservation of policy given that the EC Regulations required effective sanctions. He concluded that, unlike in *Maher*, s 3 of the Act of 1972 was not availed of for transposition. Instead, the Fisheries (Consolidation) Act 1959 was availed of for transposition, which was not designed to be used for this much. Section 3(3) of the Act of 1972 required primary legislation. Thus, the use of the statutory instrument pursuant to a section of the Act of 1959 was *ultra vires* the Minister's powers and in violation of Article 15.2.1°. On appeal to the Supreme Court, Keane CJ for the Court, held that it was not in dispute in the proceedings that the

[68] Witness how the Keane CJ held that Member State discretion had been reduced to "vanishing point" at p 185.
[69] See the discussion as to the new parliamentary scrutiny regime in Ch 6, enacted after Maher.
[70] *Browne v Ireland* [2003] 3 IR 205.
[71] *Kennedy v Attorney General* [2007] 2 IR 45.
[72] Sea Fisheries (Drift Nets) Order 1998.
[73] The Order of 1998 was made pursuant to s 223A of the Fisheries (Consolidation) Act 1959, as amended, for the stated purpose of giving effect to Council Regulation EC No. 1239/98 and provided that in relation to drift nets that an individual was not to cause or permit a person to fail to comply with provisions of the Regulation.

Minister was empowered by s 3 of the Act of 1972 to make Regulations, even where the "principles and policies" being given effect to were not in primary legislation. He held that it was clear from the decisions of *Meagher* and *Maher* that the fact that the "principles and policies" of a Regulation were not to be found in an Act of the Oireachtas but rather in the Community measure did not affect its constitutional validity.

Thus, he held the Order at issue was designed to give effect to a Council Regulation and not an Act of the Oireachtas. Section 3(3) of the Act of 1972 was unequivocal in its terms: a Minister could not create an indictable offence by way of Regulation.[74] Therefore, s 223A could not empower the Minister to make such an offence. Section 224B, on the other hand, had created an indictable offence by way of primary legislation and employing the maxim *expressio unius est exclusio alterius*, it was clear that s 223A was not intended to empower the Minister so as to create an indictable offence. Continued as follows: **[5–39]**

> "While there was some discussion in the course of the written and oral submissions as to whether the creation of an indictable offence was "necessitated" by the obligations of our membership of the communities within the meaning of Article 29.4.5° of the Constitution, having regard to the provisions of art. 31 of the Council Regulation of 1993, it seems to me that that issue does not arise in this case. *Either the Order of 1993 was intra vires s. 223A of the Act of 1959 or it was not.* If it was within the power of the second respondent to make such a Regulation for the reasons advanced on his behalf in the High Court and this court, it is not material whether the making of the Regulation in that form was "necessitated" by the obligations of the State as a Member of the communities. If, on the other hand, the order was *ultra vires* s. 223A and could only have been validly made by the second respondent under s. 3 of the Act of 1972, it follows that it was of no effect and *it is again unnecessary to consider the issue as to whether it was "necessitated" in constitutional terms by our membership of the communities.* For the reasons I have given, I am satisfied that the making of the order was *ultra vires* s. 223A of the Act of 1959".[75] (Emphasis supplied)

The lucid and helpful decision of Kearns J in the High Court, below, is in stark contrast to the reasoning of Keane CJ here, that appears less than opaque.[76] There clearly is **[5–40]**

---

[74] s 3 of the European Communities Act 1972 prior to recent amendments (considered below) provided that:

> "(1) A Minister of State may make Regulations for enabling section 2 of this Act to have full effect.
> (2) Regulations under this section may contain such incidental, supplementary and consequential provisions as appear to the Minister making the Regulations to be necessary for the purposes of the Regulations (including provisions repealing, amending or applying, with or without modification, other law, exclusive of this Act).
> (3) Regulations under this section shall not create an indictable offence.
> (4) Regulations under this section may be made before the 1st day of January 1973, but Regulations so made shall not come into operation before that day".

[75] *Browne v Ireland* [2003] 3 IR 205, 221.

[76] Another useful way of considering the decision of Kearns J is that of the authors of *Kelly: The Irish Constitution* (4th ed) (Lexis-Nexis, Dublin, 2003) para. 5.3.77, who note that the Court considered the *substance* of the domestic Regulations as necessitated but not the *method* of implementation.

considerable difficulty with the element of the reasoning of Keane CJ that suggests that either way, *intra vires* or *ultra vires*, that the same result is reached: that the question of "necessitated" is irrelevant. This begs the questions, if it is irrelevant in either instance, then when is it relevant at all? Surely, the mode of reasoning of Kearns J is the model to be adopted: is primary legislation necessary? Is the secondary instrument "necessitated" by membership? Are the "principles and policies" contained in the parent EC legislation? Is the legislation *ultra vires* the Minister? Surely, if it is found that a measure is *ultra vires* the Minister's powers, then it would logically follow that an enquiry would ensue as to whether a measure was "necessitated" by the obligations of membership of the Community.

[5–41] By contrast, for Denham J, the issue was a net one which she disposed of as follows. By virtue of s 3(3) of the Act of 1972, any Statute purporting to give power to a Minister to create an indictable offence had to set out such power in plain and clear language.[77] In this case, the Fishing (Consolidation) Act 1959 did not provide in clear and plain language that the Minister had the power to create an indictable offence. Thus, in making the Order of 1998, the Minister had acted *ultra vires.* Clearly, the reasoning of Denham J proceeds from a fundamentally different premise to that of Keane J, although the two arrive at the same conclusion as to the *vires* of the legislation. Denham J did not express any opinion as to the question of "necessitated" and instead elected to adopt her own reasoning in *Maher* and *Meagher.* It seems apparent that the Supreme Court at all costs wished to avoid the issue of "necessitated' in its disposal of the matter and it is thus most unfortunate that the Supreme Court did not elect to adopt the crystalline clear analysis of the Court below.

[5–42] At first sight, the later decision of the Supreme Court in *Kennedy v Attorney General*[78] is virtually indistinguishable from that in *Browne v Ireland* on the facts. In *Kennedy v Attorney General*, a fisherman had been prosecuted for violating the terms of a license pursuant to the Mackerel (Licensing) Order 1999. In the High Court, Ó Caoimh J held the Order to be *ultra vires* s 223A of the Fisheries (Consolidation) Act 1959, as amended, the same section that the Order in *Browne v Ireland* had offended against. On appeal to the Supreme Court, it was argued on behalf of the respondents that the measure was *intra vires,* in that unlike in *Browne v Ireland,* here the Order did not implement European Community law and the case did not involve a measure giving effect to Community law but rather a measure adopted by the State to control sea fishing. The applicant contended that the Minister had acted *ultra vires* s 3(3) of the Act of 1972 by using secondary legislation to create an indictable offence instead of s 3(3) of the Act of 1972.

[5–43] Denham J, for the majority of the Court, held that the key issue to consider was that ss 223A and 224B of the Act of 1959, as amended, established a schema. While s 223A authorised the Minister to prescribe measures to conserve fish stocks, s 224B authorised the Minister to make Regulations to restrict fishing. The latter, Denham J held, was the objective of the Order at issue and that *Browne* was not thus

[77] At pp 221-246.

[78] *Kennedy v Attorney General* [2007] 2 IR 45.

distinguishable. The specific conditions of the Order were based on Community law. She held that it could not have been the intention of the Oireachtas to use s 223A to implement Community law in light of the wording of s 224A, which created provisions for offences to be enacted. She stated that:

> "if s. 223A were considered an appropriate basis for the statutory instrument it would, as pointed out by Keane CJ in *Browne v Ireland*, be used to circumvent s. 224B (quite apart from any consideration of s. 3(3) of the Act of 1972)".

Thus the trial judge was upheld and the appeal dismissed.

However, Fennelly J found himself unable to agree with the majority. Fennelly J summarised the conclusion of the majority as being that "the Order could only have been adopted under section 224B". He concluded, that the interaction of national and Community competence was central to the decision of the High Court and that the Order fell within the Minister's powers under s 223A to conserve fish stocks and was formulated within the area of discretion of Members States. The Order could not, he held, have been made pursuant to s 224B as its terms had to be specified in a Community act to comply with that section. The decision in *Browne* did not, he concluded, determine that no Order could be made under s 223A. Rather, the Order here did not implement or give effect to any Community requirement unlike in *Browne.* Fennelly J labeled as crucial the fact that the Keane CJ in *Browne* had not based his decision upon s 3(3) of the Act of 1972 (unlike Denham J) but rather upon the terms of s 224B and the maxim *expressio unius est exclusio alterius. Browne* was distinguishable on the basis that the Order of 1998 there implemented a mandatory requirement, whilst here, there was no such mandatory requirement being implemented. **[5–44]**

The difficulty with the decision of the majority, *per* Denham J, is that it proceeds on the basis that s 3(3) of the Act of 1972 is irrelevant to the inquiry and that the Minister could have created an offence under s 224B, when in fact s 3(3) was the basis for her decision in *Browne.* Here, the respondent had been charged with an offence pursuant to both the Order and s 223A. With respect, this much (i.e., the charge) appears incorrect in law and s 3(3) appears not to have been argued with any force by the applicants whatsoever. It is difficult to see how she found the cases of *Kennedy* and *Browne* to be so indistinguishable and yet proceeded on such a different basis. Perhaps this is due the fact that her reasoning in *Kennedy* demonstrates such a degree of similarity to that of Keane CJ in *Browne* (yet who in fact the rest of the *Browne* Court agreed with and not Denham J). Furthermore, even the decision of Fennelly J is particularly problematic, in that it ignores the fact that an indictable offence had been created pursuant to the Order and s 223A instead of s 3(3). Section 224B, however, did not purport to enact an offence pursuant to s 3(3), a seemingly critical element of the jigsaw. **[5–45]**

More fundamentally to the present inquiry, the central difficulty remains that the relationship between the *ultra vires* doctrine and the question of what is "necessitated" appears still uncertain after both *Browne* and *Kennedy.* Moreover, the *dictum* of Keane CJ in *Browne* has yet to be overruled. Surely, if a Minister has acted beyond his powers, this in turn raises a question as to the relevance of Article 15.2.1°, as to whether law making was required on the part of the State and in turn as to whether the law was protected by Article 29.4.6°. A key question to consider also is the relevancy of the **[5–46]** "necessitated" test, if Keane CJ was so able to dismiss its application to a consideration of *vires*. Arguably, its redundancy is becoming increasingly apparent if it is not the first test to be considered in a *vires* challenge. Thus, its immunity, or lack thereof, would be established first, incorporating a consideration of Article 15.2.1° and then the question as to its *vires* would be established. Clearly, however, if one severs the link between the *vires* test and constitutionality (the "necessitated" question), a fundamental difficulty presents itself. Constitutional immunity is relevant in a constitutional analysis. However, the fact that it has become irrelevant entails that the provisions of Article 29.4.6° perhaps have outlived their usefulness and that no satisfactory means of testing "necessitated" has been formulated, and thus arguably that the question of what is "necessitated" ought to erased from its constitutional position.

The European Communities Act 2007

[5–47] The express purpose of the European Communities Act 2007 is to amend s 3 of the European Communities Act 1972[79] so as to permit the Ministerial creation of indictable offences by way of regulation, to give effect to European acts under statutes other than the Act of 1972 and to validate certain statutory instruments made before the passing of the Act of 2007. However, the Act has its real genesis in the Supreme Court decisions of *Browne v Ireland* and *Kennedy v Attorney General*, considered above, which it attempts to reverse in terms of result. The net result of the content of the Act of 2007 is a dramatic enhancement of Ministerial powers to create indictable offences with swingeing penalties in the absence of debate or scrutiny by the Houses of the Oireachtas, to retrospectively validate all previous statutory instruments made before the passing of the Act that purported to give effect to European acts and to constitutional proof their effects, giving them statutory force, even in the event of serious conflict with constitutional rights.

1. The Provisions of the European Communities Act 2007

[5–48] Section 2 of the Act of 2007 amends s 3 of the Act of 1972, which now provides that:

> "Regulations under this section may—
> a. make provision for offences under the regulations to be prosecuted on indictment, where the Minister of the Government making the regulations considers it necessary for the purpose of giving full effect to—
> i. a provision of the treaties governing the European Communities, or
> ii. an act, or provision of an act, adopted by an institution of the European Communities or any other body competent under those treaties, and

[79] s 3 of the Act of 1972, prior to amendment, provided that:

"(1) A Minister of State may make regulations for enabling section 2 of this Act to have full effect.

(2) Regulations under this section may contain such incidental, supplementary and consequential provisions as appear to the Minister making the regulations to be necessary for the purposes of the regulations (including provisions repealing, amending or applying, with or without modification, other law, exclusive of this Act).

(3) Regulations under this section shall not create an indictable offence.

(4) Regulations under this section may be made before the 1s day of January 1973, but regulations so made shall not come into operation before that day".

See Fahey, "The European Communities Bill 2006" (2007) 12 BR 4.

b. make such provision as that Minister of the Government considers necessary for the purpose of ensuring that penalties in respect of an offence prosecuted in that manner are effective and proportionate, and have a deterrent effect, having regard to the acts or omissions of which the offence consists, provided that the maximum fine (if any) shall not be greater than €500,000 and the maximum term of imprisonment (if any) shall not be greater than 3 years…".

Thus, swingeing penalties of a most significant nature for indictable criminal offences may be proscribed by Ministerial Order in the absence of any reasoned debate or scrutiny by the Houses of the Oireachtas. The then Minister of State, Mr Noel Treacy TD, introducing the Bill of 2006 stated that: **[5–49]**

> "…We are capping penalties in European legislation at €500,000 and a maximum of three years' imprisonment. On the principle of subsidiarity and taking account of our responsibilities, therefore, we are capping the powers that Ministers have to make regulations on all those issues even though other legislation permits much greater penalties. The penalties in this Bill of a maximum of €500,000 fine and up to three years' imprisonment — and the courts will make the decision on the actual fine and the term of imprisonment within those limits — are not especially excessive when compared with other legislation…".[80]

Clearly effectiveness, pragmatism and deterrence form the rationale behind this section, whereby a Minister may create by way of secondary legislation criminal offences to be prosecuted on indictment. While such values may be to the fore of the jurisprudence of the Court of Justice as to European law generally, it may not necessarily save s 2 from falling foul of judicial scrutiny in this jurisdiction. It is worth recalling that the status quo in s 3(3) of the Act of 1972, expressly prohibiting such Ministerial action, had been approved of for its constitutional wisdom with respect to the separation of powers by Denham J in *Kennedy v Attorney General*, when she stated that: **[5–50]**

> "The European Communities Act 1972, specifically states a principle and a policy that regulations made by a Minister enabling Community law shall not create an indictable offence: "Section 3(3) Regulations under this section shall not create an indictable offence". *It is an important principle and policy of the legislation. It is a limitation on the power of a Minister*…".[81]

Moreover, the general tenor of reforms of national legislative activity in the area of the implementation of European law has been towards increased scrutiny of European law measures and the thrust of s 2 of the Act goes entirely contrary these recent developments.[82] **[5–51]**

2. Power to Give Effect to European Acts Under Statutes Other Than the Act of 1972

Section 4 of the Act of 2007 provides for a most distinct Ministerial power that: **[5–52]**

---

[80] *Seanad Debates*, Vol. 185 No. 14 (12 December 2006).

[81] *Kennedy v Attorney General* [2005] 2 ILRM 401; [2007] 2 IR 45, (emphasis supplied).

[82] See the discussion above as to parliamentary scrutiny of EU affairs, see above Ch 8.

(1) A power to make a statutory instrument conferred on a Minister of the Government by a provision of a statute may be exercised for the purpose of *giving effect to a European act* if the obligations imposed on the State under the European act concerned relate, in whole, to matters to which that provision relates.
(2) *A statutory instrument made for a purpose referred to in subsection (1) may contain such incidental, supplementary and consequential provisions as appear to the Minister of the Government making the statutory instrument to be necessary* for the purposes of the statutory instrument (including provisions repealing, amending or applying, with or without modification, other law, exclusive of this Act, the Act of 1972 and the provision of the statute under which the statutory instrument is made) . . .
(5) This section applies to a power that, but for this section, would not be exercisable for the purpose of giving effect to a European act."

(Emphasis supplied).

[5–53] Section 4(1) purports to allow statutory instrument making powers in *existing* legislation to be used to give effect to EC law, subject matter permitting, thereby circumventing the need to use the Act of 1972. However, practical this might be, this seems to be a questionable statutory intervention in view of the fact that it renders the Act of 1972 seemingly redundant in a wide range of circumstances. The Minister of State introducing the Act (referring to the provisions of the then Bill) stated that:

"What is being proposed is no more than what was already provided for in the 1972 Act, although its remit is more extensive on this occasion. It is worth noting that section 3(2) is limited in its scope. It cannot be used to amend this Bill, the 1972 Act or the relevant section of the primary legislation being used to create the statutory instrument. The constitutional validity of this approach was accepted by the Supreme Court in the *Meagher v Minister for Agriculture* case. . .

There are safeguards in place and a Minister can only use existing primary legislation to give effect to a European Community measure if the existing primary legislation relates in whole to the subject matter of the European Community measure. For example, a Minister cannot use the Institutes of Technology Act 2006 to give effect to a European Community measure on water quality, as it is not permissible to jump from one to the other. However, it makes no sense if a Minister could not use, for example, an existing Act dealing with water quality to give effect to a European Community measure on the same subject. There would be cohesion, parallelism, linkage and commonality".[83]

[5–54] In other words, the legislator understood the Supreme Court in *Meagher* to require such provisions as a matter of technicality. However, the effects of s 4(1) are surely compounded by the extraordinary provisions of s 4(2) of the Act that accord to the Minister sweeping powers where s 4(1) is employed. Thus, in the event of the use of a statutory instrument to implement a European act pursuant to legislative powers, other than those contained in the Act of 1972, s 3(2), using the same formula that exists as contained in s 4(2) of the European Communities Act 1972, permits the Minister to create statutory instruments that:

"contain such incidental, supplementary and consequential provisions as appear to the Minister of the Government making the statutory instrument to be necessary for the

[83] Minister Noel Treacey TD, *Seanad Debates*, Vol. 185 No. 14 (12 December 2006).

purposes of the statutory instrument (including provisions repealing, amending or applying, with or without modification, other law".

Although the subsection expressly excludes, *inter alia*, the power to alter the provision of the statute under which the statutory instrument is made itself, one wonders whether such a section could ever survive judicial consideration in light of the fact that the Minister is left truly at large in the operation of the section that permits a vast array of legislation to modified with minimal democratic safeguards and a complete absence of Oireachtas scrutiny. The Minister, pursuant to the section, is given far-reaching law making powers that might be perceived as going well beyond those judicially approved of in the decision of the Supreme Court in *Meagher v Minister for Agriculture*, the decision relied upon by the Minister when introducing the Bill as evidence of its stamp of constitutionality. Here, fundamentally, however, the express purpose of the authorised act of delegation as approved by the Oireachtas in a parent Act is being stretched and expanded to European acts to include the power to amend, repeal or modify legislation, as to which the Minister may also create significant criminal penalties. *Prima facie*, it remains questionable as to whether the *ratio* of *Meagher* may extend this far.[84] [5–55]

3. Incorporation by Reference: Altering the Constitutional Status of a Statutory Instrument

Section 5 of the Act of 2007 provides that: [5–56]

"(1) Every statutory instrument made before the passing of this Act—
(*a*) under a provision of a statute that did not provide for the exercise of the power conferred by that provision for the purpose of giving effect to a European act, and (*b*) that purported to give effect to a European act, shall, in so far as it purported to give such effect, have statutory effect as if it were an Act of the Oireachtas.

(2) If subsection (1) would, but for this subsection, conflict with a constitutional right of any person, the operation of that subsection shall be subject to such limitation as is necessary to secure that it does not so conflict but shall otherwise be of full force and effect".

Thus, s 5 operates to retrospectively validate all statutory instruments that might have been perceived to be constitutionally frail in the wake of the *Browne* and *Kennedy* decisions. The formula of s 5 is significant in so far as it attempts to alter the constitutional status of a statutory instrument and represents a breathtaking act on the part of the Oireachtas to mend its own hand. It is arguable that s 5(1) could be contended to be both, on its face, prospective and retrospective. Do the usual rules of statutory interpretation then apply, that is that statutory instruments only speak prospectively unless otherwise provided for or does the purposive approach apply pursuant to the Interpretation Act 2005? More controversially, s 5(2) represents a rather botched attempt to guarantee the section constitutionality in the event of a challenge to its constitutionality with respect to proportionality. If, in retrospectively [5–57]

[84] One might legitimately question the purpose of the inclusion of s 4(3) merely mandating that a Minister specify what legislation he was using to omnibus through implementing European legislation — common sense surely would dictate that this be done.

validating a statutory instrument and giving it the status of primary legislation, a constitutional right is conflicted with, s 5(2) provides that s 5(1) shall be "subject to such limitation as is necessary to secure" the protection of constitutional rights, but rather clumsily s 5(1) "shall otherwise be of full force and effect". This is clearly a most far-reaching section, providing for haphazard reading down of legislation so as to save it in the event of challenge. Quite apart from the subjective and potentially inconsistent application of the section to legislation, one wonders whether the subsection *should* ever survive judicial challenge, whether under the Constitution or the European Convention on Human Rights Act 2003.

[5–58] However, despite the obvious difficulties associated with this type of approach to legislating and to constitutionalism generally, as outlined here, ss 5(1) and (2) would appear to have already received judicial sanction in light of the decision of the Supreme Court in *Leontjava v Minister for Justice*[85] which, authorised a particularly liberal and unchecked view of legislative powers of the Oireachtas. The decision of the Supreme Court in *Leontjava* has received trenchant criticism for its inconsistent approach to matters relating to the proper system of checks and balances inherent within the separation of powers. Senator Quinn in the Seanad Committee stage contended forcefully that:

> "[i]t [the legislation] abrogates to the Executive the power to create indictable offences by ministerial edict... We must increase rather than dilute the amount of EU business that is carried out in the full light of day Ministerial orders, in practice, are invisible".[86]

[5–59] The European Communities Act 2007 represents a striking approach on the part of the Oireachtas to European law matters, and runs contrary to the general trends in this area towards reform of the Irish legislative process, in relation to EU affairs. Unfortunately, pragmatism and efficiency prevail in this particular instance at the expense of principle, which results in an extraordinary aggrandisement of unchecked Ministerial power.

Recent Developments as to European Legislation Implemented into the Irish Legal Order

[5–60] The latest installment in the jurisprudence as to delegated legislation, the "principles and policies" test and its interaction with European law, has come in the form of the interesting twist posed by the Supreme Court decision in *McCauley Chemists*

[85] *Leontjava v Director of Public Prosecutions* [2004] 1 IR 591. See Binchy, "Emerging Trends in Irish High Court and Supreme Court Jurisprudence" Fourth Annual Brian Walsh Memorial Lecture, (ISEL, 9 November 2005); Fanning, "Reflections on the Legislative Process following *Leontjava v Director of Public Prosecutions*" (2004) 39 *Irish Jurist* 286. See also the provisions of s 3 of the Act of 2007 that allows for the annulment of regulations made pursuant to the powers of the Act without prejudice to the validity of acts done there under. This provision also seems to be constitution-proofed, unfortunately for the same reasons as discussed in the text above.

[86] *Seanád Debates*, Vol. 185 No. 14 (12 December 2006).

(Blackpool) Ltd v Pharmaceutical Society of Ireland.[87] *McCauley* concerned a challenge to the statutory instrument purporting to implement Council Directive 85/433/EEC as to the mutual recognition of pharmacist qualifications, that attempted to facilitate the effective right of establishment across the European Union.[88] The Council Directive had been implemented by way of the European Communities (Recognition of Qualifications in Pharmacy) Regulations 1991,[89] introducing a new s 2(3A) into the Pharmacy Act 1962. In practice, the Regulations had the effect of placing anti-competitive obstacles in the way of foreign trained pharmacy graduates from establishing themselves in this jurisdiction by reason of a restriction that was intended to be temporary in operation only, but in fact remained in place for well over a decade at the date of challenge at national and European level.

The domestic Regulations implementing the Directive repeated verbatim the text of the Directive. Article 2 of Council Directive provided as follows: **[5–61]**

> "1. Each Member State *shall* recognize the diplomas, certificates and other formal qualifications ...
> 2. However, Member States *need not* give effect to the diplomas, certificates and other formal certificates referred to in paragraph 1 with respect to the establishment of new pharmacies open to the public. For the purposes of applying this Directive, pharmacies which have been in operation for less than three years shall also be regarded as new.
> Five years after the date stipulated in Article 19 (1), the Commission shall submit a report to the Council on the way in which Member States have implemented the preceding subparagraph ...". (Emphasis supplied)

In the High Court, McCracken J had little difficulty in disposing of the matter with remarkable brevity. He concluded, upon analysis of the decisions in *Meagher v Minister for Agriculture* and *Maher v Minister for Agriculture*, that given that the Council Directive at issue had obliged Ireland to change the manner in which it regulated pharmacists, previously pursuant to the Pharmacy Act 1962, he concluded that the Regulations simply repeated that which was contained in the Directive and did nothing more. As Article 15.2.1° was not thus brought into play, the Regulations were "necessitated" by the obligations of membership of the European Communities and Union. However, the matter was appealed to the Supreme Court and was to subsequently become the subject of a preliminary reference to the Court of Justice.[90] At Supreme Court level, the issues had become refined to whether or not the 1991 Regulations were invalid because of the fact that they purported to amend primary **[5–62]**

---

[87] High Court, McCracken J, 31 July 2002. The decision of McCracken J was appealed to the Supreme Court and an order for a preliminary reference to the Court of Justice was made by the Supreme Court on 11 May 2005: see Case C-221/05 *Sam McCauley Chemists (Blackpool) Ltd v Pharmaceutical Society of Ireland* [2006] ECR I-6869. Final orders in the Supreme Court proceedings were made on 18 October 2006.

[88] The legislation at issue in *McCauley Chemists* had previously been subject to an unsuccessful challenge in the High Court three years after the enactment of the implementing statutory instrument, but on different grounds to those in *McCauley Chemists* in *Young v Pharmaceutical Society of Ireland* [1995] 2 IR 91.

[89] SI 330 of 1991.

[90] Case C-221/05 *Sam McCauley Chemists (Blackpool) Ltd v Pharmaceutical Society of Ireland* [2006] ECR I-6869.

legislation, thereby infringing Article 15.2.1°. The issue was further narrowed as to whether the restriction of the Recognition Directive so as to exclude EU-registered pharmacists in pharmacies of less than three years establishment, constituted the exercise of a free-standing discretion based on purely national-law considerations. Thus, ostensibly, Article 2.1 of the Directive imposed a mandatory obligation: "shall recognise" and Article 2.2. of the Directive provided for some type of discretion: "need not give effect". However, the focus of the appeal turned to interpreting Article 2.2 in light of the recital to the Directive. The recital provided that that:

> "Whereas ... certain Member States restrict the number of new pharmacies that may be established, while others have adapted no such provisions; whereas in these circumstances it is *premature* to provide that the effects of the recognition of diplomas, certificates and other evidence of formal qualifications in pharmacy must also extend to the pursuit of the activities of pharmacist as the controller of a pharmacy open to the public for *less than three years*; whereas this problem must be *re-examined by the Commission and the Council within a certain period*". (Emphasis supplied)

[5–63] Hence, the Council would consider the matter within a "certain period," a time left undefined. Moreover, the key sentence as to it being premature to provide for the effects of "less than three years" appears not to have become the focus of the dispute.

[5–64] However, the Supreme Court held that the recital referred to a "certain period" and that Article 2.2. referred initially to new pharmacies.[91] The three-year limit mentioned in Article 2.2 was not referred to further by the Court. Rather, the Court noted that the purpose of the Directive was so as to facilitate free movement. The Court stated that it was not clear whether, as a matter of Community law, Article 2.2 conferred a discretion on a Member State or, whether on the contrary, the Council faced with the fact of divergent policies had decided to postpone mutual recognition for a "certain period." With respect, this appears to be a very muddled interpretation of Article 2.2. In fact, it is suggested here, that Article 2 in fact did both of these things and provided for an obligation and a discretion in relation to pharmacists for less than three years, but in general constituted primarily a mandatory obligation. The Irish legislature had a legislative choice as to Article 2.2 by virtue of the phrase "need not give effect": in other words it could have given effect to a more full bodied form of mutual recognition but it was not a choice exercised as the Oireachtas was not involved in the domestic implementation of the Directive. Moreover, it is submitted that it is not the function of the Irish Supreme Court to examine the proposed legislative dimension to existing European legislation, even in this context, and that the recital ought not to be the starting point for a decision that required a resolution of domestic constitutional principles relating to Article 15.2.1°, Article 267 TFEU and the "necessitated" clause.

[5–65] Noting the difficulties confronting it, the Court openly acknowledged that while it was conscious of the neutrality of Community law in relation to domestic issues, it concluded that the matter was crucially dependent to the resolution of the dispute and on a literal reading of Article 267 TFEU, was one that the Court was obliged to refer as a Court of last instance. Moreover, the logic of McCracken J, diligently

[91] Murray CJ, Denham, Hardiman, Fennelly and Lavan JJ, the latter sitting on the Supreme Court.

following the established jurisprudence as to the *vires* question and the "necessitated" clause, is not adopted here. The Court of Justice, composed of a chamber of five judges, and in the absence of an opinion from the Advocate General, indicating the lack of difficulty that the proceedings presented to it in terms of novelty and jurisprudence, responded in a more limited fashion to the questions raised by the Irish Supreme Court.[92] The Court of Justice held that the Directive had to be interpreted so that a Member State complying with the minimal recognition of diplomas as laid down by the Directive, was not in fact exercising any discretion. However, the Court took care to note that the Community legislature had decided to lay down this scheme in "precise and unconditional terms"[93] and accordingly deferred to the Community legislature to attend to the ostensible unfairness arising from the Directive. The Supreme Court decision in *McCauley* appears to promote an extraordinarily stretched interpretation of the mandatory preliminary reference obligation pursuant to Article 267 TFEU in light of the fact that its reference appears largely orientated towards domestic law.[94]

Conclusion

It has been demonstrated here how major constitutional difficulties surround the domestic implementation of European law in the Irish context, thereby affecting its operation in the legal order and that, consequently, the "necessitated" clause pursuant to Article 29.4.6° is in need of reconsideration as to its inherent scope, operation and objectives. The "principles and policies" clause pursuant to Article 15.2.1 as judicially construed has operated simply to complicate the domestic implementation of European law. The failure of the Supreme Court, also in *Browne v Ireland*, to employ the necessitated clause appropriately provides ample evidence of major constitutional difficulties surrounding the necessitated clause and its impact upon the operation of European law in the domestic legal order. The European Communities Act 2007 represents a most unfortunate direction for the law to move towards and the construction of the Act by the Supreme Court could amount to a major repositioning of the Supreme Court of its case-law on the implementation of EU law in the domestic legal order. **[5–66]**

[92] Case C-221/05 *Sam McCauley Chemists (Blackpool) Ltd v Pharmaceutical Society of Ireland*, [2006] ECR I-6869.

[93] At para. 32.

[94] Final orders in the proceedings were made by the Supreme Court on 18 October 2006 where the proceedings were dismissed and the order of the High Court confirmed.

CHAPTER 6
Litigation by the Irish State at EU Level and EU Law Litigation Emanating from Ireland

Overview

It remains unusual for the Irish State to maintain much of a "presence" or "profile" in the case-law of the Court of Justice. Ireland has not litigated legislative competence issues with any degree of frequency before the Court of Justice historically, the recent Data Retention Directive litigation aside.[1] The State usually joins or supports the UK in direct actions and preliminary references before the Court of Justice and shares with the UK a concern in EU-level litigation for common law, sovereignty and criminal justice matters. Traditionally low rates of preliminary references from the Irish courts, low participation rates as interveners in litigation before the Court of Justice by the Irish States and a relatively poor compliance rate by the State in its implementation of internal market legislation until very recently have cumulatively characterised Ireland as litigator at European level.[2] Of late Ireland mounted a campaign against an unfavourable decision to the State of the Grand Chamber of the Court of Justice in *Metock v Minister for Justice*.[3] Thereafter, the State lobbied extensively for the **[6–01]**

[1] See the discussion in Ch 1.

[2] See discussion at para 6-08.

[3] Case C-127/08 *Metock and Others v Minister for Justice, Equality and Law Reform* [2008] 3 CMLR 39, where the Irish legislation implementing the Citizen Rights Directive and the controversial decision of the Court in Case C-109/01 *Secretary of State for the Home Department v Akrich* [2003] ECR I-9607 were successfully challenged. See the reaction of the State in *The Irish Times* (22 September 2008) and its unsuccessful campaign in Smyth, "How do we close information gap between Dublin and Brussels?" *The Irish Times* (29 September 2009) and see also 9 October 2010. However, the European Communities (Free Movement of Persons) (Amendment) Regulations 2008 (SI No 310/2008) were passed swiftly to give effect to the decision. The amendments sought by the State largely related to sham marriages rather curiously, a situation an issue already provided for by the Citizens Rights Directive.

amendment of the Citizens Rights Directive, engaging in an unsuccessful battle of unparalleled proportions. However, it is not likely that the State will ever become a "repeat player,"[4] given the decline in litigation volume in all EU-related areas recently. The Irish initiation of litigation as to European issues has in reality been both exceptional and remarkable although some change is evident in recent times. The failure to litigate issues and to employ EU litigation fora to resolve conflicts or to influence the outcome of proceedings or to become involved where it has not previously had influence on account of a policy opt-out, all represent a conflicting puzzle of strategic isolation and *ad hoc* activity.[5]

[6–02] Three areas are discussed here in order to consider this theme further, of Irish litigation at EU level and EU law litigation emanating from the Irish State namely: (1) preliminary reference ruling data; (2) infringement action data against the Irish State; and (3) the use of the observation procedure by the Irish State at EU level.

Ireland and Article 267 TFEU (Ex Article 234 EC) Preliminary Reference Ruling Data

[6–03] Litigation from the Irish courts to the Court of Justice has been historically statistically low. Quite what this indicates as a matter of theory is perhaps more difficult to pinpoint, although there are many ways of assessing such trends. In general terms, the numerical figures as to the number of preliminary references referred by Irish courts and quasi-judicial bodies to the European Court of Justice pursuant to Article 267 TFEU are very disappointing.[6] A total of 53 preliminary references have been made by the Irish courts to the European Court of Justice since Ireland first joined the EU in 1973 (i.e. 1973–2010).[7] In a thirty-year study by the present author of references from the inception of Ireland's membership (from 1973–2003) a total of 44 references had been made, a particularly low total comparatively.[8] Notably, no reference was made in 2009 but at the time of writing, five references from the High and Supreme Courts were pending, a massive change in pattern.[9] This figure of 53 references appears less than

4 As to litigator strategy and the concept of a "repeat player," see Galanter, "Why the 'Haves' Come Out Ahead: Speculations of the Limits of Legal Change" (1974) 9 *Law and Society* 95.

5 See generally, Panke, *Small States in the European Union: Coping with Structural Disadvantages* (Ashgate, London, 2010).

6 Fahey, *Practice and Procure in Preliminary References to Europe: 30 Years of Article 234 EC Case Law from the Irish Courts* (Firstlaw, Dublin, 2007).

7 The High Court has made slightly more references than the Supreme Court but for practical purposes, the High and Supreme Courts generate most of the references between them, although quasi-judicial bodies and the Supreme Court have been the most active referring bodies in recent times.

8 Fahey, above n6.

9 See *Annual Report of the Court of Justice 2009* (Court of Justice, 2010); In *Goshawk Dedicated Ltd v Life Receivables Irl. Ltd* [2009] IESC 7, the Supreme Court indicated that it would refer questions to the Court of Justice in January 2009 but no order for reference was made in 2009 and the proceedings were still before the Supreme Court in March 2010.

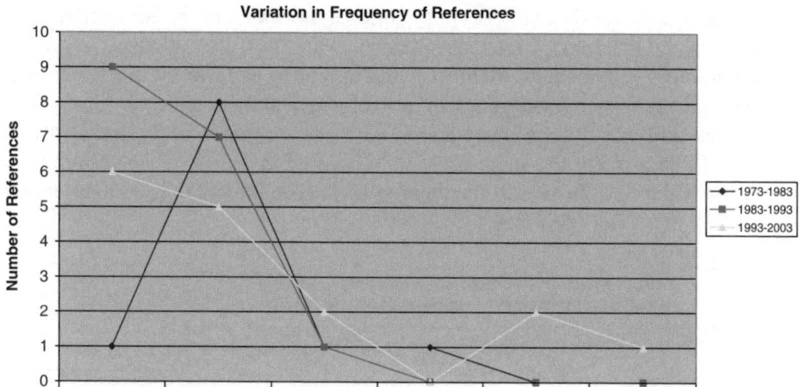

	Supreme Court	High Court	Circuit Court	District Court	Labour Court	Appeal Commissioners
1973-1983	1	8	1	1	0	0
1983-1993	9	7	1	0	0	0
1993-2003	6	5	2	0	2	1

By Court

Figure 6.1 Source: Fahey, *Practice and Procure in Preliminary References to Europe: 30 Years of Article 234 EC Case Law from the Irish Courts* (Firstlaw, Dublin, 2007).

robust against a backdrop of a *communautaire* judiciary and significantly more references (numerically at least) from nearly every other State. The Irish courts have referred, again historically, the least number of cases per year across the Member States.[10] In certain subject areas, such as to the European arrest warrant, the Irish courts may not seek a preliminary reference ruling from the Court of Justice as the State has yet to make a declaration to accept the jurisdiction of the Court.[11] If we compare the total of preliminary references emanating from the Irish courts to that of the other so-called small-sized "old" EU states such as Denmark, Austria, Finland and Portugal, we find the overall number of references from the Irish judiciary, from 1973 to the present day, to be relatively smaller than from any of these small-sized countries individually.[12] Then from 2003–2010, discounting again new accession States, the data for Irish preliminary references made in this period is still lesser than that from other Member States.

[10] Source: Stone Sweet and Brunell, "The European Court and the National Courts: A Statistical Analysis of Preliminary References 1961–1995" (Jean Monnet Working Paper No 14/1997), available at www.jeanmonnetprogram.org.

[11] Thus, the Irish State has not accepted the jurisdiction of the Court of Justice in respect of former Third Pillar matters pursuant to ex Article 35 EU (pre-Lisbon). See Fahey, "*Being a Third Pillar Guardian of Fundamental Rights? The Irish Supreme Court and the European Arrest Warrant* (2008) 33 ELR 563.

[12] This is with the exception of Finland but it must be taken into account that Finland only joined the EU in 1995. See *Annual Report of the Court of Justice 2009* (Court of Justice, 2010) for statistics as to closed and pending actions.

[6–04] Extreme reluctance has been displayed by some of the courts of the newer Member States to engage in the preliminary reference dialogue with the Court of Justice.[13] On balance, "older" pre-Nice Enlargement Member States appear to be involved in significantly more in preliminary reference proceedings by way of observations before the Court of Justice than newer post-nice Enlargement States, with the exception of Poland.[14] "Older" or Founding EU States are also more likely to be engaged in extensive "defensive" behaviour before the Court of Justice in preliminary reference proceedings, rarely missing an opportunity to set out their stall.

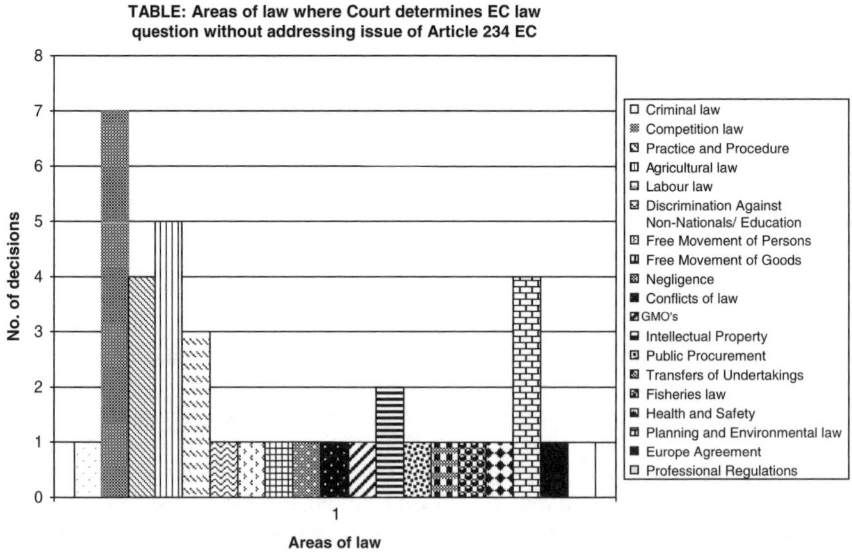

Figure 6.2 Source: Fahey, *Practice and Procure in Preliminary References to Europe: 30 Years of Article 234 EC Case Law from the Irish Courts* (Firstlaw, Dublin, 2007).

[6–05] Existing data, as set out above,[15] indicates that where EU law arises in the Irish courts that it has mostly been at High Court level and that the courts have largely resolved questions themselves in the absence of assistance from the Court of Justice in

[13] For example, in the case of Estonia this has been demonstrated to be the case: D'Sa and Lafranque, "Getting to Know You: The Developing Relationship between National Courts of the "Newer" Member States and the European Court of Justice, with particular Reference to Estonia" (2008) 19 EBLR 311.

[14] Kapko and Weslowski, "One-Shotters of Repeat Players? New Member States before the European Court of Justice" (2007) 10 EJR 55; (2007) 11 EJR 52. See also Malferrari, "The Functional Representation of the Individuals' Interests Before the EC Courts: The Evolution of the Remedies System and the Pluralistic Deficit in the EC" (2005) 12 IJGLS 667.

[15] Source: Fahey, above n 6.

Table: *Numbers Of Cases Referred, Refused, Considered (1973–2003) Superior Courts Only*

	HIGH COURT	*SUPREME COURT*	*TOTAL*
REFERENCES MADE	20 (26% OF HIGH COURT DECISIONS ON EC LAW)	16 (42% OF SUPREME COURT DECISIONS ON EC LAW)	36:32% OF TOTAL CASES ON EC LAW IN SUPERIOR COURTS
REFERENCES REFUSED	18 (24% OF HIGH COURT DETERMINATIONS)	7 (18% OF SUPREME COURT DECISIONS ON EC LAW)	25:22% OF TOTAL CASES ON EC LAW IN SUPERIOR COURTS
INCIDENCE OF EC LAW WHERE REFERENCE NOT EXAMINED	38 (50% OF HIGH COURT DTERMINATIONS)	15 (40% OF SUPREME COURT DECISIONS ON EC LAW)	53:46% OF TOTAL CASES ON EC LAW IN SUPERIOR COURTS
TOTAL	76 (67% OF CASES ON EC LAW IN SUPERIOR COURTS)	38 (33% OF CASES ON EC LAW IN THE SUPERIOR COURTS)	114 CASES ON EC LAW

Source: Fahey, *Practice and Procure in Preliminary References to Europe: 30 Years of Article 234 EC Case Law from the Irish Courts* (Firstlaw, Dublin, 2007).[16]

[16] Sources of data: The author obtained the case-law considered here from an examination of all legal IT databases, the BAILII website, the *Curia* website, the official law reports, the Central Office of the High Court, textbooks, periodicals and general enquiries and purported to be as comprehensive a study as reasonably practicable. Percentages were rounded to the nearest decimal. A number of categories are excluded from the table, such as cases where the incidence of EU law is so marginal that it is not considered: for example where a court mentions EU law related matters or case-law in passing or, for example, non superior court decisions are outside the remit of this table because of the fact that they remain unreported generally. Case-law subsequent to 2003 is excluded.

Luxembourg. Most Supreme Court decisions in the area of EUlaw delivered during the period 2003–2010 are in the area of the European arrest warrant, as to which the Supreme Court lacks preliminary reference referral powers.[17] There have been many Brussels I disputes in the courts in the last decade and the reason for the large number of cases arising in this latter area might be related to the fact that the Brussels I disputes concern procedural objections raised in litigation to the jurisdiction of the Irish courts, that are more readily invoked and litigated than substantive areas of law.[18]

[6–06] Nearly all of the Supreme Court preliminary references made during the period 2000–2010 (the Keane and Murray Supreme Courts), are made in proceedings with a public law dimension and all of the applicants, bar one, are natural or legal persons and not the State. In one particular recent Supreme Court competition law preliminary reference, the decision to refer was exclusively at the behest of the Supreme Court.[19] Few free movement disputes have, until recently, yet to reach the Supreme Court despite less than forty years of membership of the EU whereas, by contrast, one of the most important EU law free movement of persons decisions of all time, *Metock v Minister for Justice*,[20] was generated by the Irish High Court during this recent period. Thus, while matters may be at an elementary level in this regard in this particular period, a radically different trend is discernable at Supreme Court level.

---

[17] C-382/03 *Ryanair v Aer Rianta cpt* (removed from register); C-19/00 *Siac Construction Limited v County Council of the County of Mayo* [2001] ECR I-7725; C-341/04 *Eurofood IFSC* [2006] ECR I-3813; C-221/05 *McCauley Chemists v Pharmaceutical Society of Ireland* [2006] ECR I-6869; C-209/07 *Competition Authority v Beef Industry Development Society Ltd and Barry Brothers (Carrigmore) Meats Ltd* [2008] ECR I-8637; C-372/07 *Hassett (A Minor) v South Western Health Board* [2008] ECR I-7403; *Goshawk Dedicated Ltd v Life Receivables Irl. Ltd* [2009] IESC 7, the Supreme Court indicated that it would refer questions to the Court of Justice but no order for reference was made in 2009 and the proceedings were still before the Supreme Court in March 2010.

[18] However, serious delays ensue from the date of the reference of the Supreme Court, in Brussels I and Insolvency Regulation cases, to the date of the decision of the Court of Justice and then the subsequent consideration of that decision by the Supreme Court, notwithstanding the largely procedural questions posed in Brussels I and Insolvency Regulation disputes. For example, in *Eurofood*, the Supreme Court referred questions in 2004 and that Court gave judgment in the dispute in 2006, upon the receipt of the decision of the Court of Justice and the Supreme Court dismissed the appeal in July 2006: [2006] IESC 41. In *Hassett*, the Supreme Court referred the questions in July 2007 and the Court of Justice delivered judgment in October 2000, while the appeal was dismissed by the Supreme Court on 16 January 2009. See the later decision of the High Court in *Doherty (A Minor) v North Western Health Board and Others* [2010] IEHC 283.

[19] C-209/07 *Competition Authority v Beef Industry Development Society Ltd and Barry Brothers (Carrigmore) Meats Ltd* [2008] ECR I-8637.

[20] i.e, Case C-127/08 *Metock v Minister for Justice, Equality and Law Reform* [2008] 3 CMLR 39. See the recent preliminary reference from the Supreme Court on the interpretation of Council Regulation (EC) 2201/2003 after the ratification of the Treaty of Lisbon in relation to the custody rights of an unmarried father: Case C-400/10 *McB v. E* [2010] IESC 48, pursuant to the urgent preliminary reference procedure (Article 104b Rules of Procedure of the Court of Justice). The Supreme Court has suggested a negative answer and the Court of Justice responded similarly (5 October 2010.)

Transposition Deficits, Article 258 TFEU (Ex Article 226 EC) Infringement Proceedings and Ireland

Golub argues that States with poor implementation rates of Internal Market laws create situations where lawyers can easily question the conformity of national measures with European-based secondary legislation.[21] Poor implementation of internal market law has distinct legal consequences under the Treaties and the infringement action itself pursuant to Article 258 TEFU is the subject of ongoing Treaty reforms, to ensure its effectiveness.[22] The application of this theory to Ireland remains interesting, although it has diverse applications to different areas of law. Overall, transposition deficits decreased markedly in the EU over a period of a decade, from 1992 to 2002, corresponding closely to greater integration and economic prosperity achieved from the roll out of the single market. In 1992, approximately one in five Directives had not been transposed by Member States.[23] Irish transposition compliance has improved significantly only in very recent years, reducing from 5.4% at one point to 1.5% in 2006. The Irish Presidency of the European Council in 2004 resulted in an improved transposition co-ordination regime.[24] In 2009, Ireland had the best scoreboard score to date at 1%, shared by 13 of the 27 Member States. However, Ireland in 2009 had more transposition cases pending against it than in 2006[25] and Ireland, along with Austria, UK and Poland, had the highest number of open infringement actions against it. In environmental law Ireland's compliance with EU legislation remains at its worst and from 1998-2003, Ireland had the highest number of infringement actions against it, topped only by Spain.[26] The reasons for this lack of compliance are complex and multifarious but are frequently institutional or relate to the complexity of the planning law process in this jurisdiction and/or the financial cost of proactive environmental management. The alteration of the coalition Government in 2007 to include the Green Party may impact in future years on these statistics. Otherwise, it does not appear to be the case that Irish transposition trends have any bearing of the incidence of EU law in Ireland or EU law-related litigation. Infringement actions involving Ireland may decrease potentially in the future and Golub's contentions are difficult to apply to Ireland outside the realm of Environmental law. **[6–07]**

Ireland as Litigator: Interventions by Member States in Preliminary Reference Proceedings—Irish Observations

It is possible for Member States to submit observations to the Court of Justice in preliminary references and direct actions, even when they are not involved in the dispute, pursuant to the rules of procedure of the Court of Justice.[27] This extends also to cases where Member States have not accepted the jurisdiction of the Court of Justice **[6–08]**

[21] See Golub, "Modeling Judicial Dialogue in the European Community: The Quantitative Basis of Preliminary References to the ECJ" (EUI Robert Schumann Centre Working Paper No. 58/96).
[22] See the (minor) changes made to the procedure by the Treaty of Lisbon so as to enhance its effectiveness, as to Art 260 TFEU.
[23] See European Commission Internal Market (DG) at www.europa.eu.
[24] I am grateful to Dr Jane O' Mahony for this information.
[25] See *Internal Market Scoreboard 19 July 2009* (European Commission, 2009).
[26] See www.europa.eu and the *Annual Report of the Court of Justice of the European Union*, available at http://curia.europa.eu/.
[27] See Art 104 Rules of Procedure of the Court of Justice.

in a particular field.[28] The proper assessment of Member State observations before the Court of Justice in preliminary rulings and direct actions and their impact on the decisions of the Court of Justice and EU law generally is hotly contested in recent political science literature. Carrubba, Gabel and Hankla have demonstrated that small shifts in the number of governments intervening in preliminary references and direct actions have large substantive effects on the decision of the Court of Justice and that the threat of "override" and "non-compliance" with their judgment is of major relevance.[29] This much, however, has been disputed by Stone Sweet and Brunnell on the basis that, *inter alia*, their data misrepresents how the EU legal system works and the dominant place of the Commission in litigation.[30] From a non-empirical legal perspective, arguably a more cynical view of the value of observations may be offered, given the putative ineffectiveness of Member State interventions in many of the leading cases in EU law where the Court has disregarded numerically-large "opposition" to developments in a particular case, for example, *Environmental Crimes, Carpenter, Metock*.[31] In Granger's study of the number of observations made by national governments in preliminary reference proceedings originating in their own courts in the period from 1995–1999, the Irish government is shown to have made the lowest number of observations in such instances of all the Member States, demonstrating low State participation and little attempt on its part to influence EU policies at this level.[32]

[6–09] It has been shown by Granger, then, that the Irish government historically made a below average number of observations in the areas of free movement of goods, person, service, taxation, agriculture, approximation of laws, environment and consumers, competition, principles of EC law, company law and external relations. In the area of social policy, however, Ireland records an above average level of participation.[33] Older EU States (pre-Nice Enlargement) have tended to participate by way of observations in more preliminary reference cases than newer States (post-Nice Enlargement), albeit that the gap is closing and that the knowledge deficit must be overcome with time.[34] It has been suggested that Member States submitting observations in preliminary reference proceedings only do so defensively and/ or limit their interventions to areas affecting the financial interests of their own States.[35] Others, by contrast, do not miss an opportunity to participate, tending to comprise older States, wealthier and larger States.

---

[28] See Case C-105/03 *Criminal Proceedings against Maria Pupino* [2005] ECR I-5285 para 37.

[29] Carrubba, Gabel and Hankla, "Judicial Behaviour under Political Constraints: Evidence from the European Court of Justice" (2008) 102 APSR 435.

[30] Stone Sweet and Brunnell, "How the Legal System of the European Union works and does not work: Response to Carruba, Gabel and Hankla" (2010), available at http://works.bepress.com/alec_stone_sweet/36.

[31] See Case C-176/03 *Commission v Council* [2005] ECR I7879; C-60/00 *Carpenter v Secretary of State for the Home Department* [2002] ECR I-6279; Case C-127/08 *Metock v Minister for Justice, Equality and Law Reform* [2008] 3 CMLR 39.

[32] Granger, *supra*, p 8.

[33] Noticeably, however, Granger does not offer a more defined explanation of "social policy".

[34] Kapko and Weslowski, "One-Shotters or Repeat Players? New Member States before the European Court of Justice" (2007) 10 EJR 55; (2007) 11 EJR 52.

[35] *ibid.*

Ireland has been suggested to be a State that engages only in important domestic cases, but bolstered by the ability to engage in seminal cases emanating from other Member States, benefits from this cost-effective strategy.[36] This view is not necessarily shared by the current author but its refutation is more complex. While the precise tabulation numerically of observations is problematic, as the official data generated by the Court of Justice solely lists the date of decision and year of reference, that an observation may be made by a Member State in 2010 as to a case lodged before the Court of Justice in 2009, where the decision in the case is delivered in 2011 by the Court of Justice in a preliminary reference, which is referred back to the national court which delivers judgment in 2012![37] With such a large methodological caveat aside, from 1999–2003, Ireland made 18 observations in preliminary reference proceedings. From 2003–2007, Ireland made 42 observations in preliminary reference proceedings and it would appear that Ireland made less than 20 observations in the period from 2008–2010.[38] Thus, a multiple of interventions have been made in recent times. This also corresponds to a slight increase in the number of preliminary references emanating from Ireland in the same period. However, the increased figures in both instances do not necessarily correlate in that the Irish State is making observations in proceedings where the case does not emanate from the jurisdiction. **[6–10]**

The recent tranche of observations submitted by the Irish State have mostly been in finance-related areas, for example in VAT cases, and also in agriculture or economically-related (for example, company law or the free movement of capital), as well as in social law-related fields and many observations (eight) were in Grand Chamber cases. Numerically, Ireland sends many advocates to make observations (as many as three sometimes) and the cost-effectiveness relative to the outcome of this (as well as intervening generally) may come under scrutiny in straitened times. Overall, the Irish State increasingly enters observations beyond those cases originating domestically and statistically it is now engaging in a multiple of its previous intervention activities since 2003. From this much it can be deduced that a "c-change" in attitude to European litigation on the part of the State is apparent and a more proactive and aggressive stance has been adopted by it. However, whether such a pattern will continue in the future, post-Lisbon and in economically-challenging times, remains to be seen. **[6–11]**

Conclusion

The activities of the Irish State, or paucity thereof, in EU-law litigation and the scarcity of cases emanating from the Irish courts generally to the Court of Justice together contribute to the unusual phenomenon that is Ireland within the EU. The changes in patterns and variations in trends may mirror larger trends but also merely form a variable in a complex jigsaw. The increase in litigation and activity in the last decade in preliminary references from the Supreme Court, an improved transposition rate and an **[6–12]**

[36] *ibid.*

[37] While certain Member State ministries make available to researchers the observations submitted by the Member States, the author made a freedom of information request in March 2010 to obtain sight of all observations submitted by the Irish State in certain closed cases, which was refused.

[38] Source: Data provided on request from the Court of Justice as to closed cases and the date range is to June 2010.

increase in observations submitted by the State in proceedings before the Court of Justice may have indicated a renewed emphasis on European-related affairs in that time period. Nonetheless, litigation is difficult to assess in a wider sense and the stance of the State in law and policy is not coherent, which again is borne out in the above trends and data. The Irish State, as a small-sized State and a geographically-peripheral State with a common law legal system and constitutional heritage, clearly has many reasons to seek to gain influence in a larger conglomeration of States but that as a matter of politics, such influence may not be desired by the State. Nonetheless, EU law affords opportunities to gain influence or alter its policy preferences and data outlined in the above text indicates that Ireland is not availing of such possibilities.

CHAPTER 7
EU Consumer Law in Ireland: Product Liability, Package Holiday Law and Unfair Contract Terms

Overview

EU law has provided many recent legislative innovations in the realm of consumer law that have now been transposed into Irish law, with mixed success and a very limited amount of litigation. The benefits that the European legislation has sought to deliver for consumers are far-reaching all the same, despite their failure to impact upon litigation. The innovations of the European measures into traditionally private law spheres, benefiting consumers for many centuries subject to the principle of caveat emptor, are of course apparent. The few instances where the Irish Supreme Court has had an opportunity to consider EU consumer law are disappointing in terms of outcome more so than in terms of reasoning and a more developed jurisprudence may yet evolve in this area. The account following is limited to the relevant legislation and case-law and a wider discussion of the topics at issue is best left to specialist texts in tort, consumer and contract law. Two major areas of consumer law that the Supreme Court has had occasion to consider recently include product liability and package holiday law, both of which are considered here accordingly, followed by a brief consideration of contract law-related measures for consumers emanating from EU law. [7–01]

Product Liability

The Liability for Defective Products Act 1991 transposed into Irish law the Product Liability Directive (Council Directive 85/374/EEC), concerning liability for defective products.[1] The main effect of the Act is to introduce into Irish law the principle of [7–02]

[1] Council Directive 85/374/EEC of 25 July 1985 on the approximation of the laws, regulations and administrative provisions of the Member States concerning liability for defective products. See Schuster, *The New Product Liability Regime* (ICEL, 1991); McMahon and Binchy, *Casebook on the Irish Law of Torts* (3rd ed) (Tottel, Dublin, 2005); Pelly "Is European Products Liability more

"strict" or "no fault" liability. This imposes liability on the producer and, in certain circumstances, the supplier of a defective product. Whether the European regime sought to transpose a regime of strict liability into national law has been debated extensively since the introduction of the Directive, diverging markedly from the negligence based standard of reasonable care existing at common law. Many commentators had outlined the view that the regime as implemented in the Act of 1991 fell far short of strict liability, as did the Directive itself.[2] Moreover, another key question has been whether the Irish Act of 1991 had incorrectly transposed the Directive by reason of the range defences set out in the Act of 1991 and the introduction of "expectation" in the standard for defectiveness, in s 5 of the Act, thereby offsetting the putative strictness of the European product liability regime. There is precedent to the effect of successful plaintiff prosecution of Tobacco related proceedings pursuant to Council Directive EEC 85/374 on Liability for Defective Products.[3] The large number of defences present in the Act is of immense significance in so far as it offsets the "strictness" of the strict liability regime introduced in the Liability for Defective Products Act, 1991. The defences to the regime are set out in s 6 of the Act of 1991, which provides as follows:

> "A producer shall not be liable under this Act if he proves—
> a. that he did not put the product into circulation, or
> b. *that, having regard to the circumstances, it is probable that the defect which caused the damage did not exist at the time when the product was put into circulation by him or that that defect came into being afterwards,* or
> c. that the product was neither manufactured by him for sale or any form of distribution for an economic purpose nor manufactured or distributed by him in the course of his business, or
> d. that the defect concerned is due to compliance by the product with any requirement imposed by or under any enactment or any requirement of the law of the European Communities, or
> e. *that the state of scientific and technical knowledge at the time when he put the product into circulation was not such as to enable the existence of the defect to be discovered,* or
> f. in the case of the manufacturer of a component or the producer of a raw material, that the defect is attributable entirely to the design of the product in which the component has been fitted or the raw material has been incorporated or to the instructions given by the manufacturer of the product." (Emphasis supplied).

Protective than the Restatement (Third) of Torts: Products Liability?—Part I" (2001) 19 ILT 318. And see as to product safety European Communities (General Product Safety) Regulations, 1997 (SI No. 197 of 1997) and European Communities (General Product Safety) Regulations 2004 (SI No. 1999 of 2004).

[2] See generally Schuster, *The New Product Liability Regime* (ICEL, 1991); McMahon and Binchy, *Casebook on the Irish Law of Torts* (3rd ed) (Tottel, Dublin, 2005); Pelly, "Is European Products Liability more Protective than the Restatement (Third) of Torts: Products Liability?—Part I" (2001) 19 ILT 318.

[3] In December 1996, two victims of tobacco addiction brought legal proceedings against the French manufacturer for failure to provide information on the dangers of *Gauloises* cigarettes. Invoking the manufacturer's liability without fault, the victims claimed damages and interest of FRF 2 668 090 and FRF 1 158 499 respectively. See Le Monde, 20, 27 and 28 December 1996 (noted in Commission Green Paper Liability for Defective Products Brussels, 28 July 1999 COM(1999) 396 final).

The "development risks defence" afforded to the manufacturer pursuant to s 6(e) of the Act of 1991 was a defence included to meet the needs of high risk industries in which innovation is often crucial to success. It is important to distinguish between the "state of the art" defence in s 6(b) and the "development risks defence" in s 6(e). As Clark states, **[7–03]**

> "The term *state of the art* could be used to connote a product which is not defective when judged against the prevailing safety standards at the time when it was out unto circulation, but the manufacturer has the defence that existing knowledge made the defect not reasonably discoverable. Thus the state of the art arguments relate to the question of defectiveness, while the *development risks* issues arise later, as a defence to a finding of defectiveness".[4]

Insofar as the "state of the art" defence requires the proof scientifically and factually of a negative, it remains quite a burden to surmount and a defence that might be unpalatable in the public domain to raise.[5] **[7–04]**

The inclusion of the so-called "development risks" defence in the Act of 1991 is noted by Schuster and Quill to be of great significance insofar as it introduces the concept of fault, albeit in a limited form, and offsets the practical implications of strict liability.[6] So, the question arose recently as to whether the range of defences in the Act of 1991 warranted a preliminary reference to the Court of Justice to determine the strictness of the "strict liability" regime. Thus, in proceedings in Ireland relating to the liability of tobacco manufacturers for the injuries suffered by smokers in *Delahunty v Player and Wills (Ireland) Ltd*,[7] the possibility of a preliminary reference pursuant to Article 267 TFEU (ex Article 234 EC) was canvassed by Fennelly J, *obiter*, in the Supreme Court, considering by way of a motion to dismiss the claim of the plaintiff, the Court considered, *obiter*, the adequacy of the transposition and the strictness of the regime implemented, in light of the provisions of s 5 of the Act and the defences contained therein. **[7–05]**

Thus Fennelly J held that: **[7–06]**

> "For the purposes of this appeal, it must be assumed—Mr Sreenan did not ask the Court to do otherwise—that the plaintiff suffered very serious illness as a result of smoking cigarettes. Mr Cush made a very simple submission with regard to the Act of 1991. He says it imposes a strict liability. That depends on the cigarettes being regarded as defective products for the purposes of the Act ...
>
> I do not think a court could possibly decide, on a motion of the type before the Court on this appeal, whether cigarettes "fail to provide the safety which a person is entitled to expect." That will require a great deal of evidence to be given at the trial. It is also highly material that the Act of 1991 was passed in order to transpose into Irish law the provisions of the Council Directive of 1985 mentioned above. The definition of defective

---

[4] Clark, *Product Liability* (Sweet & Maxwell, London, 1989) p 151.

[5] See C-300/95 *Commission v United Kingdom* [1997] All ER (EC) 481; [1997] ECR I-2649.

[6] Schuster, *The New Product Liability Regime* (ICEL, 1991).

[7] *Delahunty v Player and Wills (Ireland) Ltd. and Others* [2006] IESC 21. Proceedings that were ultimately dismissed in separate proceedings by Gilligan J by reason of delay in *Shanaghan and Orsv PJ Carroll* [2007] IEHC 229.

> product is based on Article 6 of the Directive. The Act must be interpreted in the light of the Directive. If the matter comes before this Court in circumstances where a decision on such an interpretation is necessary for the decision of the Court, it would appear that the obligation of the Court to refer this matter to the Court of Justice of the European Communities pursuant to Article 234 of the EC Treaty would arise. That will, of course, depend on whether such an interpretation is necessary for its decision. For that reason alone, it would be impossible to determine such an important issue at this stage. Furthermore, the High Court may wish to refer such questions to the Court of Justice and may do so at any stage of the proceedings.
>
> ... the plaintiff claims that the appellant's "Silk Cut" cigarettes were targeted at vulnerable people such as the plaintiff. It was foreseeable that such people would consume cigarettes placed on the market by them. Issues of causation can be some of the most difficult in tort law. While the appellant has raised an arguable point, I cannot agree that it is decisive. Finally, if Mr Cush is correct in his interpretation of the Act of 1991, the liability of the appellant may be strict".

[7–07] However, these views do not appear to have been shared by the Court of Justice, in particular in the aftermath of its decision in *Commission v United Kingdom*,[8] where the Court held that the Directive itself, despite its array of defences, remained a regime of strict liability, perhaps casting doubt upon the comments of Fennelly J in *Delahunty* on the need for clarification of the "strictness" of the regime established in Ireland.[9] The discussion by Fennelly J of the relevance and utility of a preliminary reference on the point is particularly important but it appears that it will not arise in respect of the tobacco litigation and appetite of the Court of Justice for consumer claims appears stymied by recent case-law.

Package Holidays and Travel Law

[7–08] Another major area of consumer law, traditionally a private law sphere, where EU law has intervened and regulated to a mixed degree of success, is the Package Holiday law regulating industry and the obligations owed by tour operators to consumers, which has its genesis in EU measures.[10] The Package Holidays and Travel Trade Act 1995 transposed into Irish law Council Directive 91/314/EEC[11] on package travel, package holidays and package tours and was the subject of a recent Supreme Court decision in *Scaife v Falcon Leisure Group*.[12] In *Scaife*, the plaintiff, whilst on a package holiday in Spain, fell in the hotel at a buffet and suffered injuries. The defendant sought to appeal against a finding of the High Court in favour of the plaintiff. The issue arose in particular as to the liability of the holiday organiser and the standard of care applicable pursuant to s 20 of the Package Holiday and Trade Travel Act 1995 and whether strict

---

[8] C-300/95 *Commission v United Kingdom* [1997] ECR I-2649.

[9] There the Court was considering the UK implementation regime. See Pugh and Pilgerstorfer, "The Development Risk Defence— Knowledge, Discoverability and Creative Leaps" (2004) 4 JPIL 258.

[10] See McDonald, ed, *European Community Tourism Law and Policy* (Blackwell, Dublin, 2003); Buttimore, *Holiday Law* (Blackwell, Dublin, 1998); Johnston and Unberath "The Double-Headed Approach of the ECJ concerning Consumer Protection" (2007) 44 CMLR 1237; Weatherill, *EU Consumer Law and Policy* (Elgar European Law, Northampton, 2005); Weatherill *et al*, *Consumer Protection Law* (Aldershot/Burlington, Vt.: Ashgate/Dartmouth 2005).

[11] Council Directive 91/314/EEC of 13 June 1990, OJ 190 L 158.

[12] *Scaife v Flacon Leisure Group* [2007] IESC 57.

liability applied or whether reasonable care was the relevant standard that the trial judge had applied.

Section 20 provides that: [7–09]

> "(1) The organiser shall be liable to the consumer for the proper performance of the obligations under the contract, irrespective of whether such obligations are to be performed by the organiser, the retailer, or other suppliers of services but this shall not affect any remedy or right of action which the organiser may have against the retailer or those other suppliers of services.
> (2) The organiser shall be liable to the consumer for any damage caused by the failure to perform the contract or the improper performance of the contract unless the failure or the improper performance is due neither to any fault of the organiser or the retailer nor to that of another supplier of services, because –
> a. the failures which occur in the performance of the contract are attributable to the consumer,
> b. such failures are attributable to a third party unconnected with the provision of the services contracted for, and are unforeseeable or unavoidable, or
> c. such failures are due to –
> i. force majeure, …
> ii. an event which the organiser, the retailer or the supplier of services, even with all due care, could not foresee or forestall".

Thus, the issue arose as to whether the organiser was liable for every incident arising, howsoever arising, and whether a strict or purposive approach was appropriate to the interpretation of the section. Either way, the consumer and the travel industry would be affected by the outcome of such a dispute to a significant degree. [7–10]

The Supreme Court per Macken J,[13] dismissing the appeal, held that the organiser was not an insurer to the consumer and that this was determinative of the dispute. Macken J, after considering a range of cases mainly from the UK courts and a passage from an Advocate General,[14] held that the test to be applied was not one of strict liability. The events in question had to be judged by the standard of reasonable skill and care which, if not express, was implied into the contract between the organiser and holidaymaker. The trial judge was entitled to find on the evidence that the accident was wholly foreseeable and thus the finding in favour of the plaintiff would stand, taking into consideration the manner in which the hotel had dealt with the accident and the system in place to deal with the incident. [7–11]

The issue arises here as to whether a purposive approach (or teleological approach) to the interpretation of the Act, or even indirect effect or "conforming interpretation" was required, in place of the common law approach adopted by the Supreme Court, that appears *prima facie* at odds with the objectives of the Directive, being to assist consumers with claims against holiday organisers and to render such claims easier to [7–12]

---

[13] Hardiman, Fennelly JJ concurring.

[14] *Hone v Going Places Leisure Travel*, Unreported, 13 June 2001, a decision of the English Court of Appeal; *Wong Wee Wan v Kwan Kin Travel Services Ltd* [1996] 1 WLR 38; *Healy v Cosmoair Plc* [2005] All ER 432; Opinion of Advocate General Tizzano in C-168/00 *Leitner v TUI Deutschland* [2002] ECR I-2631.

pursue. It is difficult to see how the thrust of the Supreme Court decision could be seen to be *ad idem* with the opinion of the Advocate General in *Leitner v TUI Deutschland*[15] in the passage cited by Macken J, who had referred to the importance of considering the text and aims of the Directive, whilst arriving at an analysis most favourable to the consumer. The importance of the common law interpretive standards in contract law, adopting the literal approach thereto, remained the key feature of the decision of Macken J and, for this reason, irrespective of the outcome of the decision, *Scaife* is a disappointing analysis of European consumer law initiatives. The suggestion of Fennelly J in *Delahunty* as to the appropriateness of a preliminary reference to assess the correctness of the Irish transposition measures there stands in marked contrast to the firm rejection of the appeal in *Scaife* by Macken J, where no mention of the need for a preliminary reference on the question is made, arguably to the detriment of Irish consumers and to the benefit of the travel industry.

[7–13] It is quite remarkable the absence of case-law on EC Consumer law arising in the Irish courts in recent times given its putative importance for ordinary litigants and it potential to generate favourable outcomes for consumers.

Unfair Contract Terms

[7–14] There is remarkably little case-law in Ireland on the impact of EU measures on Unfair Contract Terms, despite the important benefits delivered by the EU-based measures. Council Directive 93/13/EEC of 5 April 1993 on unfair terms in consumer contracts was implemented into Irish law by way of secondary legislation, pursuant to the European Communities (Unfair Terms In Consumer Contracts) Regulations, 1995.[16] The European Communities (Unfair Terms in Consumer Contracts) (Amendment) Regulations 2000[17] were introduced to extend enforcement powers under Regulation 8 of the 1995 Regulations to "consumer organizations", an important development.[18] There is some evidence that the National Consumer Agency has effectively employed its powers under the Regulations to assist, *inter alia*, with practices relating to gym membership contracts and there is also evidence that the Regulations have been effective at ameliorating, *inter alia*, certain aspects of building contracts.[19] Otherwise, it seems apparent that Irish Consumer law has yet to receive adequate litigation and that a substantive jurisprudence has not yet emerged.[20]

---

[15] C-168/00 *Leitner v TUI Deutschland* [2002] ECR I-2631.

[16] SI No 27 1995.

[17] SI No 307 of 2000.

[18] *Marshall v Capital Holdings Ltd (Trading as Sunworld)* [2006] IEHC 271.

[19] Dorgan "Safe as Houses" (2002) 96 LSGI 12.

[20] Further evidence of this is clear from case-law in relation to the Consumer Credit Act 1995 and a doomed effort of a defendant to rely upon EU Consumer legislation in *AIB PLC v Higgins* [2010] IEHC 219, where an effort was made to attempt to broadly construe the definition of a consumer for the purposes of the Consumer Credit Act 1995, drawing upon Council Directive 87/102/EEC of 22nd December, 1986, as amended by Council Directive 90/80/EEC of 22nd February, 1990. However, see the challenges of the concept of a "consumer" in EU law generally: Micklitz, Reich and Rott, *Understanding EU Consumer Law* (Antwerp, Intersentia, 2009).

Consumer Protection Act 2007

The Consumer Protection Act 2007[21] purports to implement the Unfair Commercial Practices Directive, Directive 2005/29/EC and should represent an important development in (primary) Irish consumer law.[22] So far, there is only one case from the Superior Court considering this legislation and, in particular, European Community (Misleading and Comparative Marketing Communications) Regulations 2007 (SI No 774 of 2007)[23] which purported to implement the Misleading Advertising Directive, Directive 2006/114 EC[24] in *Tesco Ireland Ltd v Dunnes Stores,*[25] where Laffoy J refused a request for an injunction by the plaintiff to suppress misleading advertising comparing promotional price emanating from the defendant, although on procedural grounds, relating to the form of order that the Court could make. The interesting feature of the case is that Laffoy J refused to accept that neither the Act of 2007 nor the Regulations of 2007 altered the procedural position existing under the older Regulations and a Supreme Court decision interpreting them, to the extent that the courts, in such cases, could not grant an interlocutory injunction, but rather only a final order on account of the consequences for the advertising and retailer involved. Laffoy J, here, engaged in a rather literal reading of the two instruments and no discussion took place it would seem as to the effectiveness of EU law and the need for the Court to read the Irish provisions in light of EU law. Presumably, the fact that the plaintiff was a large-scale pan-European retailer (and not a consumer) seeking to "stamp out" a competitor's media blitz would reduce the sympathies that a Court might have for a plaintiff to fashion a suitable remedy. However, the absence of such an analysis and the rather striking result is notable, i.e. that the two new pieces of legislation with their origins in pan-European consumer protection could not be of use to the plaintiff and, instead, a rather expensive and timely re-formulation of proceedings was required. A drafting error in the Regulations[26] was noted by the Court and the level of response of the legislator to the judgment of the Court as a whole will be worthy of some consideration. **[7–15]**

---

[21] As to recent developments in Ireland the Consumer Protection Act 2007; O'Neill, "The Consumer Protection Act 2007-"Enforcing the New Rules" (2008) 26 ILT 46; Reilly, "The Consumer Protection Act 2007: Rationalising the regulation of misleading commercial practices in Ireland-Part I" (2008) 15(6) CLP 127 and 157 and Reilly, "The Rule of traders in the Enforcement of the Unfair Commercial Practices Directive — A Unfair Competition Law for Ireland?" (2009) 31 DULJ 100.

[22] Directive 2005/29/EC of the European Parliament and of the Council of 11 May 2005 concerning unfair business-to-consumer commercial practices in the internal market and amending Council Directive 84/450/EEC, Directive 97/7/EC, 98/27/EC and 2002/65/EC of the European Parliament and of the Council and Regulation (EC) No 2006/2004 of the European Parliament and of the Council.

[23] European Communities (Misleading Advertising) Regulations 1988 (SI No. 134 of 1988) were revoked by the 2007 Regulations.

[24] Directive 2006/114/EC of the European Parliament and of the Council of 12 December 2006 concerning misleading and comparative advertising

[25] *Tesco Ireland Ltd v Dunnes Stores* [2009] IEHC 569.

[26] In Reg 3 of the 2007 Regulations and its reference to a trader and not a consumer.

Conclusion

[7–16] Overall, the EU Consumer law jurisprudence to date is disappointing and the small number of relevant cases is proportionate to the success thereof. The decisions of the Supreme Court in *Delahunty* and *Scaife* pull in very different directions and the input of the Supreme Court cannot yet be definitely assessed in this area. The need for the Irish courts to consult the Court of Justice via Article 267 TFEU as to the Irish implementing legislation seems apparent. Equally so, the role of the doctrine of indirect effect in EU Consumer law is critical to the success of the legislation so as to ameliorate the domestic implementation of the European texts. However, the case-law as yet is not forthcoming and the judiciary have yet to be afforded an opportunity to develop the case-law in this area.

Chapter 8
The Legal Role of the Oireachtas in EU Affairs

Introduction

[8–01] The process of the first failed Treaty of Lisbon referendum in 2008 and then extensive political campaign to ratify the Treaty of Lisbon a second time around brought with it a valuable period of reflection, not merely for the Irish State but also Irish institutional actors, scholars and civil society alike, incomparable to any time in previous history.[1]

[1] The failure of the first Treaty of Nice referendum resulted in much more modest gains: witness the establishment of a National Forum on Europe in 2001 and the advent of a more enhanced legislative scrutiny regime for legislation resulting from the EU: see European Union (Scrutiny) Act 2002 (subsequently amended, the content of which is discussed above); Travers, "The Reception of Community Legislation into Irish law and Related Issues Revisited" (2003) 37 *Irish Jurist* 58 and Costello, "Peoples' Vengeances: Ireland's Nice Referenda" (2005) 1 ECLR 357.

Many recommendations were made in this period by this broad church of entities to reform Irish "Euro-affairs," re-evaluating several fundamental and broad ranging themes such as the Government referendum spending rules, referendum broadcasting rules and critically, the role of the Oireachtas (Irish Parliament) in EU affairs.[2] The role of the Oireachtas is evaluated here and an effort is made to assess the large question of its place in European affairs and how this bears upon EU law in Ireland, a comparative institutional question not usually posed. However, major changes are now posed by the Treaty of Lisbon as regards National Parliaments in European affairs. Also, European affairs raise unique and curious questions as to what the legislature should and could do within a national legal system. Substantively, it is questioned here whether the position of the Parliament in Ireland post-Lisbon results in any more of a substantially effective body than that already in existence. It is contended here that the absence of constitutional provision in domestic law for a distinct role for the Oireachtas in European affairs has substantially diminished its role as a result and that institutionally, the minimalist role played by it and another major institution in Ireland, the judiciary, results in a dearth of institutional contributions to a dynamic European legal order.

[8–02] The role of the Oireachtas in European affairs is considered here firstly, as to its legislative scrutiny powers, then secondly, as to the aftermath of the first failed Treaty of Lisbon referendum. The new powers bestowed upon National Parliaments by the Treaty of Lisbon are then considered, as are the activities and report of the Sub-Committee of the Houses of the Oireachtas on *Ireland's Future in the European Union*. The initial proposals of the Oireachtas to accommodate the Treaty of Lisbon changes are then assessed, followed by an analysis of the provisions of the European Union Act 2009 and the changes to the role of the Oireachtas after the Treaty of Lisbon. Then, the Joint Report on the *Implementation of the Lisbon Treaty: Provisions on the Enhanced Role for National Parliaments* is outlined, as are the changes to the legislative scrutiny regime effectuated by the European Union Act 2009. Domestic constitutional changes to role of Oireachtas to implement the Treaty of Lisbon are then briefly outlined. The powers of the German Federal Parliament are considered here as useful comparative examples, reflecting on the changes wrought by the Treaty of Lisbon and the decision of the German Federal Constitutional Court as to the Parliament.

---

[2] Sub-Committee on Ireland's Future in the European Union, *Ireland's Future in the European Union: Challenges, Issues and Options* (Oireachtas, November, 2008); Houses of the Oireachtas Joint Committee on European Scrutiny, *Special Report on the Enhanced Role for National Parliaments in the Lisbon Reform Treaty* (Prn. A8/0660, May, 2008); Barrett, Laffan, Thom, Thomas and Tonra, eds., *Ireland's Future in Europe: Scenarios and Implications* (UCD Dublin European Institute, November, 2008); Barrett, "Building a Swiss Chalet in an Irish legal Landscape? Referendums on European Union Treaties in Ireland and the Impact of Supreme Court jurisprudence" (2009) 5 ECLR 32; Kingston, "Ireland's options after the Lisbon Referendum: Strategies, Implications and Competing Visions of Europe" (2009) 34 ELR 467; Hogan, "The Lisbon Treaty and the Irish Referendum" (2009) 15 EPL 163; Broadcasting Commission of Ireland, *Guidelines in respect of coverage of the referendum on the Treaty of Lisbon and related constitutional amendments* (7 June 2009) see www.bci.ie.

The Role of the Oireachtas in European Affairs Pre-Lisbon: Legislative Scrutiny[3]

Research to date on the Oireachtas in European affairs is limited to its role in scrutinising European legislation only. The Oireachtas has not been the subject of comparative analysis with other branches of Government or with other parliamentary bodies in European States. As the Government has enjoyed a parliamentary majority for some time now, the role of parliament in European referenda has not been the subject of scholarly analysis. Since the failed referendum on the Treaty of Lisbon in 2008, Parliament has played a more significant role in considering European matters and in setting a European-related agenda but the achievements to date thereof are modest. No specific constitutional provision has been made for parliamentary analysis of European affairs in Ireland and no constitutional or legislative provision exists to govern the relationship between the Irish and European legislatures at until the Treaty of Lisbon. Whilst a modest form of parliamentary legislative scrutiny had originally been in place at the inception of Community membership, in the form of the European Communities Act 1972, it was amended on the grounds on criticism as to its deficiencies.[4] This resulted in the European Communities (Amendment) Act 1973, nonetheless still constituting a framework to analyse legislation, lacking rigour or a real resource commitment.[5] The European Union (Scrutiny) Act 2002 was enacted to ensure greater scrutiny of EU legislation by the Houses of the Oireachtas, so as to scrutinise proposed measures more rigorously and to amend the European Communities Act 1972. However, the newer Act of 2002 has origins in desires more to redress the anti-European electoral feeling after the first failed Treaty of Nice referendum rather than any benevolent pro-European governmental sentiments.[6] **[8–03]**

---

[3] This section draws heavily from Fahey, "Reflecting On the Scope of the European Union (Scrutiny) Act, 2002" (2007) 13 EPL 85. See also Conlan, Donnelly and Fahey, FIDE XXIV Congress Report — Ireland (FIDE, 2010).

[4] See Robinson, "The Irish European Communities Act, 1972" (1973) 10 CMLR 352 and 467. Professor Robinson, former President of Ireland, a Senator then in the Seanad (the Upper House of Parliament) was instrumental in the changes wrought, but nonetheless still critical of the less than full-blooded system of parliamentary scrutiny introduced in the amending legislation in 1973. s 5 of the European Communities Act 1972 provided that:

> "The Government shall make a report twice yearly to each House of the Oireachtas on developments in the European Communities".

[5] *ibid.* Originally, only two annual reports and four annual debates would have been produced, contended to be inadequate by Robinson, *supra*. However, in the amended Act of 1973, express mention was made in statute for a Joint Committee on European Affairs. By 1992, this Committee (previously entitled the Joint Committee on secondary legislation of the European Communities), had produced 14 reports.

[6] The Government adopted, with much modification, an Opposition Bill, the European Union Bill 2001, introduced by Mr Ruari Quinn TD. See, Travers, "The Reception of Community Legislation into Irish Law and Related Issues Revisited" (2003) 37 *Irish Jurist* 58 and Hogan and Whyte, *Kelly: The Irish Constitution* (4th ed) (Lexis-Nexis, Dublin, 2003), para. 5.3.103, where it is noted by the latter that the Act of 2002 was enacted to abate concerns about any democratic deficit in European affairs being perceived by the electorate.

[8–04] The European Union (Scrutiny) Act 2002 established the legislative basis for the EU scrutiny process in the Houses of the Oireachtas. The Act provides that Ministers shall forward to the Oireachtas each draft EU legislative measure, together with an statement outlining the content, purpose and likely implications for Ireland of the proposed measure; submit overall reports to the Oireachtas every six months giving details of "measures, proposed measures and other developments in relation to the European Communities and the European Union." The amount of legal measures falling within the scope of the Act of 2002 scrutiny regime was previously the subject of criticism by this author.[7] More recently, a Dáil Select Committee on European Affairs was established by Order of Dáil Éireann of 23 October 2007. The Dáil Select Committee was joined with a Select Committee of Seanad Éireann, established by Order of Seanad Éireann of 24 October 2007, to form the Joint Committee on European Affairs. The Joint Committee on European Scrutiny was first established by both Houses of the Oireachtas in October 2007.[8] These two committees, the Joint Committees (of both Houses), are the key parliamentary actors in EU Affairs in the jurisdiction.

[8–05] The output of the Committee system is far from satisfactory and its relationship with other State institutions drafting EU law appears limited. Some EU based legislation has been the subject of trenchant criticism from the Supreme Court for its lack of clarity and poor drafting. For example, the European arrest warrant Act 2003 has been stated by the Supreme Court in Ireland to be an example of extremely poor legislative drafting and is most unclear in key passages.[9] As a result of errors in legislative transposition, the primary Act has been amended on a number of occasions. There appears, then, to be some "disconnect" between the activities of the legislature as regards EU affairs.

[8–06] Prior to considering the role of the Oireachtas after the Treaty of Lisbon and the legislative changes proposed by the Oireachtas to accommodate the Treaty of Lisbon, the relevant provisions of the Treaty will be firstly be recounted here and assessed.

The Treaty of Lisbon and National Parliaments

[8–07] The Treaty of Lisbon effectuates a number of important changes, so far as national parliaments are concerned, which have been outlined in much detail elsewhere and are not the principal subject of analysis here.[10] Major innovations in the Treaty of Lisbon

[7] Fahey, "Reflecting On the Scope of the European Union (Scrutiny) Act, 2002" (2007) 13 EPL 85 and Walsh, "Parliamentary Scrutiny of EU Criminal Law in Ireland" (2006) 31 ELR 48. See generally, Barrett, ed, *National Parliaments and the European Union: The Constitutional Challenge for the Oireachtas and Other Member State Legislatures* (Clarus Press, Dublin, 2008).

[8] Before that, the work of scrutinising draft EU legislation had been done by a Sub-Committee of the European Affairs Committee. The Committee's core function is to consider all new EU legislative measures and assess what level of scrutiny is required by the Oireachtas.

[9] Discussed below in Ch 9.

[10] Louis, "The Lisbon Treaty: The Irish 'No'.: National Parliaments and the Principle of Subsidiarity—Legal Options and Practical Limits" (2008) 4 ECLR 429; Barrett, "The King is Dead, Long Live the King: The Recasting by the Reform Treaty of the Provisions of the Constitutional Treaty Concerning National Parliaments" (2008) 33 ELR 66; Barrett, ed. *National Parliaments and the European Union: The Constitutional Challenge for the Oireachtas and Other Member State Legislatures* (Clarus Press, Dublin, 2008).

relating to National Parliaments include a Protocol on National Parliaments and a Protocol on the application of the principles of subsidiarity and proportionality, which gives a role to National Parliaments to ensure decisions are taken at the appropriate level in the EU and that competence is respected. Article 5(3) TEU now gives National Parliaments the responsibility for ensuring that EU institutions comply with the principle of subsidiarity. Moreover, Article 12 TEU now explicitly details how National parliaments can contribute actively to the good functioning of the EU and enumerates their information powers, their role as to subsidiarity, their monitoring functions, their functions as to the revision of the Treaties, applications for accession and inter-parliament cooperation between National parliaments and the European Parliament, is now expressly provided for.

The most striking issue to note is that National Parliaments are now *explicitly* referred to the Treaties in a Title on Democratic Principles, as well as in two Protocols: on the role of National Parliaments in the EU and on the application of the Principles of subsidiarity and proportionality. The first Protocol is predominantly an information-based rights charter, while the second Protocol is a more procedure-based compliance monitoring system, giving teeth to the rights in the first Protocol. At a practical level, Commission consultation documents will now be forwarded directly to the National Parliaments by the Commission and their scrutiny reserve is extended from six to eight weeks. They are given an enhanced role in the area of Freedom, Security and Justice and a formal inter-parliamentary relationship between National Parliaments and the European Parliament is provided for in the Protocol on the role of National Parliaments. National Parliaments will also be involved in future Treaty changes and enlargement applications. **[8–08]**

Of most importance, however, is their negative right in the newly extended Article 7(3) of the Protocol on application of the Principles of subsidiarity and proportionality. Thus, they gain significant rights in the area of subsidiarity to send a reasoned opinion within eight weeks of the transmission of a draft legislative act that the act does not comply with subsidiarity, which may result in the review of the proposal: the new so-called "yellow" and "orange" card mechanisms entail that a draft proposal has to be reviewed. Much has been written about the rights for National parliaments as provided for in these Protocols and, in the latter provisions in particular, the content of which is outside of the scope of this current work.[11] Suffice to say that opinion is divided as to whether the revised content and procedures relating to subsidiarity in the Treaty of Lisbon is so inherently complex and political more than legal that it may not be effective or that the procedures themselves are fraught with such difficulties that they may not work, such as obtaining the necessary institutional blocking vote.[12] For example, Barrett suggests that while it may become excessively difficult to block legislation in practice on account of the complexities of the revised Protocol rights, that the greatest benefits of the new procedures will be indirect in nature and rather the **[8–09]**

[11] Barrett, "The King is Dead, Long Live the King: The Recasting by the Reform Treaty of the Provisions of the Constitutional Treaty Concerning National Parliaments" (2008) 33 ELR 66.

[12] See the evidence of Prof Dashwood and Prof Hix outlined in House of Commons European Scrutiny Committee, *Subsidiarity, National Parliaments and the Lisbon Treaty* (HC 563, 33rd Report of Session 2007–2008), Ch 3 See Dougan, "The Treaty of Lisbon 2007: Winning Minds, Not Hearts" (2008) 45 CMLR 617, 657–661.

motivation and input entitlements of National Parliaments will color the complexion of their activities. Equally, the House of Commons European Scrutiny Committee has expressed the view as to whether the revised role for National Parliaments would make much practical difference to the current status quo.[13] The "light" implementation of these provisions in Irish law suggests that their operation may not be unproblematic, discussed above.

The Aftermath of the First Failed Treaty of Lisbon Referendum

[8–10] In June 2008, for the first Treaty referendum, the Irish electorate rejected the Treaty of Lisbon for reasons adverted to earlier, shortly after a new Taoiseach (Prime Minister) came to power.[14] The role of the Oireachtas as an entity, including the Government parties and opposition parties, in the period before the first referendum was arguably quite limited and not substantive or active, in either the civic or political sense, and the referendum was conducted largely on party lines, with the non-Government opposition parties that supported the referendum making a modest effort to pass the referendum and the limited opposition to the referendum largely leading the public debates, assisted by Libertas, a party formed to oppose the Treaty of Lisbon by a businessman, Mr Declan Ganley. The Irish media were criticised in this time by the European Commission on the grounds that they were becoming increasingly Euro-sceptic, although the influence that they had on popular opinion presents a causal challenge.[15] The period of reflection which ensued after the first referendum coincided with a global economic recession, a severe downturn in the Irish economy as well as unprecedented unpopularity of the Irish Government. Extensive Government research was commissioned so as to explain the negative vote and, from the findings, distinct trends were discernable concerning class and gender in voting patterns. Ultimately, many respondents pointed to an information deficit.[16]

[8–11] By the time that the second Treaty of Lisbon referendum took place, a party founded principally to oppose the Treaty of Lisbon, Libertas, disintegrated following an abysmal performance in the MEP elections in 2009.[17] For the second referendum, the State's broadcasting rules were amended so as to facilitate the reality of the politics governing the referendum campaign, where all the major political parties supported

---

[13] *ibid,* para. 37.

[14] Mr Brian Cowen TD, formerly Tánaiste (or deputy leader), replaced Mr Bertie Ahern TD as Taoiseach (Prime Minister) in 2008.

[15] The "changing media landscape" between 2002 and 2008 is identified as an important determinant of changes in public opinion which influenced the Lisbon referendum: see "Irish media more Eurosceptic, warns EC report." See *The Irish Times*, (2 September 2008).

[16] *Post-Lisbon Treaty Research Findings* (Millward Brown IMS, Dublin, September 2008), http://www.imsl.ie/ (last visited 27 November 2009), conducted on 2,101 adults.

[17] Founded by a millionaire Irish businessman, Mr Declan Ganley. The party attracted considerable controversy in respect of its funding. The Forum on Europe, a body established by the Government prior to the first referendum campaign to promote discussion on Ireland's membership of the European Union, was not re-established for the second referendum: see http://www.forumoneurope.ie/ (last visited 28 December 2009). A Referendum Commission, an ad hoc body established by Government to outline the "Yes" and "No" arguments in the referendum campaigns, chaired by a High Court judge, was part of the landscape of the first and second referenda. See Referendum Act 1998 and www.refcom.ie (last visited 28 December 2009).

the Government in their desire to procure a successful referendum result.[18] Previously, broadcasters had been obliged to provide equal airtime to those campaigning for and against the Treaty referendum result, despite the weight of elected representatives and campaigners in favour of the Treaty. The National Forum on Europe was effectively abolished by the Minister for the Environment for the second referendum campaign, Parliament again not acting here as the instigator of such actions.

The numerous reports of the Oireachtas published in the last two years reflecting on how to accommodate the Treaty of Lisbon in Irish law are considered here now in chronological order. **[8–12]**

I: Oireachtas Reports Preparing for Lisbon

(A) Initial Report of the Oireachtas to Accommodate the Treaty of Lisbon Changes

In advance of the first Treaty of Lisbon referendum in June 2008, the report of the Joint Committee on European Scrutiny was published before this event in May 2008 (*Report on the Enhanced Role for National Parliaments in the Lisbon Reform Treaty*) as to how the Irish legislature should respond to the Protocol attached to the Treaty of Lisbon as to National Parliaments, while viewing the new subsidiary procedures as enhancing democracy, contained in reality few substantive recommendations and suggested that bye-laws be employed in the main to cope with the revised procedures contained therein.[19] The Special Report recommended that an extra sitting day per month be allocated to both Houses for EU business, where the reports of the European Scrutiny Committee on important EU draft laws would be considered, as would the ongoing work programme of the Joint Committee on European Affairs, the implementation of the Treaty of Lisbon, briefings by Ministers on major policy matters being considered by the Council of Ministers and proposals by National Parliaments to have draft laws struck down on subsidiarity grounds. The Joint Committee also considered how the Houses might implement their new powers by way of a system of delegation, by the use of Standing Orders to underpin the yellow and orange card procedures, how the Order of Reference of the Joint Committee on European scrutiny could be revised and how the resource implications of its new powers could be assessed. **[8–13]**

The report, nonetheless, was "light" on substantive recommendations on how to actually manage the rights and duties contained in the Protocols, despite the looming changes in the event of the successful ratification of the Treaty of Lisbon, and the political reality of a second referendum campaign appears to have stymied further developments in this regard. After this Report, then in 2008, the people rejected the Treaty of Lisbon in a referendum and the political system was plunged into a deep period of soul-searching as to how to proceed. **[8–14]**

---

[18] See Broadcasting Commission of Ireland, *Guidelines in respect of coverage of the referendum on the Treaty of Lisbon and related Constitutional Amendments 2009* (7 August 2009), see www.bci.ie.

[19] Joint Committee on European Scrutiny *Report on the Enhanced Role for National Parliaments in the Lisbon Reform Treaty* (23 May 2008).

(B) Sub-Committee of the Houses of the Oireachtas on Ireland's Future in the European Union

[8–15] After the first failed referendum, a Sub-Committee of the Houses of the Oireachtas was established in early October 2008 *Ireland's Future in the European Union*, which then heard extensive evidence from a range of experts and bodies on Ireland and the EU and, it is suggested here, made a number of limited and generalised recommendations in its final report in November 2008.[20] The time mandate given to the body was particularly short, despite the magnitude of its brief. Notwithstanding, this is, by far, the most substantive role ever played by Parliament in European affairs, more so than after the first failed Treaty of Nice referendum. The Sub-Committee Report on *Ireland's Future in the European Union* contained many suggestions to enhance the role of the Oireachtas, to increase accountability, to introduce a scrutiny reserve, to have more structured meetings with Ministers before Council meetings, to focus more on non legislative documents and to alter the internal procedures of the Oireachtas to give effect to the recommendations of the Committee.[21] The Report specifically criticised the lack of influence of the Oireachtas in EU decision making processes, the procedures giving effect to EU law in Ireland, the way EU business is handled in the Oireachtas and sensitive policy areas such as workers rights and socio-ethical issues.[22] The Sub-Committee concluded that the Houses of the Oireachtas should play a leading role in Ireland's engagement with the EU. Despite these high-minded goals, to the present day, no long-term vision, policy or constitutional change has been made to accommodate the multi-layered democracy envisioned by the Treaty of Lisbon, discussed below in greater detail.

[8–16] However, it is contended here, that even these more forceful criticisms fail to adequately address the root and branch reform of parliament activities as to European affairs in Ireland and that the adequate resourcing as well as the constitutional position of such committees and activities needs fundamental re-evaluation. The report, while a most significant intervention in European affairs as regards the Oireachtas generally, nonetheless pales in comparison with its UK and German counterparts, where substantial reports and evidence gathering exercises are more common parliamentary activities.

[8–17] During 2009, the first part of the year was largely spent by the body politic on preparing for the second referendum on the Treaty of Lisbon which was held in November 2008.

---

[20] Houses of the Oireachtas Sub-Committee on Ireland's Future in the European Union, *Ireland's future in the European Union: Challenges, Issues and Options* (November 2008). The more specific recommendations include (at para. 31 onwards) the adoption of a formal scrutiny reserve system and an EU Affairs panel in the Seanad but other recommendations include encouraging TD's to gain expertise in EU affairs (para. 40).

[21] See Houses of the Oireachtas Sub-Committee on Ireland's Future in the European Union, *Ireland's Future in the European Union: Challenges, Issues and Options* (November, 2008).

[22] At p 69.

(C) Joint Report on the Implementation of the Lisbon Treaty: Provisions on the Enhanced Role for National Parliaments

Finally, however, in 2009, the Joint Committees on European Affairs and European Scrutiny published the *Joint Report on the Implementation of the Lisbon Treaty: Provisions on the Enhanced Role for National Parliaments.*[23] This Joint Report represents a very important attempt on the part of the Oireachtas to outline holistically how the Houses will cope with the challenges that subsidiarity presents to them, as well as the opportunities afforded by it. The report is particularly detailed and well-written and a sense of engagement with responsibilities is evident from the report. The delay in producing such a work, however, is noticeable and the EU Affairs website on which the report is so prominently displayed as "new" while dynamic and filled with images and links, is in fact rather outdated.[24] **[8–18]**

The main recommendations of the Joint Report are that on an interim basis the new system should operate, that the Joint Committee on European Scrutiny should have responsibility for the day to day operation of s 7(3) of the Act of 2009 (the "yellow" and "orange" card procedures, discussed next), that the Committee should employ its existing powers under the Act of 2002 to assess subsidiarity compliance, that the select committees of both Houses should have the right to work independently, that Government Departments should provide the highest level of cooperation, eg. advance notice, so as to meet prospective deadlines,[25] that inter-parliamentary cooperation is critical, that the Joint Committees on European Affairs and European Scrutiny are to become the actors to litigate subsidiarity for the purposes of Article 8 of the Protocol on the application of subsidiarity and proportionality and the range of new documents to which the Houses of the Oireachtas are entitled to receive are outlined, considered next. **[8–19]**

The Joint Report notably states that the resource implications of the new role for national parliaments under the Lisbon Treaty were not clear and that both committees agreed that arrangements and procedures would be put in place pending the completion of a comprehensive consultation by the Joint Committee on the **[8–20]**

---

[23] Joint Committees on European Affairs and European Scrutiny published the *Joint Report on the Implementation of the Lisbon Treaty: Provisions on the Enhanced Role for National Parliaments* (Joint Committees on European Affairs and European Scrutiny, December 2009), see www.oireachtas.ie.

[24] For example, http://euaffairs.ie/ while containing photos of business of the Committees, still had, at the end of February 2010, an icon emphasising or advertising the Swedish Presidency of the EU in 2009. An advertisement seeking submissions on the European Citizens Initiative is located at the top of the same page, seeking submissions by end of January 2010. See the limited number of submissions made to the Houses of the Oireachtas Joint Committee on European Affairs as to the European Citizens Initiative, resulting in a rather disappointing report: See *EU Scrutiny Report No. 6 Report on the Joint Committee of European Affairs Contribution to the European Commission on its Green Paper on a European Citizens' Initiative* (Joint Committee on European Affairs, February, 2010). See *Proposal for a Regulation of the European Parliament and Council on the Citizen's Initiative* COM(2010) 119 final 2010/0074 (COD) 31.3.2010.

[25] The report notes (p 19–20) that the Joint Committee on European Scrutiny had actively participated in the COSAC pilot project on subsidiarity checking and had met all of the relevant time deadlines.

future role of the Houses of the Oireachtas on EU affairs, suggesting an uneasy and uncertain view of the future, for all the positive assertions of the value of the two new Protocols. [26]

[8–21] Next here then, the legislative and constitutional changes made to Irish law so as to implement the Treaty of Lisbon, are considered here.

II: Legislative and Constitutional Changes Made to Irish Law to Implement the Treaty of Lisbon

(A) European Union Act 2009: Changes to the Role of the Oireachtas After the Treaty of Lisbon

[8–22] The amendments made to Irish statutory law to incorporate these changes effectuated to the role of Parliament by the Treaty are far from striking and represent a lowest common denominator type of incorporation. The amendments are made by way of statute and are not constitutional in nature. Section 7(1) provides for the operation of the procedures for the revision of the Treaties in accordance with Article 48.7 TEU, while s 7(2) provides for the operation of the procedure in accordance with Article 81.3 TFEU as to proposals on judicial co-operation in civil matters. The Act provides generally for the procedure as set out in Article 7(3) the Protocol on the application of subsidiarity and proportionality, which extends the subsidiarity control applying under the ordinary legislative procedure which operates when reasoned opinions from majority of votes allocated to national parliaments comes into play. The yellow and orange card procedures are more generally provided for in s 7(3) of the Act of 2009, specifying the general time limit as set out in the Treaties of eight weeks for the issuance of a reasoned opinion on draft legislative acts. Thus, it is stated that:

> "Either House of the Oireachtas may, not later than 8 weeks after the transmission of a draft legislative act referred to in Article 6 of Protocol No. 2 to the Treaty on European Union and the Treaty on the Functioning of the European Union, send to the Presidents of the European Parliament, the Council and the European Commission a reasoned opinion in accordance with that Article if the House concerned passes a resolution in respect of the draft legislative act concerned authorising the House to so do".

Section 7(4) of the Act of 2009 makes provision for the justiciable rights accorded to national parliaments by the Treaty of Lisbon where an ex ante breach of subsidiarity is asserted by either House of the Oireachtas. The Act thus provides that:

> "where either House of the Oireachtas is of opinion that an act of an institution of the European Union infringes the principle of subsidiarity provided for in the treaties governing the European Union and wishes that proceedings seeking a review of the act concerned be brought in the Court of Justice of the European Union in accordance with Article 263 of the Treaty on the Functioning of the European Union, it shall so notify the

[26] At p 8. See more recently Houses of the Oireachtas Joint Committee on European Affairs, *EU Scrutiny Report No. 6 Report on the Joint Committee on European Affairs' Contribution to the European Commission on its Green Paper on a European Citizens' Initiative* (Houses of the Oireachtas, February 2010).

> Minister in writing for the purposes of Article 8 of Protocol No. 2 to that treaty and the Treaty on European Union and the Minister shall, as soon as may be after being so notified, arrange for such proceedings to be brought".

Section 7(4) then sets out the procedure relating to Article 8 of the Protocol whereby a perceived justiciable breach pursuant to the Protocol is litigable by the relevant Minister for Foreign Affairs upon receipt of a reasoned opinion of either of the Houses that an act of the EU institutions infringes subsidiarity (and not any composition of Parliament), albeit that this much is provided for in the Treaties. Nonetheless, a more substantive constitutional provision would arguably be more appropriate to provide the core of the subsidiarity powers, set out above, given their inherent importance. It must be said that the legislative changes made to implement the Treaty of Lisbon as a matter of law are sparse and simplistic and arguably fail to capture the change of tone that the Protocols attached to the Treaty of Lisbon set, i.e. they are rudimentary changes that are made. The consistently piecemeal manner in which European affairs as to parliament are dealt with by statute is disappointing and while it cannot be said that the provisions of the Act of 2009, as outlined above, are legally incorrect and they certainly do not represent a wholesale effort to reform parliamentary affairs as to EU law. **[8–23]**

(B) Changes to the Legislative Scrutiny Regime Effectuated by the European Union Act 2009

However, the range of measures subject to legislative scrutiny under the Act of 2002, in fact, are now technically reduced as a result of the destruction of the pillar structure of the EU in the Treaty of Lisbon. Thus, the range of instruments employed will be reduced and joint actions and common positions are no longer within the remit of the Scrutiny Committees. However, the number of instruments as to which the Oireachtas receives of a variety of forms is, of course, dramatically increased in light of the content of the Protocols and the new information-based rights therein. Hence, s 6 of the European Union Act 2009 now provides that: **[8–24]**

> "Section 1 of the European Union (Scrutiny) Act 2002 is amended by the substitution of the following definition for the definition of "measure": "'measure' means—
> a. a regulation or directive adopted under the Treaty on the Functioning of the European Union,
> b. a decision adopted under Article 28 or 29 of the Treaty on European Union, or
> c. an act (other than a regulation, directive or decision referred to in paragraph (*a*) or (*b*)) requiring the prior approval of both Houses of the Oireachtas pursuant to subsection 7° or 8° of Article 29.4 of the Constitution".

Despite this apparent reduction, the role of the National Parliaments is in fact substantially enhanced and complicated by their new range of mainly negative powers.

(C) Domestic Constitutional Changes to Role of Oireachtas to Implement the Treaty of Lisbon

Article 29 of the Irish Constitution has provided for the constitutional super-structure relating to EU membership. It has been amended in the wake of each referendum in Ireland but the amendments made have been largely minimalist and each alteration has included references to the new Treaty being ratified. The former provisions of **[8–25]**

Article 29.4.6° and Article 29.4.8° of the Constitution, as inserted by recent referenda in 1998[27] and 2002[28] respectively, put in place formally and structurally, mechanisms by which the State was able to decide to exercise particular options contained in the Treaty of Amsterdam and the Treaty of Nice: the so-called "variable geometry" clauses. Article 29.4.6° provided as follows:

> "The State may exercise the options or discretions provided by or under Articles 1.11, 2.5 and 2.15 of the Treaty referred to in subsection 5° of this section and the second and fourth Protocols set out in the said Treaty but any such exercise shall be subject to the prior approval of both Houses of the Oireachtas".

The provisions of Article 29.4.8° provided that:

> "The State may exercise the options or discretions provided by or under Articles 1.6, 1.9, 1.11, 1.12, 1.13 and 2.1 of the Treaty referred to in subsection 7° of this section but any such exercise shall be subject to the prior approval of both Houses of the Oireachtas".

[8–26] Most remarkably, it has been legally and constitutionally beyond dispute since 1998 (i.e. since the Treaty of Amsterdam) that there were aspects of membership of the Communities and Union contained in the Irish Constitution that were not objectively necessary and were legally considered to be discretionary. Articles 29.4.6° and 8° were formulated to protect State sovereignty by allowing the discretion to be exercised, conditional upon the approval of both Houses of the Oireachtas being obtained, thereby adopting an attitude of tremendous flexibility and pragmatism as to European affairs. However, the concentration of this protection is in the hands of the State in times of parliamentary majority, a factor meriting some consideration. The difficulty here, as commentators have noted, is that at what point does the prior consent of the Houses of the Oireachtas become necessary?[29]

[8–27] Of the recent constitutional changes made so as to ratify the Treaty of Lisbon, this formula is repeated. Article 29.4.7° permits the State, with only the approval of Parliament needed and not a referendum, to engage in enhanced cooperation and to take part in the Schengen Area and the Area of Freedom, Security and Justice.[30] This permission is the constitutional background to Protocol (No. 21) considered above. Article 29.4.7° provides that:

> "The State may exercise the options or discretions—
>
> i. to which Article 20 of the Treaty on European Union relating to enhanced cooperation applies,
>
> ii. under Protocol No. 19 on the Schengen *acquis* integrated into the framework of the European Union annexed to that treaty and to the Treaty on the Functioning of the European Union (formerly known as the Treaty establishing the European Community), and

---

[27] The Eighteenth Amendment to the Constitution.

[28] The Twenty-Sixth Amendment to the Constitution.

[29] See Hogan and Whyte *op.cit.*, para 5.3.86.

[30] See Fahey, "Swimming in a Sea of Law: Reflections on Water Borders, Irish (-British)-Euro Relations and Opting-Out and Opting—In After the Treaty of Lisbon" (2010) 47 CMLR 645.

iii. under Protocol No. 21 on the position of the United Kingdom and Ireland in respect of the area of freedom, security and justice, so annexed, including the option that the said Protocol No. 21 shall, in whole or in part, cease to apply to the State, but any such exercise shall be subject to the prior approval of both Houses of the Oireachtas".

Irish parliamentary approval is then needed to opt in pursuant to Article 8 of the Protocol, as a matter of domestic law.[31] This falls short of a possibly more rigorous and systematic approach, such as that being contemplated in the UK at the time of writing.[32] The European Union Act 2009, which amends Irish statutory law to incorporate the enhanced role for national parliaments as to the new Protocol on subsidiarity, as contained in the Treaty of Lisbon, is equally devoid of any system to deal with the implications of Article 4a or the remainder of the Protocol.[33] It could be contended that the constitutional amendments made recently authorise the State, by way of parliamentary authority only, to elect to opt-into the Area of Freedom, Security and Justice, pursuant to the terms of the relevant Protocol or to also join the Schengen Area. The difficulty with the simplicity of the constitutional provision drafted is that is fails to enumerate other related issues arising in the event of the State exercising such choices. **[8–28]**

However, beyond this, the activities on a public level of the Oireachtas European affairs committee have increased several fold and the proceedings of the Committees employ a range of technologies and use more effectively their websites to disseminate their activities. On a visual level, there appears to be more evidence of engagement with the public with the inception of the new website for the parliamentary EU Affairs activities generally.[34] **[8–29]**

III: A Comparative Perspective on the Role of Parliament in European Affairs: The Case of the Germany Federal Parliament Pre-Lisbon

As stated above, no constitutional or legislative provision exists to govern the relationship between the Irish and European legislatures. This is in marked contrast to Articles 23(2) and (3) of the German Constitution (GG) prior to the Treaty of Lisbon,[35] which provided as follows: **[8–30]**

[31] Twenty-Eighth Amendment to the Constitution (Treaty of Lisbon) Act 2009: see www.oireachtas.ie.

[32] See House of Lords European Union Committee *Enhanced Scrutiny of EU Legislation with a United Kingdom Opt-in* (2nd Report, Session 2008–09, HL Paper 25).

[33] Practice suggests that Irish MEP's do not vote in the plenary where Ireland has not opted into a measure: see generally House of Lords Select Committee on European Union, *The Treaty of Lisbon: An Impact Assessment* (10th Report, Session 2007–08, HL Paper 62). This, arguably, is a worrisome development in the long-term, particularly if Ireland reviews its opt-out in the future, as per the terms of Declaration (No. 56) considered above.

[34] See http://euaffairs.ie/.

[35] The details of the Bundestag's role in German European policies are set out in the Federal Statute on "co-operation between the Federal Government and the German Bundestag in European Union affairs".

> "(2) The Bundestag and, through the Bundesrat, the Länder shall participate in matters concerning the European Union. The Federal Government shall keep the Bundestag and the Bundesrat informed, comprehensively and at the earliest possible time.
>
> (3) Before participating in legislative acts of the European Union, the Federal Government shall provide the Bundestag with an opportunity to state its position. The Federal Government shall take the position of the Bundestag into account during the negotiations. Details shall be regulated by a law".

[8–31] However, as Hofmann notes, Article23 GG distinguished between information and hearing. The Bundestag has the right to be informed by the federal government about *all* matters concerning the EU (Article 23 (2) GG) but has the constitutional right to be heard expressly *only* with respect to the EU's "legislative acts" (Article 23 (3) GG).[36] Scrutiny is placed in a context where it presupposes information and both aspects of the Bundestages involvement (information and control) are regulated by the Constitution and an Act on Cooperation between the Federal Government and the German Bundestag in Matters concerning the EU of 12 March 1993 and a further Agreement on aspects of the Act was reached in 2006.[37] These rights, of the Bundestag, date from as far back as 1957, at the inception of the Treaty of Rome. Within the Bundestag, there is also a constitutionally prescribed European Affairs Committee, enjoying the highest prominence of all committees with a membership of 50 which meets on a weekly basis.[38]

[8–32] The German example is a particularly fine one of rigorous scrutiny constitutionally mandated, distinguishing itself considerably from the Irish model because of its constitutional origins and prescribed rights and correlative obligations. It is, however, arguably the most inherently empowered of all of the parliamentary bodies of the European States[39] by virtue of its notable constitutional position and the affirmative constitutional obligations owed to it by the State: its counterparts in Austria,[40] Belgium,[41]

---

[36] Hofmann, "Parliamentary Representation in Europe's System of Multi-Layer Constitutions: A Case Study of Germany" (2003) 10 MJ 1.

[37] Agreement between the German Bundestag and the Federal government on cooperation in matters concerning the EU in implementation of s 6 if the Act on Cooperation between Federal government and the German Bundestag in Matters concerning the European Union (28 September 2006).

[38] There are also European Affairs Committees in the Länder.

[39] As to which and hereafter for an outstanding comparative survey, see the House of Lords Select Committee on the European Union, *Review of Scrutiny of European Legislation* (First Report, 2002–2003, HL Paper 15, Appendix 4).

[40] As in Germany, the members of the Austrian Bundesrat are representatives of the Austrian Lander delegated by the Lander parliaments. The Austrian Bundesrat, however, has more limited constitutional rights than its German counterpart.

[41] The Belgian Parliament deals with European matters through its Joint Advisory Committee on European Affairs, which involves MEP's.

Denmark,[42] Finland,[43] France,[44] Greece,[45] Italy,[46] Luxembourg,[47] the Netherlands,[48] Portugal,[49] Spain,[50] or Sweden do not compare favourably as to its general constitutional powers or otherwise, nor as to its specific constitutional rights relating to the provision of information from the European legislature.[51] Many modes of practice of the House of

---

[42] In Denmark, the European Affairs Committee (Europaudvalget) was created in 1972 and meets throughout the year, except for August. The parties are allocated places on the Committee according to their strength in the Folketing.

[43] The Grand Committee (Suuri valiokunta/ Stora utskottet) was given its task to scrutinise EU policy in 1994 (the Committee was formed in 1906). The Eduskunta/Riksdag selects committee members to reflect party strength. However, even the smallest party normally has at least one substitute place on the committee. The Grand Committee meets twice a week.

[44] The mechanism for examining EU legislation by the national parliament has not been in place for very long, only around 10 years. It involves a "delegation" of each chamber. The objective of the French system is to allow the National Assembly and the Senat to adopt a position on legislation in preparation. The delegations in the Assembly and the Senat are at the centre of the process, and are like committees but not called that as the latter are only for working on French law.

[45] The composition of the Committee of European Affairs is mixed, consisting of national MP's and MEP's. The Committee has an advisory role but does not meet regularly. It can be convened by its Chairman, by a third of its members or by the Government. In general, the Chairman chooses topics for consideration but the Parliamentary Speaker may also do so.

[46] In the Senate, the relevant Committee is the "Giunta per gli affari delle Comunitá europee", and in the Chamber of Deputies, the "Commissione le politiche dell Unione Europea"—also known as the XIV standing committee.

Traditionally in both Houses of the Italian Parliament direct competence on EU matters is the responsibility of standing committees, the EU Committees having a consultative role. In 1999 the Chamber of Deputies reformed its rules of procedure, giving the Chamber's EU committee standing committee status, with specific tasks. The Giunta of the Senate, however remains solely consultative, with the primary competence falling to the Constitutional Affairs Committee. This is felt to have created an imbalance between the two.

[47] Luxembourg's Chamber of Deputies has a Committee for Foreign and European Affairs and Defence, which scrutinises, investigates and reports on EU documents, sometimes after taking evidence and the Committee's opinions are sent to Government.

[48] In the Tweede Kamer, membership of the Committee reflects the political weighting of the second chamber. The Tweede Kamer EU Committee broadly functions under the same terms as the Commons EU Committee, though in a more ad hoc manner. The Committee in the Eerste Kamer conducts general work on EU affairs, and refers particular issues to specialised committees. It plays a particular role in transposition.

[49] The Committee of European Affairs is the specialist committee for all matters related to the EU. The Committee has an umbrella responsibility, distributing the issues among the relevant Specialist Committees. The Committee may then request Opinions from the individual Specialist Committees on which it bases reports to the Government. These reports, whether based on other Committee opinions or not, may lead to the presentation of resolutions to the plenary. The European Affairs Committee is the only Committee with such a power.

[50] The Committee scrutinises and ranks proposed laws, and makes reports to the plenary and the government. Joint meetings are held with Spanish MEP's. There is currently a sub-committee on the 2004 IGC.

[51] The Advisory Committee on EU Affairs of the Riksdag (EU-Nämden) was established in 1995. The Advisory Committee on EU Affairs reflects the parties' strength in the Riksdag. The Committee meets weekly throughout the year, except in August.

Lords European-related affairs committees are being adopted in Ireland, such as the taking of expert evidence and the public and high-profile conduct of proceedings, although these practices are ad-hoc and not systematic and the limited staff of the Irish parliament for such matters remains less favorable than in the case of the UK. Moreover, in contrast with Germany, all other comparable parliamentary bodies are liable to be regulated by way of statute and are thus subject to ad hoc arrangements that may be altered by incoming regimes, for example, unlike the more permanent constitutional position enshrined in the German text, with transparent and affirmative rights accruing to the parliamentary body.

[8–33] Lord Mance, in a recent lecture where he endeavored to defend the opt-in opt-out positions negotiated by the UK in the Treaty of Lisbon and the role of Parliament to be played as a result,[52] suggested in a wider reflection, that the UK parliamentary regime as to European affairs was less comprehensive and less transparent than the German regime, that the proposals considered by Parliament were narrower in the UK, that confidentiality was more readily invoked in the UK in parliament, that the position taken by Parliament was not the basis for negotiations unlike in Germany and that the UK Parliament did not formally take account of devolution in European affairs. These comparisons with the German position may be applied with equal, if not more, force to the Irish context and the Irish Parliament to a degree has been playing "catch up" with the House Lords *modus operandus* until recently.

[8–34] In the decision of the German Federal Constitutional Court on the constitutionality of the ratification of the Treaty of Lisbon,[53] the Court annulled the accompanying legislation and obliged the Federal president not to ratify the Treaty of Lisbon before the powers of Parliament were specified. However, the transparency of the reasoning of the Court has been criticised on this particular point.[54] The Act Extending and Strengthening the Rights of the Federal Parliament and Federal Council in EU matters[55] was held by the Court to be in breach of Article 38 (1)[56] of the Basic Law read with Article 23.[57] So, the Court held that the Act did not provide the two Chambers with the

---

[52] Mance, "Opting into Community law and interpreting Convention rights: is the United Kingdom more or less committed?" (2009) July PL 544, 553–558.

[53] 30 June, 2009; *Judgment of the German Federal Constitutional Court on the Treaty of Lisbon* B VerGE 2 Bv E 2/08: see www.bverfg.de/en. See Editorial comments (2009) 46 CMLR 1023; Thym, "In the Name of Sovereign Statehood: A Critical Introduction to the Lisbon Judgment of the German Constitutional Court" (2009) 46 CMLR 1822, 1806; Tomuschat, "The ruling of the German Constitutional Court on the Treaty of Lisbon" (2009) 10 GLJ 1259; Doukas, "The verdict of the German Federal Constitutional Court on the Lisbon Treaty: not guilty, but don't do it again!" (2009) 34 ELR 866; Kokkott, "The Basic Law at 60: From 1949 to 2009: The Basic law and Supranational integration" (2009) 11(1) GLJ 99.

[54] See Thym, "In the Name of Sovereign Statehood: A Critical Introduction to the Lisbon Judgment of the German Constitutional Court" (2009) 46 CMLR 1822, 1901.

[55] *Gesetz über die Ausweitung und Stärkung der Rechte des Bundestages und des Bundesrates in Angelegenheiten der Europäischen Union.*

[56] "Members of the German Bundestag shall be elected in general, direct, free, equal and secret elections. They shall be representatives of the whole people, not bound by orders or instructions, and responsible only to their conscience".

[57] An Act extending and strengthening the rights of the Federal Parliament and Federal Council in European Union matters Publications of the Federal Parliament No. 16/8489.

necessary and sufficient degree of participation rights and the Treaty could not be ratified until this Act was amended in line with the requirements of the Court.[58] The amended legislation was passed by two Chambers in September 2009. The importance which the Court placed upon the role of Parliament in its important decision is notable. Thus, the position as to the German parliament is particularly significant and most remarkable and operates as a useful precedent for other parliamentary scrutiny models and for considering the proper place of parliament in European-related affairs after the Treaty of Lisbon.

Conclusion

What is the effectiveness of the Oireachtas as an institutional actor in the past, present and future, in light of its enhanced role as provided for in the Treaty of Lisbon? It appears that any answer to this question, of itself or in comparative terms, of necessity must conclude that the institutional consideration of EU affairs is limited and piecemeal and that a failure to adequately engage with challenges as they arise has resulted in rather haphazard engagement with European matters. It is suggested, here, that the Oireachtas has failed to adequately grasp and employ the full range of its new powers under the Treaty of Lisbon. As a body, it has made a limited contribution to European affairs. The absence of constitutional provision for the Oireachtas has substantially diminished its institutional role. The legislative and constitutional provisions passed so as to ratify the Treaty of Lisbon are both modest and disappointing. The German example is particularly striking and, while it may not form a realistic goal yet as to parliament given the complexities in amending the Irish Constitution, nonetheless, the contribution of dynamic and well-organised debate and actions on European affairs has the potential to strengthen an institutional actor. **[8–35]**

The crisis instigated by the first failed Treaty of Lisbon referendum brought with it a valuable period of reflection but the legal outcomes from the point of view of the role of parliament are limited. The legislative provisions passed so as to take into account the new role for National Parliaments in the Treaty of Lisbon has not been embraced adequately and the new role has been incorporated only by way of legislation and not in the domestic constitutional order.

[58] 30 June, 2009 *Judgment of the German Federal Constitutional Court on the Treaty of Lisbon*, B VerGE 2 Bv E 2/08: see www.bverfg.de/en [273] [406] and [409].

CHAPTER 9
The European Arrest Warrant in Irish Law

Introduction

The European arrest warrant[1] is considered here as a standalone subject and the reason for its inclusion is its dominance as a European-originating measures in Irish law. Despite its recent origins, the European arrest warrant has spurned a large Supreme Court jurisprudence on a range of topics that shows no sign of abating and it appears to disproportionately feature in the docket of the Court.[2] However, the Irish courts have been denied access to the Court of Justice through the guise of the preliminary ruling mechanism by virtue of the decision of the Irish State not to accept the jurisdiction of the Court of Justice in respect of former Third Pillar matters pursuant to (prior to the Treaty of Lisbon) ex Article 35 EU.[3] In a major constitutional development, the Court of Justice in its landmark decision in *Pupino*[4] transferred its **[9–01]**

[1] The Framework Decision was adopted pursuant to Title VI of the Treaty on European Union Council Framework Decision of 13 June 2002 on the European arrest warrant and the surrender procedures between Member States OJ L 190 p 1. See the *Report from the Commission based on Article 34 of the Council Framework Decision of 13 June 2002 on the European Arrest Warrant and the surrender procedures between Member States* (COM) 2006 8; final and Commission Staff Working Document *Annex to the Report from the Commission on the implementation since 2005 of the Council Framework Decision of 13 June 2002 on the European arrest warrant and the surrender procedures between Member States* SEC (2007) 979.

[2] The material here draws from Fahey, "Being a Third Pillar Guardian of Fundamental Rights? The Irish Supreme Court and the European arrest warrant" (2008) 33 ELR 563 and has been updated accordingly to take account of recent developments, of which there are many, as regards legislation and case-law.

[3] As well as UK and Denmark. While the level of acceptance of this jurisdiction has proven to be rather uneven across the Member States and some conflicting notices have been published also: See OJ 2005 L 327 p 19; 1999 OJ C 120 p. 24; OJ 2005 L 327 p 19. See also OJ 2008 C 69/1.

[4] C-105/03 *Criminal Proceedings against Maria Pupino* [2005] ECR I-5285.

longstanding former First Pillar case law on the obligations of Members State courts to interpret national law in light of European Union law, indirect effect, to the former Third Pillar, thereby extending its own jurisdiction beyond that contemplated by the Treaties before the abolition of the pillars by the Treaty of Lisbon.[5] This decision, has been of major importance in the Irish context, where the national courts used *Pupino* to "bridge the gap" in the absence of a means to refer questions to the Court of Justice. The *Pupino* decision has been followed extensively and with much approval in the Irish Supreme Court in recent case law in this area.[6] However, the manner in which *Pupino* has been applied in Ireland, largely uncritically, merits some attention. Whether the Irish courts have interpreted domestic law *contra legem* as a result of their uncritical adherence to *Pupino* remains a difficult question, considered below.

[9–02] The issue remains as to what a national Supreme Court should do to protect fundamental rights when it is unable itself to refer questions to the Court of Justice? Does an uncritical application of *Pupino* solve this difficulty? What measures can legitimately be inserted in domestic implementation laws to "bridge the gap" further, for example, to protect fundamental rights in the realm of the former Third Pillar under national constitutional law?[7] The Irish jurisprudence on extradition had traditionally been particularly favourable to the accused and had a history of being conscious of potential human rights violations.[8] This jurisprudence, however, has been disavowed with the enactment of the arrest warrant procedure.

This chapter considers recent developments in the Irish Supreme Court since the inception of the surrender procedure in Irish law. The focus of the analysis here is solely on the Irish Supreme Court only for reasons of space.

The European Arrest Warrant and Irish Law

[9–03] It is important to note that Ireland had not been consulted initially about the content of the European arrest warrant[9] and the removal of the need for "dual criminality" as contained in the European arrest warrant had at the outset presented a major challenge to key aspects of Irish case-law on extradition existing for many decades. The Framework Decision was implemented into Irish law by the European Arrest Warrant Act 2003 and was recently amended by Part 8 of the Criminal Justice (Terrorist Offences) Act 2005 and again in Part 2 Criminal Justice (Miscellaneous Provisions) Act 2009, that sought to cure errors in implementation contained in the original legislation

[5] On the abolition of the pillars, see de Witte, "The Question of the Treaty Architecture" 1957–2007" in Ott and Vos, eds., *Fifty Years of European Integration: Foundations and Perspectives* (CUP, Cambridge, 2009) p 9; Dougan, "The Treaty of Lisbon 2007: Winning Minds, not Hearts" (2008) 45 CMLR 617, 617–626.

[6] *Izevbethau v Minister for Justice, Equality and Law Reform* [2010] IESC 303, paras 82 and 83.

[7] Recital 12 of the Framework Decision provides that nothing in the Decision can "prevent a Member State from applying its constitutional rules relating to due process, freedom of association, freedom of the press and freedom of expression in other media", discussed here below in "The European Arrest Warrant and Irish Law".

[8] See the account in O'Higgins, "Pink Underwear, the European arrest warrant and the Law of Extradition" (2007) 12(3) BR 91.

[9] *The Irish Times* (21 May 2002).

arising in the case-law.[10] The amount of amendments surfacing from poor legislative drafting and judicial critique, is surely remarkable,[11] although certainly not unprecedented in Irish legislation purporting to implement EU law obligations.[12] Recital 12 of the preamble to the Framework Decision provides that the adoption of the arrest warrant procedure did not:

> "prevent a Member State from applying its constitutional rules relating to due process, freedom of association, freedom of the press and freedom of expression in other media".

In fact, the Irish Government in drafting the European Arrest Warrant Act 2003 went particularly far to ensure that the surrender procedures could satisfactorily protect fundamental rights norms pursuant to Recital 12 of the Framework Decision.[13] The end result was the adoption of s 37 of the Act of 2003, which provides that:

---

[10] See *Report On the Operation of the European Arrest Warrant Act 2003 (as amended) in the year 2008 made to the Houses of the Oireachtas by the Central Authority in the person of the Minister for Justice, Equality and Law Reform pursuant to s. 6(6) of the European Arrest Act 2003* (Department of Justice, 2009). There were 25 appeals to the Supreme Court in 2008 and 21 ongoing.

It states that 87 persons were surrendered to the State since the coming into operation of the Act of 2003. A massive increase in numbers being surrendered by the State since 2004 is evident in the statistics also: see Appendix 5 (p 19). On the new appeal procedures from the High Court to the Supreme Court where a point of law of exceptional public importance can be certified pursuant to s 16(12) of the Act of 2003, as amended by s 12(f) of the Criminal Justice (Miscellaneous Provisions) Act 2009, see *Minister for Justice, Equality and Law Reform v Rettinger* [2010] IESC 45. There was approximately a two month period between the High and Supreme Court decisions in the proceedings, which raises serious issues of fairness and fundamental rights as well as the temporal challenges of such a procedure in the first place. See the important recent decision of the Supreme Court in *Rimsa v Governor of Cloverhill* [2010] IESC 47.

[11] See the criticisms of no fewer than three Supreme Court judges of the original implementing legislation: *Minister for Justice, Equality and Law Reform v Ferenca* [2008] IESC 52. The Act as amended most recently by the Act of 2009 (signed into law in July 2009), now makes provision for certain electronic communications to transmit documents and to provide for identification of those being surrendered, although such amendments are not necessarily innovative in light of the recent origins of the Act.

As to the far-reaching complexities of the (many) amendments made to the primary Act and the failure of the Irish legislature to maintain its website up to date, to the detriment of lawyers and clients, see the appropriate but unsympathetic decision of the Supreme Court in Minister *for Justice, Equality and Law Reform v Adach* [2010] IESC 33. It should be said that the Irish legislature has been grossly in remiss in relation to its obligations to implement EU law in this area and that in light of the pan-European nature of the arrest warrant, impacting as it does on many citizens, lawyers and judges in various Member States, that greater efforts could be made to publicise legislative changes to the primary Act.

[12] See, the discussion above in Ch 1. While every effort has been made to ensure the accuracy of the text here, on account of the multitude of legislative changes to the primary Act and volume of cases, readers are advised to carefully check implementing legislation.

[13] The then Minister for Justice, introducing the European Arrest Warrant Bill 2003 in the Dáil (Irish Parliament), adopted s 37 after considerable pressure being brought to bear on him so as to protect fundamental rights in the new surrender regime: see Irish Human Rights Commission *Observations on the European Arrest Warrant Bill* (IHRC, September 2003) (see www.ihrc.ie). The Minister (577 *Dáil Debates*, 10, 17 December 2003) contended that "no state in the European Union [would] have a higher degree of real and substantial protection for those who seek the protection of its courts".

> "[a] person shall not be surrendered under this Act if … (*b*) his or her surrender would constitute a contravention of any provision of the Constitution…".

[9–04] On either a literal or purposive construction, s 37 does appear to exceed the text of the Framework Decision. The Commission has suggested that s 37 goes further than any other comparable Member State implementation measure as well as going beyond the text of the Framework Decision and gives rise to an incorrect implementation thereof.[14] Whether s 37 represents a mis-implementation of the Framework Decision remains an interesting unsolved question insofar as infringement proceedings cannot be brought against Ireland by the Commission and an individual the subject of surrender proceedings may not ask an Irish Court to refer such questions to the Court of Justice. Notwithstanding, ostensibly the Irish judiciary are under a far-reaching obligation to treat human rights concerns expressed in surrender applications in the most serious fashion. However, the practical operation of the Act of 2003 has not matched the ideal and the role of s 37 has been "read down" dramatically through judicial interpretation, as will be outlined below. Section 37 has not been amended by the two subsequent acts mending errors in the primary implementing Act.

The European Arrest Warrant in the Irish Supreme Court: Leading Decisions

[9–05] The Supreme Court has dismissed most recent challenges in surrender proceedings and there are few victorious individual appellants to date in surrender proceedings. A number of practical difficulties have emerged in this area and been resolved in the absence of a preliminary reference to the Court of Justice to resolve the questions posed. The case-law of the Irish Supreme Court is considered here under four headings: (1) fundamental rights objections to surrender proceedings; (2) evidential aspects of the arrest warrant procedure; (3) time limits in arrest warrant proceedings; and (4) access to justice in surrender proceedings. The first category, namely fundamental rights challenges, has all but disappeared as a ground of challenge in the most recent case-law which demonstrates a certain stability arising in the case law.

1. Fundamental Rights Objections in Surrender Proceedings

[9–06] The Supreme Court has rejected all challenges on fundamental rights grounds in surrender proceedings, despite the express inclusion of s 37 into the implementation legislation. It would appear that the relevance and utility of s 37 is now highly questionable, it having been "read down" most significantly, despite the judicial lacuna remaining. In the first Supreme Court decision examining the operation of s 37 in Irish law, in *Minister for Justice, Equality and Law Reform v Brennan*,[15] the appellant who had absconded from prison in the UK, sought to appeal to the Supreme Court against his surrender by order of the High Court. The appellant submitted that in light of having absconded from prison he now faced surrender for a common law offence, that of escaping from lawful custody, the maximum term being life imprisonment and resulting, he contended, in a disproportionate sentence in comparison to that

---

[14] See Commission Staff Working Document (see fn 1), pp 5–6. Italy is also criticised for similar reasons.

[15] *Minister for Justice, Equality and Law Reform v Brennan* [2007] IESC 21.

applicable in Ireland,[16] or alternatively that the proportionate nature of a sentence was a constitutionally protected right in Irish law relying, *inter alia,* on s 37. Murray CJ for the Court[17] held that while the surrender process was subject to constitutional scrutiny, the national courts remained subject to the *Pupino* interpretive obligation. Murray CJ held that it could not have been the intention of the Oireachtas (Irish Parliament) in enacting s 37 that the surrender of individuals would be refused if the manner in which a trial in the requested State would be carried out did not conform to the Constitution. He remarked that he was:

> "... not aware of any authority for the principle that the extradition or surrender of a person to a foreign country would contravene the Constitution simply because their legal system and system of trial differed from ours as envisaged by the Constitution".

However, Murray CJ was prepared to admit of some "egregious circumstances such as a clearly established and fundamental defect in the system of justice" in the issuing State that would warrant a refusal of surrender pursuant to s 37, that the Court was not prepared to speculate as to, resulting in the dismissal of the appeal. What is, thus, unmistakable as a result of the Supreme Court decision in *Brennan,* is that the potential use to which s 37 can be put is restricted to all but the most extreme or "egregious" of situations, ostensibly contrary to the intention of parliament. Whether such an instance may in fact ever result remains another question. **[9–07]**

Similarly, in *Minister for Justice, Equality and Law Reform v Stapleton,* [18] the Supreme Court overturned a decision of the High Court that had refused the surrender of an individual to an English court on the basis of s 37 of the Act of 2003. The arrest warrant in *Stapleton* had been issued in 2005 as to fraud offences allegedly committed between 1978 and 1982 and he alleged that his right to a fair trial had been prejudiced by way of delay, warranting the prohibition of his surrender, which the High Court readily acceded to. On appeal to the Supreme Court, the Court *per* Fennelly J, was less prepared to entertain the complaint of delay, finding instead that the applicant had contributed in fact to the delay asserted as being unlawful.[19] The Court reiterated its own decision in *Brennan,* that was interpreted by the Supreme Court as having set out *per* Fennelly J, "the correct approach" to the balancing of the constitutional rights of individuals subject to surrender procedures against the obligations of the State pursuant to the Framework Decision. Rather, he held mutual recognition and mutual confidence were key elements of the new system of surrender, citing with approval the **[9–08]**

[16] The European arrest warrant in *Brennan,* under the heading "Nature and Legal Classification of the Offences and the Applicable Statutory Provision/ Code" stated that:

> "Escaping from lawful custody is a common law offence and triable before a Judge and jury. It is punishable by a term of imprisonment and a fine. The term is not prescribed and is at the discretion of the Judge. As it is a common law offence, the maximum term of imprisonment that a Judge can impose is life".

[17] Murray CJ, Macken and Finnegan JJ, Murray CJ held that it had not been established nor could it be that the appellant would in fact be exposed to life imprisonment and the passages impugned by the appellant had been inserted there for informational purposes only.

[18] *Minister for Justice, Equality and Law Reform v Stapleton* [2007] IESC 30; [2006] 3 IR 26.

[19] Murray CJ, Denham, Geoghegan, Fennelly and Kearns JJ.

decision of the Court of Justice in *Advocaten voor de Wereld* that had upheld the validity of the arrest warrant as compatible with fundamental rights. However, nowhere in *Stapleton* is any reference made to the inability of the Irish Court of last instance to refer questions for a ruling to the Court of Justice. What is interesting about *Stapleton* is once again the overt willingness of the Court to downgrade the importance of s 37 of the Act of 2003.[20]

[9–09] It seems clear, however, that the Supreme Court yet again is indicating its unconditional support for the new surrender procedures, an enthusiasm that remains unabated despite the existence of s 37. Clearly s 37 cannot now be seen as having any potential to temper surrender requests falling short of Irish constitutional requirements, despite the efforts made to include such a device on the grounds of fairness. Notably, no reference is made to Dáil Debates (Parliamentary debates) as to the intention of Oireachtas (legislature) in adopting s 37 of the Act of 2003.[21] The Irish Supreme Court jurisprudence in this area demonstrates how the Recital 12 permission remains deeply problematic as a matter of national and European law. The Supreme Court jurisprudence surely gives rise to a question as to the utility of the Oireachtas inserting s 37 into the Act of 2003 in the first place. If a modified or watered down obligation was intended, surely s 37 would have been drafted so as to reflect as much. Instead, *Pupino* has been excessively fastened upon by the Irish courts, unable to consult the Court of Justice for clarification of the scope of the s 37 obligation.

---

[20] And to similar effect see the cases of *Minister for Justice, Equality and Law Reform v S.R.* [2007] IESC 54; *Minister for Justice, Equality and Law Reform v Gardener* [2007] IESC 40, where similar delay challenges are rejected by the Supreme Court on appeal and where the Court invoked in the latter *inter alia* the "scheme and spirit" of the Framework Decision to dismiss the cases. See *Butenas v Governor of Cloverhill Prison* [2008] IESC 9, where a constitutional challenge to the validity of detention powers in s 16(4) of the Act of 2003 was rejected. In *Minister for Justice, Equality and Law Reform v Johnston* [2008] IESC 11, an unsuccessful surrender challenge on the basis of *inter alia* delay, the plaintiff did not invoke s 37 at all. See also *Minister for Justice, Equality and Law Reform v Puta and Sulej* [2008] IESC 29; [2008] IESC 30, an unsuccessful challenge to the technical adequacy of the constitutional ratification of the Framework Decision, where the first appellant also alleged that his surrender to the Czech Republic, which was averred to be "more like the Wild West", would expose him to a justice system in breach of s 37. The Supreme Court, *per* Murray CJ, held that a heavy onus had to be discharged with cogent evidence to invoke s 37 and that the "irresponsible" allegations made could not prevail.

See also the recent decision of the Supreme Court in *Minister for Justice, Equality and Law Reform v Rettinger* [2010] IESC 45 on the construction of 37(1)(a) of the Act of 2003 as to the interaction of the European arrest warrant and the ECHR. S. 37(1)(a) prohibits surrender where it would be incompatible with the ECHR. In *Rettinger*, the Supreme Court remitted the proceedings to the High Court as to the burden and standard of proof applicable where there the applicant had submitted that he would be the subject of inhuman and degrading treating in breach of Article 3 ECHR (and certain case law of the Strasbourg Court) if he were surrendered to Poland to complete a prison sentence. The Supreme Court, in particular in the course of the decision of Denham J at para 27, sought to provide a useful template for the trial judge below.

[21] The use and legitimacy of the use of such parliamentary debates remains subject to considerable dispute in Ireland. Ireland has yet to have a "*Pepper v Hart*" revolution ([1993] 1 All ER 42): see *Crilly v Farrington* [2002] 1 ILRM 161.

2. Evidential Aspects of the Arrest Warrant Procedure

The challenges to the arrest warrant arising in the Irish Supreme Court in the area of evidential aspects of the warrant are particularly important in so far as they bear upon both fundamental rights and procedural matters equally and may affect the uniformity of the operation of the arrest warrant in Europe generally. A rather remarkable modification of the Irish legislation is now to be found in s 45C of the Act of 2003, as inserted by s 20 of the Act of 2009, providing for a wholesale rejection of technical complaints by respondents objecting to surrender, with a saver clause for injustice. That such a slothful and omnibus form of drafting could be included in legislation implementing EU law obligations is alarming, and its construction by the Supreme Court will be telling. **[9–10]**

2.1 Miscellaneous Case-Law

In the first major Supreme Court decision on the evidential aspects of the European arrest warrant, delivered temporally prior to *Pupino*, *Minister for Justice, Equality and Law Reform v Dundon*,[22] the appellant was the subject of an arrest warrant issued in respect of the offence of murder. The issuing judicial authority, an English court, had received a written undertaking from the Parliamentary Under Secretary and the Director of Public Prosecutions as to the information contained in the warrant. The issue arose, thus, as to whether undertakings provided by the issuing State, pursuant to s 22 of the Act of 2003, were required to be given *personally* by the judge or court concerned and whether the courts in surrender proceedings had to consider the adequacy of evidence against an individual.[23] The Supreme Court, *per* Denham J,[24] employing ordinary canons of statutory interpretation, held that there was no requirement that the undertaking "given" had in fact to be made by the issuing authority and thus that the undertakings given complied fully with the Act. Moreover, the Court held that the adequacy of the evidence against the person sought was not a matter for consideration in surrender proceedings under the Act, thereby overturning the Court below. That there is no necessity to establish a *prima facie* case against an individual for them to be surrendered is a striking conclusion indeed, in the absence of clarification from the Court of Justice and the Supreme Court has thus disavowed decades of its own case-law in the realm of extradition. Whilst probably correct, this conclusion flows directly from the consequences of full mutual recognition and not due process law and practice. **[9–11]**

To similar effect in *Minister for Justice, Equality and Law Reform v Altaravicius*[25] where a net point of law arose for consideration in the Supreme Court relating to the entitlement **[9–12]**

---

[22] *Minister for Justice, Equality and Law Reform v Dundon* [2005] IESC 13; [2005] 1 IR 261.

[23] s 22 of the Act of 2003 provides that:

> "(1) … a person shall not be surrendered under this Act unless… (*b*) an undertaking in writing is given to the High Court by the issuing judicial authority that the person will not be proceeded against, sentenced, or detained … for an offence committed before his or her surrender other than the offence … specified in the European arrest warrant concerned.".

[24] Upholding the High Court decision: Murray CJ, Denham, McGuinness, Hardiman and Geoghegan JJ.

[25] *Minister for Justice, Equality and Law Reform v Altaravicius* [2006] IESC 23; [2006] 3 IR 148. The warrant in *Altaravicius* related to robbery offences allegedly committed in 2001 in Lithuania.

of a person subject to surrender to request the domestic warrant on foot of which an arrest warrant is issued. Thus, there the Supreme Court allowed an appeal against a High Court decision ordering a copy of the warrant for surrender from Lithuania to be produced before the Irish High Court, on the grounds of fair procedures and Recital 12 of the Framework Decision.[26] The Supreme Court thus held that the European arrest warrant was based on mutual recognition and respect between judicial authorities and could not require an underlying warrant to be produced where neither the Act nor the Framework Decision explicitly so required. There was, as Denham J described it, a "presumption" that the underlying documents were in order, pursuant to s 4A of the Act of 2003, [27] which an individual could seek to rebut, thereby disentitling them to go on a general "fishing expedition". If this were not the case, Denham J held, this would defeat the development that the European arrest warrant was, that of international co-operation predicated on mutual trust and judicial co-operation.[28] Once again this outcome here flows logically from mutual recognition but the conclusion is reached in the absence of a consultation of the Court of Justice. Notably, the decision is delivered after *Pupino* but no reference is made thereto. Interestingly, *Altaravicius* is analogous to the recent decision of the House of Lords in *Dabas v High Court of Justice, Madrid*[29] discussed below, where a similar evidentiary request was dismissed.

[9–13] In *Minister for Justice, Equality and Law Reform v Rodnov*[30] the Supreme Court dismissed an appeal against a decision of the High Court, where the individual subject to surrender had complained that the arrest warrant was bad on its face in that it had omitted a formula of words at the commencement of the form that were contained in the annex to the Framework Decision.[31] Murray CJ, for the Court, held that while there had been a want of strict formal compliance in the particular warrant at issue, the defect was not "a want of formality which affected in any way the substance or effect of the European arrest warrant".[32] Murray CJ held that it would have been wholly unsatisfactory if the Court had to look for further information[33] and rather a "common sense approach" had to be adopted as to challenges to the evidentiary formalities of the warrant. There is no reference to *Pupino* here, perhaps understandably given that it is an *ex tempore* decision of the Court and thus marked by

---

[26] Pursuant to s 4A of the Act of 2003, as amended: "It shall be presumed that an issuing state will comply with the requirements of the Framework Decision, unless the contrary is shown".

[27] Murray CJ, Denham and Hardiman JJ.

[28] Denham J further noted that a discretion was provided for in s 20 of the Act of 2003, for a judge to seek further information from the issuing judicial authority, which had not yet been employed by the High Court in the instant case and that it had been open to the applicant here to have made such an application.

[29] [2007] UKHL 6; [2007] 2 AC 31; [2007] 2 CMLR 39, see below, 4.1: "Reading down s 37 and using *Pupino* to 'bridge the gap'".

[30] *Minister for Justice, Equality and Law Reform v Rodnov* (Unreported, Supreme Court, *ex tempore*, 1 June 2006).

[31] Art 8 of the Framework Decision provides that certain essential information shall be contained in the warrant as set out in the Annex. The words omitted were that:

> "This warrant has been issued by a competent judicial authority. It requests that the person mentioned below be arrested and surrendered for the purpose of conducting a criminal prosecution or executing a custodial sentence of detention order."

[32] p 2 of the decision (Murray CJ, Hardiman and Macken JJ).

[33] Pursuant to s 20 of the Act of 2003.

extreme brevity. Surely this question was one worthy of a definitive answer from the highest European Court but there is again no mention of the inability of the Supreme Court to consult the Court of Justice on this important point of procedure and essential procedural questions are determined in isolation despite their impact on practice and the uniformity in operation of the instrument. This decision is affected by the new s 45C inserted into the Act of 2003 by s 20 of the Act of 2009.

2.2 "Flight" and Surrender

In the controversial decision of the Supreme Court in *Minister for Justice, Equality and Law Reform v Tobin,*[34] the *Pupino* interpretive obligation was invoked as to the interpretation of the word "fled" in s 10 of the Act of 2003, to decide whether an Irish businessman who was convicted and sentenced in his absence for a fatal road traffic accident in Hungary, had "fled" that jurisdiction so as to warrant his surrender there.[35] Section 10 of the Act of 2003 had been amended by the Act of 2005, which had sought to particularise the circumstances where surrender could be ordered so as to relate to the European arrest warrant and s 10 as amended by the Act of 2005 had provided that surrender could be ordered on a person for "flight": [9–14]

> "on whom a sentence of imprisonment or detention has been imposed in respect of an offence to which the European arrest warrant relates, and *who fled from the issuing state before he or she—*
> *i. commenced serving that sentence, or*
> *ii. completed serving that sentence*..." (Emphasis supplied).[36]

This formula as to "flight" was to generate a vast body of law. The Supreme Court in *Tobin*, per Fennelly J in refusing his surrender, held that the term "to flee" or "fled" could not be expanded so as to include the respondent, who had paid bail and had left Hungary in the course of the prosecution with the knowledge of the authorities. The *Pupino* obligation, Fennelly J held, would not allow for any other interpretation, in so far as "fleeing" was more usually associated with escape, haste or evasion and not an instance such as this.[37] The difficultly with this much is that the respondent did not ultimately have to serve a sentence imposed by a Hungarian Court, in light of the highly restrictive interpretation adopted of the word "fled," and the decision of the [9–15]

---

[34] *Minister for Justice, Equality and Law Reform v Tobin* [2008] IESC 3.

[35] s 10 governs the obligation to surrender and provides that:

> "Where a judicial authority in an issuing state duly issues a European arrest warrant in respect of a person— (a) against whom that state intends to bring proceedings for the offence to which the European arrest warrant relates, or (b) on whom a sentence of imprisonment or detention has been imposed and who fled from the issuing state before he or she— (i) commenced serving that sentence, or (ii) completed serving that sentence, that person shall, subject to and in accordance with the provisions of this Act and the Framework Decision be arrested and surrendered to the issuing state".

[36] s 10(b) originally provided for surrender on a person:

> "...on whom a sentence of imprisonment or detention has been imposed and who fled from the issuing state before he or she—
> i. commenced serving that sentence, or
> ii. completed serving that sentence ...".

[37] Interestingly, the Tampere European Council conclusions of 1999 and the recital to the Framework Decision were dismissed by Fennelly J as inappropriate interpretive aids.

Court provoked much public outcry in Hungary. A decision of the Court of Justice as to the term "fled" would have been fruitful in such a difficult case as to the breadth of the *Pupino* interpretive obligation, given the likelihood of this issue arising in other Member State courts in the future.

[9–16] *Minister for Justice, Equality and Law Reform v Sliczynski*[38] is one of several cases after *Tobin* also as to the question of "fleeing" pursuant to s 10 of the Act. The appellant sought to appeal against an order of the High Court directing his surrender to Poland to serve four terms of imprisonment. On one of the offences as to which his surrender was sought, the appeal was tried *in absentia* and sentenced. Suspensions were imposed as to the first three offences and as a consequence of the last conviction, the suspension of the earlier terms of imprisonment was lifted. The appellant submitted that the High Court had erred in admitting evidence from the Polish Judicial Authority which was alleged to constitute inadmissible hearsay evidence, that the Court erred in applying the notion of the onus of proof, that the Court erred in finding that the appellant had fled Poland and in deciding that the Polish authorities were not obliged to provide an undertaking pursuant to s 45 of the Act of 2003.

[9–17] The High Court had found that the facts averred to by the appellant were not such as to come within the concept of innocent fleeing such as had existed in the case of *Tobin* or of a lawful departure from Poland. The Supreme Court on appeal held that it was not necessary to strain the language of the phrase "who fled from the issuing State before serving the sentence" to fit circumstances which may often arise, as those in the present case, where a sentence had been suspended but the suspension was later lifted. It was telling that the appellant admitted that he was convicted and sentenced on the first three charges in his presence and did not challenge the contents of the letters exhibited in affidavits. He had to be taken to have understood the significance of the terms attaching to the suspension of those sentences.

[9–18] The Supreme Court[39] held that the only documentation or information which came within s 20(1) or (2) of the Act of 2003 enjoyed the status of being admissible without having to be proved in the usual way. This was the intention of the subsections for the specific purpose of compliance with a statutory function and the obligations flowing from the Framework Decision. The Court held that the appellant could not be surrendered for the purpose of serving a sentence in respect of the fourth offence for which he was convicted and sentenced *in absentia* but he would be surrendered in respect of the other three offences. Thus, the Supreme Court held that the learned judge was correct in finding that the applicant had fled Poland within the meaning of s 10 of the Act. The facts of the case appear somewhat particular as regards flight and it undoubtedly is a less controversial decision than *Tobin*. However, s 20 of the Act of 2003 has also been amended to include a reference to "affidavit", taking into account the Supreme Court decision in this case. Notably, s 45 has been modified by s 20 of the Act of 2009 and provides for a global rejection of applications to refuse surrender on technical grounds (in s 45C), with a saver for potential injustice.

[38] *Minister for Justice, Equality and Law Reform v Sliczynski* [2008] IESC 73. See subsequently *Minister for Justice Equality and Law Reform v Slonski* [2010] IESC 19.

[39] Murray CJ and Macken J (delivering substantially similar decisions with respect to their reasoning), Finnegan J concurring.

Minister for Justice, Equality and Law Reform v Gheorghe[40] is also of note where there the appellants were husband and wife and were living in Ireland since 2000. Their surrender was sought by a Romanian judicial authority to serve a sentence imposed on them in their absence in 2005. The appellants had been convicted of offences of "swindling concerning contracts". The High Court had made orders that each of the appellants be delivered to the judicial authorities of Romania and the appellants made objections to their surrender on the basis that *inter alia* they had not "fled" within the meaning of s 10 of the Act of 2003 and that the requirements of s 45 of the Act of 2003 as to undertakings provided by the judicial authorities in Romania had not been complied with, in that they alleged that they had not been notified as to the time and place where they would be tried and that there was no sufficient undertaking that they would be retried in a proper manner. The appellants had sworn that they were unaware of their impending trial in Romania. The main issue arose here again as to whether they had "fled" the country within the meaning of s 10 of the Act of 2003. **[9–19]**

The Supreme Court held per Fennelly J (Denham, MacMenamin JJ concurring) that the credibility of both appellants was in serious doubt by reason of the blatantly untruthful means by which they obtained visitors visas to travel to the UK. The trial judge was correct in rejecting the submission that the appellants had not fled Romania and the ground of appeal failed. As to the undertaking provided by the Romania judicial authority, sufficient evidence did not exist of the time and date of the trial and no personal service was alleged in the first case, while in the second case the position was more ambiguous. The evidence on its face did not indicate that either appellant was personally notified of the date and place of the trial. However, the Supreme Court held that it would be a serious matter if a judicial authority were to dishonour its solemn undertaking that there would be a retrial. There was nothing in the terms of the undertaking offered to suggest this and the Court held that the second ground of appeal would be dismissed. An interesting discussion takes place in *Gheorghe* as to the essence of a retrial the subject of an undertaking and the extent to which a court can look at national procedures in other States, which relates to questions of fair procedures.[41] This remains a likely avenue for future appeals. **[9–20]**

More recently, *Minister for Justice, Equality and Law Reform v Stankiewicz*[42] concerned once again the question of whether an appellant had fled within the meaning of s 10 of the Act of 2003. The appellant had received suspended sentences in Poland on two offences and alleged that his *bona fide* departure from Poland could not have been characterised as "flight" as he alleged that he travelled to Germany to work for a substantial time and that he moved to Ireland in 2005 to improve himself. The appellant denied that he had committed the offence at issue and asserted that he had been tried *in absentia* and that he had not authorised a lawyer to appear on his behalf in Poland. **[9–21]**

Geoghegan J held that the most recent decision of the Court on the "fled" issue was delivered in the *Gheorghe* case, which had referred to the exceptional facts of the *Tobin* **[9–22]**

---

[40] *Minister for Justice, Equality and Law Reform v Gheorghe* [2009] IESC 76.

[41] See the discussion in *Minister for Justice, Equality and Law Reform v Marek* (Unreported, *ex tempore*, 5 February 2009).

[42] *Minister for Justice, Equality and Law Reform v Stankiewicz* [2009] IESC 79.

case and which had affirmed passages from the decisions of the Court in *Sliczynski*. The Court had determined that fleeing could take place *before* the imposition of a sentence of imprisonment. In the present case, the Court was satisfied that the appellant had fled within the meaning of s 10 of the Act of 2003 and the appeal would be dismissed. The Court held that it was most unlikely that a Polish lawyer would appear without proper authorisation to do so. *Stankiewicz* entails that some degree of clarity is brought to bear of the question of "flight" but the highly exceptional and controversial decision in *Tobin* is not well-dealt with by the Court. A further decision of a fuller court would appear to be necessary on this question also.

[9–23] All the more remarkable then, the legislature in s 6(c)(ii) of the Act of 2009 has *deleted* the element of s 10 of the Act: "*and who fled from the issuing state before he or she— (i) commenced serving that sentence, or (ii) completed serving that sentence*".[43] Thus, on its face, it appears that the legislature has obliterated the vast jurisprudence mounting at Supreme Court level on the question of "flight" and while it may quell the tide of appeals to that Court, it remains to be seen whether this amounts to a further mis-implementation of the Framework Decision.[44]

2.3 Other Evidential Questions—Speciality

[9–24] An exception to the rule of specialty as contained in the Framework Decision, a principle of extradition law, notably also was the subject of recent analysis. The speciality rule, a rule of extradition law, arose to protect individuals being prosecuted or sentenced for another offence on which they had not been surrendered. The judicial authority in Poland had issued two separate warrants on which surrender of the respondent was sought in *Minister for Justice, Equality and Law Reform v Gotszlik*.[45] The High Court had refused surrender on the basis of an interpretation of s 22 of the Act of 2003, as amended. Section 22(1)(a) of the Act of 2003, the key section the subject of the appeal, expressly dis-applied the rule of speciality and provided that:

> "under the law of the issuing state a person who is surrendered to it pursuant to a European arrest warrant shall not be proceeded against, sentenced, or detained for the purposes of executing a sentence or detention order, or otherwise restricted in his or her personal freedom, for an offence committed before his or her surrender other than the offence (in respect of which he or she is surrendered) specified in the European arrest warrant…".

---

[43] Emphasis supplied.

[44] On the definition of a detention order pursuant to s 10(d) of the Act of 2003, see *Minister for Justice, Equality and Law Reform v Murphy* [2010] IESC 17, where the Supreme Court held in proceedings to determine whether a hospital order with restrictions was a detention order within the meaning of the Act, that (per Denham J):

> " a detention order under s.10(d) as any order involving deprivation of liberty which has been made by a criminal court in addition to or instead of a prison sentence. In this case the detention order was made by a criminal court after conviction, for the extraditable offences of rape and assault occasioning bodily harm, instead of a prison sentence".

On the need for information as to the circumstances of flight and the conditions of a suspended sentence, see *Minister for Justice, Equality and Law Reform v Slonski* [2010] IESC 19.

[45] *Minister for Justice, Equality and Law Reform v Gotszlik* [2009] IESC 13.

Section 22 purported to implement Article 27 of the Framework Decision. The rule ostensibly did not arise on the facts here as all of the offences for which the respondent was sought were on the warrants. The Minister appealed against the judgment of the High Court and contended that the trial judge had erred in law in interpreting s 22 as requiring the court to refuse the surrender of the respondent and in holding that only a literal interpretation of s 22 was appropriate.

The Supreme Court held *per* Denham J (Fennelly J concurring), that while the second warrant was withdrawn it was an exceptional case enabling the Court to consider whether to hear a point of law in circumstances which had rendered the matter moot. The Court held that by s 22, the Oireachtas intended to implement the Framework Decision and the words of the section were clear. Section 22 provided for a specific statutory presumption and there was nothing before the Court to rebut that presumption. A purposive approach was also possible as to s 22 and the rule of specialty and Denham J thus held that the Court had to follow *Pupino*. No issue of *contra legem* applied to s 22. The Court held that it could order the surrender of a person on more than one arrest warrant. The facts of the case had altered by the time of the Supreme Court decision and the respondent was no longer sought as to one offence and the Court would order that the respondent would be surrendered on one warrant only. Macken J noted in a concurring judgment that there existed the distinct possibility that more than one judicial authority might issue an arrest warrant in respect of the same person. Once again, *Pupino* is employed by Denham J to resolve an interpretive question albeit in the absence of a reference to the Court of Justice. It is suggested here that the drafting of s 22 is arguably less clear than the Court was prepared to admit but that nonetheless the outcome was correct. **[9–25]**

2.4 Correspondence Issues

Minister for Justice, Equality and Law Reform v Dolny[46] concerned the net question of correspondence and the manner in which a court could construe the underlying facts of the warrant. The surrender of the appellant in *Dolny* was sought by authorities in Poland and the appellant objected to his surrender on the basis that the offence of which he was convicted did not correspond to any offence under Irish law. The High Court held that from the facts evidence of beating existed such as to render beating or battery as an adequate description of the offence at issue and so the High Court held that the corresponding offence was that under s 3 of the Non Fatal Offences against the Person Act 1997. The Supreme Court on appeal per Denham J held that the Court would affirm the approach taken by the High Court. In order to address the issue of correspondence, it was necessary to consider the particulars on the warrant, the acts to decide if they would constitute an offence in the State. The natural and ordinary meaning of the words on the warrant were plain- to beat on the face and head. Denham J held that the Court had to look, as it did at common law, with all the information provided, the facts and acts described and to give words their ordinary and popular meaning. The words described acts which would constitute an offence if committed in the jurisdiction and the Supreme Court dismissed the appeal. Whilst it is surprising that the Act did not govern this much, the outcome of the decision is uncontroversial. **[9–26]**

[46] *Minister for Justice, Equality and Law Reform v Dolny* [2009] IESC 48.

[9–27] *Minister for Justice, Equality and Law Reform v Ferenca*[47] is an interesting decision as to s 38 of the Act of 2003 and the implementation of a list of offences into Irish law where no correspondence is required pursuant to Article 2.2. of the Framework Decision. This embodies the idea of mutual recognition that the Framework Decision outlines. The status of the decision in the future will prove to be of tremendous importance and it is notable in a later decision of the Supreme Court, discussed next here, that no mention is made of the present decision in *Ferenca*, despite the three members of the Court being in agreement as to the poor drafting of the Act of 2003, a criticism that the Court has not shied away from in recent times.

[9–28] Section 38 of the Act of 2003, prior to its amendment by the Act of 2009, listed the offences where correspondence did not need to be proven, the essence of mutual recognition. In Ireland, however, the implementing provisions also set out in s 38 the following addition elements in s 38(1)(b):

> "(1) ... a person shall not be surrendered to an issuing state under this Act in respect of an offence unless—
> a. the offence corresponds to an offence under the law of the State, and—
> i. under the law of the issuing state ... or
> b. the offence is an offence to which paragraph 2 of Article 2 of the Framework Decision applies *or is an offence that consists of conduct specified in that paragraph*, and under the law of the issuing state the offence is punishable by imprisonment for a maximum period of not less than 3 years." (Emphasis supplied).

Section 38 (1)(b) thus made a reference to *conduct* which would define certain offences not listed that would not need to satisfy a correspondence test. However, the difficulty with this is that it ostensibly mis-implements the Framework Decision by introducing an element of subjectivity and a correspondence test into the section which Article 2.2, on its face, sought to abolish.

[9–29] The High Court in *Ferenca* had made an order directing the surrender of the appellant to the relevant authorities in Lithuania and his surrender was sought so that the appellant would serve a term of imprisonment imposed as to three offences by one composite sentence. The request for surrender did not relate to two or more offences in respect of which a term of imprisonment was imposed for each offence. The trial judge found that the second and third offences as listed in the European Arrest Warrant corresponded to offences under the law of the State but that the first offence was not an offence which corresponded to an offence under the law of the country. No box for any of the offences listed in Article 2.2 was ticked and so the trial judge concluded that none of the three offences were Article 2.2 offences. The issue arose as to the application of s 38(1)(b).

[9–30] Murray CJ for the Supreme Court, in allowing the appeal, held that s 38(1)(b) was badly drafted and, as there was no conduct specified in Article 2.2, it was impossible for a court in the executing State to decide that an offence consisted of conduct specified in Article 2.2. The first offence mentioned in the warrant was not an offence within the first two alternatives of s 38(1) and it could not be captured by some proposed alternative in s 38(1)(b). There was no basis on which the Court could

[47] *Minister for Justice, Equality and Law Reform v Ferenca* [2008] IESC 52.

apportion the sentence imposed among three offences and so the request for his surrender would be refused. Geoghegan J held that s 38(1)(b) wrongfully referred to a list of conduct. The Irish courts could not adjudicate on what courses of conduct might be criminal conduct under Lithuanian law. The Court could not draw an inference as to the similarly of Irish and Lithuanian sentencing principles. Macken J held that s 38(1)(b) went beyond what was envisaged in Article 2.2 as provided for in the template warrant annexed to the Framework Decision to cover offences whose description could have led the issuing State to tick an offence in the equivalent box. Section 38(1)(a) did not supersede or have any precedence over s 38(1)(b). Section 38 clearly constituted a problematic section warranting revisiting on the part of the legislature, which occurred through the amendment of the section in s 17 of the Act of 2009, which deleted the impugned phrase ("*or is an offence that consists of conduct specified in that paragraph*") in *Ferenca*, which the Supreme Court had found fault with.

A subsequent decision of importance which interprets Article 2.2. of the Framework Decision and s 38 of the Act of 2003 is *Minister for Justice, Equality and Law Reform v Desjatnikovs*[48] but where *Ferenca* does not feature whatsoever. There, the surrender of the appellant was sought to the Republic of Latvia on an arrest warrant relating to one offence. The offence related to taking cash from a cash desk in a pawnshop. Three options were asserted as methods by which an offence could be identified as permitting surrender- as a corresponding offence, an offence listed in Article 2.2. of the Framework Decision and in the absence of a box being ticked on the list as to the second option, that the executing judicial authority could hold that the offence was one specified on the list. The Supreme Court held per Denham J that the Irish Act had to be interpreted as far as possible in light of the wording of the framework decision in light of *Pupino*. On the plain words of the Framework Decision, an exception was made to the principle of double criminality by the creation of the list system in Article 2.2. This exception required a decision by the issuing state which had to be communicated in the form of the warrant. The issue arose as to whether the Act of 2003 introduced a third option in addition to the second option. Denham J held that it would be an extraordinary leap to give to the Irish High Court the role of deciding whether on the facts the warrant referred to an offence in the issuing state. It was the duty of the Court to interpret s 38(1)(b) of the Act of 2003 as far as possible in light of the wording and purpose of the Framework Decision. The High Court erred in determining that there was a third option by which an Irish court could go behind the warrant, consider the facts and make the determination asserted when an issuing state had not made such a decision. The Court held that it would allow the appeal and an order would not be made directing the surrender of the appellant on the arrest warrant. **[9–31]**

The difficulty with this decision is that Denham J purports to give a conclusive decision on a section of the Act in the absence of a reference to the earlier decision of the Court in *Ferenca*, where some degree of apprehension was expressed by different members of the Court as to the best course of action to adopt. As a matter of precedent, this much is simply problematic. On a more substantive level, the decision of Denham J to employ *Pupino* to resolve the interpretive question, is surely correct, in the absence of clarification of the matter from the Court of Justice or indeed the Commission.

---

48 *Minister for Justice, Equality and Law Reform v Desjatnikovs* [2008] IESC 53.

3. Time Limits in Surrender Proceedings

[9–32] The time limits that surrender proceedings are subject to remains a key procedural and fundamental rights question in so far as surrender proceedings are designed to be efficacious and judicially policed. A range of difficulties in this regard have confronted the Irish courts.[49] The second *Dundon* decision considered by the Supreme Court, *Dundon v Governor of Clover Hill,*[50] relating to the same applicant in the first *Dundon* decision is also of note, where the Court was asked subsequently to interpret Article 17 of the Framework Decision.[51] The Court was asked to decide in *habeas corpus* proceedings *before* the making of the final surrender decision[52] whether the applicant had a right to immediate release upon expiry of the sixty day period specified in the Framework Decision and if not, whether such a situation was in breach of their fundamental rights. Dundon challenged the lawfulness of his detention, where the validity of his surrender had been upheld by the Supreme Court shortly before he instituted these proceedings. No penalty is provided for a breach of the time limits in Article 17.

[9–33] Section 16 of the Irish implementing legislation, however, provides for a curious and loose implementation of the obligations in Article 17.[53] Denham J, in the Supreme

---

[49] See most recently *Rimsa v Governor of Cloverhill* [2010] IESC 47, finding that the Act of 2003 had incorrectly transposed the Framework Decision. The Court held that there was a "clear and manifest conflict" between Art 23 of the Framework Decision and s 16(5) of the Act of 2003. The latter expressly permitted any postponement of surrender by agreement by any authority in the State on a postponed surrender date not just the executing judicial authority, unlike the Framework Decision.

[50] *Dundon v Governor of Clover Hill Prison* [2005] IESC 83; [2006] 1 IR 518.

[51] Art 17 of the Framework Decision states that:

> "1. A European arrest warrant shall be dealt with and executed as a matter of urgency.
> 2. In cases where the requested person consents to his surrender, the final decision on the execution of the European arrest warrant should be taken within a period of 10 days after the consent has been given.
> 3. In other cases, the final decision on the execution of the European arrest warrant should be taken within a period of 60 days after the arrest of the requested person.
> 4. Where in specific cases the European arrest warrant cannot be executed within the time limits laid down in paragraphs 2 or 3, the executing judicial authority shall immediately inform the issuing judicial authority thereof, giving the reasons for the delay. In such case, the time limits may be extended by a further 30 days . . .".

[52] Art 23 of the Framework Decision provides for *inter alia* the surrender of an individual after the final decision on the execution of the warrant and mandates their release *after* particular time limits have passed. Denham J held that the Article was inapplicable as the final decision on the applicant's appeal had not yet been made by the Supreme Court.

[53] ss 16(10) and (11) of the Act of 2003 provide that:

> "(10) If the High Court has not, after the expiration of 60 days from the arrest of the person concerned under section 13 or 14, made an order under this section or section 15 , or has decided not to make an order under this section, it shall direct the Central Authority in the State to inform the issuing judicial authority and . . . and the Central Authority in the State shall comply with such direction.
>
> (11) If the High Court has not, after the expiration of 90 days from the arrest of the person concerned under section 13 or 14, made an order under this section or section 15 , or has decided not to make an order under this section, it shall direct the Central Authority in the State to inform the issuing judicial authority . . . and the Central Authority in the State shall comply with such direction".

Court,[54] held that the extendable time limits in the Framework were, in her opinion, "a strongly worded recommendation," but the processes remained subject to the fact that there was no mandatory time limit of sixty days *prior* to the final order for surrender in the same way as after the final order. While Denham J held that it was unfortunate that it had not been possible to process the request more expeditiously, she concluded that the applicant had exercised his right of access to the courts "fully" through his extensive initiation of proceedings.

Geoghegan J stated it was quite likely that a sixty-day period would be exceeded without fault in any European Member State where tiers of appellate courts were involved in the arrest warrant process. If he was wrong in this regard, Geoghegan J held that a purposive approach applied to the Act of 2003 and that time taken up by proceedings instigated by the applicant had to be discounted from the time limits. Similarly, Fennelly J considered the Court bound by the interpretive obligation set out in *Pupino* so as to arrive at the conclusion reached by the Supreme Court.[55] Despite the extreme importance of this procedural point, the variety of ways in which the Supreme Court judges address the point raise worrisome questions once again as to uniformity of interpretation of the instrument and its implications for fundamental rights. Whether the Supreme Court is interpreting the national legislation *contra legem* remains unclear in the absence of clarification. **[9–34]**

More recently, in *Minister for Justice, Equality and Law Reform v Johnston,*[56] the appellant appealed against an order for surrender to the UK as to a warrant issued in April 2001 as to drugs offences. The appellant alleged that the delay in seeking his surrender and his medical and psychiatric condition suffered in that period entailed that his surrender was unfair. The appellant admitted coming to Ireland to avoid the charges and to avoid the attention of those in the UK who he alleged were intent on doing him harm. He had been stopped in Holyhead by UK police investigating terrorism in 2005. The arrest warrant had been issued in July 2006. The appellant further alleged that he had a legitimate expectation that he would not be surrendered on the basis of certain conversations and exchanges in Holyhead. The Supreme Court held *per* Macken J that the appellant had fled to Ireland to avoid the charges and had been responsible for the delay suffered generally. The appellant did not have a legitimate expectation that be would not be the subject of a prosecution on the basis of the exchanges alleged. There was no error of law on the part of the High Court as the law had been outlined clearly by the trial judge and the appeal would be dismissed. **[9–35]**

The Supreme Court here followed expressly its own case law.[57] The volume of "delay" cases appears to have eased now, with a body of settled jurisprudence emerging now as a result.

---

[54] Murray CJ, Denham, Fennelly, Hardiman and Geoghegan JJ.

[55] See the subsequent interpretation of this decision in a later judgment of the Supreme Court in *Minister for Justice, Equality and Law Reform v S.R.* [2007] IESC 54, that, *per* Finnegan J, held that the requirement in Article 17 is a matter related to "internal discipline within the States and is not intended to confer individual rights".

[56] *Minister for Justice, Equality and Law Reform v Johnston* [2008] IESC 11.

[57] In particular, *Minister for Justice, Equality and Law Reform v Stapleton* [2007] IESC 30; [2006] 3 IR 26; *Minister for Justice, Equality and Law Reform v Gardener* [2007] IESC 40.

4. Access to the Courts in Surrender Proceedings

[9–36] Access to the courts is a fundamental right of tremendous importance in surrender proceedings given the fact that individuals are being pursued in this expeditious system between States through a judicial process. This area alone is one where the Supreme Court has reacted favorably to the subject of surrender proceedings and the legislature has also followed suit. In the recent decision of *Ó Fallúin v Governor of Cloverhill,*[58] the Supreme Court decided an important point relating to detention powers and the right of access to justice of an individual in surrender proceedings. The applicant in *Ó Fallúin* had been charged with conspiracy to defraud the UK Passport Office and his surrender had been ordered by the Irish High Court, subject to a committal to prison pending the carrying out of the order for 15 days.[59] The Supreme Court there was asked to interpret in *habeas corpus* proceedings s 16(7) of the Act of 2003[60] and whether it entailed that a person whose surrender had been ordered but who was not in fact surrendered could be detained in custody pending an appeal to the Supreme Court. While the Act, thus, clearly provided for the immediate release of an individual in detention in the ordinary course, the Act had failed to provide for the scenario of the surrender decision being contested in the ordinary way in the appellate process through the Irish Courts. Thus, the outcome of the decision was likely to have a profound effect on the liberty of those subject to surrender proceedings. The applicant in this case notably had failed to make a *habeas corpus* application for his release within the fifteen day period from the making High Court surrender order.

[9–37] The Supreme Court *per* Fennelly J concluded that the applicant had been in unlawful detention and that there was no necessary connection between the applicant's right to pursue his appeal and his right to liberty while it was pending. Rather the appeal did not depend on his detention in custody. Section 16(7) of the Act of 2003 was silent in respect of the appellate process and thus the maxim "*expressio unius est exclusio alterius*" applied.[61] Fennelly J then turned to the Article 23 of the text of the Framework Decision to Article 23, by virtue of the fact that the Irish law had to be read in light thereof.[62] Article 23 provided that:

> "upon expiry of the time limits referred to in paragraph 2 [which provides for the ten-day period] to 4, if the person is still being held in custody he shall be released".

[9–38] Fennelly J held that the true meaning and intent of Article 23 had not been properly argued in the instant proceedings and so the Court would have to await a decision of

---

58 *Ó Fallúin v Governor of Cloverhill* [2007] IESC 20.

59 s 13 of the Act of 2003 provides that "An order under this section shall not take effect until the expiration of 15 days beginning on the date of the making of the order".

60 s 16(7) of the Act of 2003 formerly provided that:

> ". . . a person (to whom an order for the time being in force under this section applies) who is not surrendered to the issuing state in accordance with subsection (5), *shall be released from custody immediately* upon the expiration of the 10 days referred to in subsection (5), unless, upon such expiration, proceedings referred to in subsection (6) are pending." (emphasis supplied).

61 Meaning, approximately: "To say one thing is to exclude another".

62 Pursuant to the *Pupino* decision of the Court of Justice, which is not explicitly referred to in the decision of Fennelly J but by implication is being referred to.

the Court of Justice. In fact, the implementation of Article 23 of the Framework Decision in Irish law has received some criticism from the Commission.[63] What again is noticeable is the absence of any comment from the Supreme Court to the effect that they had no ability to access the Court of Justice as to this important practical question and its operation in the Member State courts. The outcome of the *Ó Fallúin* decision at least is favourable to the accused. However, the result was obtained through the *habeas corpus* proceedings, a constitutionally enshrined remedy, that must be dealt with expeditiously as a matter of right.[64] Again, the importance of access to the courts in this area would surely entail that the Court of Justice would be in a position to decide this important procedural question. Notably, the legislature has responded to this and s 16(7) now provides after modification by s 12 of the Act of 2009 that:

> "Where a person (to whom an order for the time being in force under this section applies) is not surrendered to the issuing state within the relevant period specified in subsection (5) and the surrender is not prohibited by reason of subsection (6) the High Court may remand the person in custody or on bail for such further period as is necessary to effect the surrender *unless it considers it would be unjust or oppressive to do so.*" (Emphasis supplied).

Butenas v Governor Cloverhill Prison[65] addressed the thorny question of access to justice and the drafting errors in the Act of 2003 that the Court has been called upon to address, despite its limited legal resources. *Butenas* follows on from the key decision of the Supreme Court on this issue of *Ó Fallúin v Governor of Cloverhill.*[66] The High Court in *Butenas* had made an order for the surrender of the appellant to Lithuania pursuant to s 16 (1) of the Act of 2003. A consequential order was made committing the appellant to prison pending his surrender, pursuant to s 16(4) of the Act of 2003. The appellant did not appeal against those orders. The appellant subsequently sought orders pursuant to Article 40.4.2 of the Constitution directing his release on the basis that he had been unlawfully detained. The High Court dismissed the application and rejected the submission that s 16(4) was unconstitutional. The appellant alleged that s 16(4) was unconstitutional in that it failed to permit the Court in the exercise of an inherent discretion to release a person on bail. **[9–39]**

The Supreme Court held per Murray CJ that when the High Court had made an order for surrender of a person pursuant to s 16 of the Act, that s 16(4) did not oust its inherent jurisdiction to admit the person concerned to bail pending surrender in the exercise of its discretion, even if other sections of the act made express provision for bail. Thus, the Court held that the claim of the appellant was unfounded that s 16(4) was unconstitutional, albeit on different grounds from the High Court. The High Court had the power to grant bail because the appellant was refused bail in the original and earlier proceedings pursuant to s 16 of the Act of 2003. The appellant had chosen **[9–40]**

[63] Not strictly relating to the point raised in *Ó Fallúin*. See Commission Staff Working Document, fn 1 (p 31), referring to the lack of clarity in Ireland as to the implementation of Art 23.
[64] Irish law has now been amended to take into account the Supreme Court decision in *Ó Fallúin*: s 16(7), as substituted by s 76(f) of the Criminal Justice (Terrorist Offences) Act 2005.
[65] *Butenas v Governor Cloverhill Prison* [2008] IESC 9.
[66] *Ó Fallúin v Governor of Cloverhill* [2007] IESC 20.

not to appeal the original order. The appellant was entitled to apply to the High Court for bail pending his surrender. The application of the appellant for release pursuant to Article 40 was refused and the appeal would be dismissed.

It must be questioned how s 16 could ever be held to be unconstitutional for constitutional reasons as to EU law and fundamental rights outside of the scope of the present work, despite the obvious drafting errors therein. The decision of the Court here in particularly practical but legally is rather suspect. The legislature has previously responded to similar concerns as to the Act of 2003 through the first amendment of the Act in 2005 and now again s 16 has been substantially amended by the Act of 2009, but not s 16(4).[67]

Conclusion

[9–41] The *Pupino* decision appears to now form a key part of most recent decisions of the Supreme Court in surrender proceedings in order to "bridge the gap" between national implementing legislation of the arrest warrant and the absence of an ability to refer questions of law to the Court of Justice. No conflict, however, is evident in any of the Irish Supreme Court jurisprudence as to whether the use of the *Pupino* "conforming" or consistent interpretation would in fact be *contra legem*, i.e. that the asserted interpretation of the Act of 2003 in light of the Framework Decision would go beyond the actual scope or provisions of the Framework Decision wrongfully, *contra legem*. By contrast, in a recent judgment of the House of Lords as to the European arrest warrant in *Dabas v High Court of Justice, Madrid*, a notable conflict emerged as to the proper use of the *Pupino* decision and the limits of the interpretative obligation.[68] There, a split Lords divided on the application of *Pupino* "conforming" or consistent interpretation, to the (UK) Extradition Act 2003. *Dabas* raised a net point of law, as to whether the actual arrest warrant document had to be produced in the absence of a certificate, in light of the wording of s 64 of the Act of 2003 which reads as follows:

> The conduct constitutes an extradition offence in relation to the category 1 territory if these conditions are satisfied–.... (b) a certificate issued by an appropriate authority of the category 1 territory shows that the conduct falls within the European framework list...".

[9–42] The appellant in *Dabas* had been sought by the Spanish High Court in respect of the Madrid Train bombings in 2004. The arrest warrant in that case, which otherwise complied with the form which the Framework Decision provided, was not accompanied by the certificate specified in s 64, as above. The Framework Decision made no

[67] Only four *habeas corpus* complaints were made in 2008 pursuant to Art 40.4 of the Constitution. See Report above (fn 10) (p 9). See the difficult case of *Covaciu v Governor of Cloverhill Prison* [2010] IEHC 182 (High Court) where Peart J upheld the remand of an applicant on the basis of a Supreme Court warrant (arising from an appeal to the Supreme Court), where the applicant could not be surrendered on the basis of the volcanic ash saga. See also to similar effect "Detention lawful despite withdrawal of European arrest warrant, " noted in *The Irish Times* (12 April 2010).

[68] *Dabas v High Court of Justice, Madrid* [2007] UKHL 6; [2007] 2 AC 31; [2007] 2 CMLR 39. See further Mackarel, "'Surrendering' the fugitive—the European arrest warrant and the United Kingdom" (2007) 71(4) *European Journal of Crime, Criminal Law and Criminal Justice* 362.

specific reference to such a certificate.[69] The appellant contended thus that the warrant did not comply with the Act of 2003 because of the fact that it had not been accompanied by a certificate of the kind referred to in s 64. The Law Lords by a majority, employing the *Pupino* duty of construction, sought to construe the Act of 2003 in light of the Framework Decision and held that the evidential condition contended for by the appellant would if adopted have been unhelpful and inefficient and would be in breach of the spirit of co-operation that the instrument was founded on. Lord Scott, dissenting as to the application of *Pupino* only and not the result, expressed the view that it was not possible to interpret s 64, a clear statutory provision, in light of the Framework Decision without construing the Act of 2003 *contra legem*, given the precise wording of s 64 of the UK legislation.[70] A split such as that occurring between the majority and minority in *Dabas* is a sign of the healthy operation of judicial protection in former Third Pillar matters, particularly where no Court in the UK (similar to Ireland) can refer such proceedings to the Court of Justice. A rigorous and critical application of the *Pupino* decision is of much importance in deciding whether a particular interpretation of implementing legislation is *contra legem* the Framework Decision. It is evident that the Irish Supreme Court has uncritically applied the *Pupino* decision. That such a divergence as to the application of *Pupino* has yet to arise in Ireland is thus most regrettable indeed.

The political decision of the Irish State not to accept the jurisdiction of the Court of Justice in this area and to opt out of the "Communitarisation" of the Area of Freedom, Security and Justice in the Treaty of Lisbon, discussed above, for reasons outwardly to do with sovereignty and control over the national legal system in criminal justice, is now proving to have major legal consequences. Their decisions have been criticised extra-judicially by Fennelly J of the Irish Supreme Court, who has stated that: **[9–43]**

> "[i]t is apparent that the decision to decline jurisdiction to the Court of Justice is rooted in objection to the enlargement of the powers of the Court. It is difficult to see how the policy serves the presumed purpose...The most fundamental aspects of criminal procedure such as the burden and method of proof, the right to bail, trial by jury may be at stake...The absence of capacity to consult the Court of Justice may have the consequence that the Court of Justice is less likely to become aware of ... specific concerns".[71]

The validity of these concerns appears indisputable as a matter of law and policy in light of the case-law to date. The Irish Supreme Court has arguably failed to "bridge the gap" between the domestic constitutional protection it is supposed to be affording **[9–44]**

[69] Lords Bingham, Hope, Brown and Mance; Lord Scott dissenting.

[70] He stated that [2007] 2 AC 31, 57 (para. 66):

> "In my opinion the normal construction of section 64, in the context of the Act as a whole, would require the answer that it does. The section certainly reads as though a separate and express certification signed by a judicial authority and additional to the arrest warrant itself is required. And there is good reason to suppose that the normal construction reflects Parliament's intention.... Article 34(2)(b) [TEU] requires no more than that the result of the member states implementation be consistent with and give proper effect to the Framework Decision in questions...".

[71] Fennelly, "Preliminary Reference Procedure: A Factual and Legal Review" (2006) 13 IJEL 55, 80.

to those subject to surrender pursuant to s 37 and the *Pupino* interpretive obligation, shadowed by its inability to access the Court of Justice in construing an instrument that lacks direct effect. The force and utility of s 37 appears to have been cast aside by the Irish Supreme Court in favour of full mutual recognition. Whether such a response is satisfactory in light of its inability to consult the Court of Justice as to the correct interpretation of the instrument, on so many practical points affecting liberty and fundamental rights and freedoms, appears to become more self-evidently not the case. The *Pupino* solution does not appear to be an adequate response to the Irish judicial dilemma. While the judicial protection that can be offered in the realm of the former Third Pillar is questionable where the Court of Justice has such a truncated jurisdiction, the challenge remains for national courts, in Member States such as Ireland as guardians of fundamental rights, to truly "bridge the gap" effectively.

[9–45] The most recent case-law of the Supreme Court appears to be relatively uncontroversial and a measure of stability appears to have been achieved in the case-law. There still remains the issue of why the Irish judges are unable to seek the advices of the Court of Justice to resolve practical and procedural questions as to the arrest warrant procedure. The majority of the case-law considered here is factually weak, affecting the resulting case-law. Undoubtedly there have been a multitude of unsatisfactory drafting errors in the Irish implementing legislation. *Pupino* may not always be able to resolve such errors, which will spurn further case-law if the legislature continues to adopt such a piecemeal approach to its duties.

APPENDIX A

SELECTED LEGISLATION EXTRACTS

[Note: amendments to earlier legislation are not indicated in these extracts]

EUROPEAN COMMUNITIES ACT 1972

Number 27 *of* 1972

ARRANGEMENT OF SECTIONS

AN ACT TO MAKE PROVISION WITH RESPECT TO MEMBERSHIP OF THE STATE OF THE EUROPEAN COMMUNITIES.

[16*th December*, 1972]

BE IT ENACTED BY THE OIREACHTAS AS FOLLOWS:

Definitions

1.—(1) In this Act—

"the European Communities" means the European Economic Community, the European Coal and Steel Community and the European Atomic Energy Community;

"the treaties governing the European Communities" means—

(*a*) "the ECSC Treaty", that is to say, the Treaty establishing the European Coal and Steel Community, signed at Paris on the 18th day of April, 1951,

(*b*) "the EEC Treaty", that is to say, the Treaty establishing the European Economic Community, signed at Rome on the 25th day of March, 1957,

(*c*) "the Euratom Treaty", that is to say, the Treaty establishing the European Atomic Energy Community, signed at Rome on the 25th day of March, 1957,

(*d*) the Convention on certain Institutions common to the European Communities, signed at Rome on the 25th day of March, 1957,

(*e*) the Treaty establishing a single Council and a single Commission of the European Communities, signed at Brussels on the 8th day of April, 1965,

(*f*) the treaty amending certain Budgetary Provisions of the Treaties establishing the European Communities and of the Treaty establishing a single Council and a single Commission of the European Communities, signed at Luxembourg on the 22nd day of April, 1970,

(*g*) the Treaty relating to the accession of Ireland to the European Economic Community and to the European Atomic Energy Community, signed at Brussels on the 22nd day of January, 1972,

(*h*) the decision, of the 22nd day of January, 1972, of the Council of the European Communities relating to the accession of Ireland to the European Coal and Steel Community, as supplemented or amended by treaties or other acts of which the dates of entry into force are dates not later than the 1st day of January, 1973.

(2) (*a*) In the foregoing subsection "treaties or other acts of which the dates of entry into force are dates not later than the 1st day of January, 1973" does not include a treaty or other act of which the date of entry into force is later than the 22nd day of January, 1972, unless the Government have, not later than the 1st day of January, 1973, by order declared that this section applies to it.
(*b*) Where an order under this section is proposed to be made, a draft thereof shall be laid before each House of the Oireachtas and the order shall not be made until a resolution approving of the draft has been passed by each such House.

General provision

2.—From the 1st day of January, 1973, the treaties governing the European Communities and the existing and future acts adopted by the institutions of those Communities shall be binding on the State and shall be part of the domestic law thereof under the conditions laid down in those treaties.

Power to make regulations

3.—(1) A Minister of State may make regulations for enabling section 2 of this Act to have full effect.

(2) Regulations under this section may contain such incidental, supplementary and consequential provisions as appear to the Minister making the regulations to be necessary for the purposes of the regulations (including provisions repealing, amending or applying, with or without modification, other law, exclusive of this Act).

(3) Regulations under this section shall not create an indictable offence.

(4) Regulations under this section may be made before the 1st day of January, 1973, but regulations so made shall not come into operation before that day.

Effect and confirmation of regulations

4.—(1) Regulations under this Act shall have statutory effect and, unless they are confirmed by Act of the Oireachtas passed within six months after they are made or are regulations merely revoking wholly regulations previously made under this Act, they shall cease to have statutory effect on the expiration of that period, but without prejudice to the validity of anything preciously done thereunder.

(2) If when regulations under this Act are made, or at any time thereafter and before the regulations are confirmed or cease to have statutory effect, Dáil Éireann stands adjourned for a period of more than ten days and if, during the adjournment, at least one-third of the members of Dáil Éireann by notice in writing to the Ceann Comhairle require Dáil Éireann to be summoned, the Ceann Comhairle shall summon Dáil Éireann to meet on a day named by him being neither more than twenty-one days after the receipt by him of the notice nor less than ten days after the issue of the summons.

Report to Houses of Oireachtas

5.—The Government shall make a report twice yearly to each House of the Oireachtas on developments in the European Communities.

Short title

6.—This Act may be cited as the European Communities Act, 1972.

EUROPEAN UNION (SCRUTINY) ACT 2002

Number **25** *of* **2002**

ARRANGEMENT OF SECTIONS

Acts Referred to

European Communities Act, 1972	1972, No. 27
European Communities Acts, 1972 to 2001	

AN ACT TO PROVIDE FOR THE SCRUTINY BY THE HOUSES OF THE OIREACHTAS OF CERTAIN PROPOSED MEASURES, TO AMEND THE EUROPEAN COMMUNITIES ACT, 1972, AND TO PROVIDE FOR RELATED MATTERS.

[23*rd October*, 2002]

BE IT ENACTED BY THE OIREACHTAS AS FOLLOWS:

Interpretation

1.—(1) In this Act, save where the context otherwise requires—

"European Communities" has the meaning assigned to it by the European Communities Act, 1972;

"measure" means—

(*a*) a regulation or directive adopted under the Treaty establishing the European Community;
(*b*) a joint action adopted under Article 14 of the Treaty on European Union;
(*c*) a common position adopted under Article 15 of the Treaty on European Union;
(*d*) a measure requiring the prior approval of both Houses of the Oireachtas pursuant to Article 29.4.6° of the Constitution not otherwise mentioned in this definition;

"Minister", in relation to a measure, means the Minister of the Government performing functions in relation to the measure or, if there is more than one such Minister of the Government, such one of them as may be agreed upon by them.

(2) In this Act—

(*a*) a reference to a section is a reference to a section of this Act unless it is indicated that reference to some other provision is intended,
(*b*) a reference to a subsection or paragraph is a reference to a subsection or paragraph of the provision in which the reference occurs, unless it is indicated that reference to some other provision is intended, and

(*c*) a reference to any enactment shall be construed as a reference to that enactment as amended, adapted or extended by or under any subsequent enactment.

Scrutiny of measures by Houses of Oireachtas

2.—(1) As soon as practicable after a proposed measure is presented by the Commission of the European Communities or initiated by a Member State, as the case may be, the Minister shall cause a copy of the text concerned to be laid before each House of the Oireachtas together with a statement of the Minister outlining the content, purpose and likely implications for Ireland of the proposed measure and including such other information as he or she considers appropriate.

(2) The Minister shall have regard to any recommendations made to him or her from time to time by either or both Houses of the Oireachtas or by a committee of either or both such Houses in relation to a proposed measure.

(3) *Subsections (1)* and *(2)* shall not apply, if in the opinion of the Minister, there is insufficient time for the carrying out of the procedures aforesaid and the performance of the functions of the Houses of the Oireachtas in relation to the text aforesaid.

(4) Where, pursuant to *subsection (3)*, a text of a proposed measure has not been laid before each House of the Oireachtas and the measure concerned is adopted by an institution of the European Communities, the Minister shall cause a copy of the text of the measure to be laid before both Houses of the Oireachtas together with a statement outlining the implications for Ireland of the measure and the circumstances of its adoption and including such other information as he or she considers appropriate.

(5) Every Minister of the Government shall make a report to each House of the Oireachtas not less than twice yearly in relation to measures, proposed measures and other developments in relation to the European Communities and the European Union in relation to which he or she performs functions.

Exempt measures

3.—(1) *Subsections (1)* and *(2)* of *section 2* shall not apply to a proposed measure which, in the opinion of the Minister, is confidential.

(2) Where by virtue of *subsection (1), subsections (1)* and *(2)* of *section 2* do not apply to a proposed measure, the Minister may make a report to either or both Houses of the Oireachtas or to a committee of either or both such Houses in relation to the proposed measure as he or she deems appropriate in the circumstances.

Amendment of European Communities Act, 1972

4.—The European Communities Act, 1972, is hereby amended by the substitution of the following section for section 5:

> "5.—In each year, beginning with the year 2003, the Government shall make a report to each House of the Oireachtas on developments in the European Communities and the European Union.".

Annual Report to Houses of Oireachtas

5.—In each year, beginning with the year 2003, the Joint Committee on European Affairs shall make a report to each House of the Oireachtas on the operation in the preceding year of this Act.

Short title and collective citation

6.—(1) This Act may be cited as the European Union (Scrutiny) Act, 2002.

(2) The European Communities Acts, 1972 to 2001, and *section 4* may be cited together as the European Communities Acts, 1972 to 2002.

EUROPEAN COMMUNITIES ACT 2007

Number **18** *of* **2007**

ARRANGEMENT OF SECTIONS

Acts Referred to

European Communities Act 1972	1972, No. 27
European Communities Acts 1972 to 2006	
Ministers and Secretaries (Amendment) (No. 2) Act 1977	1977, No. 28

AN ACT TO AMEND THE EUROPEAN COMMUNITIES ACT 1972 FOR THE PURPOSE OF ALLOWING OFFENCES UNDER REGULATIONS UNDER THAT ACT TO BE PROSECUTED ON INDICTMENT; TO MAKE PROVISION IN RELATION TO THE TRANSPOSITION OF PROVISIONS OF THE TREATIES GOVERNING, AND ACTS OF THE INSTITUTIONS OF, THE EUROPEAN COMMUNITIES UNDER ACTS OF THE OIREACHTAS OTHER THAN THAT ACT; AND TO PROVIDE FOR MATTERS CONNECTED THEREWITH.

[21*st April*, 2007]

BE IT ENACTED BY THE OIREACHTAS AS FOLLOWS:

Definitions

1.— In this Act—

"Act of 1972" means the European Communities Act 1972;

"European act" means—

(*a*) a provision of the treaties governing the European Communities, or
(*b*) an act, or provision of an act, adopted by an institution of the European Communities or any other body competent under those treaties;

"European Communities" has the same meaning as it has in the Act of 1972;

"statute" means—

(*a*) an Act of the Oireachtas, or
(*b*) a statute that was in force in Saorstát Éireann immediately before the date of the coming into operation of the Constitution and that continues to be of full force and effect by virtue of Article 50 of the Constitution;

"statutory instrument" means an order, regulation, rule, scheme or bye-law made in exercise of a power conferred by statute;

"treaties governing the European Communities" has the same meaning as it has in the Act of 1972.

Amendment of section 3 of Act of 1972
2.— Section 3 of the Act of 1972 is amended by—

(*a*) the substitution of the following subsection for subsection (3):

"(3) Regulations under this section may—

(*a*) make provision for offences under the regulations to be prosecuted on indictment, where the Minister of the Government making the regulations considers it necessary for the purpose of giving full effect to—

(i) a provision of the treaties governing the European Communities, or
(ii) an act, or provision of an act, adopted by an institution of the European Communities or any other body competent under those treaties,

and

(*b*) make such provision as that Minister of the Government considers necessary for the purpose of ensuring that penalties in respect of an offence prosecuted in that manner are effective and proportionate, and have a deterrent effect, having regard to the acts or omissions of which the offence consists, provided that the maximum fine (if any) shall not be greater than €500,000 and the maximum term of imprisonment (if any) shall not be greater than 3 years.",

and

(*b*) the insertion of the following subsection:

"(5) In this section—

'maximum fine' means the maximum fine to which a person shall be liable on conviction on indictment of an offence;

'maximum term of imprisonment' means the maximum term of imprisonment to which a person shall be liable on conviction on indictment of an offence.".

Regulations to which section 3(3) of Act of 1972 applies
3.— The Act of 1972 is amended by the insertion of the following section:

> "3A.— Every regulation to which subsection (3) (inserted by *section 2 (a)* of the *European Communities Act 2007*) of section 3 of this Act applies shall be laid before each House of the Oireachtas as soon as may be after it is made and, if a resolution annulling the regulation is passed by either such House within the next 21 days on which that House sits after the regulation is laid before it, the regulation shall be annulled accordingly but without prejudice to the validity of anything previously done thereunder.".

Power to give effect to European acts under statutes other than Act of 1972
4.— (1) A power to make a statutory instrument conferred on a Minister of the Government by a provision of a statute may be exercised for the purpose of giving effect to a European act if the

obligations imposed on the State under the European act concerned relate, in whole, to matters to which that provision relates.

(2) A statutory instrument made for a purpose referred to in *subsection (1)* may contain such incidental, supplementary and consequential provisions as appear to the Minister of the Government making the statutory instrument to be necessary for the purposes of the statutory instrument (including provisions repealing, amending or applying, with or without modification, other law, exclusive of this Act, the Act of 1972 and the provision of the statute under which the statutory instrument is made).

(3) Where a statutory instrument is made for a purpose referred to in *subsection (1)*, the statutory instrument, or the preamble or recital to the statutory instrument, shall specify the European act to which the statutory instrument gives effect.

(4) Section 2 of the Ministers and Secretaries (Amendment) (No. 2) Act 1977 shall not apply to a power to make a statutory instrument for a purpose referred to in *subsection (1)*.

(5) This section applies to a power that, but for this section, would not be exercisable for the purpose of giving effect to a European act.

Validation of certain statutory instruments

5.— (1) Every statutory instrument made before the passing of this Act—

(*a*) under a provision of a statute that did not provide for the exercise of the power conferred by that provision for the purpose of giving effect to a European act, and

(*b*) that purported to give effect to a European act,

shall, in so far as it purported to give such effect, have statutory effect as if it were an Act of the Oireachtas.

(2) If *subsection (1)* would, but for this subsection, conflict with a constitutional right of any person, the operation of that subsection shall be subject to such limitation as is necessary to secure that it does not so conflict but shall otherwise be of full force and effect.

Short title and collective citation

6.— (1) This Act may be cited as the European Communities Act 2007.

(2) The European Communities Acts 1972 to 2006 and this Act may be cited together as the European Communities Acts 1972 to 2007.

TWENTY-EIGHTH AMENDMENT OF THE CONSTITUTION (TREATY OF LISBON) ACT 2009

ARRANGEMENT OF SECTIONS

SCHEDULE

AN ACT TO AMEND THE CONSTITUTION.

[15*th October*, 2009]

WHEREAS by virtue of Article 46 of the Constitution any provision of the Constitution may be amended in the manner provided by that Article:

AND WHEREAS it is proposed to amend Article 29 of the Constitution:

BE IT THEREFORE ENACTED BY THE OIREACHTAS AS FOLLOWS:

Amendment of Article 29 of Constitution

1.— (1) Article 29 of the Constitution is hereby amended as follows:

(*a*) in subsection 3° of section 4 of the Irish text—

(i) the words "den Chomhphobal Eorpach do Ghual agus Cruach (do bunuigheadh le Connradh do sínigheadh i bPáras an 18adh lá d'Aibreán, 1951), de Chomhphobal Eacnamaíochta na hEorpa (do bunuigheadh le Connradh do sínigheadh insan Róimh an 25adh lá de Mhárta, 1957) agus", and

(ii) the second sentence,

shall be repealed,

(*b*) in subsection 3° of section 4 of the English text—

(i) the words "the European Coal and Steel Community (established by Treaty signed at Paris on the 18th day of April, 1951), the European Economic Community (established by Treaty signed at Rome on the 25th day of March, 1957) and", and

(ii) the second sentence,

shall be repealed,

(*c*) subsections 4°, 5°, 6°, 7°, 8°, 9°, 10° and 11° of section 4 of both the Irish text and the English text shall be repealed,

(*d*) the subsections, the texts of which are set out in Part 1 of the Schedule, shall be inserted after subsection 3° of section 4 of the Irish text, (*e*) the subsections, the texts of which are set out in Part 2 of the Schedule, shall be inserted after subsection 3° of section 4 of the English text.

(2) The amendment of section 4 of Article 29 of the Constitution effected by this Act shall—

(*a*) subject to paragraph (*b*), have effect upon and from the entry into force of the Treaty of Lisbon amending the Treaty on European Union and the Treaty establishing the European Community, signed at Lisbon on the 13th day of December 2007, and
(*b*) in so far as it inserts subsection 5° of that section, have effect upon and from the passing of this Act.

(3) Subsection 5° (inserted by this Act) of section 4 of Article 29 of the Constitution shall, before the entry into force of the treaty referred to in paragraph (*a*) of subsection (2), be numbered subsection 12°.

Citation
2.—(1) The amendment of the Constitution effected by this Act shall be called the Twenty-Eighth Amendment of the Constitution.

(2) This Act may be cited as the Twenty-Eighth Amendment of the Constitution (Treaty of Lisbon) Act 2009.

SCHEDULE

PART 1

. . .

PART 2

4° Ireland affirms its commitment to the European Union within which the member states of that Union work together to promote peace, shared values and the well-being of their peoples.

5° The State may ratify the Treaty of Lisbon amending the Treaty on European Union and the Treaty establishing the European Community, signed at Lisbon on the 13th day of December 2007 ("Treaty of Lisbon"), and may be a member of the European Union established by virtue of that Treaty.

6° No provision of this Constitution invalidates laws enacted, acts done or measures adopted by the State, before, on or after the entry into force of the Treaty of Lisbon, that are necessitated by the obligations of membership of the European Union referred to in subsection 5° of this section or of the European Atomic Energy Community, or prevents laws enacted, acts done or measures adopted by—

(i) the said European Union or the European Atomic Energy Community, or institutions thereof,
(ii) the European Communities or European Union existing immediately before the entry into force of the Treaty of Lisbon, or institutions thereof, or
(iii) bodies competent under the treaties referred to in this section,

from having the force of law in the State.

7° The State may exercise the options or discretions—

(i) to which Article 20 of the Treaty on European Union relating to enhanced cooperation applies,
(ii) under Protocol No. 19 on the Schengen *acquis* integrated into the framework of the European Union annexed to that treaty and to the Treaty on the Functioning of the European Union (formerly known as the Treaty establishing the European Community), and
(iii) under Protocol No. 21 on the position of the United Kingdom and Ireland in respect of the area of freedom, security and justice, so annexed, including the option that the said Protocol No. 21 shall, in whole or in part, cease to apply to the State,

but any such exercise shall be subject to the prior approval of both Houses of the Oireachtas.

8° The State may agree to the decisions, regulations or other acts—

(i) under the Treaty on European Union and the Treaty on the Functioning of the European Union authorising the Council of the European Union to act other than by unanimity,
(ii) under those treaties authorising the adoption of the ordinary legislative procedure, and
(iii) under subparagraph (*d*) of Article 82.2, the third subparagraph of Article 83.1 and paragraphs 1 and 4 of Article 86 of the Treaty on the Functioning of the European Union, relating to the area of freedom, security and justice,

but the agreement to any such decision, regulation or act shall be subject to the prior approval of both Houses of the Oireachtas.

9° The State shall not adopt a decision taken by the European Council to establish a common defence pursuant to Article 42 of the Treaty on European Union where that common defence would include the State.

EUROPEAN UNION ACT 2009

Number 33 *of* 2009

ARRANGEMENT OF SECTIONS

Acts Referred to

European Communities Act 1972	1972, No. 27
European Communities Act 2007	2007, No. 18
European Communities Acts 1972 to 2007	
European Union (Scrutiny) Act 2002	2002, No. 25
Interpretation Act 2005	2005, No. 23

AN ACT TO MAKE PROVISION WITH RESPECT TO THE STATE'S MEMBERSHIP OF THE EUROPEAN UNION; TO PROVIDE FOR THE APPLICATION UNDER THE LAW OF THE STATE OF THE TREATY OF LISBON AMENDING THE TREATY ON EUROPEAN UNION AND THE TREATY ESTABLISHING THE EUROPEAN COMMUNITY, SIGNED AT LISBON ON THE 13TH DAY OF DECEMBER 2007; FOR THOSE PURPOSES TO AMEND THE EUROPEAN COMMUNITIES ACT 1972; AND TO PROVIDE FOR MATTERS CONNECTED THEREWITH.

[27*th October*, 2009]

BE IT ENACTED BY THE OIREACHTAS AS FOLLOWS:

Definitions

1.— In this Act—

"Act of 1972" means the European Communities Act 1972;

"European Union" has the same meaning as it has in the Act of 1972;

"Minister" means the Minister for Foreign Affairs; and

"treaties governing the European Union" has the same meaning as it has in the Act of 1972.

Amendment of section 1 of Act of 1972

2.— Section 1 of the Act of 1972 is amended, in subsection (1), by the insertion of the following definitions:

'European Union' means the European Union, established by virtue of the Lisbon Treaty, and the European Atomic Energy Community;

'Lisbon Treaty' means the Treaty of Lisbon amending the Treaty on European Union and the Treaty establishing the European Community, signed at Lisbon on the 13th day of December 2007;

'treaties governing the European Union' means—

(*a*) the Treaty on European Union,
(*b*) the Treaty on the Functioning of the European Union,
(*c*) the Lisbon Treaty, and
(*d*) the treaties governing the European Communities,

but shall not include the provisions to which the first paragraph of Article 275 of the treaty referred to in paragraph (*b*) applies;".

Amendment of section 2 of Act of 1972

3.— Section 2 of the Act of 1972 is amended by the substitution of the following subsection for subsection (1):

"(1) The following shall be binding on the State and shall be part of the domestic law thereof under the conditions laid down in the treaties governing the European Union:

(*a*) the treaties governing the European Union;
(*b*) acts adopted by the institutions of the European Union (other than acts to which the first paragraph of Article 275 of the Treaty on the Functioning of the European Union applies);
(*c*) acts adopted by the institutions of the European Communities in force immediately before the entry into force of the Lisbon Treaty; and
(*d*) acts adopted by bodies competent under those treaties (other than acts to which the first paragraph of the said Article 275 applies).".

Amendment of section 3 of Act of 1972

4.— Section 3 of the Act of 1972 is amended by the substitution, in paragraph (*a*) of subsection (3) (inserted by section 2 of the European Communities Act 2007) of the following subparagraphs for subparagraphs (i) and (ii):

"(i) a provision of the treaties governing the European Union, or
(ii) an act, or provision of an act, adopted by an institution of the European Union, an institution of the European Communities or a body competent under those treaties, and".

Construction of references

5.— (1) References in any enactment (other than this Act and the Act of 1972) to the European Communities shall be construed as including references to the European Union.

(2) References in any enactment (other than this Act and the Act of 1972) to the treaties governing the European Communities shall be construed as references to the treaties governing the European Union.

(3) References in any enactment to the Treaty establishing the European Economic Community or the Treaty establishing the European Community shall be construed as references to the Treaty on the Functioning of the European Union.

(4) In this section "enactment" has the same meaning as it has in the Interpretation Act 2005.

Amendment of European Union (Scrutiny) Act 2002

6.— Section 1 of the European Union (Scrutiny) Act 2002 is amended by the substitution of the following definition for the definition of "measure":

" 'measure' means—

(*a*) a regulation or directive adopted under the Treaty on the Functioning of the European Union,

(*b*) a decision adopted under Article 28 or 29 of the Treaty on European Union, or

(*c*) an act (other than a regulation, directive or decision referred to in paragraph (*a*) or (*b*)) requiring the prior approval of both Houses of the Oireachtas pursuant to subsection 7° or 8° of Article 29.4 of the Constitution;".

Role of Houses of Oireachtas

7.— (1) (*a*) Either House of the Oireachtas may, not later than 6 months after receiving a notification under the third subparagraph of Article 48.7 of the Treaty on European Union, pass a resolution opposing the adoption of the decision to which the notification relates.

(*b*) A resolution referred to in *paragraph (a)* shall constitute an opposition to the decision concerned for the purposes of the third subparagraph of Article 48.7 of the Treaty on European Union, and the European Council shall be informed accordingly thereof.

(2) (*a*) Either House of the Oireachtas may, not later than 6 months after receiving a notification under the third subparagraph of Article 81.3 of the Treaty on the Functioning of the European Union, pass a resolution opposing the adoption of the decision to which the notification relates.

(*b*) A resolution referred to in *paragraph (a)* shall constitute an opposition to the decision concerned for the purposes of the third subparagraph of Article 81.3 of the Treaty on the Functioning of the European Union, and the Council shall be informed accordingly thereof.

(3) Either House of the Oireachtas may, not later than 8 weeks after the transmission of a draft legislative act referred to in Article 6 of Protocol No. 2 to the Treaty on European Union and the Treaty on the Functioning of the European Union, send to the Presidents of the European Parliament, the Council and the European Commission a reasoned opinion in accordance with that Article if the House concerned passes a resolution in respect of the draft legislative act concerned authorising the House to so do.

(4) Where either House of the Oireachtas is of opinion that an act of an institution of the European Union infringes the principle of subsidiarity provided for in the treaties governing the European Union and wishes that proceedings seeking a review of the act concerned be brought in the Court of Justice of the European Union in accordance with Article 263 of the Treaty on the Functioning of the European Union, it shall so notify the Minister in writing for the purposes of Article 8 of Protocol No. 2 to that treaty and the Treaty on European Union and the Minister shall, as soon as may be after being so notified, arrange for such proceedings to be brought.

Continuation in force of certain statutory instruments

8.— (1) Where a European act (in this subsection referred to as a "repealed act"), to which effect or further effect has been given, in whole or in part, by a statutory instrument, is repealed and replaced by another European act (in this subsection referred to as a "codify ing act") without any material modification of the repealed act, that statutory instrument shall, upon and after the repeal of the repealed act, have effect as if it had been made for the purpose of giving effect or further effect, in whole or in part (as the case may be), to the codifying act, and accordingly—

(*a*) references in that statutory instrument to the repealed act shall be construed as references to the codifying act, and
(*b*) references in that statutory instrument to a provision of the repealed act shall be construed as references to the provision of the codifying act that corresponds, in accordance with the codifying act, to the first-mentioned provision.

(2) Where, before the passing of this Act, a European act (in this subsection referred to as a "repealed act"), to which effect or further effect was given, in whole or in part, by a statutory instrument, was repealed and replaced by another European act (in this subsection referred to as a " codifying act ") without any material modification of the repealed act, that statutory instrument shall, from the date of the repeal of the repealed act, be deemed to have been made for the purpose of giving effect or further effect, in whole or in part (as the case may be), to the codifying act, and accordingly shall have effect, and be deemed from that date to have had effect, subject to—

(*a*) references in that statutory instrument to the repealed act being construed as references to the codifying act, and
(*b*) references in that statutory instrument to a provision of the repealed act being construed as references to the provision of the codifying act that corresponds, in accordance with the codifying act, to the first-mentioned provision.

(3) In this section—

"European act" means—

(*a*) a provision of the treaties governing the European Union, or
(*b*) an act or provision of an act, adopted by an institution of the European Union, an institution of the European Communities or any other body competent under those treaties;

"statutory instrument" means an order, regulation, rule, scheme or bye-law made in exercise of a power conferred by—

(*a*) an Act of the Oireachtas (including the Act of 1972), or
(*b*) a statute that was in force immediately before the date of the coming into force of the Constitution and that continues to be of full force and effect by virtue of Article 50 of the Constitution.

Short title, collective citation and commencement
9.— (1) This Act may be cited as the European Union Act 2009.

(2) The European Communities Acts 1972 to 2007 and this Act may be cited together as the European Communities Acts 1972 to 2009.

(3) This Act (other than *section 8*) shall come into operation on such day or days as the Minister may appoint by order or orders either generally or with reference to any particular purpose or provision and different days may be so appointed for different purposes or provisions.

APPENDIX B

SELECTED CASE EXTRACTS

(in alphabetical order)

An Taoiseach v Commissioner for Environmental Information

[2010] IEHC 241

Author's note: This case is a particularly important consideration of the operation of the doctrine of Primacy and the powers of quasi-judicial bodies.

1. Background

1.1 These proceedings come before this Court by way of statutory appeal under Article 13 of the E.C. (Access to Information on the Environment) Regulations 2007 (S.I. No. 133 of 207) ("the regulations") against a decision of the respondent made on the 10th October, 2008, wherein she directed the appellant to disclose to the notice party a record, in the form of a hand-written note, of discussions and the outcome of those discussions at a meeting of the Government on the 24th June, 2003.

1.2 The appellant seeks an order setting aside the impugned decision. He also seeks a declaration that the record is exempt from disclosure pursuant to the provisions of the regulations and, in particular, regulation 8(a) (iv) and/or regulation 8 (b). He seeks a further order remitting the notice party's request for access to the record to the respondent for further consideration or determination by her, should this Court consider it necessary or appropriate.

2. Legislative Background

2.1 Directive 2003/4/EC of the European Parliament and of the Council of the 28th January 2003 on Public Access to Environmental Information ("the directive") was adopted to guarantee a right of access by the public to environmental information held by or for public authorities and to set out "*the basic terms and conditions of, and practical arrangements for*" the exercise of this right, as stated in Article 1. In addition, it is designed to ensure that "*as a matter of course, environmental information is progressively made available and disseminated to the public in order to achieve the widest possible systematic availability and dissemination to the public of environmental information*". Article 3 imposes an obligation on Member States to ensure that public authorities provide environmental information held by or for Member States once a request is made. It states:–

> "*Member States shall ensure that public authorities are required, in accordance with the provisions of this Directive, to make available environmental information held by or for them to any applicant at his request and without his having to state an interest.*"

This obligation is subject to Article 4 of the Directive which sets out discretionary exceptions to it. However, when a request for environmental information relates to information on emissions into the environment a Member State may not rely on certain of the exceptions set out to refuse access to such information. Article 4 states:–

> "*1. Member States may provide for a request for environmental information to be refused if:*
>
> ...
>
> *(e) the request concerns internal communications, taking into account the public interest served by disclosure.*
>
> *2. Member States may provide for a request for environmental information to be refused if disclosure of the information would adversely affect:*
>
> *(a) the confidentiality of the proceedings of public authorities, where such confidentiality is provided for by law;*
>
> ...

> *The grounds for refusal mentioned in paragraphs 1 and 2 shall be interpreted in a restrictive way, taking into account for the particular case the public interest served by disclosure. In every particular case, the public interest served by disclosure shall be weighed against the interest served by the refusal. Member States may not, by virtue of paragraph 2(a), (d), (f), (g) and (h), provide for a request to be refused where the request relates to information on emissions into the environment."*

2.2 Article 6 of the directive provides for "access to justice" as follows:–

> *"(1) Member States shall ensure that any applicant who considers that his request for information has been ignored, wrongfully refused (whether in full or in part), inadequately answered or otherwise not dealt with in accordance with the provisions of Articles 3, 4 or 5, has access to a procedure in which the acts or omissions of the public authority concerned can be reconsidered by that or another public authority or reviewed administratively by an independent and impartial body established by law. Any such procedure shall be expeditious and either free of charge or inexpensive.*
> *(2) In addition to the review procedure referred to in paragraph 1, Member States shall ensure that an applicant has access to a review procedure before a court of law or another independent and impartial body established by law, in which the acts or omissions of the public authority concerned can be reviewed and whose decisions may become final. Member States may furthermore provide that third parties incriminated by the disclosure of information may also have access to legal recourse.*
> *(3) Final decisions under paragraph 2 shall be binding on the public authority holding the information. Reasons shall be stated in writing, at least where access to information is refused under this Article."*

2.3 The regulations transposed the above directive into Irish law on the 28th March, 2007. Article 7(1) purports to replicate Article 3, in that, it sets out the general obligation under the regulations, on public authorities to make available to applicants, access to environmental information. It states:–

> *"7. (1) A public authority shall, notwithstanding any other statutory provision and subject only to these Regulations, make available to the applicant any environmental information, the subject of the request, held by, or for, the public authority."*

2.4 Mandatory exceptions to the provision of environmental information, which are subject to the provisions of Article 10, are set out in Article 8 which provides:–

> *"8. A public authority shall not make available environmental information in accordance with article 7 where disclosure of the information—*
> *(a) would adversely affect—*
> ...
> *(iv) without prejudice to paragraph (b), the confidentiality of the proceedings of public authorities, where such confidentiality is otherwise protected by law (including the Freedom of Information Acts 1997 and 2003 with respect to exempt records within the meaning of those Acts);*
> *or*
> *(b) to the extent that it would involve the disclosure of discussions at one or more meetings of the Government, is prohibited by Article 28 of the Constitution."*

2.5 Article 9 of the regulations outlines discretionary grounds for refusal as follows:–

"...

(2) A public authority may refuse to make environmental information available where the request—

...

(d) concerns internal communications of public authorities, taking into account the public interest served by the disclosure."

2.6 Article 10 has the effect of creating an exception to the exceptions, in that, it provides for information to be released when it relates to information on emissions into the environment. However in its second paragraph, it preserves the confidentiality of Government discussions, even where the information sought relates to emissions into the environment. It states:–

"10. (1) Notwithstanding articles 8 and 9 (1) (c), a request for environmental information shall not be refused where the request relates to information on emissions into the environment.

(2) The reference in sub-article (1) to information on emissions into the environment does not include a reference to any discussions on the matter of such emissions at any meeting of the Government.

(3) The public authority shall consider each request on an individual basis and weigh the public interest served by disclosure against the interest served by refusal.

(4) The grounds for refusal of a request for environmental information shall be interpreted on a restrictive basis having regard to the public interest served by disclosure.

(5) Nothing in article 8 or 9 shall authorise a public authority not to make available environmental information which, although held with information to which articles 8 or 9 relates, may be separated from such information.

..."

2.7 Article 13 of the regulations provides for an appeal "*on a point of law*" to this Court from a decision of the respondent. The respondent is empowered under article 12(9) to refer "*any question of law*" arising in an appeal before her to this Court for determination. That did not happen in this case.

2.8 As this case concerns a record of government discussions, the guarantee of confidentiality under Article 28.4.3 of the Constitution is relevant. That provision states as follows:–

"3° The confidentiality of discussions at meetings of the Government shall be respected in all circumstances save only where the High Court determines that disclosure should be made in respect of a particular matter -

(i) in the interests of the administration of justice by a Court, or

(ii) by virtue of an overriding public interest, pursuant to an application in that behalf by a tribunal appointed by the Government or a Minister of the Government on the authority of the Houses of the Oireachtas to inquire into a matter stated by them to be of public importance."

3. The Facts

3.1 The Department of An Taoiseach ("the Department") received a series of requests from the notice party in letter[s] dated the 30th March, 2007, seeking access to (i) any documents showing Cabinet decisions or conclusions on Ireland's greenhouse gas emissions for the years 2002-2007 and (ii) any documents, including, but not limited to, minutes of meetings, that reported any Cabinet discussions on Ireland's greenhouse gas emissions for the years 2002-2007. The notice party indicated in his letters to the Department that he was making the request pursuant to the provisions of the directive. Having not received a reply to his requests, the notice party wrote a further letter to the Department advising it, that due to its failure to respond that he assumed that his requests were refused and that, accordingly, he wished to appeal that refusal under article 11 of the regulations, which had come into force since he first made his request.

3.2 On the 17th May, 2007, the matter was referred for internal review in the Department. By letter dated the 13th June, 2007, the Department informed him that no records were held by it within the scope of the first request and that twenty six records were held within the scope of the second. It further stated that eight of the records were being released to him and were enclosed but that the remaining eighteen records, descriptions of which were set out, were not being released on the basis that the documents were records of the government and were specifically excluded from public disclosure, as mandated by article 8 of the regulations and s.19 of the Freedom of Information Act 1997. The letter then went on to outline the notice party's right to appeal the decision to the respondent.

...

3.5 In an email of the following day an official of the respondent set out the central submissions made by the notice party and invited the Department's comments. The notice party's arguments were summarised in that email as follows:–

> *"Even though article 8(b) of SI 133 makes reference to Article 28 of the Constitution in relation to cabinet confidentiality, it is a fundamental principle of EU law that the EU measure is supreme and cannot be overridden by domestic legal provisions even where this is a constitutional provision [see Costa v ENEL [1964] ECR 585; Handelgsellschaft [1970] ECR 1125].*
>
> *The relevant sections (articles 3(1) and 4(2) of the Directive are sufficiently clear to have direct effect [Van Duyn v Home Office [1974 ECR 1337].*
>
> *Cabinet confidentiality cannot be considered if it conflicts with rights under the Directive – given that information on emissions is being sought, the Directive states that there are no grounds for refusal.*
>
> *Article 8 (b) and article 10(2) of SI 133 contradict the provisions of the Directive and must be disapplied.*
>
> *The doctrine of supremacy requires that the Commissioner exercise powers that she would not normally have under domestic law."*

3.6 On the 29th January, 2008, the Department replied to the respondent indicating that it had consulted with the Attorney General's Office and the Department of the Environment, Heritage and Local Government (the Department that introduced the regulations). Their advice was to the effect that the regulations were fully compatible with the directive and that there was no conflict between them. The directive, it was pointed out, gave Member States discretion as to whether to exempt disclosure of certain information and those exemptions were set out in article 10 of the regulations.

3.7 In her decision, the respondent took the view that only one of the eighteen documents could be regarded as constituting a "*report*" of discussion at Cabinet on Ireland's greenhouse gas emissions, thereby confining the appeal to the notice party's right of access to this document alone. The notice party does not take issue with this. The respondent, in her decision, then set out the Department's decision and the respective positions of the notice party and of the Department. She identified the relevant parts of the legal provisions at issue, that is, the directive, the regulations and Article 28.4.3 of the Constitution. She observed that the Freedom of Information Act 1997 applied only to decisions made under that Act and did not enshrine a legal protection for confidentiality generally.

...

3.9 The respondent then considered whether the notice party's requests related to information on emissions into the environment. If they did, she noted that the grounds for the refusal of a request, as contained in Article 8 were subject to Article 10. She stated that the Department did not take any issue with her office proceeding on the basis that the request related to emissions into the environment. The wording of the notice party's request indicated that it was a request relating to emissions into the environment. She found the nature of the document in issue was such, that part of it disclosed factual information on emissions into the environment and the remaining portion related to, in a general sense, information on emissions into the environment. She concluded that "*the record portion which discloses factual information on emissions into the environment also relates to emissions into the environment*".

3.10 The respondent then went on to consider whether the regulations were in conflict with the directive. She noted the provisions of Article 3 and 4 of the directive. In respect of Article 4 she stated:–

> "*While all the grounds for refusal are subject to a public interest test, article 4 of the Directive provides that, 'where the request relates to information on emissions into the environment', five of the eight 'harm based grounds for refusal may not be invoked. The five 'harm based' grounds for refusal are those at paragraph 2(a), (d) (f), (g) and (h) of article 4. Of particular relevance here is paragraph 2(a) which provides the potential to refuse environmental information where disclosure would adversely affect 'the confidentiality of proceedings of public authorities, where such confidentiality is protected by law.'*

3.11 To the extent that Article 10(1) of the regulations restricts the operation of the exception provisions of Article 8 of the regulations in the case of requests that relate to information on emissions into the environment, she found that it did conflict with Article 4 of the directive. As to whether Article 10(2) of the regulations accorded with the directive she stated as follows:–

> "*Article 10(2) of the Regulations qualifies article 10(1) by providing that the latter 'does not include a reference to any discussions on the matter of such emissions at any meeting of the Government'. The effect of article 10(2) is to disapply article 10(1) in the case of a record which refers to discussions, at any meeting of the Government, on emissions into the environment. The Department argues that, taken in conjunction with article 10(5) of the Regulations, this approach is perfectly compatible with the Directive. It says that the application of article 10(2) simply serves to confine release of environmental information which pertains to emissions to 'factual information'. I do not accept that the Department is correct in this. I cannot find anything explicit or implicit in the Directive or in its objectives to support the making of exceptions for certain classes of information within the category described in paragraph 2(a) of Article 4 of the Directive. Neither can I find anything in the Directive which would allow a Member State to confine the exception to factual information as argued by the Department. While elements of paragraph 2 of article 4 of the Directive as transposed by article 9(1) of the Regulations (international relations, public security, national defence, the course of justice, intellectual property rights) do not attract the prohibition on refusal, I consider that the exception in paragraph 2(a) – the confidentiality of the proceedings of public authorities, where such confidentiality is provided for by law – is definitely subject to it.*
> *The Department has not brought to my attention any provision in the Directive or any case law which would support its approach to the application of paragraph 2(a) and the transposing of the provision so as to provide for the omission of certain categories of information from its prohibition. It appears to be suggesting that it is open to me to confine my consideration to the wording of the provisions of the Regulations. My view is that the option of applying the Regulations in isolation from the Directive is not one which is open to me.*"

3.12 The respondent stated that she was adopting the teleological approach in her analysis of the transposition of the directive. She did not think that there was any alternative remedy open to the notice party in order to seek the information he was seeking. The purpose of the existence of exceptions or grounds for refusal was, in her view, because some information, if disclosed, would adversely affect the confidential proceedings of public bodies. She noted that Member States are expressly prohibited from invoking Article 4 (2) (a), (d), (f), (g) and (h) in order to refuse a request where the request relates to information on emissions into the environment, but that where a request for information related to information on emissions into the environment it could be refused under Article 4(2) (b), (c) and (e) (*i.e.* international relations, public security, national defence, the course of justice and intellectual property rights). The blanket prohibition in Article 4(2) (b), (c) and (e) did not apply, she found, in respect of confidentiality which was provided for in Article 4(2) (a). She stated:–

> *"Clearly, the Directive was framed to specifically exclude the refusal of a request on confidentiality – based grounds where the request relates to information on emissions to the environment. It seems to me that this is indicative of a conscious decision that confidentiality – even confidentiality provided for by law – was not sufficient to displace the presumption that environmental information relating to emissions will be released. Thus, environmental information in cabinet discussions relating to such matters as security, defence or the course of justice may be withheld even where such information relates to emissions whereas a blanket prohibition on matters 'confidential' is not envisaged by the directive."*

3.13 For the above reasons she concluded that article 10(2) of the regulations was not in conformity with article 4(2) of the directive. She found that the directive was directly effective but that it was incorrectly transposed into Irish law. She relied on a line of jurisprudence from the European Court of Justice [E.C.J.] to the effect that a public body must disapply national procedural rules in order to protect individual rights derived from directly effective E.C. law, in finding that the requirements of Article 4(2) of the directive could not properly be set aside by Article 10(2) of the regulation; (*Gervais Larsy v. Institut national d'assurances socials pour travaillerurs independents*) (INASTI) ECR-I-05063; *Colson and Kamann v. Land Nordrgein – Westfalen* [1984] Case C-14/83 ECR 1891 and *Henkel KGaA* case [2004] ECR 1-1725). She also referred to the decision of this Court (Keane J.) in *Murphy v. Telecom Éireann* [1989] I.L.R.M. 53.

3.14 As to her jurisdiction to determine the above matters, the following passage from her decision is significant:–

> *"I am conscious of the fact that while my Office is a creature of the Regulations, its creation arose from the 'Access to justice' provisions set out at Article 6 of the Directive. Specifically Article 6(2) of the Directive provides that 'Member States shall ensure that an applicant has access to a review procedure before a court of law or other independent and impartial body established by law, in which the acts or omissions of the public authority concerned can be reviewed and whose decision may become final." Having considered the matter, including the objectives of the Directive, I find that where a provision of the Directive is as clear and precise as the provision at issue here, I must exercise my functions in carrying out a review and proceed on the basis that the requirements of paragraph 2 of Article 4 of the Directive cannot properly be set aside by article 10(2) of the Regulations."*

3.15 The appellant instituted judicial review proceedings around the time of this appeal in order to challenge the *vires* of the respondent to reach such a decision. The parties agreed that this issue could be dealt with within the confines of this appeal.

...

3.17 During the hearing of these proceedings the respondent applied for a reference by this Court to the E.C.J. under Article 234 of the E.C. Treaty. The appellant opposed this and the notice party took a neutral position.

4. Jurisdiction

4.1 The first matter that must be examined is the jurisdiction of the respondent. The parameters of that jurisdiction must be identified to assess whether she was entitled to look to the directive to interpret the true meaning of the regulations and whether her jurisdiction properly encompasses the disapplication of national law.

. . .

7. Decision

7.1 The problem in this case is not securing supremacy or primacy of Community law over domestic law, but discerning the correct procedural means for doing this. The notice party has rights under Art 3 of the Directive and Art 7 of the Regulations to the disclosure to him of the material in issue in this case which it is accepted concerns emissions into the environment unless that material can be withheld on the grounds of cabinet confidentiality. As it is clear that the regulations [Art 10[2]] do unequivocally provide for the exclusion from disclosure of this material, because the documents sought record cabinet discussion, the core issue is whether the respondent is entitled to disapply that provision in the Regulations and Art 28.4.3 of the Constitution and to give direct effect to the directive, which does not contain a similar express exclusion in respect of cabinet confidentiality.

7.2 Disapplication it was submitted by Ms Butler, in this sense does not mean that the regulation in question is deemed to be or becomes invalid, merely that in the discrete circumstances of this case it is not applied. This outcome could be seen as the worst of all worlds, in that a law or rule which is said to be inconsistent with a superior EU law is not declared invalid by a court of competent jurisdiction, but remains in force where its validity and enforceability is in doubt, there being circumstances in which it cannot apply and perhaps others where it can. It is to be envisaged that over time and with the expanding role of the EU in so many areas of life and commerce, the national legal landscape would become littered with the moribund remains of hitherto valid national laws. Such a state of affaires would greatly undermine the clarity and certainty that are necessary and fundamental to the integrity of legal systems in societies and communities based on the rule of law. In effect the vast array administrative bodies across the entire spectrum of public administration could claim or have imposed on them, a jurisdiction to hear and determine all questions of law and fact relating to the application or enforcement of EU rights, in preference to national laws, once EU rights were asserted by a party to a dispute.

7.3 Manifestly under our domestic law this could not occur as disputes of this nature are reserved exclusively to the Courts and issues such as arose in this case, *i.e.* the consistency of the regulations with the Directive, could only be litigated in the High Court at first instance. The problem with all this, apart from the violence done to the judicial architecture of the State, is that the party who may wish to rely on domestic law, either as a protection of his rights or as establishing a binding duty, will be denied a hearing of his case in a forum, *i.e.* the Courts, established by law for that purpose and which by virtue of such, over time have acquired the professional expertise, experience and competence to deal with these matters with the constitutional guarantee of independence and impartiality. As the focus of the concern of many of these public bodies, many of whom are purely administrative in character, would be the enforcement of the EU rights relying on the supremacy of EU law, attaining that supremacy might too easily be achieved by the suppression of rights and duties based on national laws, without adequate or appropriate consideration of correct constitutional and legal tests and balances.

7.4 The approach advocated in the respondent's submission puts to the hazard a variety of EU legal principles some of which are also well established in our domestic constitutional law. The principle of legal certainty and clarity of laws in force would be undermined if national laws could not be enforced because of conflict with EU laws but were not lawfully repealed or declared invalid by a Court of competent jurisdiction. The principle of judicial protection would manifestly be breached if the rights and duties of parties to disputes concerning the application of EU laws could not be considered and determined by Courts established by law with competence to deal with these matters. The principle of proportionality would be at risk where the procedural route chosen to enforce EU law inflicted disproportionate damage on the national system of law and the rights and duties of the parties affected. The principle of subsidiarity would be ignored as the forum chosen might bear no resemblance to the appropriate forum for consideration and determination of the issue involved. The principle of equivalence would in effect be stood on its head. This principle requires that EU rights can be applied and enforced in national courts on no less favourable terms and conditions than similar actions arising under national law. The respondent's submission would result in EU rights enjoying a degree of procedural supremacy which not only far exceeds that available to similar actions based on national law, but virtually eliminates national procedural safeguards for rights and duties based on national law.

7.5 It was argued by the respondent and the notice party that if the notice party were required to litigate his right to the disclosure sought in the High Court, this would breach the principle of effectiveness, in that the cost and delay involved in taking his case to the High Court would amount to a very serious obstacle if not a an actual impediment to the exercise of his rights under the Directive. This submission seems to overlook the Access to Justice provision in Art 6[2] of the Directive. As quoted above this provides for a review procedure to a court of law or an independent impartial body established by law. Art 13 of the Regulations transposes this aspect of the Directive and creates the right of appeal to this Court which is the proceeding now before me. Although the appeal is limited to an appeal on a point of law, as all of the issues which have arisen and are in issue between the parties are questions of law, the appeal procedure contains ample jurisdiction so as to fulfill the requirement in Art 6[2] of providing a review procedure in this case. I would construe the term "review" in a wide general sense rather than the more familiar judicial review concept in Irish law or the review type appeal such as the appeal from the High Court to the Supreme Court. I would treat this appeal as full rehearing of the appeal or review before the respondent on all legal issues arising, including the jurisdictional issue now under discussion and all issues of interpretation of the Directive and the Regulations. To that extent, the jurisdiction of this Court on this appeal may be greater than that of the respondent on the review now under appeal, that seems to me to be necessary to ensure that the full original jurisdiction of this Court, is made available to determine the issues that necessarily arise in the consideration of the notice party's rights under the Directive and Regulations, thereby achieving full compliance with Art 6 of the Directive.

7.6 In my view it cannot be said that recourse to the High Court by the notice party would breach the principle of effectiveness when the Directive itself provides for a review before a court of law. That review is there for the benefit of all parties to a disputed application for disclosure and is not merely an instrument to enforce the notice party's rights under the Directive and Regulations.

7.7 Whilst there can be no doubt but that where there is a conflict between an EU law and a national law the EU law must prevail, the question must be asked whether it is necessary to ensure the supremacy of EU law, to undermine, national systems of law, which would be the inevitable outcome if the respondent's submission is correct, or do the relevant judgments of the ECJ demand such a response from national legal systems.

7.8 As set out above there is a clear line of authority from the ECJ to the effect that member states enjoy procedural autonomy subject to the principle of equivalence and effectiveness. It is submitted on behalf of the respondent and the notice party that the line of authority stemming from the *Fratelli Constanzo Spa* case to the effect that where a national law conflicts with a an EU law the doctrine of supremacy requires that the national law be disapplied in favour of the EU law, and that it was the function and duty of all public bodies confronted with such conflict in the discharge of their functions to disapply the national law at that point. On the face of it, there would appear to be a conflict between these two lines of authority emanating from the ECJ. That of course would be very surprising if it were the case. I am not at all satisfied that it is. Whilst there are statements in these cases apparently requiring national law to be disapplied, which taken in isolation seem to require as was submitted by the respondent and notice party, that conflicting national laws be disapplied at the point of application by whatever public body is dealing with them, these statements taken in the overall context of the cases in which they arise but more particularly in the context of the general jurisprudence of the ECJ and the well established principles of EU law as mentioned above, would not seem to have the kind of meaning contended for by the respondent and the notice party, as this would create a very clear conflict in the jurisprudence of the ECJ, with the well established line of authority on national procedural autonomy, and the variety of EU legal principles mentioned above, which could be either ignored or breached in the process.

7.9 The opinion of Advocate General Jacobs in the *Van Schijndel*, quoted above, in my opinion, correctly elucidates the problem, namely, that the primacy of EU law is secured by a general rule to that effect, which of course must be universally applied across all the member states. It is then left to the member states within the architecture of their own legal systems to determine procedures for the enforcement of EU law subject to the principles of equivalence and effectiveness.

7.10 I am satisfied therefore that in transposing the Directive in the Regulations this state was entitled to and did establish a procedure for dealing with claims for disclosure of environmental material and for refusals of same, when such might occur, as in this case. Clearly those regulations did not purport to confer on the respondent the kind of jurisdiction she asserted in her ruling, namely to consider the validity of the regulations in light of the Directive, a jurisdiction unquestionably reserved under the Constitution to a Court of law. Thus notwithstanding the patient and full hearing she afforded the parties and the careful consideration she gave to the difficult issues in the case, I must conclude that she exceeded her jurisdiction and was not entitled to embark on a consideration of whether the regulations correctly transposed the Directive and she had no jurisdiction to disapply the Regulations and in particular Art 10[2] or Art 28.4.3 of the Constitution. The jurisdiction given to her under the laws of this state was confined to the Regulations and no more. In this respect, it should be noted that Art 12[9][a] of the Regulations permits the respondent to refer any question of law to the High Court for determination and can postpone her decision until after such determination. This procedure is there *inter alia* to assist the respondent when confronted with the kind of problems that arose in this case.

7.11 As mentioned earlier this appeal is a full rehearing on all legal issues which arose in the case. Thus notwithstanding the foregoing conclusion, it remains necessary for this Court to consider the findings of the respondents on other aspects of the case which could affect the ultimate determination of the issue of whether the notice party is entitled to the disclosure of the document in issue. Although the respondent did not have jurisdiction to consider whether the Regulations incorrectly transposed the Directive, this Court does.

9. Decision

9.1 In her decision the respondent acknowledged that the document at issue, as a record of discussions of a meeting of the government, enjoyed protection under Article 28.4.3 of the Constitution and, as such, fell within the ambit of article 8(b) of the regulations, subject to article 10 of the regulations. Therefore, the regulations, properly construed, preclude the disclosure of the document in issue on the basis of Article 28.4.3.

9.2 As is apparent from the summary of the submissions above, much of the debate in the case concerned whether a meeting of the government should be catagorised as "*the proceedings of a public authority*", or as "*internal communications*" of a public authority. The first issue to be confronted is whether the appellant is entitled to raise in this appeal the issue of whether Art

9[2][d] of the Regulations and Art 4[1][e] of the Directive apply, given that these were not relied on in the appeal or review before the respondent. I have already held that this appeal is a rehearing and therefore new material can be introduced. I am satisfied that the respondent and notice party had ample notice of the appellant's reliance on Art 9[2][d] of the Regulations and Art 4[1][e] of the Directive in advance of the hearing of this appeal. Therefore, having regard to the importance of the issue I permitted the appellant to rely on it.

9.3 It is clear that the Regulations expressly and unequivocally make provision for discussions at meeting of the government in regulations 8[b] and 10[2]. Hence in my view, applying the primary canon of construction, namely ascertaining the true meaning of the words used and applying same unless absurdity is produced, I am of opinion that for the purpose of the Regulations, it must be taken that the only provisions of the Regulations that govern or affect cabinet confidentiality are Art 8[b] and Art 10[2] and not Art 8[a][iv] or 9[2][d]. The opening phrase in Art 8[2][iv] namely *"without prejudice to paragraph [b]",* tends to reinforce this conclusion. Art 10[2] has the effect of protecting from disclosure a record of discussion at a meeting of the government of emissions into the environment.

9.4 As it is apparent that the provisions in the Regulations which expressly deal with meetings of the government are not replicated in the Directive, the Court must consider whether Art. 8[b] and 10[2] are inconsistent with the Directive and hence invalid. It is in this context that the issue as to the correct categorisation of meetings of the government arises and whether Art 4.1[e] or 4.2[a] applies.

9.5 Meetings of the government are but one aspect of its constitutional role and its many and varied functions as described briefly in the Constitution and set out in great detail in a vast array of legislation. To describe meetings of the government as "the proceedings" of the government as the public authority in question seems to me somewhat artificial and strained. Applying the natural and ordinary meaning of these terms as used in Art 4.2[a] in the Directive, would in my opinion result in a conclusion that Art 4.2[a] did not and was not intended to apply to meetings of the government such as and in so far as these are provided for in our Constitution and laws.

9.6 On the other hand meetings of the government are the occasions when as provided for in Art 28.4.2 of the Constitution the members of the government come together to act as a collective authority, collectively responsible for all departments of State. Meetings of the government are the constitutionally mandated means or system of communication between its members for the purpose of discharging their collective responsibility. These meetings and their records are required by the Constitution to be private and confidential unless otherwise directed by the High Court under Art 28.3 of the Constitution. Whereas many aspects of the functions of the government are essentially public and external in nature, meetings of the government are quintessentially private and internal to the overall functions of the government. Thus in my judgment, this constitutionally mandated form of communication between members of the government can only be regarded as the internal communications of a public authority. Any other conclusion would lead to absurd results as pointed out by Collins, in that communications between members of the government in any other context apart from formal meetings of the government would have to be regarded as internal communications, and protected from disclosure, but the same communications at a government meeting would as *"the proceedings of a public authority"* attract disclosure. Manifestly such a state of affaires, apart from its obvious absurdity, would seriously undermine the discharge of collective responsibility by the government, as required by Art 28.4.2 of the Constitution. In this regard, I should further add, that I am quite satisfied that the distinction sought to be drawn between communications between the members of a public authority and between officials of that authority or between officials of the authority and the members of the authority is devoid of any rational merit and has no discernible basis either in the express provisions or by way of necessary implication, in the Directive or the Regulations.

9.7 Hence in my view Art 4.1[e] of the Directive clearly applies to meeting of the government and thus there is no conflict between Art 8[b] and 10[2] of the Regulations and the Directive.

10. Application for a reference to the ECJ under Art 234 of the EU treaty

10.1 As this Court is not a Court of last resort in this jurisdiction with competence to deal with the issues of EU law that have arisen in the case, I have decided to exercise my discretion to refuse the respondents application for such a reference.

11. Conclusion

11.1 For the reasons set out above, I must allow the appeal, set aside the determination of the respondent and grant declarations to the following effect:

(a) That the respondent did not have the requisite legal power to consider whether Art 10[2] of the Regulations was inconsistent with Art 4.2 of the Directive and to disapply Art 28.4.3 of the Constitution and Art 10[2] of the Regulations.
(b) Art 8[b] alone and not Arts 8[a][iv] or 9[2][d] of the Regulations apply to discussions at meetings of the government.
(c) For the purposes of the Directive, discussions at meetings of the government are "*internal communications*" within the meaning of Art 4.1[e] of the Directive.

Crotty v An Taoiseach

[1987] IESC 4

Judgment of the Court delivered pursuant to the provisions of Article 34.4.5° by Finlay CJ, 9 April 1987.

Finlay C.J.:

Part of the plaintiff's appeal in this case is against the dismiss by the High Court of his claim for a declaration that the European Communities (Amendment) Act, 1986, is invalid having regard to the provisions of the Constitution. The Court in this decision deals with that issue only.

The European Communities (Amendment) Act, 1986, ("the Act of 1986") purports to amend the European Communities Act, 1972, and to bring into the domestic law of the State Article 3, s. 1; Title II; Article 31; Article 32; and in part Articles 33 and 34 of the Single European Act ("the SEA"). The Act of 1986 was enacted by the Oireachtas in December, 1986, but does not come into effect until the making of a statutory order which has not yet been made. The other provisions of the SEA largely consisting of the provisions on European cooperation in the sphere of foreign policy contained in Title III are not affected by the Act of 1986 and do not fall to be dealt with in this decision of the Court.

In the High Court the plaintiff's claim was rejected on the grounds that because the SEA had not yet been ratified by the State and because the Act of 1986 had not yet been brought into effect the plaintiff failed to establish that he had a *locus standi* to challenge the validity of the Act of 1986 having regard to the provisions of the Constitution. The Court is satisfied, in accordance with the principles laid down by the Court in *Cahill v. Sutton* [1980] IR 269, that in the particular circumstances of this case where the impugned legislation, namely the Act of 1986, will if made operative affect every citizen, the plaintiff has a *locus standi* to challenge the Act notwithstanding his failure to prove the threat of any special injury or prejudice to him, as distinct from any other citizen, arising from the Act.

The net issue therefore here arising is as to whether the provisions of Article 29, s. 4, sub-s. 3 of the Constitution authorise the ratification by the State of the provisions of the SEA intended to amend the Treaties establishing the European Communities. These provisions are the Articles and Title of the SEA referred to in the Act of 1986. Article 29, s. 4, sub-s. 3 reads as follows:–

> "3° The State may become a member of the European Coal and Steel Community (established by Treaty signed at Paris on the 18th day of April, 1951), the European Economic Community (established by Treaty signed at Rome on the 25th day of March, 1957) and the European Atomic Energy Community (established by Treaty signed at Rome on the 25th day of March, 1957). No provision of this Constitution invalidates laws enacted, acts done or measures adopted by the State necessitated by the obligations of membership of the Communities or prevents laws enacted, acts done or measures adopted by the Communities, or institutions thereof, from having the force of law in the State."

This provision was enacted as the Third Amendment to the Constitution by virtue of a referendum held in 1972 and permitted the State to join the European Communities. The Court is satisfied that the first sentence of this provision authorised the State to join three Communities identified as to each by reference to the Treaty which established it. It is clear and was not otherwise contended by the defendants that the ratification by the State of the SEA (which has not yet taken place) would not constitute an act "necessitated by the obligations of membership of the Communities". It accordingly follows that the second sentence in Article 29, s. 4, sub-s. 3 of the Constitution is not relevant to the issue as to whether the Act of 1986 is invalid having regard to the provisions of the Constitution. It was contended on behalf of the plaintiff that any amendment of the Treaties establishing the Communities made after the 1st January, 1973, when Ireland joined those Communities would require a further amendment of the Constitution. It was contended on behalf of the defendants that the authorisation contained in the first sentence of Article 29, s. 4, sub-s. 3 was to join Communities which were established by Treaties as dynamic and developing entities and that it should be interpreted as authorising the State to participate in and agree to amendments of the Treaties which are within the original scope and objectives of the Treaties. It is the opinion of the Court that the first sentence in Article 29, s. 4, sub-s. 3 of the Constitution must be construed as an authorisation given to the State not only to join the Communities as they stood in 1973, but also to join in amendments of the Treaties so long as such amendments do not alter the essential scope or objectives of the Communities. To hold that the first sentence of Article 29, s. 4, sub-s. 3 does not authorise any form of amendment to the Treaties after 1973 without a further amendment of the Constitution would be too narrow a construction; to construe it as an open-ended authority to agree, without further amendment of the Constitution, to any amendment of the Treaties would be too broad. The issue then arises as to whether the effect of the amendments to the Treaties proposed by the SEA is such as would bring the introduction of them into the domestic law by the Act of 1986 outside the authorisation of Article 29, s. 4, sub-s. 3 as above construed.

The only provisions affecting the European Coal and Steel Community proposed in the SEA are Articles 4 and 5 thereof, and the only provisions affecting the European Atomic Energy Community proposed in the SEA are Articles 26 and 27 thereof. These Articles have essentially the same effect as Articles 11 and 12 with regard to the European Economic Community (the EEC). All of these Articles give a power to the European Council at the request of the Court of Justice of the European Communities to attach to that Court a court of first instance for the trial of certain classes of cases. It is sufficient, therefore, for the purpose of this decision to consider the EEC Treaty (the Treaty of Rome) and the proposed amendments and additions to it.

The Act of 1986 enjoys the presumption of constitutional validity, so the onus is on the plaintiff to show that it is in some respect invalid, having regard to the provisions of the Constitution. The contention made on behalf of the plaintiff on this issue was under four headings.

(1) Changes which are proposed in the decision-making process of the Council in six instances from unanimity to a qualified majority were asserted to be an unauthorised surrender of sovereignty.
(2) The power given to the Council by unanimous decision at the request of the Court of Justice of the European Communities (the European Court) to attach to it a court of first instance with an appeal from the latter on questions of law to the European Court was said to be an unauthorised surrender of the judicial power.
(3) It is submitted that Article 20 dealing with cooperation in economic and monetary policy, Article 21 dealing with social policy, Article 23 dealing with economic and social cohesion, Article 24 dealing with research and technological development, and Article 25 dealing with the environment, all add new objectives to the Treaty of Rome which make them additions to the original Treaty which are outside the existing constitutional authorisation.
(4) It is submitted that powers granted to the Council by Articles 18 and 21 of the SEA would enable it by a qualified majority to direct the approximation of laws concerning the provision of services and concerning the working environment, health and safety of workers which amount to new powers outside the existing constitutional authorisation

and which could encroach on existing guarantees of fundamental rights under the Constitution.

In discharging its duty to interpret and uphold the Constitution the Court must consider the essential nature of the scope and objectives of the Communities as they must be deemed to have been envisaged by the people in enacting Article 29, s. 4, sub-section 3. It is in the light of that scope and those objectives that the amendments proposed by the SEA fall to be considered.

Article 2 of the Treaty of Rome provided as follows:–

"The Community shall have as its task, by establishing a common market and progressively approximating the economic policies of Member States, to promote throughout the Community a harmonious development of economic activities, a continuous and balanced expansion, an increase in stability, an accelerated raising of the standard of living and closer relations between the States belonging to it."

Article 3 of that Treaty set out what the activities of the Community should include for the purposes stated in Article 2, and amongst these activities are:–

"(*c*) the abolition, as between Member States, of obstacles to freedom of movement for persons, services and capital;
(*f*) the institution of a system ensuring that competition in the common market is not distorted;
(*g*) the application of procedures by which the economic policies of Member States can be coordinated and disequilibria in their balances of payments remedied;
(*h*) the approximation of laws of Member States to the extent required for the proper functioning of the common market;
(*i*) the creation of a European Social Fund in order to improve employment opportunities for workers and to contribute to the raising of their standard of living;
(*j*) the establishment of a European Investment Bank to facilitate the economic expansion of the Community by opening up fresh resources;
(*k*) the association of the overseas countries and territories in order to increase trade and to promote jointly economic and social development."

For the purpose of attaining its objectives and implementing its provisions the Treaty of Rome established certain institutions. Amongst these is the Court of Justice of the European Communities which was established to ensure that in the interpretation and the application of the Treaty the law is observed. The decisions of that Court on the interpretation of the Treaty and on questions covering its implementation take precedence, in case of conflict, over the domestic law and the decisions of national courts of Member States:

Another institution of the EEC is the Council, whose decisions have primacy over domestic law and which for the purpose of ensuring that the objectives of the Treaty are attained is charged with ensuring the co-ordination of the general economic policies of the Member States. Some of its decisions must be unanimous, others may be taken by qualified majority, and still others by simple majority. The capacity of the Council to take decisions with legislative effect is a diminution of the sovereignty of Member States, including Ireland, and this was one of the reasons why the Third Amendment to the Constitution was necessary.Sovereignty in this context is the unfettered right to decide: to say yes or no. In regard to proposals coming before the Council which the State might oppose, unanimity is a valuable shield. On the other hand, in proposals which the State might support, qualified or simple majority is of significant assistance. In many instances the Treaty of Rome provided a requirement that a decision on a particular topic should be unanimous, but would after the expiry of a particular stage or of the transitional period require only a qualified majority. The Community was thus a developing organism with diverse and changing methods for making decisions and an inbuilt and clearly expressed objective of expansion and progress, both in terms of the number of its Member States and in terms of the mechanics to be used in the achievement of its agreed objectives.

Having regard to these considerations, it is the opinion of the Court that neither the proposed changes from unanimity to qualified majority, nor the identification of topics which while now separately stated, are within the original aims and objectives of the EEC, bring these proposed amendments outside the scope of the authorisation contained in Article 29, s. 4, sub-s. 3 of the Constitution. As far as Ireland is concerned, it does not follow that all other decisions of the Council which now require unanimity could, without a further amendment of the Constitution, be changed to decisions requiring less than unanimity.

The power of the Council to attach to the European Court a court of first instance with limited jurisdiction which would be subject to appeal on questions of law to the European Court, does not affect in any material way the extent to which the judicial power has already been ceded to the European Court. This Court is therefore of the opinion that the establishment of an additional court, if it occurs, has not been shown to exceed the constitutional authorisation.

The existing Treaty contains various provisions dealing with the approximation of laws in general, with freedom for the provision of services in the Member States, with working conditions and with the prevention of occupational accidents and diseases. The proposals contained in Articles 18 and 21 of the SEA have not been shown to contain new powers given to the Council which alter the essential character of the Communities. Neither has it been shown that they create a threat to fundamental constitutional rights. Therefore, it is the opinion of the Court that the appeal under this heading also fails.

For the foregoing reasons, it has not been shown to the satisfaction of the Court that any of the provisions of the European Communities (Amendment) Act, 1986, are invalid having regard to the provisions of the Constitution.

Finlay C.J.:

In addition to the appeal against the dismiss of his claim for a declaration that the European Communities (Amendment) Act, 1986, is invalid having regard to the provisions of the Constitution, which has been dealt with in the decision of the Court, the plaintiff has appealed against the dismiss of a claim for a declaration and injunction restraining the Government from ratifying the Single European Act ("the SEA"). The grounds for that claim, other than those already dealt with by the decision concerning the Act of 1986, are that the provisions contained in Article 30 under Title III of the SEA are inconsistent with the Constitution.

These provisions are entitled "Provisions on European cooperation in the sphere of foreign policy." They do not purport to constitute amendments of or additions to any of the Treaties establishing the Communities. Adherence to these provisions of the SEA by the State could not be an act necessitated by any obligation of membership by the State of the Communities nor could such provisions be laws enacted, acts done or measures adopted by the Communities or institutions thereof. Article 29, s. 4, sub-s. 3 of the Constitution accordingly does not apply to the provisions concerning European Political Cooperation (EPC) contained in Article 30 under Title III of the Single European Act.

Article 29, s. 6 of the Constitution therefore applies to those provisions since they can derive no immunity from it by virtue of Article 29, s. 4, sub-s. 3 and they do not become part of the domestic law of the State unless and until the Oireachtas validly so determines. The Oireachtas has passed no law purporting to bring these provisions into the domestic law of the State. The provisions of the SEA contained in Article 30 therefore rank as part of an international treaty negotiated by the Government but not yet ratified, the terms of which have been approved by resolution of Dáil Éireann but which has not been brought into our domestic law.

Article 30 of the SEA is divided into twelve sub-articles. It constitutes an agreement between states adhering to the SEA, described in Title III as "High Contracting Parties", which are in fact the Member States of the Communities. From the preamble to the SEA and from the terms of Article 30 themselves, it is clear that the agreements contained in that Article are arrived at with the possible ultimate objective of a form of European political union between the Member States of the Communities as an addition to the existing economic union between them. There can be no doubt that if that aim were ever achieved it would constitute an alteration in the essential scope and objectives of the Communities to which Ireland could not agree without an amendment of the Constitution. Article 30 in summary provides for:–

(1) Cooperation in the formation of foreign policy between the parties, with the aim of formulating and putting into effect a joint foreign policy.
(2) Cooperation with the Commission of the Communities.
(3) Cooperation with the Parliament of the Communities.
(4) Cooperation on European security.
(5) The adoption of common positions at international conferences and in international institutions.
(6) The state holding the Presidency of the Council of the Communities at any time shall hold the Presidency of the EPC which shall be responsible for initiating action and representing the position of Member States with third countries in relation to EPC activities.
(7) A Secretariat is to be established, the members of which will have diplomatic status.

The detailed terms of these provisions impose obligations to consult; to take full account of the position of other partners; to ensure that common principles and objectives are gradually developed and defined; as far as possible to refrain from impeding the formation of a consensus and the joint action which this could produce; to be ready to cooperate policies more closely on the political aspects of security. They do not impose any obligations to cede any national interest in the sphere of foreign policy. They do not give to other High Contracting Parties any right to override or veto the ultimate decision of the State on any issue of foreign policy. They impose an obligation to listen and consult and grant a right to be heard and to be consulted.

The net issue which arises in this part of this appeal is whether, having regard to the general nature and effect of Article 30 of the SEA and its status in relation to our law as above outlined, this Court is entitled under the Constitution, at the instance of the plaintiff, to intervene so as to prevent the Government from ratifying this treaty. It is an issue of a fundamental nature, the importance of which, in my view, transcends by far the significance of the provisions of the SEA. The separation of powers between the legislature, the executive and the judiciary, set out in Article 6 of the Constitution, is fundamental to all its provisions. It was identified by the former Supreme Court in *Buckley and Others (Sinn Féin) v. Attorney General* [1950] IR 67 and has since been repeatedly acknowledged and implemented by this Court. It involves for each of the three constitutional organs concerned not only rights but duties also; not only areas of activity and function, but boundaries to them as well.

With regard to the legislature, the right and duty of the Courts to intervene is clear and express.

(1) Article 15, s. 4, Article 34, s. 3, sub-s. 2 and Article 34, s. 4, sub-s. 4 of the Constitution vest in the High Court and, on appeal, in this Court the right and duty to examine the validity of any impugned enactment of the Oireachtas and, if it be found inconsistent with the Constitution, to condemn it in whole or in part.

(2) Article 26 of the Constitution confers on this Court the duty, upon the reference to it by the President of a Bill passed or deemed to have been passed by both houses of the Oireachtas, to decide whether such Bill or any specified provision or provisions of such Bill is or are repugnant to the Constitution or to any provision thereof.
(3) The Courts do not, in my opinion, have any other right to intervene in the enactment of legislation by the Oireachtas.

With regard to the executive, the position would appear to be as follows:- This Court has on appeal from the High Court a right and duty to interfere with the activities of the executive in order to protect or secure the constitutional rights of individual litigants where such rights have been or are being invaded by those activities or where activities of the executive threaten an invasion of such rights.

This right of intervention is expressly vested in the High Court and Supreme Court by the provisions of Article 34, s. 3, sub-s. 1 and Article: 34, s. 4, sub-s. 3 of the Constitution and impliedly arises from the form of the judicial oath contained in Article 34, s. 3, sub-s. 1 of the Constitution.

Article 29, s. 4, sub-s. 1 of the Constitution provides:–

> "The executive power of the State in or in connection with its external relations shall in accordance with Article 28 of this Constitution be exercised by or on the authority of the Government."

Article 28, s. 2 of the Constitution provides:–

> "The executive power of the State shall, subject to the provisions of this Constitution, be exercised by or on the authority of the Government."

The combined effect of these two constitutional provisions clearly is that the executive power of the State in connection with its external relations shall be exercised by or on the authority of the Government but that in so exercising that power the Government is subject to the provisions of the Constitution.

Article 29, s. 5, sub-s. 1 provides:–

> "Every international agreement to which the State becomes a party shall be laid before Dáil Éireann."

Article 29, s. 5, sub-s. 2 provides:–

> "The State shall not be bound by any international agreement involving a charge upon public funds unless the terms of the agreement shall have been approved by Dáil Éireann."

I have already referred to the provisions of s. 6 of Article 29 of the Constitution vesting in the Oireachtas the right to determine the extent and manner in which an international agreement shall be part of the domestic law of the State. From these constitutional provisions, it seems reasonable to infer a scheme under the Constitution that by virtue of Article 29, s. 5, sub-s. 1, Dáil Éireann should have a primary control over the exercise by the Government of its executive power in relation to entering into international agreements, and that under Article 29, s. 5, sub-s. 2 no international agreement of major importance being one that involved a charge upon public funds could bind the State without the approval of Dáil Éireann as to its terms. This scheme is consistent with the provisions of Article 28, s. 3, sub-s. 1 which provide:–

"War shall not be declared and the State shall not participate in. any war save with the assent of Dáil Éireann."

A declaration of war and participation in war is necessarily part and parcel of the external relations of the State. This provision again emphasises the control by Dáil Éireann of the Government in its exercise of executive power in external relations.

The overall provisions concerning the exercise of executive power in external relations do not contain any express provision for intervention by the Courts. There is nothing in the provisions of Articles 28 and 29 of the Constitution, in my opinion, from which it would be possible to imply any right in the Courts in general to interfere in the field or area of external relations with the exercise of an executive power. This does not mean that the executive is or can be without control by the Courts in relation to carrying out executive powers even in the field of external relations. In any instance where the exercise of that function constituted an actual or threatened invasion of the constitutional rights of an individual, the Courts would have a right and duty to intervene.

In this case where the plaintiff adduced no evidence at the hearing in the High Court but relied on matters pleaded and not denied, I am satisfied that he has not established any actual or threatened invasion of any constitutional right enjoyed by him as an individual arising from the terms of Article 30 of the Single European Act.

It was submitted that, whereas the plaintiff acknowledged that the Courts had no function to intervene with the Executive in the formation or statement of policy, either in external relations or in any other part of Government activity, a difference arose where the declaration of policy involved, as it is stated Article 30 of the SEA involves, a commitment to other states for consultation, discussion and an endeavour to coincide policies. I cannot accept this distinction. It appears probable that under modern conditions a state seeking cooperation with other states in the sphere of foreign policy must be prepared to enter into not merely vague promises but actual arrangements for consultation and discussion. I can find no warrant in the Constitution for suggesting that this activity would be inconsistent with the Constitution and would, as is suggested, presumably in each individual instance, require a specific amendment of the Constitution.

I am confirmed in the view which I have reached with regard to the constitutional limits of the intervention by the Courts in the exercise by the Government of its executive functions by the decision of this Court in *Boland v. An Taoiseach* [1974] IR 338. FitzGerald C.J., in the course of his judgment in that case, at p. 362, stated as follows:–

"Consequently, in my opinion, the Courts have no power, either express or implied, to supervise or interfere with the exercise by the Government of its executive functions, unless the circumstances are such as to amount to a clear disregard by the Government of the powers and duties conferred on it by the Constitution."

In the course of his judgment in the same case, Budd J., at p. 366, stated as follows:–

"The judiciary has its own particular ambit of functions under the Constitution. Mainly, it deals with justiciable controversies between citizen and citizen or the citizen and the State and matters pertaining thereto. Such matters have nothing to do with matters of State policy. Viewing the matter from another angle, as to the nature of any relief that could properly be claimed in proceedings of this nature, I ask whether it could be said that the Courts could be called upon to pronounce adversely or otherwise on what the Government proposed to do on any matter of policy which it was in the course of formulating. It would seem that that would be an attempted interference with matters which are part of the functions of the Executive and no part of the functions of the judiciary. From a practical standpoint alone, what action would be open to the Courts? The Courts could clearly not state that any particular policy ought not to be pursued.

> The Constitution goes further in indicating how far the policies involved in government decisions as to policy such as this are removed from the purview of the Courts in that it makes the Government responsible to the Dáil which can support or oppose those policies and review them. Ultimately, there is the responsibility of the Government to the people who must be consulted by way of referendum where any change of the Constitution is contemplated."

Griffin J., in the course of his judgment in that case, at p. 370, stated as follows:–

> "In the event of the Government acting in a manner which is in contravention of some provisions of the Constitution, in my view it would be the duty and the right of the Courts, as guardians of the Constitution, to intervene when called upon to do so if a complaint of a breach of any of the provisions of the Constitution is substantiated in proceedings brought before the Courts."

I do not consider that it has been established that adherence by the State to the terms of Article 30 of the SEA amounts, in the words of FitzGerald C.J., "to a clear disregard by the Government of the powers and duties conferred on it by the Constitution." Furthermore, I interpret the decision of Griffin J. in *Boland v. An Taoiseach* [1974] IR 338 as being consistent with the view already expressed by me that where an individual person comes before the Courts and establishes that action on the part of the Executive has breached or threatens to breach one or other of his constitutional rights that the Courts must intervene to protect those rights but that otherwise they can not and should not.

I, therefore, am satisfied that this appeal on this issue should be dismissed.

Walsh J.:

This part of the proceedings deals only with Title III of the Single European Act. The heading of that title is "Provisions on European cooperation in the sphere of foreign policy." This title is not included in the European Communities (Amendment) Act, 1986. Neither is the preamble to the Single European Act incorporated in or referred to by the said Act. The terms of the preamble are however relevant to the issue now before the Court concerning Title III. In its first paragraph the preamble refers to the will to continue work to transform relations between the Member States of the European Communities into a European Union. It goes on to say that the signatories are resolved to implement "this European Union" firstly on the basis of the Communities operating according to their own rules and, secondly, of European Cooperation among the Signatory States "in the sphere of foreign policy" and to invest this union "with the necessary means of action". It is abundantly clear, and indeed was not contested in the present case, that so far as Ireland is concerned the creation of a European Union which would include Ireland would require an amendment of the Constitution. Title III of the Single European Act, which in reality is itself a separate treaty although not so in form, does not purport to create a European Union; but on the other hand openly acknowledges that such is the objective.

The preamble goes on to state that the parties are determined "to work together to promote democracy on the basis of the fundamental rights recognised in the constitutions and laws of the Member States, in the Convention for the Protection of Human Rights and Fundamental Freedoms and the European Social Charter, notably freedom, equality and social justice." So far as the latter aspirations are concerned no objection could be taken to them having regard to the fact that the preamble of the Constitution of Ireland sets out that one of the aims of the Constitution is to safeguard the dignity and freedom of the individual and to assist in establishing concord with other nations. Article 5 of the Constitution says that Ireland is a sovereign, independent and democratic state. Article 29, s. 1 of the Constitution contains the affirmation that Ireland is devoted to the ideal of peace and friendly co-operation amongst nations founded on international justice and international morality (see the Irish language text of the Constitution).

The preamble to the Single European Act further refers to "the responsibility incumbent upon Europe to aim at speaking ever increasingly with one voice and to act with consistency and solidarity in order more effectively to protect its common interests and independence, in particular to display the principles of democracy and compliance with the law and with human rights to which they are attached, so that together they may make their own contribution to the preservation of international peace and security in accordance with the undertaking entered into by them within the framework of the United Nations Charter." The sentiments there expressed are also unexceptionable as a general objective of the European Community and of the individual Member States, and as such would appear to be in no way incompatible with the aims and aspirations of the Constitution in those fields.

It is however the treaty provisions set out in Title III which have given rise to the plaintiff's claim for an order to restrain the Government from ratifying the treaty already executed by them. Article 33, s. 1 of the Single European Act provides that it will be ratified "by the High Contracting Parties in accordance with their respective constitutional requirements." In essence therefore this part of the case is concerned with whether or not, as a matter of Irish law, the method of ratification proposed by the Government is in accordance with the Constitution, namely, whether it can now be ratified on the basis that its terms have been approved in their entirety by Dáil Éireann in accordance with Article 29, s. 5, sub-s. 2 of the constitution.

This brings me to a consideration of the relevant provisions of the Constitution and the treaty-making powers of the executive organ of Government (the "Government"). Article 6 of the Constitution refers to "all powers of government" and goes on to differentiate between the legislative, executive and judicial organs of government. It refers to the powers of government as being derived "under God, from the people, whose right it is to designate the rulers of the State and, in final appeal, to decide all questions of national policy, according to the requirements of the common good." It must follow therefore that all the powers of government are to be exercised according to the requirements of the common good. Section 2 of the same Article provides that these powers of government are exercisable "only by or on the authority of the organs of State established by this Constitution." So far as external or foreign relations are concerned Article 29, s. 4, sub-s. 1 of the Constitution provides that "the executive power of the State in or in connection with its external relations shall in accordance with Article 28 of this Constitution be exercised by or on the authority of 1the Government." Article 28, s. 2 provides that "the executive power of the State shall, subject to the provisions of this Constitution, be exercised by or on the authority of the Government."

The Constitution confers upon the Government the whole executive power of the State, subject to certain qualifications which I will deal with later, and the Government is bound to take care that the laws of the State are faithfully executed. In its external relations it has the power to make treaties, to maintain diplomatic relations with other sovereign States. The Government alone has the power to speak or to listen as a representative of the State in its external relations. It is the Government alone which negotiates and makes treaties and it is the sole organ of the State in the field of international affairs. For these functions it does not require as a basis for their exercise an Act of the Oireachtas. Nevertheless the powers must be exercised in subordination to the applicable provisions of the Constitution. It is not within the competence of the Government, or indeed of the Oireachtas, to free themselves from the restraints of the Constitution or to transfer their powers to other bodies unless expressly empowered so to do by the Constitution. They are both creatures of the Constitution and are not empowered to act free from the restraints of the Constitution. To the judicial organ of government alone is given the power conclusively to decide if there has been a breach of constitutional restraints.

The powers of external sovereignty on the part of the State do not depend on the affirmative grant of this in the Constitution. They are implicit in the provisions of Article 5 of the Constitution. The State would not be completely sovereign if it did not have in common with other members of the family of nations the right and power in the field of international relations equal to the right and power of other states. These powers of the State include the power to declare war or to participate in a war, to conclude peace, to make treaties, and maintain diplomatic relations with other states.

However the exercise of the power is limited. In the first instance the Government alone has the power, as already mentioned, to speak and listen as the representative of the State, and, subject to the constitutional restraints, to make treaties. Article 28, s. 3, sub-s. 1 of the Constitution provides that war shall not be declared and the State shall not participate in any war save with the assent of Dáil Éireann. That is one express constitutional prohibition on the exercise by the Government of its powers in its international relations. So far as treaties or international agreements are concerned Article 29, ss. 5 and 6 deal further with the matter. They provide that (a) every international agreement to which the State becomes a party shall be laid before Dáil Éireann, (b) the State shall not be bound by any international agreement involving a charge upon public funds unless: the terms of the agreement shall have been approved by Dáil Éireann (save where the agreements or conventions are of a technical and administrative character) and (c) no international agreement shall be part of the domestic law of the State save as may be determined by the Oireachtas. As a general rule neither the Government nor the Oireachtas can be restrained until their intentions are translated into acts. In proper cases they are subject to judicial cognisance, and judicial review and restraint. Thus statements of the Government policy as such are not restrainable by the Courts. But if the policies arc translated, for example, into treaties then different considerations arise.

In the present case counsel for the defendants submitted that even in the case of treaties the Courts are not empowered to interfere unless the treaties are translated into domestic legislation. To do so, the defendants asserted, would be for one of the organs of State to trespass upon the functions of another in a manner unauthorised by the Constitution. The defendants relied upon the decision of the former Supreme Court of Justice in *Buckley and Others (Sinn Féin) v. Attorney General* [1950] IR 67 in support of this proposition. That was a case in which legislation was impugned. The power to review legislation is expressly granted by the Constitution. What the Court was doing in that case was to interfere in what it regarded and described at p. 84 of the report as "an unwarrantable interference by the Oireachtas with the operation of the Courts in a purely judicial domain." It does not follow from that conclusion that the actions of the executive can never be reviewed by the Courts even in respect of matters which are on their face apparently within the exclusive domain of the Government. It is beyond dispute and well settled in many cases that one of the functions of the Courts is to uphold the Constitution. That includes restraining the Government from freeing themselves or purporting to free themselves from the restraints of the Constitution.

This issue was discussed at some length in this Court in the case of *Boland v. An Taoiseach* [1974] IR 338. The subject of that litigation was what became known as the "Sunningdale Agreement", and in particular clause 5 thereof. It was held by this Court that it was not an agreement or treaty but a communiqué containing declarations and assertions of policy, and therefore was not restrainable. In the course of his judgment in that case FitzGerald C.J. at p. 362 stated:–

> "Consequently, in my opinion, the Courts have no power, either express or implied, to supervise or interfere with the exercise by the Government of its executive functions, unless the circumstances are such as to amount to a clear disregard by the Government of the powers and duties conferred upon it by the Constitution."

O'Keeffe P. in the course of his judgment at p. 363 stated that it was clearly not within the competence of the Government to agree to depart from the terms of the Constitution. He found that the document in question was not such an agreement but simply a statement of policy. Budd

J. stated, and in my view correctly so, that the Courts could clearly not state that any particular policy ought not to be pursued and was of opinion that nothing more than a declaration of policy had been made and that there was not any agreement between the parties. It is to be inferred from his judgment that if an agreement were in existence different considerations would apply. Griffin J. in his judgment was also of opinion that the stage had not been reached in that case where the Courts could intervene as no formal agreement had been reached between the parties, and furthermore that if the contemplated agreement were reached it would have led to legislation which itself could be the subject of a constitutional challenge in the Courts. Pringle J. agreed that the appeal in that case should be dismissed for the reasons stated in the judgments, and that the Courts had no power to interfere with the exercise by the Government of its executive functions in the circumstances relied upon by the plaintiff. That, as I understand it, meant that Pringle J. was in agreement with his colleagues that nothing beyond the pronouncemment of a policy had taken place and that therefore the Courts could not intervene at that stage.

What is at issue in the present case is not simply a declaration of policy but an actual treaty. As it will obviously involve a charge upon the public funds the requirement of the Constitution in Article 29, s. 5, sub-s. 2, that it should be approved by Dáil Éireann, has been complied with. The State is not yet bound by this Treaty even though it has been laid before Dáil Éireann because its binding effect depends upon ratification in accordance with Irish "constitutional requirements". The question therefore is whether the State in attempting to ratify this Treaty is endeavouring to act free from the restraints of the Constitution.

The object of this Treaty, so far as Ireland is concerned, is to bind this State in its relations with the other Member States of the European Communities. Adherence to the Treaty, or indeed the Treaty itself, is not in any sense an obligation arising from or necessitated by membership of the European Communities. I do not accept the submission made on behalf of the defendants that unless and until the terms of the Treaty are translated into domestic legislation the Court has no competence in the matter. In international law the State in entering into a treaty must act in good faith. That is why the provision in the Treaty itself for ratification in accordance with the constitutional requirements of this State is so important. If some part or all of the Treaty were subsequently translated into domestic legislation and found to be unconstitutional it would avail the State nothing in its obligations to its fellow members. It would still be bound by the Treaty. Therefore if the ratification of this Treaty under the Irish Constitution requires a referendum to amend the Constitution to give effect to it, the fact that the State did not hold a referendum would not prevent the State from being bound in international law by the Treaty. If a referendum were to be held or had been held and the Treaty were rejected then the State would not be in breach of its international obligations because it would not have ratified the Treaty. It is not for the other states to the Treaty to satisfy themselves that the Government of Ireland observed its own constitutional requirements. This is solely a matter for the Government of Ireland and if it fails to take the necessary steps, the State cannot afterwards be heard to plead that it is not bound by the Treaty.

The Treaty does not purport to commit the State to agreeing to the establishment of a European Union of which Ireland would be a part. That is manifestly something to which the Government could not commit the State. What the Treaty does is to commit the State to pursuing a policy which has, *inter alia*, as one of its objectives the transformation of the relations of Ireland with the other Member States of the European communities into a European Union. If this were simply a unilateral statement of policy on the part of the Government or part of a multilateral declaration of policy to the like end it could not be called into question in this Court. As was pointed out by Budd J. in *Boland v. An Taoiseach* [1974] IR 338 at p. 366 it would, as such, be outside "the purview of the Courts in that it makes the Government responsible to the Dáil which can support or oppose those policies and review them." The present Treaty provisions go much further than that and, notwithstanding that, they have been approved by Dáil Éireann. As was pointed out in the decision of the Court in the first part of this case the essential nature of sovereignty is the right to say yes or to say no. In the present Treaty provisions that right is to be materially qualified.

It commits the State, and therefore all future Governments and the Oireachtas, to the other Member States to do the following things:–

(1) To endeavour to formulate and to implement a European foreign policy.
(2) To undertake to inform or consult the other Member States on any foreign policy matters of general interest (not just of common interest) so as to ensure that the combined influence of the States is exercised as effectively as possible through co-ordination, the convergence of their positions and the implementation of joint action.
(3) In adopting its position and in its national measures the State shall take full account of the position of the other Member States and shall give due consideration to the desirability of adopting and implementing common European positions.
(4) The State will ensure that with its fellow Member States common principles and objectives are gradually developed and defined.
(5) The State shall endeavour to avoid any action or position which impairs the effectiveness of the Community States as a cohesive force in international relations or within international organisations.
(6) The State shall so far as possible refrain from impeding the formation of a consensus and the joint action which this could produce.
(7) The State shall be ready to co-ordinate its position with the position of the other Member States more closely on the political and economic aspects of security.
(8) The State shall maintain the technological and industrial conditions necessary for security of the Member States and it shall work to that end at national level and, where appropriate, within the framework of the competent institutions and bodies.
(9) In international institutions and at international conferences which the State attends it shall endeavour to adopt a common position with the other Member States on subjects covered by Title III.
(10) In international institutions and at international conferences in which not all of the Member States participate the State, if it is one of those participating, shall take full account of the positions agreed in European Political Cooperation.

One other matter expressed in somewhat ambiguous terms at Article 6 (c) in Title II is as follows:–

> "Nothing in this Title shall impede closer cooperation in the field of security between certain of the High Contracting Parties within the framework of the Western European Union or the Atlantic Alliance."

One interpretation of that is that the Member States who are members of the Western European Union or the Atlantic Alliance (Ireland is not a member of either) can develop their own co-operation in those fields without being impeded by anything in Title III of this Treaty. However, it can also amount to an undertaking on the part of this State that in the exercise of whatever powers it may have under Title III it shall do nothing to impede such co-operation in the field of security in the framework of the Western European Union or the Atlantic Alliance on the part of those Member States which belong to those institutions.

All of these matters impinge upon the freedom of action of the State not only in certain areas of foreign policy but even within international organisations such as the United Nations or the Council of Europe. That latter effect of the Treaty could amount to the establishment of combinations within these organisations. In touching upon the maintenance of the technological and industrial conditions necessary for security the Treaty impinges upon the State's economic, industrial and defence policies. The obligation on the High Contracting Parties after five years to examine whether any revision of Title III is required does not give the Treaty a temporary character.

I mentioned earlier in this judgment that the Government is the sole organ of the State in the field of international relations. This power is conferred upon it by the Constitution which provides in Article 29, s. 4 that this power shall be exercised by or on the authority of the Government. In this area the Government must act as a collective authority and shall be collectively responsible to Dáil Éireann and ultimately to the people. In my view it would be quite incompatible with the freedom of action conferred on the Government by the Constitution for the Government to qualify that freedom or to inhibit it in any manner by formal agreement with other States as to qualify it. This view is, in my opinion, corroborated by the provisions of Article 29, s. 4, sub-s. 2 of the Constitution which provides:–

> "For the purpose of the exercise of any executive function of the State in or in connection with its external relations, the Government may to such extent and subject to such conditions, if any, as may be determined by law, avail of or adopt any organ, instrument, or method of procedure used or adopted for the like purpose by the members of any group or league of nations with which the State is or becomes associated for the purpose of international co-operation in matters of common concern."

The history of this particular provision is too well known to require elaboration but the wording is such that for the particular purpose of that provision the European Economic Community is in my view such a group or league of nations with which the State is associated for the purpose of international co-operation in matters of common concern. However the limitations are very clear. This provision relates solely to the exercise of the executive functions of this State in its external relations and is subject to such conditions, if any, as may be determined by law. Furthermore it simply provides for the adoption of any organ or instrument or method of procedure for the exercise of the executive functions of the State. It does not require prior consultation with any other State as to the policy itself. It also provides that there must be enabling legislation. The framers of the Constitution, and the people in enacting it, clearly foresaw the possibility of being associated with groups of nations for the purpose of international co-operation in matters of common concern and they provided for the possibility of the adoption of a common organ or instrument. Equally clearly they refrained from granting to the Government the power to bind the State by agreement with such groups of nations as to the manner or under what conditions that executive function of the State would be exercised.

In enacting the Constitution the people conferred full freedom of action upon the Government to decide matters of foreign policy and to act as it thinks fit on any particular issue so far as policy is concerned and as, in the opinion of the Government, the occasion requires. In my view, this freedom does not carry with it the power to abdicate that freedom or to enter into binding agreements with other States to exercise that power in a particular way or to refrain from exercising it save by particular procedures, and so to bind the State in its freedom of action in its foreign policy. The freedom to formulate foreign policy is just as much a mark of sovereignty as the freedom to form economic policy and the freedom to legislate. The latter two have now been curtailed by the consent of the people to the amendment of the Constitution which is contained in Article 29, s. 4, sub-s. 3 of the Constitution. If it is now desired to qualify, curtail or inhibit the existing sovereign power to formulate and to pursue such foreign policies as from time to time to the Government may seem proper, it is not within the power of the Government itself to do so. The foreign policy organ of the State cannot, within the terms of the Constitution, agree to impose upon itself, the State or upon the people the contemplated restrictions upon freedom of action. To acquire the power to do so would, in my opinion, require a recourse to the people "whose right it is" in the words of Article 6 "...in final appeal, to decide all questions of national policy, according to the requirements of the common good." In the last analysis it is the people themselves who are the guardians of the Constitution. In my view, the assent of the people is a necessary prerequisite to the ratification of so much of the Single European Act as consists of title III thereof. On these grounds I would allow this appeal.

Henchy J.:

The Single European Act ("the SEA") is something of a misnomer, for it is a treaty rather than an instrument with the legislative connotations usually attaching to an Act. As a treaty it has a dual purpose: (1) to amend and supplement the Treaties on which the European Communities are founded; and (2) to put on a formal basis co-operation between the Member States in the field of foreign policy. It is with the latter objective, which is dealt with in Title III of the SEA, that we are concerned in this part of the plaintiff's appeal.

Title III (which is headed "Provisions on European cooperation in the sphere of foreign policy") deals with matters which are outside the scope of the existing treaties. This is evidenced by the two opening paragraphs of the preamble to the SEA:–

> "MOVED by the will to continue the work undertaken on the basis of the Treaties establishing the European Communities and to transform relations as a whole among their States into a European Union, in accordance with the Solemn Declaration of Stuttgart of 19 June 1983,
> RESOLVED to implement this European Union on the basis, firstly, of the Communities operating in accordance with their own rules and, secondly, of European Cooperation among the Signatory States in the sphere of foreign policy and to invest this union with the necessary means of action."

It is clear, therefore, that, so far as Title III is concerned, Ireland's constitutional authority for ratifying the SEA is not to be found in Article 29, s. 4, sub-s. 3 of the Constitution, which is the constitutional amendment which allowed Ireland to become a member of the European Communities. One must look elsewhere in the Constitution to see if there are express or implied provisions which would make Ireland's ratification of Title III consistent with the Constitution.

It is first necessary to make clear the scope and objective of Title III, all of which is contained in Article 30 of the SEA. Article 30, s. 1 provides that the Member States of the European Communities "shall endeavour to formulate and implement a European foreign policy." Thus, unlike the main part of the SEA. Article 30 is not intended to be an amendment of the existing Treaties but sets the Member States on a course leading to an eventual European Union in the sphere of foreign policy. Pending the attainment of that objective, which is outside the stated aims of the existing Treaties, the Member States become bound to formulate and conduct their foreign policy according to the terms stated in Article 30. What had been no more than an objective declared by the Stuttgart Declaration of 1983 is now to become a matter of solemn treaty.

The essence of this fundamental transformation in the relations between the Member States of the European Communities is that they are no longer to have separate foreign policies but are, as far as possible, to merge their national foreign policies in a European (i.e. Community) foreign policy and to work together in the manner indicated, so as to implement what is called European Political Cooperation, with a view to achieving eventual European union.

The principal courses of conduct to which the High Contracting Parties bind themselves are set out in s. 2 of Article 30:–

> "(*a*) The High Contracting Parties undertake to inform and consult each other on any foreign policy matters of general interest so as to ensure that their combined influence is exercised as effectively as possible through coordination, the convergence of their positions and the implementation of joint action.

(*b*) Consultations shall take place before the High Contracting Parties decide on their final position.
(*c*) In adopting its positions and in its national measures each High Contracting Party shall take full account of the positions of the other partners and shall give due consideration to the desirability of adopting and implementing common European positions.

In order to increase their capacity for joint action in the foreign policy field, the High Contracting Parties shall ensure that common principles and objectives are gradually developed and defined.

The determination of common positions shall constitute a point of reference for the policies of the High Contracting Parties.
(*d*) The High Contracting Parties shall endeavour to avoid any action or position which impairs their effectiveness as a cohesive force in international relations or within international organizations."

Without going further into Article 30, it is clear from those provisions that once the Member States ratify this Treaty each state's foreign policy will move from a national to a European or Community level. Apart from becoming bound to *endeavour* jointly to formulate and implement a European foreign policy, each Member State will become specifically bound to inform and consult its fellow-members, to refrain from deciding on a final position as to an issue of foreign policy without prior consultations, to *take full account* of the positions of the other partners in adopting its positions and in its national measures, to *ensure* that common principles and objectives are gradually developed and defined, and to recognise that the determination of common positions *shall* constitute a point of reference.

Those and other commitments expressed in Article 30 make manifest that, although the approach to the ultimate aim of European Union is to be reached by a pathway of gradualism, each Member State will immediately cede a portion of its sovereignty and freedom of action in matters of foreign policy. National objectives and ideological positions must defer to the aims and decisions of an institution known as European Political Cooperation, which is to work in tandem with the European Communities. A purely national approach to foreign policy is incompatible with accession to this Treaty. The methods of co-operation between the Member States, which hitherto have been informal, aspirational or, at most, declaratory (as under the Stuttgart Declaration), now pass into a realm of solemnly covenanted commitment to the conduct of foreign policy in a way that will lead to European political union, at least in the sphere of foreign policy. In that respect, Title III of the SEA is the threshold leading from what has hitherto been essentially an economic Community to what will now also be a political Community.

In the case of Ireland, it is proposed that this transformation be effected not by any amendment of the Constitution, nor by any statutory change in the domestic law, but by simply depositing an instrument of ratification of the SEA. The fundamental and far-reaching changes in the conduct of the State's foreign policy to which I have referred would thus be effected by the Government, without reference to the people and without an Act of parliament. Counsel for the Government has sought to justify this approach by submitting that, because Article 29, s. 4, sub-s. 1 of the Constitution has committed the conduct of foreign policy to the Government, the Courts are not entitled to control the Government in the way it decides to conduct foreign policy. It is therefore contended that the plaintiff's claim is ill-founded.

I am unable to accept the submission that the powers of Government in the conduct of foreign policy are not amenable to control by the Courts. It is true that Article 29, s. 4, sub-s. 1 of the Constitution provides that "the executive power of the State in or in connection with its external relations shall in accordance with Article 28 of this Constitution be exercised by or on the authority of the Government." However, when one turns to Article 28 one finds that s. 2 of that Article clarifies the position by declaring that "the executive power of the State shall, *subject to the provisions of this Constitution*, be exercised by or on the authority of the Government." (Emphasis added). It follows, therefore, that in the conduct of the State's external relations, as in the exercise of the executive power in other respects, the Government is not immune from judicial control if it acts in a manner or for a purpose which is inconsistent with the Constitution. Such control is necessary to give effect to the limiting words "subject to the provisions of this Constitution."

In testing the constitutional validity of the proposed ratification of the SEA (insofar as it contains Title III) it is important to note that the Constitution at the very outset declares as follows in Article 1:–

> "The Irish nation hereby affirms its inalienable, indefeasible, and sovereign right...to determine its relations with other nations...in accordance with its own genius and traditions."

It appears to me that this affirmation means that the State's right to conduct its external relations is part of what is inalienable and indefeasible in what is described in Article 5 as "a sovereign, independent, democratic State." It follows, in my view, that any attempt by the Government to make a binding commitment to alienate in whole or in part to other states the conduct of foreign relations would be inconsistent with the Government's duty to conduct those relations in accordance with the Constitution.

The ultimate source and limits of the Government's powers in the conduct of foreign relations are to be found in Article 6, s. 1 of the Constitution: -

> "All powers of government, legislative, executive and judicial, derive, under God, from the people, whose right it is to designate the rulers of the State and, in final appeal, to decide all questions of national policy, according to the requirements of the common good."

It follows that the common good of the Irish people is the ultimate standard by which the constitutional validity of the conduct of foreign affairs by the Government is to be judged. In this and in a number of other respects throughout the Constitution the central position of the common good of the Irish people is stressed as one of the most fundamental characteristics of Ireland as a sovereign, independent, democratic state.

A perusal of Title III of the SEA satisfies me that each ratifying Member State will be bound to surrender part of its sovereignty in.the conduct of foreign relations. That is to happen as part of a process designed to formulate and implement a European foreign policy. The freedom of action of each state is to be curtailed in the interests of the common good of the Member States as a whole. Thus, for example, in regard to Ireland, while under the Constitution the point of reference for the determination of a final position on any issue of foreign relations is the common good of the Irish people, under Title III the point of reference is required to be the common position determined by Member States. It is to be said that such a common position cannot be reached without Ireland's consent, but Title III is not framed in a manner which would allow Ireland to refuse to reach a common position on the ground of its obligations under the Irish Constitution. There is no provision in the Treaty for a derogation by Ireland where its constitutional obligations so require. On the contrary, Title III expressly provides:–

> "In adopting its positions and in its national measures [which presumably would include Acts of the Oireachtas] each High Contracting Party shall take full account of the positions of the other partners and shall give due consideration to the desirability of adopting and implementing common European positions."

Thus, if the other Member States were to take up a common position on an issue of external relations, Ireland, in adopting its own position and in its national measures, would be bound by Title III to "take full account" of the common position of the other Member States. To be bound by a solemn international treaty to act thus is, in my opinion, inconsistent with the obligation of the Government to conduct its foreign relations according to the common good of the Irish people. In this and in other respects Title III amounts to a diminution of Ireland's sovereignty which is declared in unqualified terms in the Irish Constitution.

It is urged on behalf of the Government that the changes in existing inter-state relations effected by Title III are slight, that it does little more than formalise existing practices and procedures by converting them into binding obligations. This, I fear, is to underestimate the true nature in international law of a treaty as distinct from a mere practice or procedure, and to misinterpret the commitments for the future involved in Title III. As a treaty, Title III is not designed in static terms. It not alone envisages changes in inter-state relations, but also postulates and requires those changes. And the purpose of those changes is to erode national independence in the conduct of external relations in the interests of European political cohesion in foreign relations. As I have pointed out, the treaty marks the transformation of the European Communities from an organisation which has so far been essentially economic to one that is to be political also. It goes beyond existing arrangements and practices, in that it establishes within the framework of the Communities new institutions and offices (such as European Political Cooperation, the Political Director and the Political Committee) and charts a route of co-ordination, by means such as working parties, a secretariat and regular meetings, so as to give impetus to the drive for European unity.

All this means that if Ireland were to ratify the Treaty it would be bound in international law to engage actively in a programme which would trench progressively on Ireland's independence and sovereignty in the conduct of foreign relations. Ireland would therefore become bound to act in a way that would be inconsistent with the Constitution. The Government's constitutional mandate requires it to act in accordance with the Constitution. In proposing to ratify this treaty it is in effect seeking to evade that obligation and to substitute for it an obligation, or a series of obligations, in international law which cannot be reconciled with the constitutional obligations.

There is, of course, nothing in the Constitution to prevent the Government, or any person or group or institution, from advocating or campaigning for or otherwise working for a change in the Constitution. Likewise there does not appear to be any constitutional bar to a non-binding arrangement by the State to consult with other states in the conduct of its foreign policy. It is quite a different matter when, as here, it is proposed that the State be bound by an international treaty which requires the State to act in the sphere of foreign relations in a manner which would be inconsistent with constitutional requirements. What would be an imperative under international law would be proscribed under the Constitution. In such circumstances it is the Constitution that must prevail.

For the foregoing reasons I am of the opinion that, without the appropriate constitutional amendment, the ratification of the SEA (insofar as it contains Title III) would be impermissible under the Constitution. I would declare accordingly.

Griffin J.:

I agree with the judgment delivered by the Chief Justice. I should like however to add some observations of my own.

Title III, although included in the Single European Act (SEA), and set out in Article 30 in that Act, is effectively a separate treaty between the twelve countries who are the Member States of the European Communities. They are referred to throughout that Title as the High Contracting Parties ("the parties"), the designation usually applied to states in international treaties. The long term aim and objective of Title III is the formation of a European union. It is not in issue that if the State were to join such a union, a constitutional amendment would be necessary, but a European union is neither sought to be created nor is it created by the Treaty.

There has been European Political Cooperation (EPC) since October, 1970, (prior to the entry of the State to the Communities), when the first report of the Foreign Ministers of the Members States was adopted at Luxembourg. In that report the governments undertook to co-operate in the field of foreign policy by consulting regularly, harmonising views and opinions, concerting attitudes, and, where possible, undertaking joint action. There were three subsequent reports in 1973, 1981 and 1983, and Article I of the SEA provided that political co-operation should be governed by Title III and that the provisions of that Title should confirm and supplement the *procedures* agreed in the four reports and the *practices* gradually established among the Member States. The purpose of Title III-which is entitled "Treaty Provisions on European Cooperation in the sphere of foreign policy"-appears to be to formalise the procedures and practices of the EPC and to do so by means of a treaty. By virtue of Article 32 of the SEA, nothing in Title III is to affect the Treaties establishing the Communities, so it does not purport to amend the Treaties in any way.

Details or summaries of the provisions of Article 30 have been included in the judgments already delivered and I go not propose to repeat them, although I will refer to some of those provisions. The language used in Article 30 would appear to have been chosen with extreme care to ensure that the obligations of the parties under the treaty would permit the utmost freedom of action to each of the parties in the sphere of foreign policy, and is in stark contrast to that used in Title II. For example, the parties are to *endeavour* to formulate and implement a foreign policy; to *inform* and *consult* each other on foreign policy matters; *consultations* are to take place before deciding on their final position; they are to *endeavour to avoid* any action or position which impairs their effectiveness as a cohesive force; they are *as far as possible* to refrain from impeding a consensus; in international institutions and at international conferences they are to *endeavour to adopt* common positions on the subjects covered by the Title, and where not all the parties participate in such institutions or conferences, they are to take full account of positions agreed in EPC. On security, the parties are expressed to be ready to co-ordinate their positions more closely on the political and economic aspects of security-military and defence aspects of security are not included and in my view should accordingly be considered to be excluded. Under clause 6 (c) nothing in Title III is to impede closer co-operation in the field of security between certain of the parties within the framework of the Western European Union or the Atlantic Alliance-this provision would appear clearly to have been inserted to ensure that the declared stand on neutrality and military alliances taken by the State is fully respected, as the State is the only party which is not a member of either alliance, although four other parties are also not members of the Western European Union.

Having regard to the terms in which the provisions of Title III are expressed, I am in complete agreement with the Chief Justice in concluding that those provisions do not impose any obligations to cede any sovereignty or national interest in the field of foreign policy, nor do they in any way allow a decision of the State on any issue of foreign policy to be overridden or vetoed. The Treaty, being an international agreement to which the State is a party, has been laid before and been approved by Dáil Éireann in compliance with the provisions of Article 29, s. 5, sub-ss. 1 and 2 of the Constitution. The Government is therefore, in my opinion, as the organ of government by which the executive power of the State is to be exercised pursuant to Article 29, s. 4 of the Constitution, entitled to ratify the Treaty without the necessity of an amendment of the Constitution.

However, there remains, as the Chief Justice pointed out in his judgment, an issue of a fundamental nature, i.e., as to whether the Court is entitled, at the instance of the plaintiff, to prevent the Government from ratifying the Treaty. In presenting the argument on behalf of the plaintiff, his counsel Mr. Browne, in relation to Title III, based his right to seek the intervention of this Court to prevent ratification of the Treaty on an apprehension on the part of the plaintiff that Title III would affect the independence of the State in relation to foreign policy, even though, as he put it, the Treaty had not become part of the domestic law of the State under Article 29, section 6.

This brings into question the power of the Court to intervene in the acts of the Executive and inevitably to consideration of the separation of powers provided for in the Constitution.

Article 6 of the Constitution reads as follows:–

> "1. All powers of government, legislative, executive and judicial, derive, under God, from the people, whose right it is to designate the rulers of the State and, in final appeal, to decide all questions of national policy, according to the requirements of the common good.
> 2. These powers of government are exercisable only by or on the authority of the organs of State established by this Constitution."

The effect of this Article has been considered and interpreted in a number of cases, which include *Buckley and Others (Sinn Féin) v. Attorney General* [1950] IR 67 and *Boland v. An Taoiseach* [1974] IR 338. In *Buckley's Case* O'Byrne J. delivered the judgment of the Court and said at p. 81 that the object of Article 6 was:–

> "...to recognise and ordain that, in this State, all powers of government should be exercised in accordance with the well- recognised principle of the distribution of powers between the legislative, executive and judicial organs of the State and to require that these powers should not be exercised otherwise. The subsequent articles are designed to carry into effect this distribution of powers."

Under Article 15, s. 2, sub-s. 1 the Oireachtas is the organ of State in which the sole and exclusive power of making laws is vested. Article 15, s. 4, sub-s. 1 provides that the Oireachtas shall not enact any law which is in any respect repugnant to the Constitution or to any provision thereof; and sub-s. 2 of that section provides that every law enacted by the Oireachtas which is in any respect repugnant to the Constitution or to any provision thereof shall, but to the extent only of such repugnancy, be invalid. Under Article 34, s. 1 the judicial power of government can be exercised only by judges duly appointed in the manner provided by the Constitution in courts established by law under the Constitution. The High Court and this Court on appeal from the High Court are by Article 34, s. 3, sub-s. 2 expressly given jurisdiction to examine the validity of any law enacted under Article 15 which may be challenged as being repugnant to the Constitution or to any provision thereof. If the challenged Act or any provision thereof is found to be invalid by the High Court or by this Court, the Court so finding is bound to declare that the impugned Act or provision thereof is invalid. Those Articles provide the only power given to the Courts by the Constitution to declare invalid legislation enacted by the Oireachtas.

In the case of a Bill referred to this Court by the President, pursuant to Article 26 of the Constitution, for a decision on the question as to whether such Bill or any specified provision or provisions of such Bill is or are repugnant to the Constitution or to any provision thereof, this Court is by Article 26, s. 2, sub-s. 1 given express power, and has the duty, to consider such question and pronounce its decision on such question. This is the only power given to any Court to consider a Bill which has not yet become law.

In my opinion, the Courts have no power, either express or implied, to interfere with the Oireachtas in the course of the passage of a Bill, and all efforts seeking to prevent by Court interference the introduction or passage of a Bill have failed, the most recent example being the unsuccessful attempt by the plaintiff in this case to prevent the introduction of the European Communities (Amendment) Bill, 1986.

Article 28, s. 2 provides that the executive power of the State shall, subject to the provisions of the Constitution, be exercised by or on the authority of the Government. Under s. 4, sub-s. 1 of Article 28 the Government shall be responsible to Dáil Éireann. Article 29, s. 4, sub-s. 1 provides that the executive power of the State in or in connection with its external relations shall in accordance with Article 28 of the Constitution be exercised by or on the authority of the Government.

No express power is given by the Constitution to the Courts to interfere in any way with the Government in exercising the executive power of the State. However, the Government, and all of its members and the administration in respect of which the members are responsible, are subject to the intervention of the Courts to ensure that in their actions they keep within the bounds of lawful authority. Where such actions infringe or threaten to infringe the rights of individual citizens or persons, the Courts not only have the right to interfere with the executive power but have the constitutional obligation and duty to do so. But that right to interfere arises only where the citizen or person who seeks the assistance of the Courts can show that there has been an actual or threatened invasion or infringement of such rights.

As stated earlier, the executive power of the State in or in connection with its external relations shall, in accordance with Article 28, be exercised by or on behalf of the Government. Under Article 29, s. 5, sub-s. 1 every international agreement to which the State becomes a party shall be laid before Dáil Éireann, and under sub-s. 2 of that section the State shall not be bound by any international agreement involving a charge upon public funds unless the terms of the agreement shall have been approved by Dáil Éireann, Dáil Éireann being the body to which the Government is expressly answerable under Article 28, s. 4, sub-s. 1. The constitutional scheme in respect of international agreements would appear therefore to be that the Government, exercising the executive power, may enter into international agreements, but such agreements must be laid before Dáil Éireann, and if the agreement involves a charge on public funds, the State is not to be bound by the agreement unless the terms of the agreement have been approved of by Dáil Éireann.

The power of the Court to interfere with the exercise by the Government of the executive power of the State was considered by this Court in *Boland v. An Taoiseach* [1974] IR 338. FitzGerald C.J., having referred to the statement of O'Byrne J. in *Buckley & Others (Sinn Féin) v. Attorney General* [1950] IR 67 and to the separation of the executive, legislative and judicial powers of government in Article 6 of the Constitution, said at p. 362:–

> "Consequently, in my opinion, the Courts have no power, either express or implied, to supervise or interfere with the exercise by the Government of its executive functions, unless the circumstances are such as to amount to a clear disregard by the Government of the powers and duties conferred upon it by the Constitution."

And in the same case, I said at p. 370:–

> "Counsel for the defendants argued that in no circumstances may the Courts interfere with the Government in the exercise of its executive functions. For the purpose of this action it is not necessary to determine this question in the form in which the argument was made, as the defendants need only show that the Courts cannot and should not intervene having regard to the circumstances of the present case. In the event of the Government acting in a manner which is in contravention of some provisions of the constitution, in my view it would be the duty and right of the Courts, as guardians of the Constitution, to intervene when called upon to do so if a complaint of a breach of any of the provisions of the Constitution is substantiated in proceedings brought before the Courts."

I see no reason to resile from what is stated in that passage, which was said in the context of an unqualified submission by counsel for the defendants that it is no part of the function of the judicial organ of the State to interfere with the Government in the exercise by it of the executive power of the State. In that case, in discussions arising out of that submission, members of the Court put to counsel for the defendants the example of a declaration of war by the Government without the assent of Dáil Éireann, in clear breach of the provisions of Article 28, s. 3 of the Constitution, as being a circumstance in which the Court would be bound to intervene to protect a citizen against what would undoubtedly be an invasion of his rights and a justiciable matter. I fully endorse the opinion of the Chief Justice that there is nothing in the provisions of Articles 28 and 29 of the Constitution from which it would be possible to imply any general right in the Courts to interfere with the exercise of the executive power in the sphere or area of external relations, but that in any instance where the exercise of that power constitutes an actual or threatened invasion or breach of the constitutional rights of an individual the Courts must have both the right and the duty to intervene to protect those rights. The decision in *Boland v. An Taoiseach* [1974] IR 338 is in my opinion consistent with that view.

In my judgment, the plaintiff has failed to establish any such invasion or breach of any of his rights resulting from the State being a party to the Treaty the provisions of which are set out in Title III.

I would accordingly dismiss this appeal.

Hederman J.:

I agree with the judgments of Walsh J. and Henchy J. for the reasons given by them. There is little I can usefully add.

It appears to me that the essential point at issue is whether the State can by any act on the part of its various organs of government enter into binding agreements with other states, or groups of states, to subordinate, or to submit, the exercise of the powers bestowed by the Constitution to the advice or interests of other states, as distinct from electing from time to time to pursue its own particular policies in union or in concert with other states in their pursuit of their own similar or even identical policies.

The State's organs cannot contract to exercise in a particular procedure their policy-making roles or in any way to fetter powers bestowed unfettered by the Constitution. They are the guardians of these powers -not the disposers of them. For the reasons already stated I would allow the appeal.

Delahunty v Player & Wills (Ireland) Ltd.

[2006] IESC 21

Author's note: This case is an interesting first consideration of the Product Liability Directive. No preliminary reference followed.

This is an appeal from the decision of the High Court (O'Leary J) refusing to dismiss the plaintiff's claim against the second-named defendant (hereinafter the appellant) on the grounds that the pleadings disclose no reasonable cause of action or, alternatively, under the inherent jurisdiction of the court.

The plaintiff, a life-long smoker, has sued the first two defendants, both well-known tobacco manufacturers, for personal injuries allegedly caused by the cigarettes she smoked over many years. The third, fourth and fifth named defendants were joined in the action so that the plaintiff could claim failure on the part of the state effectively to regulate the sale of tobacco products. Neither that claim nor the claim against the first-named defendant has anything to do with the present appeal.

The appellant issued a notice of motion in the High Court seeking:

(*a*) An order pursuant to Order 19 Rule 28 of the Rules of the Superior Courts dismissing the plaintiff's claim against the appellant as disclosing no reasonable cause of action.
(*b*) Further or in the alternative, an order pursuant to the inherent jurisdiction of that Court dismissing the plaintiff's claim against the appellant on the grounds that it has no reasonable prospects of success or, alternatively, is bound to fail.

The plaintiff's pleads causes of action founded on alleged negligence, breach of duty, and breach of statutory duty including, in particular breaches of the Liability for Defective Products Act 1991 and of Council Directive 85/374/EEC of 5th July 1985.

The statement of claim did not differentiate between the first two defendants and contained the following general plea:

> *"The Plaintiff has smoked cigarettes produced, manufactured, promoted and/or sold by the first and second named Defendants their respective servants and/or agents, for more than fifty years and she has now learned that the said cigarettes were defective in that they, inter alia, were and are addictive and did at all material times hereto contain and produce substances and additives which were inherently dangerous to the health and welfare of all those who consumed the said cigarettes, including the Plaintiff. The first and second named Defendants, their respective servants and/or agents deliberately and knowingly used substances and/or chemical additives in their cigarettes to create dependency and addiction amongst those, including the Plaintiff, who consumed such products."*

The foregoing paragraph contains the essence of the case made by the plaintiff, though it is particularised in much greater detail both in the statement of claim and the replies to notices for particulars delivered on behalf of the plaintiff. In effect, the tobacco manufacturers are alleged to have manufactured and placed on the market products which they knew to be dangerous to health and to have advertised and promoted their sale on the basis that they were safe. The plaintiff lays particular emphasis on the allegation that the cigarettes were, to the knowledge of the manufacturers, addictive and, moreover, that the manufacturers caused or permitted chemical additives to be used in their manufacture with the effect of enhancing nicotine delivery and facilitating the onset and maintenance of nicotine dependence.

As a result of the delivery of detailed particulars by the plaintiff on 23rd September 2003, a sharp distinction emerged between the first two defendants so far as the plaintiff's claim is concerned. I will recount the basic facts as briefly as I can.

The plaintiff was born in 1926. She commenced smoking cigarettes manufactured by the first-named defendant in 1938. She became addicted at that time. She continued to smoke cigarettes—twenty to thirty per day— manufactured by the first-named defendant, though she changed to a tipped brand in the 1960's. The plaintiff became ill in 1995, suffering from coughing, including coughing blood, recurrent chest infections, weight loss and shortness of breath. Following extensive tests, she underwent an upper lobectomy operation on 16th October 1995 and a poorly differentiated squamous cell carcinoma was found with extensive necrosis. This was removed.

The plaintiff pleads in the particulars that she learned of the harm caused by cigarettes, including addiction, from her medical practitioners after the diagnosis of her cancer in October 1995. At that time, she states that she changed her brand to "Silk Cut Extra Mild," manufactured by the appellant. She has smoked and continues to smoke that brand at the rate of about twenty a day. Because of her addiction, she is unable to give up smoking.

It is complained on her behalf that she has suffered continuing injury since 1995 and that that such injury was cause by smoking cigarettes manufactured by the appellant. The appellant disputes whether this is indeed properly pleaded and I will discuss that matter later.

Mr Paul Sreenan, Senior Counsel, accepted, on behalf of the appellant that the statement of claim, taken in isolation, does contain a plea of a reasonable cause of action. It is common case, however, that the Court may take the particulars into account, in assessing the pleadings.

Mr Sreenan makes the following points:

- There is no reasonable cause of action in respect of the alleged defects in the cigarettes manufactured and sold by the appellant. It is not alleged that the cigarettes were in any way different from or defective by comparison with other cigarettes or any standard for cigarettes. They were lawfully marketed and sold. Indeed, in recent years their advertising, packaging, labelling and sale have been highly regulated. The cigarettes manufactured by the appellant were not defective in the sense of providing *"the safety which a person is entitled to expect"* for the purposes of section 5 of the Liability for Defective Products Act 1991. That Act does not cover products which carry an inherent risk;
- By reason of the foregoing, it was perfectly lawful to sell the products. Mr Sreenan posed the question: what could the appellant have done? In reality, it could have avoided liability only by withdrawing their cigarettes from the market. It cannot be reasonable to say that a manufacturer can avoid liability only by going out of business;
- The plaintiff had sustained her injury before she ever smoked a cigarette manufactured by the appellant. It is not pleaded that she suffered any additional damage after October 1995, when she commenced smoking the appellant's cigarettes, which could be attributed to the appellant;
- Mr Sreenan argued that the injuries alleged by the plaintiff could not be attributed to the appellant. The plaintiff pleads that she was addicted to cigarettes, as a result of smoking the cigarettes of the first-named defendant and long before she ever smoked those manufactured by the appellant. At the time she commenced smoking the appellant's cigarettes, she accepts that she knew that smoking cigarettes had caused her cancer. If it were not for her addiction, she could not reasonably make the case that the appellant was liable to her. She knew perfectly well that smoking was liable to cause damage to her health. Insofar as she explains her behaviour by reference to her addiction, that was not the responsibility of the appellant.

Mr Michael Cush, Senior Counsel, for the plaintiff responded to these points:

- He accepted that there was scope for argument in respect of Mr Sreenan's first point, but such arguments should take place at the trial and were not the basis for dismissing the action. The plaintiff's claim is based on negligence at common law as well as under the Act of 1991. In the latter respect, Mr Cush submits that the Act imposes absolute liability. Insofar as the appellant relies on state regulation of the sale of its products, an issue will arise as to the extent to which full disclosure was made to state authorities in respect of the contents of and risks associated with the smoking of cigarettes.
- As to the pleading of injury after 1995, Mr Cush refers to a report of Professor O'Neill exhibited in the affidavit sworn on this motion by the plaintiff's solicitor, which discloses fresh injury at a time when the plaintiff was smoking only the appellant's cigarettes. He says that Mr Sreenan had argued that the particulars given of the plaintiff's post-1995 injuries were referable to her pre-existing injury, but had placed no affidavit evidence before the Court;
- In response to the argument that the appellant was not responsible for causing the plaintiff's addiction, Mr Cush stated that the plaintiff would make the case that the appellant specifically aimed the marketing of its "Silk Cut Extra Mild," brand of cigarettes, at least in part at people such as the plaintiff who, though already addicted, were concerned about the health risks.

The foregoing replicated very largely the argument made by the appellant in the High Court, though I have the impression that the principal emphasis there was on the causation argument, namely that the plaintiff's addiction was not caused by the appellant. O'Leary J ruled on that matter as follows:

> *"It is a matter for evidence at the trial to assess whether the nature of the addiction to cigarettes (the existence of which the Court must presume for this application) renders it impossible or unreasonable for a person so addicted to stop smoking when confronted with a life-threatening situation. It is not a matter to be decided without evidence at this stage. If it is decided that the addiction was such as to make it impossible or unreasonable for the plaintiff to stop smoking she may well be entitled to damages for any post operative injury subject of course to the other defence pleas.*
>
> *If it is found by the trial Court that the plaintiff is entitled to post operative damages (based on her continued smoking by reason of addiction) it would be open to the Court to find both the supplier who caused her addiction and the supplier who fed that addiction jointly and/or severally liable for post operative damage. The submission that the later supplier who fed but did not create her addiction could not be liable is rejected.*
>
> *The Court has considered whether there could be a causal link between the matters identified in the pleadings i.e. the alleged damage on the one hand and the alleged negligence and breach of duty listed above on the other, is satisfied that such a link could be established. Whether such a link will ever be established depends on the strength of the evidence before the Court of trial."*

However, O'Leary J also expressed the view that the report of Prof Shane O'Neill "(on one reading) links the continued smoking by the plaintiff to progressive lung damage."

The two bases invoked by the appellant in seeking to have the plaintiff's claim dismissed are complementary. They are designed to prevent actions being pursued in the courts which are entirely devoid of merit. The jurisdiction under the rules depends on the moving party—for the burden is on him—being able to show that the pleadings "d*isclose no reasonable cause of action"* or to be *frivolous or vexatious."* The alternative basis involves reliance on the inherent jurisdiction of the Court and can be traced back to the judgment of Costello J in *Barry v Buckley* [1981] I.R. 306. The circumstances in which that exceptional jurisdiction will be exercised were explained by Costello J (on 2nd October 1992) in *D.K. v King* [1994] 1 I.R. 166, at page 170:

> *"The principles on which the court will exercise its inherent jurisdiction to strike out a plaintiff's action can be shortly stated. Basically, the jurisdiction exists to ensure that an abuse of the court's process does not take place. If it is established by satisfactory evidence that the proceedings are frivolous or vexatious or if it is clear that the plaintiff's claim must fail then the court may stay the action. But it will only exercise this jurisdiction sparingly and in clear cases......"*

That passage received the express approval of this Court in the judgment of Blayney J in *O'Neill v Ryan and others* [1993] I.L.R.M. 557. Although this remedy is available in the case of any cause of action, it is clear from the cases that it is likely to be more suitable for use in cases where there is no room for dispute about the evidence. For example, orders have been made under this jurisdiction in some cases of written contracts, where the terms of the law and the applicable principles are readily ascertainable.

In my opinion, this is not a suitable case for the remedy either under the Rules of the Superior Courts or the inherent jurisdiction of the Court. There are complex and difficult issues of both law and fact to be decided, which are more appropriately argued and tested at the full hearing of the action. The plaintiff seeks to make the tobacco companies amenable for selling cigarettes which they sold but which she voluntarily consumed. It is well known that there has been tobacco litigation of many types in many jurisdictions. It is neither necessary nor appropriate that I say more than the minimum required to dispose of this appeal and this motion.

For the purposes of this appeal, it must be assumed—Mr Sreenan did not ask the Court to do otherwise—that the plaintiff suffered very serious illness as a result of smoking cigarettes. Mr Cush made a very simple submission with regard to the Act of 1991. He says it imposes a strict liability. That depends on the cigarettes being regarded as defective products for the purposes of the Act. Section 5(1) of the Act provides:

> *"For the purposes of this Act a product is defective if it fails to provide the safety which a person is entitled to expect, taking all circumstances into account, including—*
> (*a*) the presentation of the product,
> (*b*) the use to which it could reasonably be expected that the product would be put, and
> (*c*) the time when the product was put into circulation."

I do not think a court could possibly decide, on a motion of the type before the Court on this appeal, whether cigarettes *"fail to provide the safety which a person is entitled to expect."* That will require a great deal of evidence to be given at the trial. It is also highly material that the Act of 1991 was passed in order to transpose into Irish law the provisions of the Council Directive of 1985 mentioned above. The definition of defective product is based on Article 6 of the Directive. The Act must be interpreted in the light of the Directive. If the matter comes before this Court in circumstances where a decision on such an interpretation is necessary for the decision of the Court, it would appear that the obligation of the Court to refer this matter to the Court of Justice of the European Communities pursuant to Article 234 of the EC Treaty would arise. That will, of course, depend on whether such an interpretation is necessary for its decision. For that reason alone, it would be impossible to determine such an important issue at this stage. Furthermore, the High Court may wish to refer such questions to the Court of Justice and may do so at any stage of the proceedings.

I am also of the view that the claim based on liability for defective products at common law cannot be dismissed at this stage. In a situation where it has to be assumed that the product admittedly sold caused damage to the plaintiff's health, it would require very clear authority to convince a court that it is unarguable that the manufacturer is liable. I will say no more.

I am also satisfied that it is sufficiently pleaded that the plaintiff suffered injury as a result of smoking the appellant's cigarettes after 1995. Firstly, the statement of claim contains sufficient general and undifferentiated pleadings, for the purposes of Order 19, rule 28, that the plaintiff suffered personal injuries as a result of the negligence and other wrongdoing of all the defendants. Secondly, the particulars furnished in September 2003 contain allegations of extensive health difficulties after 1995, though not making any distinction between the effects of smoking the cigarettes of the respective defendants. Thirdly, in his affidavit sworn on behalf of the plaintiff in reply to the present motion, the plaintiff's solicitor exhibited the report of Professor Shane O'Neill dated 27th November 2003 already mentioned. In the course of that report, Professor O'Neill mentions the fact that the plaintiff had smoked Player cigarettes until 1995 and then began smoking "Silk Cut." He describes her continuing symptoms of "progressive external dyspnoea secondary to chronic obstructive pulmonary disease *with emphysema as a consequence of her cigarette smoking in addition* to her prior lobectomy..." (emphasis added). In his concluding opinion, he stated that she *"has evidence of progressively severe chronic obstructive pulmonary disease as a consequence of her continued smoking habit."* (emphasis added). Mr Sreenan may, of course, be right to say that it is not reasonable to attribute these symptoms to her smoking after 1995. On the other hand, it is reasonable to expect that there would be some damage due to continued heavy smoking. It is not sufficiently clear, however, that there is no pleading of further injury due to smoking after 1995.

Finally, I turn to the apparently attractive argument based on causation, which I have summarised above. On the hypothesis that the plaintiff was addicted as a result of smoking the cigarettes of the first-named defendant and that she knew smoking causes cancer when she commenced smoking the appellant's cigarettes, the appellant was neither responsible for the addiction nor for the consequences of the addiction. On the other hand, the plaintiff claims that the appellant's "Silk Cut" cigarettes were targeted at vulnerable people such as the plaintiff. It was foreseeable that such people would consume cigarettes placed on the market by them. Issues of causation can be some of the most difficult in tort law. While the appellant has raised an arguable point, I cannot agree that it is decisive. Finally, if Mr Cush is correct in his interpretation of the Act of 1991, the liability of the appellant may be strict.

In all the circumstances, I am satisfied that the learned High Court judge was correct. I would dismiss the appeal.

Digital Rights Ireland Ltd v Minister for Communication

[2010] IEHC 221

Author's note: This Art 267 TFEU Reference contains an interesting discussion on the impact of the European Charter of Fundamental Rights and *locus standi* for EU law issues.

Judgment of Mr Justice William M. McKechnie delivered on the 5th day of May 2010

1. The Plaintiff is a limited liability company, limited by guarantee, incorporated under the Companies Acts 1963-2003, on the 4th November 2005, and has its registered office at 1 Caiseal na Rí, Cashel, Co. Tipperary. It has as one of its objects, in its Memorandum of Association, the promotion and protection of civil and human rights, particularly those arising in the context of modern communication technologies.

2. The First and Second Named Defendants are Ministers of Government and corporations sole and have their principal offices at 29/31 Adelaide Road and St. Stephen's Green in the City of Dublin, respectively.

3. The Third Name Defendant ("The Garda Commissioner") is the person charged with responsibility for the Garda Síochána and has his principal offices at Garda HQ Phoenix Park in the City of Dublin. He is entrusted with a purported power under section 63(1) of the Criminal Justice (Terrorist Offences) Act 2005 to issue a Direction or Directions to telecommunications services providers.

4. The Fourth Named Defendant is Ireland and the Fifth Named Defendant is the law officer of the State designated by the Constitution of Ireland and is sued in his representative capacity.

5. The Notice Party, joined as such in these proceedings, is a statutory body corporate established by section 4 of the Human Rights Commission Act 2000. It is so joined pursuant to section 8(h) of the aforesaid Act and appears as *amicus curiae* in the above entitled proceedings.

6. This judgment relates to the following three matters, the first two moved by the Defendants and the third by the Plaintiff, all of which were heard by way of preliminary issues:

(i) The *locus standi* of the Plaintiff;
(ii) Whether security for costs should be granted against the Plaintiff;
(iii) Whether a reference to the Court of Justice ("CoJ") under Article 267 of the Treaty on the Functioning of the European Union ("TFEU") (formerly Article 234 of the Treaty establishing the European Communities ("TEC")) should be made.

Background:

7. The background to the case, as the Plaintiff alleges, is that in or around the 25th April 2002 the Minister for Public Enterprise, the predecessor of the First Named Defendant, issued a direction under s. 110(1) of the Postal Telecommunications Services Act 1983 (as amended by the Interception of Postal Packets and Telecommunication Messages (regulations) Act 1993) to certain telecommunications services providers to retain telecommunications data. Such direction was to be treated as confidential. Following this direction the First Named Defendant came into possession of, and had and exercised control over, data relating to the Plaintiff, its members and other users of mobile phones.

8. By letter dated 19th December 2002 the Data Protection Commissioner advised the Department of Communications, Marine and Natural Resources that the above-mentioned direction was *ultra vires*, constitutionally invalid and was in breach of the Data Protection Acts 1988/2003 and S.I. 192 of 2002; with the grounds therefor being that as the objectives sought by the direction amounted to a derogation from the then existing data protection legislative scheme, the same could only be enacted through primary legislation. The Data Protection Commissioner advised the Defendants that failing a satisfactory response he would issue judicial review proceedings to challenge the validity of any direction(s) the Minister purported to make under the Postal Telecommunications Services Act 1983.

9. Some of the concerns of the Data Protection Commissioner were addressed in Part 7 of the Criminal Justice (Terrorist Offences) Act 2005 ("CJ(TO)A 2005"), which made provision for the retention of traffic and location data, relating to communications transmitted by fixed line or mobile telephone, and access to such data retained for law enforcement and security purposes.

10. The Plaintiff alleges that on a date or dates unknown, following the coming into force of the above Act of 2005, the Garda Commissioner issued a direction under the provisions thereof to telecommunications service providers to retain data.

11. The European legal framework in place at the time was governed by Directive 95/46/EC ('on the protection of individuals with regard to the processing of personal data and on the free movement of such data') and Directive 97/66/EC ('concerning the processing of personal data and the protection of privacy in the telecommunications sector'), later repealed by Directive 2002/58/EC ('concerning the processing of personal data and the protection of privacy in the electronic communications sector (Directive on privacy and electronic communications)'). These Directives aimed to harmonise the position of Member States:

> *"[T]o ensure an equivalent level of protection of fundamental rights and freedoms, and in particular the right to privacy, with respect to the processing of personal data in the electronic communication sector and to ensure the free movement of such data and of electronic communication equipment and services in the Community"* (Article 1, Dir. 2002/58/EC)

The focus of these Directives was thus the protection of privacy rights arising from data retention.

12. On 6th May 2006 Directive 2006/24/EC ('on the retention of data generated or processed in connection with the provision of publicly available electronic communications services or of public communications networks and amending Directive 2002/58/EC') was published. Article 1 of Directive 2006/24/EC states:

> *"1. This Directive aims to harmonise Member States' provisions concerning the obligations of the providers of publicly available electronic communications services or of public communications networks with respect to the retention of certain data which are generated or processed by them, in order to ensure that the data are available for the purpose of investigation, detection and prosecution of serious crime, as defined by each Member State in its national law.*
> *2. This Directive shall apply to traffic and location data on both legal entities and natural persons and to the related data necessary to identify the subscriber or registration user. It shall not apply to the content of electronic communications, including information consulted using an electronic communications network."*

The ultimate purpose of this Directive was to clarify the right of Member States to legislate obligations of disclosure upon communications services providers in relation to traffic and location data, and to harmonise the minimum and maximum periods of retention of the specified data, namely to six months and 2 years respectively (Article 6).

13. In this case the Plaintiff alleges that the Defendants have wrongfully exercised control over data, in that they have illegally processed and stored data relating to the Plaintiff, its members, and other mobile phone users contrary to: (i) statute, (ii) EC law, and (iii) the Constitution, in particular having regard to the Plaintiff's asserted rights to privacy, to travel and to communicate (Arts. 40.3.1, 40.3.2 and 40.6.1), and (iv) the European Convention on Human Rights ("ECHR"), in particular the right to private life, to family life, and to privileged communication (Arts. 6(1), 8 and 10). These allegations involve a claim that s. 63(1) of the CJ(TO)A 2005 is invalid on the within grounds and further that Directive 2006/24/EC is contrary to the Charter of Fundamental Rights ("CFR") and the ECHR.

14. The synopsis last given is simply that: the proceedings as shown by the pleadings are detailed and complex. For present purposes I would adopt as useful the following summary of the remedies sought by the Plaintiff:

(i) Declarations to the effect that the Minister for Communications and/or the Garda Commissioner have acted in breach of the Data Protection Acts 1988/2003 and/or in breach of EU law;
(ii) Declarations to the effect that s. 63(1) of the CJ(TO)A 2005 is null and void for breach of the Constitution and/or EU law, and/or is incompatible with Ireland's obligations under the ECHR;
(iii) A Declaration that the State has failed in its obligation to give effect to EU law;
(iv) A Declaration that Directive 2006/24/EC is null and void for breach of the EC Treaty and/or on the grounds that it was adopted without any legal basis;
(v) Reliefs including injunctive reliefs directed towards the lawfulness of the April 2002 communication by the Minister for Public Enterprise;
(vi) If necessary, a Declaration that s. 110 of the Postal and Telecommunications Services Act 1983, as amended, is repugnant to the Constitution;
(vii) Injunctions restraining the Defendants from acting under or giving effect to the impugned instruments including the EC Directive;
(viii) An Order pursuant to Art. 267 TFEU referring the following questions to the CoJ for a preliminary ruling:
- Whether Directive 2006/24/EC is valid notwithstanding:
  (a) Article 6(1) and (2) of the Treaty on European Union ("TEU")
  (b) Article 3a TEU and 21 TFEU (formerly Articles 10 and 18 TEC)
  (c) Articles 7, 8, 11 and 41 of the CFR
  (d) Article 5 TEU (formerly Article 5 TEC) (the principle of proportionality)
- Whether Directive 2006/24/EC regulating data protection is invalid insofar as it lacks a correct legal basis in EU law (this question has now been abandoned in light of Ireland v. European Parliament and Council of the European Union (Case C-301/06) (delivered on the 10th February 2009)).

(ix) Damages;
(x) Such other consequential reliefs and costs.

Locus Standi:

. . .

43. A more flexible approach may also be necessary where questions of European law are raised. The CoJ noted as far back as 1963 that:

> *"The European Economic Community is based on the rule of law, inasmuch as neither its Member States nor its institutions can avoid a review of the question whether the measures adopted by them are in conformity with the basic constitutional charter, the Treaty. ... [T]he Treaty established a complete system of legal remedies and procedures designed to permit the Court of Justice to review the legality of measures adopted by the instutions.*

> *Natural and legal persons are thus protected against the application to them of general measures which they cannot contest directly before the Court by reason of the special conditions of admissibility laid down . . . Where the Community institutions are responsible for the administrative implementation of such measures, natural and legal persons may bring a direct action before the Court against the implementing measures which are addressed to them or which are of direct and individual concern to them and, in support of such an action, plead the illegality of the general measure on which they are based. Where implementation is a matter for the national authorities, such persons may plead the invalidity of general measures before the national Courts and can cause the latter to request the Court of Justice for preliminary ruling."* (*Plaumann & T Co. v. Commission* [1963] ECR 95 at para. 23)

Considering this extract, Cooke J., a former member of the Court of First Instance and now a member of the High Court of Ireland, noted when speaking extra judicially, in October 2005:

> *"Membership of the Union involves radical transfer of regulatory competence to the organs of the Community from the Member states. What the European Court is saying in this judgment is that the far-reaching effects of this hand-over of power to the institutions is balanced by the guarantee that the legal order of the Treaty will protect the individual against the excessive and oppressive exercise of that power in a manner which is incompatible with superior rules of law and of fundamental human rights which the European Court will imply into the legal Order of the Community for the purpose."*

. . .

45. In summary, the Court held that the principle of effective judicial protection is a general principle of Community law, which flowed from the common traditions of the Member States, and the Member States must ensure judicial protection of an individuals rights under Community law. National procedural rules must therefore not undermine this right to effective judicial protection.

46. It is therefore clear that where issues of EU law arise in litigation, the Courts may be required to take a more liberal approach to the issue of standing so that a person's rights thereunder are not unduly hampered or frustrated. The rules on standing should be interpreted in a way which avoid making it "*virtually impossible*", or *"excessively difficult"*, or which impedes or makes "*unduly difficult*", the capacity of a litigant to challenge EU measures of general application under Art. 267 TFEU (see also *Van Schijnel v. SPF* [1995] ECR I-4705, para. 17; *Amministrazione delle Finanze v. San Giogio* [1983] ECR 3595, para. 14). That is not to say that where questions of EU law are raised and a preliminary reference requested, the Court is automatically precluded from refusing a plaintiff standing. However, as was the case with regards to the power to grant interim relief in *The Queen v. Secretary of State for Transport, ex parte Factortame Ltd & Ors.* [1990] ECR I-2433, if the Court would be otherwise minded to allow standing in relation to the questions raised, but for a strict application of the national rules on *locus standi*, the Court should nonetheless grant standing where to do otherwise would render the plaintiff's Community rights effectively unenforceable.

. . .

48. As can therefore be seen from the above case law, a plaintiff may be granted *locus standi* where, having regard to the rights in question, it can show either that it has a *bona fide* concern or interest in the provisions seeking to be impugned, or else that the rights which it seeks to protect are of general importance to society as a whole; this provided the Plaintiff is not a crank, meddlesome or a vexacious litigant. I should say that this latter point was not seriously argued, and I am firmly of the opinion that the Plaintiff herein is not such a litigant.

49. I would emphasise, however, that the Court should keep in mind the tension, on the one hand, between the public interest, as represented by public bodies established by the State, and, on the other, the right of access to the Court to litigate issues relating to whether the public interest is being protected (*per* Denham J. in *Lancefort (No. 2)*). Ultimately, the Court has a duty to prevent the unconstitutional abuse of public power, be it through legislation or otherwise. Thus where it is clear that a particular public act could adversely affect the constitutional, European, or Convention rights of a Plaintiff, or indeed society as a whole, a more relaxed approach to standing may be called for in order for the Court to uphold that duty, and vindicate those rights.

...

56. Despite such concerns, I am satisfied, as Hanna J. was, that there must exist a right to privacy in respect of business transactions carried out by corporate bodies. However, this right, given the legal and factual nature of such artificial persons, will inevitably be narrower than that applicable to natural persons. No serious suggestion could be made that regulations which sought annual returns or required the keeping of proper books and accounts would be invalidly interfering with a company's right to privacy. In contrast, a requirement to divulge trade secrets may be quite a different matter. In general, I am satisfied that such a right to privacy must extend to companies as legal entities, separate and distinct from their members as natural persons. Such entities are an integral part of modern day business. It is therefore paramount that the interests of such legal persons are protected in the Courts. Much of the case law considering a company's right to privacy is considered in the context of the invasion of its premises, however this is not the only way in which a company's privacy might be invaded. As I have said, access may be sought to confidential information or research, or to information or documents generated as part of delicate business negotiations. Commerce and industry could not survive if such access was unregulated. It is therefore clear to me that in principle some right of privacy must exist at least over some areas of a company's activity. Having so decided, it is not necssary to determine where precisely on the spectrum such rights may fall.

57. In European law such a right is readily apparent from Arts. 7 and 8 CFR and Article 8 ECHR. For the sake of clarity it is worthwhile setting out these provisions. Article 7 CFR, headed "*Respect for private and family life*" provides:

> *"Everyone has the right to respect for his or her private and family life, home and communications."*

Article 8 CFR, headed "*Protection of personal data*" states:

> *"1. Everyone has the right to the protection of personal data concerning him or her.*
> *2. Such data must be processed fairly for specified purposes on the basis of the consent of the person concerned or some other legitimate basis laid down by law. Everyone has the right of access to data which has been collected concerning him or her, and the right to have it rectified.*
> *3. ..."*

Article 8 ECHR states:

> *"1. Everyone has the right to respect for his private and family life, his home and his correspondence.*
> *2. There shall be no interference by a public authority with the exercise of this right except such as is in accordance with the law and is necessary in a democratic society in the interests of national security, public safety or the economic well-being of the country, for the prevention of disorder or crime, for the protection of health or morals, or for the protection of the rights and freedoms of others."*

58. In *Hoechst AG v. Commission* [1989] ECR 2859, and two companion cases (*Dow Benelux NV v. Commission* [1989] ECR 3137 and *Dow Chemical Iberica SA v. Commission* [1989] ECR 3165) the

Court of Justice held that corporate privacy protection was a fundamental principle of Community law. However, referring to Art. 8 ECHR, the Court noted that this should not be taken as being a right to inviolability of business premises:

> *"The protective scope of that article is concerned with the development of man's personal freedom and may not therefore be extended to business premises. ... Nonetheless ... any intervention by the public authorities in the sphere of private activities of any person, whether natural or legal, must have a legal basis and be justified on the grounds laid down by law, and, consequently, those systems provide, albeit in different forms, protection againt arbitrary or disproportionate intervention. The need for such protection must be recognised as a general principle of Community law."* ([1989] ECR 2859 at paras. 18 – 19)

59. Subsequently, however, this issue was considered by the European Court of Human Rights ("ECtHR") in *Niemietz v. Germany* (1992) 16 EHRR 97. In that case the ECtHR ruled explicitly that the right to respect for private life in Art. 8 ECHR did extend to business premises since:

> *"to interpret the words 'private life' and 'home' as including certain professional or business activities or premises would be consonant with the essential object and purpose of Article 8 (art. 8), namely to protect the individual against arbitrary interference by public authorities (see, for example, Marckx v. Beligium...)."*

Nonetheless such a right could be legitimately interfered with under Art. 8(2), and such interference "might well be more far-reaching where professional or business activities or premises were involved than would otherwise be the case."

60. The ECtHR, in *Société Colas Est and Others v. France* [2002] III-421, reiterated this point, noting that:

> *"[T]he Convention is a living instrument which must be interpreted in the light of present-day conditions (see, mutatis mutandis, Cossey v. the United Kingdom, judgment of 27 September 1990, Series A no. 184, p. 14, § 35 in fine). As regards the rights secured to companies by the Convention, it should be pointed out that the Court has already recognised a company's right under Article 41 to compensation for non-pecuniary damage sustained as a result of a violation of Article 6 § 1 of the Convention (see Comingersoll v. Portugal [GC], no. 35382/97, §§ 33-35, ECHR 2000-IV). Building on its dynamic interpretation of the Convention, the Court considers that the time has come to hold that in certain circumstances the rights guaranteed by Article 8 of the Convention may be construed as including the right to respect for a company's registered office, branches or other business premises (see, mutatis mutandis, Niemietz, cited above, p. 34, § 30)."*

61. These cases were later acknowledged by the CoJ in, *inter alia*, *Roquette Frères SA v. Commission* [2002] ECR I-9011, which noted that it was now clear from the jurisprudence of the ECtHR that the protections afforded to the family home under Article 8 may apply to business premises, although potentially subject to a greater level of legitimate interference.

62. Despite being supportive of some level of privacy right for corporate persons, it should be noted that the above European case law was primarily concerned with privacy in the context of premises and search and seizures. Whether such rights could therefore be said to extend to the collection of call data is, as a result, open to question. However, I am satisfied that there is recognised in both Irish and European law a right to privacy in business. Admittedly, such a right may be subject to a high level of justified interference, compared with the equivalent rights of natural persons; however for present purposes it is unnecessary to enter into discussion as to the legitimate scope of such rights; it is enough that they exist, and that they may have been infringed. In any event, it is clear that privacy with regards to personal data is explicitly within the contemplation of Art. 8 CFR. I can see no reason why such a right, although possibly more limited, may not apply to companies. Indeed such information may be commercially sensitive. The company would therefore have a great interest in protecting such data. I would thus allow the Plaintiff *locus standi* to raise issues relating to interference with its rights of privacy, whatever they might ultimately be found to be.

...

72. Thus in the context of this application it would appear to me that the storage of communications data, even without use, may be an interference with a person's rights under Art. 8 ECHR. Therefore I would reject any assertion by the Defendants that it would be necessary for this information to be used before any challenge could be mounted to its collection. It is clear that the retention of such data, *prima facie*, may be an interference with the Plaintiff's rights to privacy. In this regard I would draw support from Art. 8 FCR which provides for the protection of personal data. Consequently I would therefore allow the Plaintiff *locus standi* in this regard. However, I would stress, that is not to say that such interference is not legitimately justified or that the Plaintiff would be ultimately successful in its action; that is, and must be, a matter for the full hearing.

...

91. In coming to my conclusions, and in light of the case law considered above, I have taken into account:

(i) The Plaintiff is a sincere and serious litigant – it is not a vexatious litigant or a crank;
(ii) This case raises important constitutional questions;
(iii) The impugned provisions affect almost all of the population;
(iv) It would be an effective way to bring the action – individual owners of mobile phones would be unlikely to litigate the matter;
(v) The Plaintiff's right of access to the Court, and the Court's duty to uphold the Constitution and ensure that suspect actions are scrutinised;
(vi) The public good which is being sought to be protected.

92. Therefore, for the reasons given above, I grant *locus standi* to the Plaintiff in relation to alleged infringements, potential or otherwise, of rights to privacy and communication, and having regard to all of the circumstances of the case, including the nature of the Plaintiff company, the Plaintiff should be able to litigate these matters fully; that is both with regards to the infringement of the Plaintiff's rights as a legal person, and also with regards to natural persons. As stated, the level of interference between these two persons may not be the same. Natural persons may be afforded greater protection of these rights than companies. It would therefore seem to me, pragmatically speaking, that it would be sensible to allow the Plaintiff to advance these arguments in full. Were the Plaintiff only allowed to advance its arguments on the grounds that it would infringe a company's rights it could leave open the question of whether natural persons' rights were nevertheless infringed. It must be in the interests of justice and Court time, that such be litigated in circumstances where the Plaintiff is not in reality put at any disadvantage in pleading on behalf of citizens in general.

93. I would reiterate that it is clear that the Plaintiff has, purely in its personal capacity, *locus standi* with regards to infringements of its rights to privacy and communication. This I would hold even if there were no other greater interests in the matter. However, given that the impugned legislation could have a possible effect on virtually all persons, I would also grant the Plaintiff *locus standi* to litigate these matters generally as what might be termed an *actio popularis.*

...

Article 267 of TFEU Reference:

109. The Plaintiff has brought a motion calling for a Reference to the CoJ under Article 267 of TFEU. The questions to be asked all relate to the validity of Directive 2006/24/EC, in particular with rights under the EU and EC Treaties, the CFR and the ECHR. Questions relating to whether the Directive was issued under the appropriate Treaty heading were live matters at the time of the hearing as the Irish Government was then involved in ongoing litigation in the CoJ on this point. Since the hearing, the CoJ has ruled against the Irish government on the issue (*Ireland v. European Parliament and Council of the European Union* (Case C-301/06) (delivered on the 10th February 2009)). The Court found that Directive 2006/24/EC was properly enacted under Art. 95 TEC, since it was apparent that differences between national rules adopted for the retention of data were liable to have a foreseeable direct impact on the functioning of the internal market which would become more serious over time. Further, the provisions of the Directive are essentially limited to the activities of service providers and do no not govern access to data, or its use by police or judicial authorities. However, the CoJ expressly stated that the action related solely to the choice of legal basis for the Directive, and "*not to any possible infringement of fundamental rights arising from interference with the exercise of the right to privacy...*" (*ibid.* at para. 57).

110. The Plaintiff notes that there is a complete discretion, under Article 267(2), for a judge to refer a question when he considers that a decision on it is necessary to enable it to give judgment. However in this case the Plaintiff also seeks to ground its application under Article 267(3), which states:

> "*Where any such question is raised in a case pending before a court or tribunal of a Member State against whose decision there is no judicial remedy under national law, that court or tribunal* shall *bring the matter before the Court of Justice*" (emphasis added)

The Plaintiff argues that where a question of the validity Community law is raised the national court must make a reference since there is no effective judicial remedy under national law because a national judge may not declare a Community instrument invalid (*Foto-Frost v. Hamptzollant Lübeck-Ost* (Case 314/85) [1987] ECR 4199).

111. Attention is drawn to the exceptions to the requirement to make a Reference. These are that, firstly, the matter is not required in order for the national court to rule on the matter case (see *Weinand Meilickev. ADV/ORGA F.A. Meyer AG* [1992] ECR I-4871; *Corsica Ferries Italia Slr v. Corpo dei Piloti del Porto di Genova* [1994] ECR I-1783; *Monin Automobiles-Maison de Deux-Roues* [1994] ECR I-195). Secondly the Community law issue is governed by previous authority (see *CILFIT*; D*a Costa en Schaake NV v. Nederlandse Belastingadministratie* [1963] ECR 31; *Foglia v. Novello II* [1981] ECR 3045). Thirdly the application of Community law is so obvious as to leave no doubt to the national court (see *CILFIT v. The Minister for Health* [1982] ECR 3415). In the Plaintiff's opinion none of these operate in this case. A useful summary in relation to references to the CoJ can be found in *Kelly v National University of Ireland* [2008] IEHC 464.

112. The Defendants admit that, in relation to the Article 267 Reference, it is a matter of discretion for the Court, but argues that at this point a Reference would be premature. They say that, in circumstances where the Plaintiff has elected to bring proceedings by way of plenary action, and must therefore provide evidence, including *viva voce* evidence, to be examined in open court, and where this has yet to be done, there is therefore as of now, no way of evaluating what the final evidential framework will be. What evidence exists is, by definition, one-sided. In this regard reliance is placed upon *Irish Creamery Milk Suppliers Association v. Ireland* (Joined Cases 36 and 71/80) [1981] ECR 735, where the CoJ stated at paragraph 6 that:

> "*The need to provide an interpretation of Community law which will be of use to the national court makes it essential ... to define the legal context in which the interpretation requested should be placed. From that aspect it might be convenient, in certain circumstances, for the*

facts in the case to be established and for questions of purely national law to be settled at the time the reference is made to the Court of Justice so as to enable the latter to take cognisance of all the features of fact and of law which may be relevant to the interpretation of Community law which it is called to give."

Thus where the legal and factual context in the case has yet to be properly defined a Reference at this stage should be refused. The Plaintiff, the Defendants submit, fails to acknowledge that significant factual and national law issues remain to be determined concerning the nature and extent of the fundamental rights directly affected by the provisions of the Directive, as well as the extent, if any, to which any such rights are capable of being enjoyed or invoked by an artificial legal entity.

113. In relation the Article 267 Reference, I am satisfied that there is sufficient information before me to make such a Reference to the CoJ. I do not think that the application is premature; it is possible to define the context of the Reference (*Irish Creamery Milk Suppliers Association v. Ireland* [1981] ECR 735 considered). This is not a case which requires significant *viva voce* evidence to properly define the context or issues in the case. It is a challenge to specific legislative provisions which speak for themselves. I am also satisfied that the Reference is required since I am unable to rule on the validity of Community law (see *Foto-Frost v. Hamptzollant Lübeck-Ost* (Case 314/85) [1987] ECR 4199). I would therefore grant the application for a Reference under Article 267 TFEU.

114. With regards to the questions to be referred I do not propose to deal with those at this juncture. Instead I would invite the parties to submit suggestions, either individually or in the form of agreed questions between them, as to the content and wording of the questions to be referred, taking into account my findings in this decision.

Conclusion

115. Thus in summary:

(i) I grant the Plaintiff *locus standi* to bring an *actio popularis* in respect of whether the impugned provisions violate citizens' rights to privacy and communications, but not with regards to family and marital privacy or travel;
(ii) I refuse the Defendants' motion for security for costs;
(iii) I grant the Plaintiff's motion for a Reference to the Court of Justice under Article 267 TFEU.

Farrell v Whitty

[2008] IEHC 124

Author's note: The Motor Insurance Directive saga spurned much litigation including the following case and *Smith v Meade* (see below), raising important questions of direct effect and the Emanation of the State doctrine.

Judgment of Mr. Justice Birmingham delivered the 31st day of January, 2008

1. Factual background to the present proceedings

1.1 On January, 26th, 1996, the plaintiff was travelling in a van driven by the first named defendant when it was involved in an accident. The vehicle was not fitted with seating in the rear; it was in this area that at the time of the accident the plaintiff was seated on the floor. This area was intended not for carrying passengers but for carrying goods.

1.2 It is the plaintiff's case that at or near Cookstown/Fortunestown, Tudor Lane, Tallaght the first named defendant lost control of the vehicle causing it to collide with a wall, as a result of which she suffered personal injuries.

1.3 Subsequent to the accident it transpired that the first named defendant was an uninsured driver. Accordingly, the plaintiff sought to recover compensation from the fifth named defendant, the Motor Insurance Bureau of Ireland ("MIBI"). The plaintiff sought to do so pursuant to the terms of an agreement between the second named defendant, the Minister for the Environment ("the Minister") and the MIBI dated 21st December, 1988.

1.4 The MIBI refused to become involved in the claim and refused to compensate the plaintiff. It did so on the basis that the plaintiff was travelling in a part of the vehicle not fitted with seating and accordingly insurance was not compulsory.

1.5 In July, 2001 the plaintiff obtained judgment by default against the first named defendant. The question of assessment of damages was deferred to the trial of the action.

2. The legal background to the present proceedings

2.1 It appears convenient to set out the legal background both under Irish domestic law and under EU law. Section 56 of the Road Traffic Act, 1961 (as amended) imposes the general obligation on the user of a motor vehicle to be covered by liability insurance for injury or damage to third parties. The obligation is to be insured in respect of all sums for which the user shall be liable to any person exclusive of "excepted persons".

2.2 The question of who is or who is not an excepted person is thus of critical significance. The question of excepted persons is dealt with at s. 65(1) of the Road Traffic Act, 1961 (as amended). It provides as follows:—

> "In this Part of this Act "excepted persons" means the following persons:
>
> (a) any person claiming in respect of injury to himself sustained while he was in or on a mechanically propelled vehicle (or a vehicle drawn thereby) to which the relevant document relates, other than a mechanically propelled vehicle, or a drawn vehicle, or vehicles forming a combination of vehicles, of a class specified for the purposes of this paragraph by regulations made by the Minister, provided that such regulations shall not extend compulsory insurance in respect of civil liability to passengers to-;.

(i) any part of a mechanically propelled vehicle, other than a large public service vehicle, unless that part of the vehicle is designed and constructed with seating accommodation for passengers..."

2.3 The approach to exemption in s.65 (1) is a somewhat unusual one which was categorised as something of a "reverse definition" by counsel who appeared for the plaintiff in the case of *Delargy v. The Minister for the Environment and Local Government,* [2005] IEHC 94, a case to which I will refer later.

2.4 In summary, the position would appear to be that one is obliged to be covered by insurance in respect of injuries to any person other than an "excepted person". However, everybody is an "excepted person" unless positively included by a ministerial order. The power of the Minister is constrained by the stipulation that the obligation of compulsory insurance shall not be extended to passengers in any part of a vehicle, unless that part of the vehicle is designed and constructed with seating accommodation.

2.5 Article 7(1) of the European Communities (Road Traffic) (Compulsory Insurance) (Amendment) Regulations, 1992 (S.I. No. 347 of 1992) substituted a new s.65(1)(a) of the Act of 1961 which specified the classes of vehicles to which the section applied. The change effected by the Regulations of 1992 extended the category of vehicle and passengers who were covered with effect from the 20th November 1992, but even under this new more expansive regime the compulsory obligation to insure does not apply to passengers travelling in a part of a vehicle not designed or constructed for passengers.

2.6 Accordingly, passengers in the rear of vehicles not fitted with seating are persons in respect of whose injuries the MIBI would not appear as a matter of domestic law to be obliged to compensate.

3. The EC Legislative Framework

3.1 A number of directives are relevant. In particular, Council Directive 72/166/EEC of 24 April 1972 on the approximation of the laws of Member Sates relating to insurance against civil liability in respect of the use of motor vehicles, and to the enforcement of the obligation to insure against such liability (hereafter known as "the First Directive"); Second Council Directive 84/5/EEC of 30 December 1983 on the approximation of the laws of Member States relating to insurance against civil liability in respect of the use of motor vehicles (hereafter known as "the Second Directive"); and Third Council Directive 90/232/EEC of 14 May 1990 on the approximation of the laws of the Member States relating to insurance against civil liability in respect of the use of motor vehicles (hereafter known as "the Third Directive").

The First Directive

3.2 This directive was adopted with the objective of facilitating the free movement of goods and persons. The operative portion of the First Directive was article 3(1) which provides:—

> "Each Member State shall, subject to Article 4, take all appropriate measures to ensure that civil liability in respect of the use of vehicles normally based in its territory is covered by insurance. The extent of the liability covered and the terms and conditions of the cover shall be determined on the basis of these measures"

3.3 Article 1(1) of the First Directive defined vehicles in the following terms:—

> "...any motor vehicle intended for travel on land and propelled by mechanical power, but not running on rails, and any trailer, whether or not coupled."

This definition of a vehicle remains in force for the purpose of the Second and Third Directives.

The Second Directive

3.4 The Second Directive required the Member States to make provision for a body to guarantee that the victims of an accident would not remain without compensation where the vehicle which caused the accident was uninsured or unidentified. Article 1(4) is particularly relevant and provides as follows:—

> "Each Member State shall set up or authorize a body with the task of providing compensation, at least up to the limits of the insurance obligation for damage to property or personal injuries caused by an unidentified vehicle or a vehicle for which the insurance obligation provided for in paragraph 1 has not been satisfied. This provision shall be without prejudice to the rights of the Member States to regard compensation by that body as subsidiary or non-subsidiary and the right to make provision for the settlement of claims between that body and the person or persons responsible for the accident and other insurers or social security bodies required to compensate the victim in respect of the same accident."

3.5 It should be noted that the Second Directive did not in any way restrict the Member State's entitlement to derogate as provided by the First Directive and accordingly the Second Directive did not as a matter of European Law affect the legality of the Regulations of 1962. See the decision of the Court of First Instance in *Withers v. Delaney and the Motor Insurance Bureau of Ireland (Case 158/01)*[2002] ECR I-08301.

The Third Directive

The Third Directive was the most ambitious to date. It was designed to fill gaps which were identified as existing in respect of compulsory insurance for passengers in motor vehicles. So, the preamble to the Third Directive states:—

> "Whereas there are, in particular, gaps in the compulsory insurance cover of motor vehicle passengers in certain Member States; whereas, to protect this particularly vulnerable category of potential victims, such gaps shall be filled."
> Article 1 of the Third Directive states in unequivocal terms:—
> "...the insurance referred to in Article 3(1) of Directive 72/166/EEC shall cover liability for personal injuries to all passengers, other than the driver, arising out of the use of a vehicle".

Ireland was obliged to comply with the terms of article 1 and 2 of the Third Directive by the 31st December, 1995, as regards passengers of vehicles exclusive of pillion passengers of motorcycles.

3.6 It will be recalled that the original European Communities (Road Traffic) (Compulsory Insurance) Regulations, 1975 (S.I. No. 178 of 1975) were amended by the Regulations of 1992. These amendments extended the area of compulsory insurance to liability for injury to passengers travelling in vehicles with seating and passengers on motor cycles, but did not appear to extend those requirements to persons sustaining injury when travelling in the part of a vehicle that was not fitted with seating.

4. The History of the Present Proceedings

4.1 On 18th September, 1997, a plenary summons was issued on behalf of the plaintiff claiming:—

(a) Damages for personal injuries arising out of the negligence, breach of duty including breach of statutory duty of the first named defendant and;

(b) A declaration that the plaintiff is entitled to rely upon the provisions of Council Directive 72/166/EEC as amended by Council Directive 90/232/EEC in respect of the matters complained of in the proceedings;

(c) A declaration that the European Communities (Road Traffic)

> (Compulsory Insurance) (Amendment) Regulations, 1992 failed to implement adequately or at all the relevant provisions of Council Directive 72/166/EEC which was amended by Council Directive 90/232/EEC.

4.2 Defences were filed which, *inter alia,* denied that the plaintiff was entitled to rely on the provisions of Council Directive 72/166/EEC as amended by Council Directive 90/232/EEC and further denied that the European Communities (Road Traffic) (Compulsory Insurance) (Amendment) Regulations, 1992 (S.I. 347 of 1992) failed to implement adequately or at all the relevant provisions of Council Directive 72/166/EEC as amended by Council Directive 90/232/EEC.

4.3 Thereafter, the plaintiffs and defendants agreed to a number of points of law being determined by the High Court as preliminary issues pursuant to Order 25 rule 1 of the Rules of the Superior Courts. These issues were as follows:—

(1) In so far as s. 65 (1) of the Road Traffic Act, 1961, as amended by article 7 of the European Communities (Road Traffic) (Compulsory Insurance) (Amendment) Regulations,1992 provide that regulations made by the second named defendant:

> "......shall not extend compulsory insurance in respect of civil liability to passengers to – (i) any part of a mechanically propelled vehicle, other than a large public service vehicle, unless that part is designed and constructed with seating and accommodation for passengers..."
>
> does s. 65(1) as amended implement EC Council Directives 72/166/EEC, 84/5/EEC and 90/232/EEC in a proper and permissible manner?

(2) If the answer to question (a) is in the negative, are the relevant provisions of EC Council Directives 72/166/EEC, 84/5/EEC and 90/232/EEC directly effective so that the plaintiff is entitled to rely on same in respect of the matters complained of in these proceedings?

(3) If the answer to question (b) is in the affirmative, is the plaintiff entitled to make recovery from the fifth named defendant pursuant to the terms of the agreement between the second named defendant and the fifth named defendant dated the 21st December, 1988?

4.4 When the matter came before the High Court on 30th July, 2004, the Court (Ó'Caoimh J) decided to refer the matter to the European Court of Justice (ECJ) for a preliminary ruling under Article 234 EC Treaty. He did so on the following two questions:

(1) As of December, 31st, 1995, the date by which Ireland was obliged to implement the provisions of the Third Directive in respect of passengers on vehicles other than motor cycles, did article 1 of the Third Directive oblige Ireland to render insurance compulsory in respect of civil liability for injury to individuals travelling in that part of a motor vehicle not designed and constructed with seating accommodation for passengers?

(2) If the answer to question 1 is in the positive, does article 1 of the Third Directive confer rights on individuals that may be relied upon directly before the National Courts?

It can be seen by the reference, Ó'Caoimh J was in effect seeking a preliminary ruling on the points of law 1 and 2 that had been identified.

4.5 However, no such ruling was sought in relation to point 3 as to whether the plaintiff was entitled to recover from the MIBI pursuant to the terms of the agreement between it and the Minister. I have been informed that when the question of a reference was raised, that the MIBI expressed a preference that this third issue should not be the subject of a preliminary reference.

On 19th April, 2007, the ECJ (in ***Farrell*** *v. Whitty, Minister for Environment (Case 356/05)* [2007] E.C.R. I-03067) gave the following answers to the questions that had been referred to it:—

> "[The Court] (First Chamber) hereby rules:
> (1) Article 1 of the Third Council Directive 90/232/EEC of the 14 May, 1990 on the approximation of the laws of the Member States relating to insurance against civil liability in respect of the use of motor vehicles is to be interpreted as precluding national legislation whereby compulsory motor vehicle liability insurance does not cover liability in respect of personal injuries to persons travelling in a part of a motor vehicle which has not been designed and constructed with seating accommodation for passengers.
> (2) Article 1 of the Third Directive 90/232 satisfies all the conditions necessary for it to produce direct effect and accordingly confers rights upon which individuals may rely directly before the national courts. However, it is for the national court to determine whether that provision may be relied upon against a body such as the Motor Insurers' Bureau of Ireland."

In essence, the ECJ gave clear answers to the two issues that had been referred to it but withheld expressing a view on whether the plaintiff could recover from the MIBI. This of course, was the aspect of the preliminary legal issues on which the High Court decided not to seek a preliminary ruling.

5. The Net Issues before the Court

5.1 Against this background it is agreed that the net issue now for determination by the court is the following:—

> "May a Directive (in this case article 1 of Third Directive 90/232) which confers rights upon which individuals may rely directly before the National Court be relied upon against the Motor Insurance Bureau of Ireland".

It is further agreed this issue can be determined by deciding whether the Motor Insurance Bureau of Ireland is or is not "emanation of the State" as this phrase is understood in European Law.

. . .

7. The judgment of the ECJ in the present case

7.1 In summary, the ECJ in *Farrell v. Whitty*, while adverting to the possibility of proceedings against the MIBI, declined to express a concluded view.

7.2 The issues dealt with by the court are to be found at paras. 37 to 44 of the judgment. Insofar as it is the manner of treatment of this issue which has seen this case come back before the High Court, it seems appropriate to quote paras. 37 to 44 in full:—

> "(37) As regards Question 2, which asks whether individuals may rely directly upon Article 1 of the Third Directive before the national courts, it should be pointed out that it has consistently been held that a provision in a directive has direct effect if it appears, as far as its subject matter is concerned to be unconditional and sufficiently precise (Case 8/81 Becker [1982] ECR 53; Joined Cases C-253/96 to C-258/96 Kempelmann and Others [1997] ECR I-6907, paragraph 37; and Case C-292/02 Meiland Azewijn [2004] ECR I-7905, paragraph 57).
> (38) It must be held in the present case that, as the Commission argues, those criteria are satisfied by Article 1 of the Third Directive. That article allows both the obligations of the Member State and the beneficiaries to be identified, and its provisions are unconditional

> and precise. Article 1 of the Third Directive may accordingly be relied upon in order to set aside provisions of national law which exclude from the benefit of the guarantee provided by compulsory insurance cover persons travelling in any part of a vehicle which is not designed and constructed with seating accommodation for passengers.
> (39) The question remains whether that provision may be relied on against a body such as the MIBI.
> (40) A Directive cannot be relied on as against individuals, whereas it may be relied on as against a State, regardless of the capacity in which the latter is acting, that is to say, whether as employer or as public authority. The entities against which the provisions of a directive that are capable of having direct effect may be relied upon include a body, whatever its legal form, which has been responsible, pursuant to a measure adopted by the State, for providing a public service under the control of the State and have for that purpose special powers beyond those which result from the normal rules applicable in relations between individuals (Case C-188/89 Foster and Others [1990] ECR I-3313 paragraph 20; Case C-343/98 Collino and Chiappero [2000] ECR I-6659, paragraph 23; and Case C-157/02 Rieser Internationale Transporte [2004] ECR I-1477, paragraph 24).
> (41) Since the national court has not provided sufficient information regarding the MIBI for it to be possible to determine whether the latter can be assimilated to such a body, it is for the national court to ascertain, taking account, on the basis of the above considerations, of the status of the MIBI and its relationship with the Irish State, whether the directive may be relied upon against it.
> (42) Should the national court decide that the directive cannot be relied upon against the MIBI, it will be bound, when applying domestic law and, in particular, legislative provisions specifically adopted for the purpose of implementing the requirements of a directive, to interpret national law, so far as possible, in the light of the wording and the purpose of the Directive concerned in order to achieve the results sought by it (Case C-408/01 Adidas-Salomon and Adidas Benelux [2003] ECR I-12537, paragraph 21, and Joined Cases C-397/01 to C-403/01 Pfeiffer and Others [2004] ECR I-8834, paragraph 113).
> (43) In any event the liability of the Member State to make good damage caused by a failure to transpose a Directive, within the meaning of the judgment in Joined Cases C-6/90 and C-9/90 Francovich & Ors. [1991] ECR I-5357, may arise.
> (44) The answer to Question 2 should therefore be that Article 1 of the Third Directive satisfies all the conditions necessary for it to produce direct effect and accordingly confers rights upon which individuals may rely directly before the national courts. However, it is for the national court to determine whether that provision may be relied upon against a body such as the MIBI."

Paragraph 40 of the ECJ judgment is particularly relevant and at this stage it is sufficient to note the language of the paragraph would appear to have its origin in a case of *Foster & Ors. (Case C-188/89)* [1990] ECR I-3313, at para. 20.

Before moving on from the European Court of Justice's dealings with this case it is appropriate to refer briefly to the opinion of the Advocate General in *Farrell v. Whitty* delivered on 5th October 2006 and the stance taken by the Commission. In para. 69, Advocate General Stix-Hackl opines as follows:—

> "With regard to a body governed by private law, the members of which are insurance companies operating on the vehicle insurance market in Ireland, linked to the State by a private law agreement with a view to undertaking the functions of the body provided for in Article 1(4) of the Second Directive, it is to be determined whether the MIBI may be regarded as an emanation of the State for the purposes of the yardsticks referred to in *Foster*. According to the Court, 'unconditional and sufficiently precise provisions of a Directive [can] be relied on against organisations or bodies . . . subject to the authority or

control of the State or [having] special powers beyond those which result from the normal rules applicable to relations between individuals'. It follows that 'a body, whatever its legal form, which has been made responsible, pursuant to a measure adopted by the State, for providing a public service under the control of the State and has for that purpose special powers beyond those which result from the normal rules applicable in relations between individuals is included in any event among the bodies against which the provisions of a directive capable of having direct affect may be relied upon'."

At para. 71 of her opinion she goes on to say:—

"71. Considering how little information was supplied by the national court concerning the MIBI, it seems difficult to claim at the outset that the latter is subject to the State's authority or control and it is uncertain whether it possesses special powers beyond those which result from the normal rules applicable to relations between individuals. On the other hand, it is not denied that the MIBI performs the functions of a body authorised for the purposes of Article 1(4) of the Second Directive, charged with compensating victims of accidents caused by unidentified or uninsured vehicles. This responsibility is public in nature, for it is provided for by the Second Directive itself, State control being exercised by means of the authorisation – in this case contained in an agreement – of the body in question.
72. In conclusion, it seems to me that the MIBI may, as a body authorised for the purposes of Article 1(4) of the Second Directive responsible for the function entrusted to those bodies by that directive, be put on the same footing as the State, with the result that Article 1 of the Third Directive may be relied upon by individuals before the national courts."

The reasoning of the Advocate General echoes the submissions that had been made by the Commission. This issue was addressed in paragraph 35 and subsequent paragraphs of its submissions. After reciting the information in relation to the MIBI that they gleaned from the written submissions lodged on behalf of the MIBI it nonetheless went on to observe as follows:—

"However, the Commission would emphasise that the MIBI has nevertheless been established as the authorised body for the purpose of Article 1(4) of the Second Directive with the special task for providing compensation for damage to property or personal injuries caused by a non-identified vehicle or a vehicle for which the compulsory insurance obligations have not been satisfied. In the Commission's view such a task merely resembles a specific public function or mission within the meaning of *Foster* and it therefore tends to be of the opinion that the MIBI is to be considered as an emanation of the State."

The jurisprudence of the ECJ

...

8. Submissions of the Parties in this Case

8.2 Because of the centrality of the *Foster* case to the arguments, I have deferred until now attempting to set out the basic contentions of the parties. On behalf of the plaintiff, Mr. Eoin McCullough S.C. has submitted that the plaintiff is indeed entitled to pursue compensation from the MIBI and that it is an emanation of the State. In that submission he receives strong support from Mr. James Connolly S.C. on behalf of the State defendants who argues to like effect. It is argued that the jurisprudence of the ECJ takes a very broad approach to the concept of an emanation of the State. Reference is made to Article 1(4) of the Second Directive obliging the Member States to set up or authorise a body with the task of providing compensation. It is said that it is beyond doubt that the MIBI is the body authorised and that the fact that it had an existence prior to any of the directives and, indeed, prior to Ireland's membership of the EEC is quite irrelevant.

8.3 Attention is drawn to the Memorandum which accompanied the 1988 Agreement and the statement therein contained that the 1988 Agreement is being made as part of the implementation of the Second EC Directive on motor insurance – directive 84/5/EEC of 30/12/1983. Attention is also drawn to the fact that the MIBI has accepted responsibility in other areas for the State's extended obligations under the Third Directive and it is asked why the situation should be different now that the situation of persons travelling in vehicles without passenger seats in the rear has been clarified.

8.4 On behalf of the fifth named defendant Mr. Patrick Connolly S.C. stresses the private nature of the MIBI, a company set up under the Companies Act as far back as 1955. It is said that the obligations of the Bureau are obligations voluntarily assumed by the Bureau under the various agreements that it has entered into with numerous Ministers and that therefore the obligations are contractually limited to those to be found in the agreement. With some firmness it is said that no further or other obligations on the part of the Bureau arise at law from any other external source. Mr. Patrick Connolly S.C. stresses that, apart from the entitlement of the Minister to require the Bureau to honour its contractual obligations, the State is not in a position to give any directions to the Bureau in the conduct of its business. In summary, Mr. Patrick Connolly S.C. submits that the tests established by *Foster* are not met in respect of the MIBI. He says this is because the Bureau is manifestly not an organisation or body which is subject to the authority or control of the State. It carries out its obligations which it has voluntarily undertaken entirely of its own accord and is under the authority or control of nobody in so doing. In carrying out the obligations which it has voluntarily assumed under the various agreements, it is not acting "pursuant to a measure adopted by the State". The ordinary meaning of the word 'measure', in the context of the State means, and is always understood to mean, a legal enactment such as either an Act of Parliament or a Statutory Instrument of a Minister. The Bureau is not responsible under any such heading. The Bureau is not providing a public service "under the control of the State". It is under no such control. The Bureau has not been given "special powers beyond those which result from the normal rules applicable in relations between individuals".

The parties join issue in relation to the significance of the *Foster* case. On behalf of the plaintiff and the State defendants it is argued that the matters referred to at para. 20 are not mandatory but are essentially illustrative in nature. As an alternative, it is suggested that if there is a requirement to meet the individual factors referred to at para. 20 in *Foster*, that the MIBI does in any event meet each of those considerations.

On behalf of the fifth named defendant it is submitted that the definition of 'emanation of the State' is to be found within para. 20 of *Foster* and that the MIBI does not meet any of the conditions there referred to.

By way of emphasising how inappropriate it is to regard the MIBI as an "emanation of the State" Mr. Patrick Connolly S.C. draws attention to the dictionary definition of the words 'emanation' and 'emanate'. The Oxford Dictionary of emanation he submitted is "the process of going forth, issuing or proceeding from anything as a source".

9. Conclusion

9.1 At the outset I should say that I am not significantly influenced by the dictionary definition point. The situation would be quite different if we were considering the phrase "emanation of the State" as a phrase that had appeared in a statute. However, here we are dealing with a situation where it has long been recognised that certain entities fall into a class such that individuals may rely on directives against them. The phrase "emanation of the State" is little more than a convenient label that can be applied once it is decided that a particular entity is one that possesses the characteristics such that an individual should be permitted to proceed against it.

9.2 In those circumstances I propose to review a number of authorities to which I have been referred with a view to identifying how to approach the task of deciding whether the MIBI falls within or without the category under consideration. In arguing for a broad or purposive approach, Mr. McCullough S.C. and Mr. James Connolly S.C. have relied on a number of decisions of the European Court of Justice as well as on the views of a number of commentators in this area. *Kampelmann v. Landschastsverband Westfalen-Lippe (Case 253/96)* [1997] E.C.R. I-4907 appears to move the matter on beyond any rigid interpretation of para. 20 of *Foster*. Paragraph 46 in *Kampelmann* states in these terms:—

> "In addition, it has consistently been held that a directive cannot of itself impose obligations on an individual and cannot therefore be relied upon as against such an individual (see, *inter alia*, Case C-91/92 Faccini Dori v Recreb [1994] ECR I-3325, paragraph 20).It may, however, be relied on against organizations or bodies which are subject to the authority or control of the State or have special powers beyond those which result from the normal rules applicable to relations between individuals, such as local or regional authorities or other bodies which, irrespective of their legal form, have been given responsibility, by the public authorities and under their supervision, for providing a public service (Case 103/88 Fratelli Costanzo v Comune di Milano [1989] ECR 1839, paragraph 31, and Case C-188/89 Foster and Others v British Gas [1990] ECR I-3313, paragraph 19)."

9.3 It will be noted that in this paragraph the ECJ, rather than speaking of the three individual elements of *Foster* para. 20, speaks of organisations or bodies which are subject to the authority or control of the State **or** have special powers. In effect, the emphasis appears to be on whether the body has been given a responsibility for providing a public service.

9.4 That a broad and purposive approach is appropriate receives the endorsement of a number of commentators. Tridimas on *General Principles of EU Law*, 2nd Edition (Oxford University Press, 2006) at p. 46 observed:

> "It is submitted therefore that, in order to be regarded as an emanation of the State, it suffices for a body to have been made responsible, pursuant to a measure adopted by the State, for providing a public service under the control of the State. This definition seems sufficiently wide to encompass private bodies which have been entrusted with the performance of functions traditionally reserved to the State and over which the State retains residual control."

9.5 Steiner, Woods and Twigg-Flesner (*EU Law*, 9th Ed., (Oxford University Press, 2006)) are of a similar view. Support for that position is also offered by Elaine Fahey in an article entitled "Preliminary Reference from the Circuit Court: The 'Emanation of the State' Doctrine in the Irish Courts" (2004) 1 I.L.T. 6

9.6 The broad approach favoured in *Kampelmann* is to be found in such cases such as *Haim v. Kassenzahnärtzliche Vereinigung Nordrhein (Case 424/97)* [2000] E.C.R. I-5123 and *Konle v. Austrian Republic (Case 302/97)* [1999] ECR I-3099. The ECJ had this to say in *Konle* at para. 62:—

> "It is for each Member State to ensure that individuals obtain reparation for damage caused to them by non-compliance with Community law, whichever public authority is responsible for the breach and whichever public authority is in principle, under the law of the Member State concerned, responsible for making reparation. A Member State cannot, therefore, plead the distribution of powers and responsibilities between the bodies which exist in its national legal order in order to free itself from liability on that basis."

10. The English Motor Insurers Bureau (MIB) Cases

10.1 Mr. Patrick Connolly S.C. on behalf of the MIBI has relied heavily on a number of cases before the English courts which dealt with the status of the Motor Insurance Bureau ("MIB"). While both Mr. Eoin McCullough S.C. and Mr. James Connolly S.C. point to areas where they say the MIBI diverges from its English counterpart, these cases require careful consideration.

10.2 The first is a bundle of three cases entitled *Mighell v. Reading, Evans v. The Motor Insurance Bureau* and *White v. White* [1999] 1 C.M.L.R. 1251 which were heard together before the Court of Appeal. Mr. Mighell and Mr. White were each injured whilst passengers in cars driven by uninsured defendants. Mr. Mighell knew that his driver was uninsured. On the finding of facts made by the court of first instance, Mr. White did not know that his driver was uninsured but ought to have known it, while Mr. Evans was injured by a hit and run driver and his case was concerned exclusively with the MIB'S liability to pay interest on an award made in his favour. In summary, each of the three judges at first instance had taken the view that, since the Motor Insurance Bureau had in effect been nominated by the State to carry out the task of compensating those injured persons who could not look to an insurance company, therefore the directive could be regarded as having direct effect. In the Court of Appeal the case is noteworthy because of a very strong and clear statement by Hobhouse L.J. Because the approach taken by Hobhouse L.J. is central to the position taken by the MIBI, it is necessary to quote from his judgment *in extenso* wherein he stated at p.1272 that:—

> "In my judgment the correct view to take of the role and status of the Bureau is that it is a private law contractor and no more and as such is not capable of being covered by any direct effect the Directive may have. It cannot be disputed that this was its status prior to the making of the Second Directive. Independently of any intervention of Community law, the Bureau was brought into existence by the insurance companies which were its original members. It provided a vehicle through which these independent insurance companies could enter into private law agreements with the Secretary of State. Their motivation does not alter or affect the nature of the relationship. It was contractual and no more.
>
> This is clearly demonstrated by the position regarding untraced drivers. The United Kingdom Government did not consider that it need take any step in this connection as a result of the making of the Second Directive. It already had in place what it regarded as an adequate and satisfactory contractual arrangement with the Bureau. The Bureau is not constitutionally an emanation of the State; it is a private law company. It is not functionally an emanation of the State; it acts on its own behalf in the commercial interests of it members, not on behalf of the State or as a delegate of the State. ...

10.3 The statement by Hobhouse L.J. is a very clear, even trenchant one. However, there are some other aspects of the judgment of the Court of Appeal that must be noted. Neither of the two other judges endorsed his views. So, Schiemann L.J. entered this reservation at p.1264 of his judgment:—

> "For my part, I accept that there is substantial uncertainty surrounding the concept of 'emanation of the State'.
>
> That uncertainty springs in part from the uncertainty of the legal concept and in part from the difficulty of applying that concept to a particular factual situation. The latter is a task which the national courts have to fulfil although they may be helped by a reference. I would not regard it as *acte clair* that the MIB was not an emanation of the State, although that is my current opinion. I do not find it necessary to express a concluded opinion on the point."

Schiemann L.J. was joined in this approach by the third member of the court, Swinton Thomas L.J. Accordingly, it would appear that in expressing the views that he did, Hobhouse L.J. was not speaking for the majority of the court.

10.4. There have been developments since which, if they do not actually undermine the persuasive authority of *Mighell, Evans* and *White*, certainly do nothing to enhance its authority. One of these three cases, that of Mr. White, *sub nom White v. White* [2001]1 W.L.R. 481, was appealed to the House of Lords which reversed the decision of the Court of Appeal, but the House of Lords decided the case on an entirely different basis relating to how the word 'knew' in the Directive was to be interpreted. Another of the three original plaintiffs, Mr. Evans, launched a collateral attack on the outcome in the Court of Appeal and before the ECJ was in part successful in that the court held, in interpreting the Second Directive, that the compensation awarded for damages must take account of the effluxion of time until actual payment of the sums awarded in order to guarantee adequate compensation in *Evans v. Secretary of State for the Environment, Transport and the Regions & Anor. (Case 63/01)* [2003] E.C.R. I- 14447.

. . .

10.6 However, with all respect to Flaux J., adopting a checklist approach by reference to para. 20 of *Foster* does not accord with the approach taken by the Court of Appeal in other cases. In *The National Union of Teachers v. Governing Body of St. Mary's Church of England (Aided) Junior School* [1997] 3 C.L.M.R. 630 the Court of Appeal was of the view that the concept of emanation of the State for the purposes of the doctrine of vertical effect was very broad and went on to indicate that the tripartite test for what constituted an emanation of the State in *Foster* was indicative rather than a statutory definition. The Court of Appeal was of the view that the Employment Appeals Tribunal erred in failing to fully appreciate the significance of the undoubted fact that the Community case law indicates that a body could be an emanation of the State without being under the control of central government. Interestingly, when for completeness sake and contrary to the views of the Court that this was not necessary, the Court went on to consider the position of the school by reference to the tripartite test, the Court appears to have been of the view that the existence of special powers could not be established. It is significant that the judgment of the Court, with which judgment the other members agreed, was delivered by Schiemann L.J. who was, of course, a member of the Court in *Mighell, White and Evans.*

11. The Irish MIBI cases

11.1 The issue of the status of the MIBI has been addressed in a small number of cases in this jurisdiction. In the case of *Dublin Bus v. The MIBI,* (Unreported, Circuit Court, October 29th, 1999) Judge Bryan McMahon, as he then was, had this to say at p.11 of the judgment:—

> "I hold that the M.I.B. of I. must be associated with the State in answering the question who is responsible for the proper implementation of Directive 84/5/EEC. Since an individual affected adversely by an improper implementation can sue the State, so also, in the circumstances of this case, can the individual claim against the State's partner in the implementation process. Furthermore, under the general scheme the M.I.B. of I. is the managing partner which is responsible for the administration and the processing of all claims under the scheme, and as such is the party which carries all litigation contemplated by the scheme. Unlike, ordinary contracts, the 1988 Agreement is also unusual in that not only does it contemplate, but it specifically provides for third parties to have rights under the agreement and for such third parties to take actions against the M.I.B. of I. Clause 2(2) of the 1988 agreement provides as follows: ... In these circumstances there can be little argument that the M.I.B. of I. is a public body, an emanation of the State which would make it liable for the failure to properly implement the Directive."

Judge McMahon considered the same issues in *Withers v. Delaney and MIBI* (Unreported, Circuit Court, 9th March, 2001), where, when invited by counsel for the MIBI to revisit the issue of whether the MIBI was an emanation of the State, he declined to reopen the issue observing that he was now even more convinced the MIBI was indeed an emanation of the state.

11.2 The decisions in question are decisions of the Circuit Court and as such are of persuasive authority only. However, the judgments in question which would seem to be reserved judgments, are elaborate and closely reasoned and accordingly, carry considerable weight. It is only right to add that Mr. Patrick Connolly S.C. points out that the *Dublin Bus* judgment does not specifically refer to the *Foster* case and the extent to which the test there set out are relevant and indeed, this is also true of the *Withers* case.

11.3 The matter was also addressed in *Delargy v the Minister for the Environment and Local Government*, [2005] IEHC 94 a decision of Murphy J. Notwithstanding that I have been informed that the case is at present under appeal, I would be very slow indeed not to follow the case if the conclusions in relation to the status of the MIBI formed part of the *ratio decidendi,* in accordance with the approach set out in the judgment of Parke J. in *Irish Trust Bank Limited v. Central Bank of Ireland* [1976-77} I.L.R.M. 50. Murphy J. concluded his judgment with the following paragraph:—

> "Moreover, the Court is not satisfied that there is evidence that the MIBI could be considered an 'emanation of the State'. In *Mighell v. Redding & Anor.*, *Evans v. The Motor Insurance Bureau* and White *v. White* [1999] 1 C.M.L.R. 1251 in the High Court and *White v. White (2)* [2001] 2 All E.R. 42 in the House of Lords, the English MIB was held not to be an emanation of the State. This appears to be more persuasive than the finding in *Dublin Bus v. MIBI.* Accordingly, the MIBI has no duty to indemnify."

11.4 The primary conclusion that the MIBI had no duty to indemnify would seem to have been grounded on the fact that at the time of the accident, when the plaintiff, a pillion passenger, suffered injuries, there was no requirement to have cover for pillion passengers and there was no issue regarding the application of European Community law. The accident in question had occurred in September, 1987 and judgment had been obtained against the uninsured defendant in 1996. Accordingly, the court was of the view that the Third Directive had no relevance of any kind, either against a public body or a private body or individual. In these circumstances it would seem that the comments in relation to the fact that the evidence had not established that the MIBI could be considered as an emanation of the State are *obiter.*

11.5 The case turned principally on the conclusion by Murphy J. that certain provisions of the Road Traffic (Compulsory Insurance) Regulations, 1962 (S.I. 14 of 1962) were invalid, having regard to the provisions of the Constitution and, moreover, that the Minister in making the orders he had, was acting *ultra vires* the powers conferred upon him by the Oireachtas and that the orders were, accordingly, null and void. In these circumstances I will not repeat the views that I have expressed about the significance of *Mighell, Evans* and *White*, as well as the House of Lords case of *White v. White,* to which Murphy J. made reference.

12. Decision

12.1 I have already indicated that much time was spent during the hearing debating the question of how determinative of the issue was the tripartite approach of the *Foster* case, though all sides had fall back positions in that counsel for the plaintiff and the State while arguing that the tripartite test was not to be approached as if it is was a statutory test argued in the alternative that even if the tripartite test applied that they can establish that the three tests are met by MIBI. In contrast, counsel for the MIBI lays heavy emphasis on the test, arguing that no aspect of the test is applicable to the MIBI but going on to say that any conceivable alternative formulation could not embrace the MIBI as it is purely a private entity.

12.2 I have concluded that the tripartite test is not to be read as if it is a statutory requirement. The *Foster* formula is a guide or illustration and no doubt a useful guide or illustration but no more than that. I take that view primarily as a result of a consideration of the language of the relevant paragraph of the *Foster* judgment itself. Paragraph 20 it will be recalled is in the following terms:—

> "It follows from the forgoing that a body, whatever its legal form, which has been made responsible, pursuant to a measure adopted by the State, for providing a public service under the control of the State and has for that purpose special powers beyond those which result from the normal rules applicable in relations between individuals *is included in any event* among the bodies against which the provisions of a directive capable of having direct effect maybe relied upon." [Emphasis added.]

12.3 I am of the view that reference to "*is included in any event*" is quite inconsistent with any suggestion that what is being offered is a comprehensive, all embracing test. On the contrary it seems to me that the phrase *"is included in any event"* signals that the category of bodies is wider than those that meet the three tests and that bodies that do meet the three tests constitute only a subset of the entire category.

12.4 The opening words of this paragraph "it follows from the foregoing" point in the same direction. What has preceded paragraph 20 are a number of paragraphs setting out general principles. This phrase roots what is to come later in paragraph 20 in what is gone before. The view that I have arrived at that it is not appropriate to apply the tripartite test as though it were a statutory definition accords with the views of the Court of Appeal in England as expressed in *NUT and others v. St. Mary's Church of England Junior School and Others* [1997] 3 C.L.M.R. 630, a judgment of Scheimann L.J.

12.5 The basic principle at issue is put very succinctly in the opinion of Advocate General Van Gervan delivered 8 May 1990 in *Foster's* case who at para. 21 observed:—

> "As I have already repeatedly emphasized, the point of departure must be the reasoning behind the Marshall and Johnston cases; a Member State, but also any other public body charged with a particular duty by the Member State from which it derives its authority, should not be allowed to benefit from the failure of a Member State to implement the relevant provisions of the Directive in national law".

12.6 The closer the subject matter under consideration to those that were at issue in *Foster,* the more helpful will be the application of the tripartite test. Conversely, if the facts to be considered and the nature of the body to be considered diverge significantly from *Foster,* the value of the test will be undermined. *Foster* concerned a commercial undertaking operating in the market place. A similar situation existed in *Rolls-Royce v. Doughty* [1992] ICR 538. The present situation is quite different in that we are concerned not with a commercial undertaking but with the vehicle by which a long-term social policy is delivered.

12.7 It seems almost beyond dispute that the MIBI performs the functions of a body authorised for the purpose of article 1(4) of the Second Directive. Equally, the responsibility is public in nature for it is a responsibility created by the Second Directive itself. In that connection, the observations of Advocate General Stix – Hackl at para. 71 of her opinion when this case was before the ECJ to which I have already referred to are worth recalling.

12.8 The fact that the MIBI, like its British counterparts was in existence well before either state joined the EEC is of no relevance. At the time the Second Directive came into being, all concerned must have been well aware that there were already in existence in at least a number of Member States bodies providing compensation and it must have been obvious to all concerned that these existing structures were likely to continue and to be authorised. Neither, do I think it significant that the authorisation took the form of an agreement rather than a statute or statutory instrument.

12.9 While there is no doubt at all that in form the MIBI is private body, a company incorporated by guarantee, I am of the view that in practice there is a considerable degree of state control or influence. The essential nature of the obligation under the 1988 agreement is to be found in Clause 4(1) to the effect that the Bureau shall satisfy judgments in respect of liability for injury to persons or damage to property which is required to be covered by an approved policy of insurance under s. 56 of the Road Traffic Act, 1961, the use of the vehicle was not in fact covered by insurance. It is accepted this encompasses later amendments enacted during the currency of the agreement. If this is so, the State is in a position to expand the scope of the responsibilities of the Bureau. By any standard this has to be regarded as a significant element of control.

12.10 I do of course accept that subject to one qualification, the State, certainly through its executive arm, is not in a position to dictate how the MIBI deals with individuals claims. There is, however, one significant exception to that general position. Clause 3(7) deals with the obligation on a claimant to take all reasonable steps against a person against whom there might be a remedy and goes on to provide that in the event of any dispute as to the reasonableness of the step, the matter is referred to the Minister for the Environment whose decision is final. It is certainly an unusual feature of a contract that it should provide that in the event of a disagreement one party to the contract should determine how the dispute is to be resolved.

13.1 It does seem to me that this provision is of a significantly different character to the provision in the English agreement that an arbitrator chosen from a panel of Queen's Counsel appointed by the Secretary of State hears an appeal when a claimant is dissatisfied with the amount of compensation offered.

13.2 A further indication of the level of public control as a matter of reality, is that amendments to the Memorandum and Articles of Association of the company require the consent of the Minister for Employment and Enterprise.

13.3 There is another area that merits examination as illustrating that the MIBI is not a typical private body entering into obligations on a voluntary basis. By virtue of s. 78 of the Road Traffic Act, 1961 as substituted by article 9 of the European Communities (Compulsory Insurance) (Amendment) Regulations, 1992 (S.I. 347 of 1992), in order for an undertaking to issue an approved policy of insurance it must be a member of the Motor Insurance Bureau of Ireland. Perhaps, even more unusually, before a body can become an exempted person and so be freed of the obligations of compulsory insurance it must provide an undertaking to deal with third party claims in respect of its vehicles on terms similar to those agreed between the Minister and the Motor Insurance Bureau of Ireland.

13.4 All these factors lead me to the view that the MIBI, in substance, if not in form operates as a *quasi*-State claims agency giving effect to an important aspect of public social policy. As such it falls to be identified with the State and is to be regarded as an emanation of the State.

13.5 In seeking to determine whether the MIBI is as a matter of European Law an emanation of the State I have been conscious that European Law in this area is not static. That this is so is illustrated by the decision of the ECJ in *Riksskatteverket v. Gharehveran (Case 441/99)* [2001] E.C.R. I-07687. That case considers the same Directive as had been the issue in two of the very early cases in this area; *Francovich v. Italy (Cases 6/90 and 9/90)* [1991] ECR I-5357 and *Wagner Miret v. Fondo de Garanatia Salarial(Case 334/92)* [1993] ECR I-6911 and proceeded to distinguish the earlier judgments in permitting the claimant to enforce the Directive directly against the Swedish State in the national courts

13.6 I have stated my view that it is not appropriate to apply rigorously the *Foster* tripartite test to establish the status of the MIBI. However, I should, before concluding state briefly that even had I been minded to apply that test more rigidly I believe I would have reached the same conclusion.

13.7 For reasons that will already be apparent I would have had no hesitation in concluding that the Bureau performs a public service. The position in relation to State control and special powers is less clear cut. Nonetheless I am of the view that aspects such as the operation of a veto on the alteration on the memorandum and articles as well as the entitlement of the Minister to give a binding direction in the event of a disagreement between a claimant and the bureau are indicative of a significant level of State control. This is hardly surprising given that it is the State that ultimately controls the scope of the obligations of the Bureau as it is the State that determines the extent of the requirements for compulsory insurance.

The third test, that of "special powers", is obviously the most difficult but here too I would have been prepared to identify special powers particularly in the area of the requirement for membership of the Bureau on the part of those bodies seeking to conduct insurance business.

13.8 In summary, I am of the view that the Motor Insurance Bureau of Ireland is to be regarded as an emanation of the State and that accordingly the plaintiff is entitled to make recovery from the fifth named Defendant pursuant to the terms of an agreement between the second named Defendant and the fifth named Defendant dated 21st December, 1998.

Kelly v U. C. D.

[2008] IEHC 464

Author's note: This pending reference considers the Equality Tribunal and the provisions of Art 267 TFEU

Judgment of Mr. Justice William M. McKechnie delivered on the 14th day of March, 2008:

1. The plaintiff in this case is a qualified teacher and resides at 11 Deansrath Avenue, Clondalkin, Dublin 22.

2. The defendant is an educational establishment descended from the body founded in 1854 as the Catholic University of Ireland, re-formed in 1880 and chartered in its own right in 1908. The university is a constituent university of the National University of Ireland. The Universities Act 1997 renamed the university as "National University of Ireland, Dublin", and the National University of Ireland, Dublin (Change of Name) Order 1998 (S.I. 447/1998) renamed the university as "University College Dublin-National University of Ireland, Dublin". At all material times it was offering a course leading to a Masters in Social Science (Social Worker) mode A for the academic period 2002 – 2004.

3. The notice party is the statutory appointee of a body established by the Employment Equality Act 1998, namely the Equality Tribunal. That body has the powers, functions and duties assigned to it by virtue of the provisions of the aforesaid Act, together with additional powers granted to it under the Equal Status Act 2000.

4. On the 23rd of December 2001, the plaintiff submitted his completed application form to University College Dublin ("UCD") seeking admission to the aforesaid course for the cycle in question. Having been interviewed in February 2002 as part of the selection process, he was informed by letter dated the 15th March 2002 that he was not being offered a place on the course. Being dissatisfied with this decision and with the follow on correspondence between himself and the college, he made a formal complaint in late-April 2002 of gender discrimination to the Director of the Equality Tribunal. He did so pursuant to s. 7 of the 2000 Act and based his claim on alleged breaches of ss. 3(1)(a) and 3(2)(a) thereof. A Mr. Hugh O'Neill, an Equality Officer with the notice party, was deputed to investigate and determine this complaint. He did so following an oral hearing on the 22nd of September 2006, and committed his decision to writing on the 2nd of November 2006. He concluded that the plaintiff had failed to establish *prima facie* discrimination on gender grounds.

5. Given the issue which this Court is concerned, it is not necessary to set out in any detail the precise nature of the complaints made by Mr. Kelly or UCD's detailed response to them. However a brief description of a general nature is required. Apparently, in February 2002, 93 candidates were interviewed for this course, 87 female and 6 male. A Professor Gabriel Kiely (male) and a Ms. Elaine Purcell (female), who interviewed the plaintiff, were obliged to complete a "selection interview guide", which has been described as a "scoring sheet". Apparently Mr. Kelly did poorly in this process. In response, relying on the numerous reasons set out (and repeated) in much of the documentation, including an affidavit sworn on the 6th of November 2006, he takes indignant issue with both the process and the result. In any event, after the interview and selection process had been completed, the top 50, two of whom were male and placed first and second, were offered immediate places on the course. A further 24, including two other males and the plaintiff (who was rated 65th overall) were placed on a waiting list. Subsequently by letter dated the 19th of August

2002, Mr. Kelly was offered a place on the course which he declined, offering as one of the reasons, the fact that he had been accepted on an equivalent postgraduate Social Work course at Trinity College, Dublin. Arising out of the entire process, both procedural and substantive, the basis of Mr. Kelly's complaint, which in essence is one of gender discrimination, is that at all times he was better qualified than the least qualified female candidate who was offered a position on round one.

6. In his initial complaint he alleged discrimination in the following respects:–

> "1. In a course for which the overwhelming number of applicants were women, no demonstrable effort was made to address the gross under-representation of men;
> 2. At the time of his interview for a place on the course he suffered hostility bias and resentment due to his gender;
> 3. There was a failure on the part of the relevant authorities at The University to demonstrate adherence to the principles of equal opportunities and positive discrimination, constituting a breach of European Union law, as interpreted by the European Court of Justice;
> 4. Because of his gender he was not treated fairly at the time of his interview for the course and was the victim of prejudice."

These grounds were later added to by way of a ten page written submission which is annexed as appendix A to the decision of the Equality Officer.

7. Some days after the decision of this officer, the plaintiff issued a notice of motion under O. 57A, r. 6(1) of the Circuit Court Rules appealing that decision to the Circuit Court which is provided for by s. 28 of the Equal Status Act 2000. A trial date of the 14th of June 2007 was subsequently set for this appeal. In the meantime however, he issued a further motion dated the 4th of January 2007, in which he sought from UCD copies of certain specified documents, again under O. 57A but this time under rule 6(6) of the Circuit Court Rules. By the issue date of this motion the plaintiff had been informed by letter of the 21st of December 2006, from Mr. Eugene O'Sullivan's solicitor for UCD, that the defendant body had retained the application forms of 49 of the 93 applicants above-mentioned and had disposed of the other applications. What Mr. Kelly therefore sought was firstly copies of "the retained applications", secondly copies of the documents "appended to or included with" the "retained applications", and thirdly copies of the "scoring sheets" of the 49 candidates, whose application forms had been retained. In a subsequent affidavit sworn by one Suzanne Quin, Head of the School of Applied Social Science at UCD, she averred at para. 3 thereof that application material was only retained in respect of those candidates who actually commenced the course and that in accordance with the college's records retention policy, the material which had been submitted by the other candidates was destroyed in March 2006. Nothing, however, turns on the precise date upon which the material was disposed of or on the correctness or otherwise of this policy.

8. The disclosure application was argued before the Circuit Court, having previously been in a list for the County Registrar. The President of that court refused the application on the 12th of March 2007 and by notice dated the 14th of March 2007, Mr. Kelly appealed to this Court against that order. For the following reasons, neither that appeal nor the substantive appeal against the decision of the Equality Officer have as yet been determined by the courts.

9. On the 23rd of April 2007, Mr. Kelly appeared before this Court and sought to have three questions, to which a fourth was added at a subsequent date, referred to the European Court of Justice under Article 234(1) and (3) of the EC Treaty. These questions are as follows:–

> 1. Does Article 4(1) of Council Directive 97/80/EC entitle an applicant for vocational training who believes that he or she has been denied access to vocational training because the principal of equal treatment was not applied to him or her, to information on the respective qualifications of the other applicants for the course in question and in

particular the applicants who were not denied access to vocational training, so that the applicant can, "establish, before a court or other competent authority, facts from which it may be presumed that there has been direct or indirect discrimination"?
2. Does Article 4 of Council Directive 76/207/EEC entitle an applicant for vocational training who believes that he or she has been denied access to vocational training "on the basis of the same criteria" and discriminated against "on grounds of sex" in terms of accessing vocational training to information held by the course provider on the respective qualifications of the other applicants for the course in question and in particular the applicants who were not denied access to vocational training?
3. Does Article 3 of Council Directive 2002/73/EC prohibiting "direct or indirect discrimination on the grounds of sex" in relation to "access" to vocational training entitle an applicant for vocational training who claims to have been discriminated against "on the grounds of sex" in terms of accessing vocational training to information held by the course provider on the respective qualifications of the other applicants for the course in question and in particular, the applicants who were denied access to vocational training?
4. Does the nature of the obligation under Article 234(3) EC differ in a member state with an adversarial (as opposed to inquisitional) legal system and, if so, in what respect?

It is in respect of this reference request that this Court now gives judgment.

10. Council Directive 76/207/EEC of 9th of February 1976 'on the implementation of the principle of equal treatment for men and women as regards access to employment, vocational training and promotion, and working conditions' (the "Equal Treatment Directive"), introduced "the principle of equal treatment for men and women as regards access to employment, including promotion, and to vocational training..." (Article 1). Article 2 defined the principle of equal treatment as meaning that "there shall be no discrimination whatsoever on grounds of sex either directly or indirectly..." (Article 2). Article 4 requires member states to take all necessary measures to ensure that "...vocational training, advanced vocational training and retraining shall be accessible on the basis of the same criteria and at the same levels without any discrimination on grounds of sex" (Article 4(c)). That directive was subsequently amended by Council Directive 2002/73/EC, which took effect only as and from the 23rd of September 2002.

11. The second Directive referred to is Council Directive 97/80/EC of 15th December 1997, 'on the burden of proof in cases of discrimination based on sex' (the "Burden of Proof Directive"), and in particular Article 4(1) thereof which reads:

> "Member States shall take such measures as are necessary, in accordance with their national judicial systems, to ensure that, when persons who consider themselves wronged because the principle of equal treatment has not been applied to them establish, before a court or other competent authority, facts from which it may be presumed that there has been direct or indirect discrimination, it shall be for the respondent to prove that there has been no breach of the principle of equal treatment.".

12. This Directive has ostensibly been given effect to in Irish law by the European Communities (Burden of Proof in Gender Discrimination Cases) Regulations 2001 (S.I. 337/2001), but only in respect of certain Acts of the Oireachtas, which do not include the Equal Status Act 2000.

13. The plaintiff relies upon the Equal Treatment Directive and the Burden of Proof Directive, as conferring upon him a right, by virtue of Community law, to have sight of the documents referred to at para. 7 of this judgment. He claims that having this information, which relates to the qualifications and suitability of the successful applicants, is critical so that he can establish his allegation of discriminating conduct, or at least can establish facts to which Article 4(1) of the Burden of Proof Directive could then apply. This right, he asserts on the one hand, is separate and distinct from his appeal presently before this Court, but on the other, if established, is such as must have a direct influence on domestic law. The latter appeal on the disclosure application has its foundation in domestic law, whereas the Directive point is based on Community law. Accordingly, Mr. Kelly submits that this Court is duty bound, by virtue of Article 234 of the EC Treaty, to refer the above questions to the European Court of Justice ("ECJ") for a preliminary ruling from that Court.

14. The plaintiff's substantial argument on this application is strikingly simple. He asserts that this Court is the court of final instance in his appeal against the order of the Circuit Court, which it will be recalled was made on foot of the disclosure application; that being so, it is submitted that in accordance with Article 234(3), this Court has no discretion, but must refer the suggested questions to the ECJ for its opinion thereon. In furtherance of his claim, the plaintiff has filed several books of legal submissions supported by authorities, articles, opinions and publications. These run to several hundred pages and it would be neither feasible nor desirable, or indeed necessary, to substantially repeat those submissions or the authorities in this judgment. This because in my view, the issue raised can be disposed of by reference to the material above mentioned, as well as the cases hereinafter discussed.

15. In addition to his principal request, Mr. Kelly has made two subsidiary arguments which conveniently can be dealt with at this point. The first submission, which I reject, is to the effect that once a party raises a question of Community law before a court acting as a court of final instance, that Court must make the reference as sought; it has no discretion to do otherwise. Arising out of a similar or comparable submission, the ECJ in *CILFIT v. The Minister for Health* [1982] ECR 3415 took the opportunity of clarifying what the true position was. As part of its decision the Court dealt specifically with this point at para. 9, where it stated:

> *"... Article [234] does not constitute a means of redress available to the parties to a case pending before a national court or tribunal. Therefore the mere fact that a party contends that the dispute gives rise to a question concerning Community law does not mean that the Court or Tribunal concerned is compelled to consider that a question has been raised within the meaning of Article [234]. On the other hand, a national Court or Tribunal may, in an appropriate case, refer a matter to the Court of Justice of its own motion."*

Therefore no party to an action has the right to insist upon a reference being made or to assert a right of veto against the making of such a reference.

16. The second point is the suggestion that para. 3 of Article 234 is entirely unrelated to the preceding paragraph. Whilst there are significant differences, as noted *infra.*, both have in common the requirement that the court of final instance must consider that the views of the ECJ are *necessary* in order to enable it to give judgment (emphasis added). Therefore, unless the domestic court felt unable to give a decision without making a reference, it would not do so. But where such conclusion is reached a reference must be made.

17. The defendant, UCD, has made two submissions in response, both in support of its opposition to the making of any reference. The College's views can be summarised as follows:–

> (1) In considering this application, the exact wording of Article 234 shows that the following four requirements must be satisfied before this court should accede to the request made:–
>
> (a) The questions must relate to provisions of Community la w upon which the European Court has jurisdiction to give a ruling,
> (b) The questions must relate to the interpretation and/or validity of those provisions,
> (c) The questions must have been raised before a national court or tribunal, and
> (d) A decision on the questions must be necessary so as to enable the national court or tribunal to give judgment.

(2) Where a court, before which the above requirements are satisfied, is a court of final instance, then a reference must be made subject only to the *acte clair* principles. These principles, which describe a number of circumstances in which a reference, even under para. (3) of Article 234, is not mandatory, takes its name from the decision of the ECJ in *CILFIT v. The Minister for Health* [1982] ECR 3415. Relying upon this decision it is suggested that the plaintiff's request for a reference should be refused as he has failed to surmount the criteria specified in that case.

(3) In particular it is said:

i) that, in the context of this case, the Court envisaged in Article 234(2) is not this court, but the Circuit Court, as that court has seisin over the substantive appeal (*Fratelli Pardini v. Ministero del Commercio con L'estero* [1988] ECR 2041);

ii) that the reference is unnecessary as any ruling would have no impact on the outcome of the case; and,

iii) that as the interpretation of community law is so obvious on the points at issue, no benefit could be derived from such a reference (*CILFIT v. The Minister for Health* [1982] ECR 3415).

(4) It is further claimed that the Equal Status Act 2000 is purely a domestic piece of legislation from which no question of Community law could arise: whereas if the discrimination claim has been brought under s. 12 of the Employment Equality Act 1998 (which it was not), some question of Community law could possibly have arisen. Moreover, the course in question was not in fact a vocational course, and therefore the Equal Treatment Directive is inapplicable.

(5) Neither does a reference have to be made when it could be regarded as frivolous or vexatious, an example of which would be where the issue in question can be determined solely by reference to domestic law (see *Riordan v. An Taoiseach* [2000] 4 IR 537).

(6) Finally, the defendant also claims that the principle of confidentiality as understood in both domestic and European case law, makes it clear that in any event the plaintiff's request for sight of all applications of the successful parties in unredacted form cannot succeed.

18. Article 234 of the EC Treaty reads:–

(1) "The Court of Justice shall have jurisdiction to give preliminary rulings concerning:

(a) the interpretation of this Treaty;

(b) the validity and interpretation of acts of the institutions of the Community and of the ECB;

(c) the interpretation of the statutes of bodies established by an act of the Council, where those statutes so provide."

(2) "Where such a question is raised before any court or tribunal of a Member State, that court or tribunal may, if it considers that a decision on the question is necessary to enable it to give judgment, request a Court of Justice to give a ruling thereon."

(3) "Where any such question is raised in a case pending before a court or tribunal of a Member State, against whose decisions there is no judicial remedy under national law, that court or tribunal shall bring the matter before the Court of Justice."

Purely for convenience I have numbered the paragraphs in the Article as (1), (2) and (3).

19. Before I look at these provisions in detail I should say a word about the relationship between Community law and national law. As a matter of general principle there is no doubt but that Community law constitutes an autonomous system of law and that in all respects it is a system which is superior to any domestic system of a Member State. In any case of conflict, inconsistency, or discord, national measures must give way. This means that where conflict exists:

(i) Community law takes precedence over domestic law;

(ii) Community law renders automatically inapplicable any relevant national provision;

(iii) Community law prohibits the adoption of any new measures which are incompatible with it; and finally,

(iv) A national court, in order to give full effect to this principle, must set aside conflicting provisions, whether passed before or after the Community measure.

20. These principles are non-controversial and well established (see *Stato v Simmenthal* [1978] ECR 629). These provisions have been supplemented by what might be described as subsidiary rules, established by the ECJ over time. One such rule emerged from the *Marleasing* case (*Marleasing SA v. La Comercial Internacional de Alimentacion SA* [1991] 1 ECR 4135) and is now known as the "Marleasing principle" or the "principle of conforming interpretation". This means that a national court has an obligation to interpret domestic legislation "so far as possible" in a manner both compatible with and in conformity to European law. This phrase "so far as possible" has been the subject matter of several decisions. Broadly speaking this interpretive method cannot be stretched to a point which involves a departure from the fundamental or cardinal feature of the provision in question. Subject however to this qualification, the Marleasing principle pervades all pieces of domestic law which necessarily are or ought to be influenced by Community law (see *Commissioners for Her Majesty's Revenue and Customs v. IDT Card Services Ireland Ltd* [2006] EWCA Civ 29 and *Pfeiffer v. Deutsches Rotes Kreuz* [2005] ICR 1307).

21. As can therefore be seen, Article 234 effectively has three parts to it. Para. (1) outlines the parameters of the Court's jurisdiction to give a preliminary ruling. Para. (2) confers a discretion on a national body to make a reference if it considers it necessary "to enable it" to give judgment on an issue before it. Para. (3) is similar to para. (2), but with two vital differences: firstly it refers to a court against which there is no judicial remedy under national law (court of final instance); and secondly, once the qualifying criteria exist, the national court must make such a reference – it has no discretion in so doing.

22. To come within this Article, a plaintiff must meet the positive requirements which are inherent in its provisions, and must also disapply all of the exceptions underlining the mandatory element of para. 3 thereof. In the first instance, this means:

(1) that the suggested questions must relate to the validity and interpretation of acts of the institutions of the Community;

(2) that such questions are raised in a case pending before the referring national court;

(3) that such court considers that a ruling from the ECJ on such question(s) is necessary so as to enable it to give judgment in the case pending before it; and,

(4) that such court is a court of final instance in that there is no judicial remedy against its decision under national law.

23. In *CILFIT v. The Minister for Health* [1982] ECR 3415 the disputed question, which arose in proceedings between wool importers and the Italian Minister of Health, concerned the payment of a fixed health inspection levy in respect of wool imported from outside the Community. The point in question depended on whether "wool" was included within a list of certain specified products, with the Minister arguing that the correct interpretation of the domestic measure was so obvious that a reference to the ECJ was not required. In the course of its judgment the court set out the essential purpose of the Article, as being to establish a uniform interpretation of Community law in all Member States, and to that effect para. 3 of Article 177 was designed to prevent the emergence of national judgments which differed from one Member State to another (para. 7). It then continued by laying down some general principles, which cumulatively are now known as the *acte clair* doctrine; these remain applicable to this day.

24. The *acte clair* principles are designed to ensure that notwithstanding what appears to be the mandatory wording of Article 234(3), a national court will not have to make a reference where the opinion of the ECJ can have no utility in the case or issue pending before it. To that end a series of cases, including, but not limited to *CILFIT*, have declared that a reference is not necessary:

(1) where a ruling could have no impact or affect on the outcome of the case (see Weinand Meilickev. ADV/ORGA F.A. Meyer AG [1992] ECR I-4871; Corsica Ferries Italia Slr v. Corpo dei Piloti del Porto di Genova [1994] ECR I-1783; Monin Automobiles-Maison de Deux-Roues [1994] ECR I-195);
(2) where the true meaning of the provision in question is "so obvious as to leave no scope for any reasonable doubt", a conclusion to be arrived at only when the same meaning would be equally obvious to courts of other Member States (see CILFIT);
(3) where the provision has been interpreted previously by the court, disregarding the nature of the earlier proceedings, and irrespective of whether or not the question raised is identical to the previous question decided upon (see CILFIT; Da Costa en Schaake NV v. Nederlandse Belastingadministratie [1963] ECR 31; Foglia v. Novello II [1981] ECR 3045); and,
(4) where the ruling is sought only for the purpose of obtaining an advisory opinion on general or hypothetical questions (see Foglia v. Novello II [1981] ECR 3045; Criminal Proceedings against Gasparini and others [2006] ECR I-9199).

25. There can be no doubt but that Directives of the Council, are acts of the Community Institutions, and therefore are within sub-paragraph (b) of Article 234(1), which it should be noted embraces not only the validity of an act, but also its interpretation. Equally so, there can be no dispute but that this Court, which is established by law and has constitutional status, is a Court as envisaged by Article 234. Therefore what must be considered is whether the other requirements of the Article are satisfied and, even if they are, whether there are any countervailing reasons against such a reference.

26. At the outset it can immediately be said that the reference application cannot be classified as being frivolous or vexatious, no matter how broad such a phrase is interpreted. Secondly this court has not been referred to any previous decision of the ECJ on this or any similar or analogous point. Thirdly, in light of the presenting circumstances, it cannot be said that the suggested questions seek an advisory opinion on general or hypothetical issues (see *Mangold* [2005] ECR I-9981 and *Adeneler v. Ellinikos Organismos Galaktos* (ELOG) [2006] ECR I-6057). And finally, in my view it cannot be concluded, with any degree of certainty, that the true meaning of the measures in issue are so obvious, to all Courts of the Member States, as to make a reference superfluous.

27. Furthermore, I do not feel that I have to make any decision as to whether or not the course to which Mr. Kelly sought admission was a course of "vocational training" for the purposes of s. 12 of the Employment Equality Act 1998. As a result, I do not have to decide whether the views of the Equality Officer in this regard are correct. The reason for this is that in my view it is at least arguable and perhaps strongly so, that as a matter or European law, a postgraduate course in Social Work is "vocational training" for the purposes of Council Directive 76/207/EEC. In *Gravier v. City of Liège* [1985] ECR 593 the ECJ, when defining or describing "vocational training", said the following at para. 30:–

> *"It follows... that any form of education which prepares for a qualification for a particular profession, trade or employment or which provides the necessary training and skills for such a profession, trade or employment is vocational training, whatever the age and the level of training of the pupils or students, and even if the training programme includes an element of general education."*

See also *Blaizot v. the University of Liège* [1989] 1 CMLR 69; in particular paras. 19 and 20 of the court's judgment. Given the nature of Mr. Kelly's application, it is sufficient in my opinion for him to establish that the relevant course is arguably a course "of vocational training" for the purposes of European law, whatever this phrase might mean in domestic law. When established, any "interest qualification" requirement of Article 234 is thus satisfied.

28. In addition, the defendant argues that the complaint of gender discrimination instituted by the plaintiff has no connection with European law, and accordingly this Court lacks jurisdiction to make a reference even if it was otherwise minded to so do. This argument is to the effect that the Equal Treatment Directive (Council Directive 76/207/EEC) was given effect to by the Employment Equality Act 1998 and not by the Equal Status Act 2000. As the application was made under s. 7 of the latter Act, all issues theretofore are purely of a domestic nature and do not touch upon and are otherwise not connected to any Directive.

29. I agree that only the 1998 Act gave effect to the Equal Treatment Directive. I also agree that the Burden of Proof Directive was only incorporated into domestic law in 2001 by the European Communities (Burden of Proof in Gender Discrimination Cases) Regulations 2001, (S.I. 337/2001), and did not cover the Equal Status Act 2000. However, this is not determinative of the matter for two reasons. Firstly, where the 2000 Act was not covered by the implementing Regulation, there may be a question as to whether the Directive was properly transposed into Irish law. Secondly, the Court must, where a Directive touches on a matter, interpret any national legislation in a manner consistent with that Directive (the *Marleasing* principle). In those circumstances, there may be a question of Community law, for the purposes of Article 234, with regards to how and if the Burden of Proof Directive affects the Equal Status Act 2000, and if it was properly transposed into Irish law. An Article 234 reference may therefore still be required, notwithstanding the fact that the Act under which the plaintiff has moved does not specifically refer to any Community legislation.

30. It is unclear whether the defendant accepts that this Court, in the applying context, is a court of final instance: on the one hand it seems to so accept: on the other it seems not to. The defendant supported the latter viewpoint by suggesting that this court is not the court which ultimately will give judgment on the appeal from the decision of the equality officer, and so it does not require any opinion from the ECJ to determine those issues. For this reason, it is therefore not the court of final instance on the issue before it. In this regard, it relies upon the case of *Fratelli Pardini v. Ministero del Commercio con L'estero* [1988] ECR 2041, which I will come back to later in the judgment.

31. In assessing the status of the Court at this stage of the appeal process, it is important to identify precisely what relief Mr. Kelly is seeking before me, and which provisions of domestic law he is invoking. Among the most contentious documents in issue are the personal statements of the successful applicants who commenced the course. That such documents are relevant and material to the substantive appeal cannot be disputed. Ms. Quin, on behalf of UCD has stated in evidence that those statements are "*part of the documents that make up the total application for the Master of Social Science (Social Work) Course*". She also explained that:

> *"applicants for the course are requested to provide two personal statements in response to the following question 'How did your interest in social work arise?' and 'What particular qualities and personal experience which you posses do you consider would be of help to you in this field of work?' These are open questions and candidates make their own decisions as to the content of their responses."*

In a letter written by Miss Richardson in January 2002, who was then the course Director, she said "*Selection for the course is based on the candidate's completed application form, personal statements, references and performance at interview.*" There cannot be an argument therefore on the relevance of said documents for comparative purposes, as it has always been the plaintiff's case that he was better qualified than the least qualified female who obtained a place in the first round. Whilst it is impossible to re-create that part of the process which related to the interview and how that impacted on the eventual outcome, it cannot be doubted however but that the personal statements must have been an influential part of it, and thus of the success or failure of each applicant.

32. As stated above, the provisions governing the substantive appeal, *i.e.* the re-hearing on facts and law against the decision of the Equality Officer, are to be found in s. 28 of the Equal Status Act 2000. That section designates the Circuit Court and not this Court as the appellate court. Section 28(3), however, states that:

> *"(3) No further appeal lies, other than an appeal to the High Court on a point of law."*

It is therefore clear that this Court could never have seisin of the appeal in the sense stated and indeed that would remain the situation even if the Circuit Court had already disposed of the appeal. However, the questions sought to be referred have been raised before this Court on an appeal from the Circuit Court rejection of the disclosure application. Such an appeal, which is permitted under Part IV of the Court of Justice Act 1936, is heard by way of re-hearing (s. 37), with the decision of the High Court thereon being "*. . . final and conclusive and not appealable*" (s. 39). Therefore this Court is the court of final instance on the disclosure application: there is no judicial remedy available in national law against such a decision.

33. The only submission to the contrary is that the Circuit Court is the court seised of the appeal proper. No reliance is placed on the provisions of s. 28(3) of the 2000 Act: therefore it is unnecessary to comment on the effect (if any) of the restricted and limited nature of that form of appeal. I am unaware as to whether the plaintiff relied upon the Directives in the application under appeal: if he did, it is clear beyond question that this court would be the final court with regards to document disclosure: Mr. Kelly either by issue estoppel, abuse of process or otherwise would not be allowed to re-open that issue in the substantive appeal. The matter would have been dealt with at first instance and finally disposed of on appeal. If he did not rely upon those Directives, one could potentially argue that he should raise this issue in the appeal proper, and if dissatisfied, attempt to re-litigate the point *via* s. 28(3) of the Equal Status Act 2000. That approach would be both most unsatisfactory and circuitous. Unsatisfactory in that, unless successful in the application, the full appeal on the facts and merits would proceed without reference to such documents. If thereafter the appellate court should grant disclosure, a mechanism would have to be found, which is not immediately apparent, to have the case entirely re-heard in the Circuit Court. Neither possibility should be allowed to occur. In my view the effect of the legal regime is that the issues relating to the disputed documents cannot be re-litigated elsewhere. The plaintiff either succeeds or fails in this court. There is therefore no judicial remedy against this Court's decision on the production of the contested documents. Consequently I am satisfied that for the purpose of the disclosure application, this Court is a "*Court*" referred to in Article 234(3).

34. The case of *Fratelli Pardini v. Ministero del Commercio con L'estero* [1988] ECR 2041 has been relied upon by the respondent as supporting the submission that no reference should be made unless the referring court requires an answer so as to determine an issue before it. In *Fratelli*, proceedings were instituted by way of an interlocutory application seeking as its sole object interim measures in respect of a dispute which arose between the company and the Italian Ministry of Foreign Trade ("*Ministero del Commercio con l'Estero*"). Having granted the interim measure, the court nevertheless made a reference to the ECJ. As a result, the Commission expressed doubts about the ECJ's jurisdiction to give a ruling on the questions raised; given the fact that the proceedings before the requesting court were concluded. According to the argument, any such opinion could have no bearing on that court, but could only have an influence, if any, on the substantive proceedings, which on the relevant date had yet to be commenced. When commenced, the substantive proceedings would be brought before a Court or Tribunal different to that of the requesting court.

35. Having referred to the wide discretion vested in the national courts as to when and at what stage of the process a reference may be made, the ECJ at para. 10 said:–

> *"In that respect it is not possible to uphold the interpretation put forward by the plaintiff in the main proceedings that the concept of a court or tribunal for the purposes of Article [234] covers all the courts or tribunals amongst which the various functions leading to a final decision on the merits are distributed, regardless of which judicial bodies are seised at various stages of a single dispute. It follows from both the wording and the scheme of Article [234] that only a national Court or Tribunal which considers that the preliminary ruling requested 'is necessary to enable it to give judgment' may exercise the right to bring a matter before the court. That right is therefore limited to a Court or Tribunal which considers that a case pending before it raises questions of Community law requiring a decision on its part."* (emphasis added)

Therefore the opinion of the ECJ could be of use to it.

36. There is no doubt but that *Fratelli* is authority for the proposition that not every court which might be involved at some stage, in a single case process, can be regarded, merely by virtue of that fact, as being a court within Article 234(3). A court which was "*functus officio*" or one which at a future date might be accessed, could not be so classified.

37. Incidentally, what saved the Pretore in *Fratelli* was his power to review. This had come about by default, in that the requesting court had erroneously failed to follow certain procedural rules, and as a result had retained a function, albeit a limited one, in that it could recall the parties at any time in order to confirm, vary, or discharge the *interim* order. If however he had become *functus officio* the result would clearly have been different.

38. It could not be said that this Court is *functus officio*, or that its involvement, is hypothetical or prospective only. Clearly, neither is so: the application is currently pending before it. True it is not the substantive appeal, but in my view that is irrelevant: this because it is the appeal proper regarding the disclosure application. A judgment, indeed the final judgment on it, has to be given, not by the Circuit Court but by this court. Therefore I am *seised* of this appeal, the result of which could be influenced by Community law: more specifically by the opinion of the Court of Justice on the questions raised. This is subject only to what is stated at para. 40 *infra*. Consequently I cannot see how *Fratelli* is of assistance to the defendant. In fact, in my view it is supportive of the conclusion herein reached.

39. It has also been claimed that the application pending is truly an interlocutory matter and therefore a reference would be inappropriate; I cannot agree that this is so. In *Hoffmann-La Roche AG v. Centrafarm Vertribsgesellschaft Pharmazeutischer Erzeugnisse* [1977] ECR 957 the Court stated at para. 6:

> *"The third paragraph of [Article 234] of the [EC] Treaty must be interpreted as meaning that a national court or tribunal is not required to refer to the court a question of interpretation or of validity mentioned in that article when the question is raised in interlocutory proceedings for an interim order . . ., even where no judicial remedy is available against the decision to be taken in the context of those proceedings provided that each of the parties is entitled to institute or to require proceedings to be instituted on the substance of the case and that during such proceedings the question provisionally decided in the summary proceedings may be re-examined and may be the subject of a reference to the Court under [Articles 234]."*

For the reasons given there cannot be a re-opening of the disclosure issue in the appeal proper. I am therefore satisfied that the present application cannot be described as interlocutory in nature.

40. There is however one problem facing the plaintiff which renders his present application premature. It is this: the ultimate purpose of relying upon the Directives is to obtain the contested documentation in unredacted form; if such documents should otherwise became available, a reference would serve no purpose and would have no utility to this Court. Until the disclosure appeal is presented to and ruled upon by this Court it will not be possible to say, even *prima facie* or provisionally, whether, as a matter of domestic law, the decision of the Circuit Court was or was not correct. It may be that this Court would take a view contrary to that of the lower Court and as a result order the production of the disputed documents. If that occurred, a reference would be entirely unnecessary. In my view therefore, the appeal must be presented before this Court, as otherwise it will not know whether a reference is or is not required. For that reason the application is premature at this point in time and its final determination must therefore await the appeal process. However, I would note, albeit *obiter*, that I am satisfied that should the disclosure of the contested documentation be refused, a reference to the ECJ may be appropriate.

Maher v Minister for Agriculture, Food and Rural Development

[2001] IESC 32; [2001] 2 IR 139; [2001] 2 ILRM 481

Judgment delivered on the 30th day of March 2001 by Keane C.J.

Introduction

1. What has become known as the milk quota system has given rise to much litigation, both at the level of the member States and in the Courts of Justice of the European Communities. The present case arises out of the making by the first named respondent (hereafter *"the Minister"*) of the European Communities (Milk Quota) Regulations 2000 (S.I. No. 94 of 2000) (hereafter *"S.I. 2000"*). These provided for certain changes in the system which I shall endeavour to summarise at a later point. The validity of S.I. 2000 is challenged by the appellants on the ground that it constitutes the exercise of legislative power by the Minister contrary to Article 15.2.1 ° of the Constitution, violates the property rights of the applicants guaranteed by the Constitution and is not afforded immunity by the provisions of Article 29.4.7 of the Constitution, providing for the consequences of our accession to the European Economic Communities. The appellants' claim was dismissed in the High Court in a reserved judgment by Carroll J. and they have now appealed from that judgment and order to this court.

2. The milk quota scheme was first introduced in 1984 by the Council of EEC in order to cope with problems which had arisen from the implementation of the Common Agricultural Policy (hereafter *"the CAP"*) established under the Treaty of Rome as it affected the market in dairy products. The measures establishing the scheme were, accordingly, part of the common organisation of the market in the milk sector in the EEC, deriving from the CAP and known as the COM.

3. One of the features of the COM was a guaranteed price for milk producers throughout the EEC. This ultimately had it as its consequence a supply of milk and milk products throughout the EEC which was hugely in excess of the demand, resulting in massive costs to the community and severe downward pressure on milk prices. Attempts to deal with the problem in other ways having proved abortive, the scheme adopted in 1984 provided for a ceiling on milk production in each of the member States and the allocation to individual producers of a ceiling on their annual production. This was effected by the imposition of what was described as a *"super levy"* on any producer who exceeded the ceiling which would render uneconomic the production of any milk in excess of the relevant figure. This was done by the allocation of what were called *"reference quantities"* to the individual producers which became known as *"quotas"* and it will be seen that it was an essential part of the scheme that the total of the quotas in any member State, including Ireland, should not exceed the quota allocated by the EEC to the member State in question.

4. The scheme was originally intended to run for five years up to the 31st March 1989, but was in fact successively extended up to the 31st March 1993. A new, but substantially similar, system was then adopted which expired on 31st March 2000.

5. While the scheme achieved its objective of halting the growth in milk production in the EEC, the quota was initially set at a level which was substantially above the consumption of milk and milk products in the EEC. Accordingly, there continued to be a surplus of milk in the community. Various methods were adopted by the EEC of dealing with the resultant problems. Eventually, what was called *"Agenda 2000"* was adopted by the EEC Commission with a view to preparing the dairy sector for the further problems which would arise from the enlargement of the European Union and the liberalisation of trade within the World Trade Organisation. The latter developments would mean, not merely a new threat of surpluses in milk production, but also an undermining of the effectiveness of the quota regime in maintaining milk prices.

6. Agenda 2000 proposed to continue the milk quota regime for six years to March 2006 and also envisaged other proposals which were of particular relevance to the present proceedings. These related to what was seen by the Commission as a particular problem, i.e. the extent of quotas held by persons who were no longer actively involved in the production of milk. Under the scheme as originally introduced, the milk quota was attached to the land and could only be transferred to another person if the land to which it was attached was being transferred to that person. An exception was introduced, however, in 1987 which enabled producers to lease any part of the quota which he or she did not intend to utilise in a particular year until the end of the milk quota year.

7. The new measures adopted by the EEC to give effect to Agenda 2000 required the member States to adopt detailed rules as to what was to happen in relation to the transfer of quotas. It also conferred certain discretions on the member States as to provisions which might or might not be included in any such detailed rules. The relevant rules in Ireland are contained in S.I. 2000 which is challenged in these proceedings.

8. The effect of S.I. 2000 is that, subject to certain exceptions, it is no longer possible for persons who are not actively engaged in milk production to transfer their quota with the land by way of sale. Nor, again, subject to certain exceptions, is it possible to lease a quota with the land. While a quota can be transferred upon the renewal of a lease of lands, a person who has not been involved in milk production for three years or more, can make a temporary lease or transfer of the quota for one further year and no more. The regulations also provided for a *"restructuring scheme"* under which a quota holder can offer all or part of his or her quota to the purchaser of the milk in return for payment. The maximum price is to be determined by the Minister. There are exceptions to these various requirements when the lands were being sold, leased, given to or inherited by a spouse or family member.

9. The first applicant in an affidavit said that he was the owner of 130 acres of land in Cashel, Co. Tipperary and that there was a milk quota attached to the lands which amounted to approximately 28,170 gallons. He said that as a result of borrowings which he had to make at high interest rates in the 1970s to develop his dairy business and the wiping out of his dairy herd by brucellosis between May and September 1980, he found it necessary to earn an income outside dairy farming. He and his wife, accordingly, in 1986 started up an oil distribution company and in the year 1996 he leased his lands and milk quota to one Maurice Ryan: the lease expired on the 31st March 2000. He said that, as a result of the introduction of S.I. 2000, if he wished to retain his quota, he had only three options:

(a) to resume milk production;
(b) to renew the lease to Mr. Ryan;
(c) to lease the quota temporarily for one year.

10. He said that neither of the first two options were available to him and the third would only enable him to retain the quota for a year. However, if he were to dispose of the milk quota, his options would be to sell it under the restructuring scheme at the maximum price fixed by the Minister of £1.36 per gallon or do the same in a year's time, after temporarily leasing it for one year. He would also be entitled to sell it to his former lessee, Mr. Ryan, but the latter was not interested in acquiring it. He said that the figure fixed by the Minister did not represent the market value of the milk quota. He said that his two children were aged 14 and 16 and that he wished to retain his milk quota so that they could take up dairy farming in a few years' time if they so chose.

11. The second applicant said that he was the joint owner with his wife of lands and premises at Fethard, Co. Tipperary together with the milk quota attaching to the lands: the lands comprised approximately 77 acres and the milk quota amounted to approximately 24,404 gallons. He said that some years ago he began to suffer from ill health and it became necessary for him to cease milk production and sell his cows. Since then most of his income had been earned from leasing some of the lands together with part of his milk quota and temporarily leasing the balance of the milk quota. He said that his only options as a result of the introduction of S.I. 2000 were to resume milk production or sell his quota under the restructuring scheme. He said that, as he was now nearly 76 and no longer in full health, he was not in a position to resume milk production. As to the sale of his quota under the restructuring scheme, his complaints were the same as those of the first applicant.

12. The third applicant is the owner of 20 acres of land at Clonoulty, Co. Tipperary together with the milk quota attaching to the lands amounting to 11,844 gallons. She said in her affidavit that for a number of years she had temporarily leased the quota to the local creamery and that most of her income had come from that temporary lease. Her only other income was the sale of weanling calves born in the winter/spring months and sold the following autumn/winter. As in the case of the other two applicants, she said that her only options as a result of S.I. 2000 were to resume milk production or sell her milk quota under the restructuring scheme and that she was not in a position to resume milk production as she could not afford the cost of installing a new milking parlour. Her complaints as to the option of selling under the restructuring scheme were to the same effect as those of the first and second named applicants.

The regulatory framework

13. The relevant EEC Regulations are Council Regulation (EEC) No. 3950/92 of 28th December 1992 as last amended by Council Regulation (EC) No. 1256/99 of 17th May 1999 (hereafter *"the EC Regulations"*).

14. Article 6 requires member States, before a specified date, to authorise for a twelve month period temporary transfers of individual reference quantities which producers who were entitled thereto do not intend to use. It also provides that the member States may vary transfer operations depending on the category of producers or dairy production structures, may limit them at the level of the purchaser within regions and may determine to what extent transfer operations may be renewed. It also permits a member State to decide not to comply with this requirement, on the basis of certain criteria. The last mentioned discretion was not exercised in the case of Ireland.

15. Article 7.1 provides that

> *"Reference quantities available on a holding shall be transferred with the holding in the case of sale, lease or transfer by inheritance to the purchasers taking it over in accordance with the detailed rules to be determined by the member States taking account of the areas used for dairy production or other objective criteria and, where applicable, of any agreement between the parties.*
> *"Any part of the reference quantity, which is not transferred with holding, shall be added to the national reserve..."*

16. As already noted, the detailed rules in Ireland are set out in S.I. 2000. However, Article 8a of the EC Regulations provided that

> *"Acting in compliance with the general principles of community law, member States may take the following measures, with the aim of ensuring that reference quantities are solely attributed to active milk producers:...(b) member States may decide not to apply the provisions on transfer of reference quantities in Article 7(1)."*

17. The Minister availed of this power by providing as follows in Article 5(1) of S.I. 2000:–

> *"Subject to the exceptions provided for in Regulations 6, 7, 8, 9, 10 and 11, where any holding, or part thereof, is transferred the milk quota attached to that holding or part thereof shall not be transferred to the person to whom that transfer is made."*

18. Sub-paragraph (2) goes on to provide that, where there is a transfer of land to which the milk quota attaches, the milk quota is to be added to the *"national reserve"* unless one of the relevant exemptions in the regulations has been availed of. The concept of the *"national reserve"*, which has been a feature of the EEC milk quota scheme since its inception in 1984, means in effect that, where a milk quota ceases to be attached to a particular farm, it may remain available as part of the total quota to which the member State is entitled. Under S.I. 2000, such milk quotas become available to active milk producers, with priority being given to small and medium producers.

19. The exemptions provided for under S.I. 2000 from Article 5(1) must next be considered. Article 7, in effect, enables the Minister to grant a certificate of entitlement to transfer a milk quota to a person who satisfies him that he has been actively engaged in the production of milk for the previous three years. Article 6 enables the quota to be transferred to the spouse and defined members of the family of the transferor. Article 9 enables the lessee of land and a quota to purchase the leased quota with or without the land from the lessor on the termination of the lease, provided he or she is a producer. Article 10 provides for the transfer of the quota on a renewal of the lease. Article 12 provides for the transfer of the quota to the lessor where a lease of land which the milk quota attaches terminates.

20. Article 8 of the EC Regulations provides that

> *"With a view to completing restructuring of milk production or to environmental improvement, member States may take one or more of the following actions in accordance with detailed rules which they shall lay down taking account of the legitimate interests of the parties ...".*

21. There follow five options which were available to the member States. That contained in sub-paragraph (b) was availed of by the Minister in S.I. 2000 and was as follows:–

> *"... determine on the basis of objective criteria the conditions under which producers may obtain, in return for payment, at the beginning of a twelve month period, through allocation by the competent authority or by the body designated by that authority, of reference quantities released definitively at the end of the preceding twelve month period by other producers in return for compensation in one or more annual instalments equal to the above mentioned payment ..."*

22. Article 26 of S.I. 2000 enables the Minister, pursuant to Article 8(b), to introduce a scheme called the *"milk quota restructuring scheme"* for the surrender of a milk quota at the end of each milk quota year and its reallocation at the beginning of the following year. Sub-paragraph (5) provides that the maximum payment for a surrendered quota and the reallocation price is to be set by the Minister.

23. The Minister also availed of the power conferred on the member State by Article 6.1 of the EC Regulations as to the temporary transfer of quotas which producers who were entitled thereto did not intend to use. Article 27 of S.I. 2000 provides inter alia as follows:–

> *"(2) A person may, subject to paragraphs (3) and (4), offer for temporary transfer such part of his or her milk quota as he or she does not intend to use during that milk quota year.*

(3) The holder of a quota who neither made milk deliveries to a purchaser, or sold milk or milk products directly for consumption, during any three successive milk quota years since 1st April 1997 and who made a temporary transfer of his or her quota under Regulation 16 of the Regulations of 1995 or under paragraph (2) during each of the three milk quota years in question shall not be entitled to make a temporary transfer under paragraph (2).
(4) A person who neither made milk deliveries to a purchaser or sold milk or milk products directly for consumption, has leased his or her land and milk quota for a period of three successive years or more, since April 1st, 1997 shall be entitled to make a temporary transfer of his or her quota under paragraph (2) for one year only."

24. There follow provisions enabling the Minister to authorise a temporary transfer of the quota for one further milk quota year in *"exceptional circumstances"*.

25. Finally, it should be noted that recital (6) of the EC Regulation sets out the rationale of the relevant provisions of the EC Regulations as follows:–

"Whereas the experience with the additional levy scheme has shown that the transfer of reference quantities through legal constructions such as leases which do not necessarily lead to a permanent allocation of the reference quantities concerned to the transferee, can be an additional cost factor for milk production hampering the improvement of production structures;
Whereas in order to strengthen the reference quantities' character as a means of regulating the market of milk and milk products, the member States should be authorised to allocate reference quantities, which have been transferred through leases or comparable legal means, to the national reserve for redistribution, on the basis of objective criteria, to active producers in particular, to those who have used them before;
Whereas member States should also have the right to organise the transfer of reference quantities in a different way than by means of individual transactions between producers;
Whereas it should be explicitly provided, in particular with a view to taking account adequately of existing legal rights, that, when using these authorisations, member States are to take the necessary measures to comply with the general principles of community law..."

. . .

Delegated legislation: Community Law

321. The case which is most material to the present discussion is *Meagher* and not merely because it concerned the implementation in Irish law of a directive adopted by the Community legislature.

322. Before embarking on a consideration of the relevance of *Meagher* to the present case, it is necessary to recall the changes to the constitutional and legal structure of this State resulting from membership of the European Communities and later the European Union and to refer to the provisions of the EC Treaty which are principally concerned. The import of *Meagher* cannot be considered in isolation.

323. The first important constitutional provision is Article 29.4.3 introduced by the Third Amendment to the Constitution in 1972 under which it was provided that *"The State* [might] *become a member of the.........European Economic Community."* Article 29.4, paragraphs 3, 4, and 5, respectively authorised the State by means of successive constitutional amendments to ratify the Single European Act in 1987, the Treaty on European Union (the Maastricht Treaty) in 1992 and the Treaty of Amsterdam in 1997. It emerges clearly from the judgment of this Court in *Crotty v An Taoiseach* [1987] IR 713 that the legislative capacity of the Council (and, since then, increasingly the European Parliament as co-legislator) seriously encroaches on the legislative sovereignty of the State.

324. Article 29.4.7 provides in addition that:

> *"No provision of this Constitution invalidates laws enacted, acts done or measures adopted by the State which are necessitated by the obligations of membership of the European Union or the Communities, or prevents laws enacted, acts done or measures adopted by the European Union or by the Communities or by the institutions thereof, or by the bodies competent under the Treaties establishing the Communities, from having the full force of law in the State."*

325. The Community regulations giving effect to the common organisation of the market in milk and milk products are "first pillar Community measures, i.e. they were adopted under the EC Treaty. Accordingly, it is unnecessary, in the present case, to have regard to any acts or measures adopted under the Treaty on European Union. Furthermore, it is probable that the authority to ratify the respective Treaties, in particular, the EC Treaty provide sufficient basis, in Community law terms, for the full effect in Irish law of directly applicable Community measures, even without the additional protection provided by Article 29.4.7.

326. The first two paragraphs of Article 249EC provide:

> *"In order to carry out their task and in accordance with the provisions of this Treaty, the European Parliament acting jointly with the Council, the Council and the Commission shall make regulations and issue directives, take decisions, make recommendations or deliver opinions.*
> *"A regulation shall have general application. It shall be binding in its entirety and directly applicable in all the Member States."*

327. The first paragraph of Article 10EC (formerly Article 5), which is also relevant, provides:

> *"Member States shall take all appropriate measures, whether general or particular, to ensure fulfilment of the obligations arising out of this Treaty or resulting from action taken by the institutions of the Community. They shall facilitate the achievement of the Community's tasks."*

328. Community regulations are directly applicable; their entry into force and their application are *"independent of any measure adopting* [them] *into national law."* (Case 94/77 *Zerbone v Amministrazione delle Finanze dello Stato* [1978] ECR 99, paragraph 23.) As Denham J. explains, in different words, they do not require any national act of implementation for their binding effect. Indeed, where they are, in their own terms, capable of being directly applied, it has been said that: *" Member States must not adopt or allow national institutions with a legislative power to adopt a measure by which the Community nature of a legal rule and the consequences which arise from it are obscured."* (*ibid.* paragraph 26.)

329. Where, however, as frequently happens especially in the case of a common organisation of the market, regulations, in addition to being directly applicable, allow Member States discretion in their implementation, some national act of implementation or transposition will be required. Then the principle cited by the applicants from the judgment of the Court of Justice in *Eridania* comes in. The Court there, at paragraph 34 of the judgment, said:

> *"The fact that a regulation is directly applicable does not prevent the provisions of that regulation from empowering a Community institution or a Member State to take implementing measures. In the latter case the detailed rules for the exercise of that power are governed by the public law of the Member State in question; however, the direct applicability of the measure empowering the Member State to take the national measures in question will mean that the national courts may ascertain whether such national measures are in accordance with the content of the Community regulation.".*

330. Clearly, the last sentence refers to the right of the courts of the Member States to refer questions of interpretation to the Court of Justice pursuant to Article 234EC (then Article 177 of the Treaty).

331. Counsel for the applicants drew attention specifically to the remark of Advocate General, at page 2787:

> *"But where a provision in Community legislation confers a discretion on a Member State it is open to that Member State to enact legislation for the purpose of implementing that provision. To what extent such legislation may be necessary, o r administrative action may suffice, is a matter to be determined by that Member State 's own law, including where appropriate its constitutional law."*

332. As was observed succinctly by Lord Hoffman, *"Community law is indifferent to the internal arrangements of power within a member state." (R v Secretary of State for Heath [2001] 1 All ER, 850 at 860).*

333. These passages must be read with those, also cited by the applicant, from the more recent case-law on milk quotas. It will suffice to quote the following from the judgment in *Dominikanerinnen-Kloster* (paragraph 26):

> *"It should, first, be recalled that........ the Court* [has held] *that according to the general principles on which Community law is based and which govern the relations between the Community and the Member States, it is for the Member States, by virtue of Article 5 of the Treaty, to ensure that Community regulations are implemented within their territory. In so far as Community law, including its general principles, does not include common rules to this effect, the national authorities when implementing Community regulations act in accordance with the procedural and substantive rules of their own national law; however, these national rules must be reconciled with the need to apply Community law uniformly so as to avoid unequal treatment of producers and traders. Furthermore, such rules must not have the effect of making it virtually impossible to implement Community regulations......"*

334. The applicants claim that a broad measure of competence has been returned to the Member States will be examined on its merits by reference to Regulation 3950/92 and Regulation 1256/99. However, Member States have limited scope for independent action when dealing with milk quotas. They cannot take action to grant them to fill a gap left by the amendment of a Community Regulation (Case C-127/94 *R v MAFF esp. Eckroyd* [1996] ELR I-2741.) I believe it is possible to say that the passages just quoted do not give any support to the applicants' claim that Member States act autonomously in making choices when implementing Community rules. They establish the following propositions.

335. Firstly, in the absence of common rules, or where Community law authorises such action, Member States may adopt their own national rules. Secondly, by virtue, *inter alia, of* Article 10EC (formerly Article 5 of the Treaty), Member States must ensure the implementation of Community regulations and take no action to undermine them. Thirdly, in doing so, they are implementing Community law, with the result that general principles of Community law, notably the principle of equal treatment but also the fundamental rights protected in the Community legal order must be respected. Fourthly, Community law is indifferent as to the national method of implementation (subject to the principle of effectiveness as explained in the passage from *Dominikanerinnen-Kloster* as well as the principle of equivalence, i.e., that rights under Community law are treated no less favourably than those granted by national law). For present purposes, that indifference relates to the choice between legislation and regulation.

336. In summary, Member States, acting within the framework of Community regulations, exercise powers or discretions which are conferred on them for the furtherance of the objectives of the scheme in question. Community law does not require any particular form of implementation. That is a matter for the legal system of the Member State concerned, except that the implementation must not have the effect of impeding the effectiveness of Community law.

337. The European Communities Act, 1972 contains the following provisions:

> *"2. From the 1 st day of January, 1973, the treaties governing the European Communities and the existing and future acts adopted by the institutions of those Communities shall be binding on the State and shall be part of the domestic law thereof under the conditions laid down in those treaties."*
> *"3.(1) A Minister of State may make regulations for enabling section 2 of this act to have full effect.*
> *(2) Regulations under this section may contain such incidental, supplementary and consequential provisions as appear to the Minister making the regulations to be necessary for the purposes of the regulations (including provisions for the repealing, amending or applying, with or without modification, other law, exclusive of this Act."*

338. Whatever view might be taken by the Court of Justice regarding the direct effect of treaty provisions or acts of secondary legislation, section 2 was clearly an essential part of the machinery for giving effect to those provisions as a matter of Irish law, in view of

339. Article 29.6 of the Constitution. For the purposes of the present case, it has the effect of making Articles 10EC and 249EC part of the law of the State.

340. It is the effect of section 3(1) which is in issue. The applicants accept, as they must, that the act of 1972, as was found in *Meagher* is compatible with the Constitution. However, they rely on the reiteration in the judgment of the Court, on that issue, of the principle that legislation must be so interpreted as not to be in conflict with the Constitution, in particular that an act cannot be interpreted so as to invade the exclusive legislative domain of the Oireachtas. Finlay C. J., delivering the judgment of the court stated at page 352:

> *"In so far as it may be possible to point to hypothetical instances of certain types of laws, measure or acts of the Community or Union which in their implementation or application within the national law might not, as to the method of implementation or application, be necessarily carried out by ministerial regulation, but rather should have been carried out by enactment of law by the Oireachtas, the Court is satisfied, without deciding that such instances do occur, that the principles laid down by this Court in the decision of East Donegal Co-Operative Livestock Marts Ltd. v. Attorney General [1970] I.R. 317, must be applied to the construction of the impugned subsection in the manner in which it was applied by the decision of this Court in Harvey v. The Minister for Social Welfare [1990] 2 I.R.. 232 to the construction of the section of the statute impugned in that case, namely, s. 75 of the Social Welfare Act, 1952. That principle is that it must be implied that the making of regulations by the Minister, as is permitted by the section, is intended by the Oireachtas to be conducted in accordance with the principles of constitutional justice, and therefore that it is to be implied that the Minister shall not in exercising the power of making regulations pursuant to the section, contravene any provision of the Constitution.*
> *"If therefore in such an instance challenge were to be made to the validity of a ministerial regulation having regard to the absence of necessity for it to be carried out by regulation instead of legislation and having regard to the nature of the content of such regulation it would have to be a challenge made on the basis that the regulation was invalid as ultra vires being an unconstitutional exercise by the Minister of the power constitutionally conferred upon him by the section."*

341. The early part of this passage might be read as implying that, in some circumstances, the implementation of Community law is necessarily, by reasons of the demands of Community law itself, carried out by regulation. It is clear, however, from the second quoted paragraph that this reading is not what was intended; in any event, as shown above, Community law makes no such demands. The issue of "necessity" is appropriately considered by reference to the content, not the form, of the instrument.

342. Consequently, it is perfectly possible for the courts, at least at the level of general principle, to apply the principles and policies test laid down in the case-law on Article 15.2.1 without any conflict with Community law. That test is designed, as is clear from the judgment of Denham J in *Laurentiu,* to protect the democratic basis of government, a principle which finds expression in the EC Treaty and in the judgments of the Court of Justice. Article 6 of the Treaty on European Union records that:

> *"The Union is founded on the principles of liberty, democracy, respect for human rights and fundamental freedoms, and the rule of law, principles which are common to the Member States."*

343. The second part of the decision in *Meagher* deals with the application of the principles and policies test to the implementation by means of a regulation made under the act of 1972 of Community law in the form of a Council directive. Blayney and Denham JJ delivered individual judgments, with which Finlay C. J. and O'Flaherty and Egan JJ agreed.

344. The two directives at issue concerned the prohibition of use of certain animal-growth hormonal substances. The State had included respectively a power to search farms and an extension of the time fixed by statute for commencing prosecutions of offences in ministerial implementing regulations. Blayney J decided that the directives could not be implemented without the first provision and that an extension of the time for prosecution was necessary. He reiterated the principle of the supremacy of Community law over national law and held that the national measures in controversy were *"necessitated by the directive."* His determination of the issue followed from an analysis of Community law provisions. The respondents argued in this case that, on a true analysis of the Community directives, Ireland as a Member State had discretion and was not bound to adopt the particular implementing measures and that the Court still found them to be *"necessitated"*. That is, in my view, to miss the point and to confuse the interpretation of Article 29.4.7 of the Constitution with the interpretation of Community law. The fact is that, rightly or wrongly, Blayney J held that the provisions in question were required by Community law. Denham J shortly expressed the same opinion (page 363). This result is the same as would have followed if questions of interpretation of the relevant provisions had been referred to the Court of Justice and the latter had ruled that the adoption of the two provisions in controversy constituted Community-law obligations of the State.

345. Denham J made it clear, however, that this was not the end of the matter. She said:

> *"If the directive left to the national authority matters of principle or policy to be determined then the "choice" of the Minister would require legislation by the Oireachtas. But where there is no case made that principles or policies have to be determined by the national authority, where the situation is that the principles and policies were determined in the directive, then legislation by a delegated form, by regulation, is a valid choice. The fact that an act of the Oireachtas has been affected by the policy in a directive, is a "result to be achieved" wherein there is now no choice between the policy and the national act. The policy of the directive must succeed. Thus where there is in fact no choice on a policy or a principle it is a matter appropriate for delegated legislation. If the directive or the minister envisaged any choice of principle or policy then it would require legislation by the Oireachtas."*

Meagher is clear authority for the proposition that, where a provision of Community law imposes obligations on the State, leaving no room (or perhaps no significant room) for choice, then Article 15.2.1 of the Constitution is not infringed by the use of ministerial regulation to implement it. Both the judgment of the Court and that of Denham J expressly preserve the force of that provision, as it has been interpreted, for cases where such an obligation does not exist. The "principles and policies" test applies *mutatis mutandis* where the delegated legislation represents an exercise of a power or discretion arising from Community-law secondary legislation. It applies with particular clarity to the case of directives where Article 249EC leaves the choice of forms and methods to the Member States. The question will not arise so frequently in the case of regulations since they are directly applicable without the need for national implementing measures. Where a regulation leaves open a range of choice, the test will apply. Each case will have to be decided on its own merits. The mere existence of a Community regulation implies some sort of Community policy. Article 253EC obliges the Community legislature to state in such acts *"the reasons on which they are based."* Member State implementing measures come inherently within the scope of such a stated policy. However, the principle of the applicability of the test is a recognition of the possibility that the choices left to the Member States may be of such significance in their nature or scope or so unconnected with Community policies and aims that they require legislation and that resort to regulations in such cases would infringe Article 15.2.1. On its facts, *Greene v Minister for Agriculture [1990] 2 I.L.R.M.* could have been such a case, though Article 15.21 was not in issue. The Community rules allowed Member States to "*lay down additional or restrictive conditions*" one of which was held by Murphy J. to infringe Article 41 of the Constitution.

346. I should say that I fully agree with the judgment of the Chief Justice in his analysis of *Meagher* and with his conclusion that none of the measures impugned in this case was *"necessitated by the obligations of membership."* I also agree, consequently, that the essential question is whether the Minister was in breach of Article 15.2.1 of the Constitution. If he was, the 2000 Regulations will be invalid, since, unlike those involved in *Meagher*, they are not "necessitated".

Applying the test

347. I will deal, firstly, with the change in the rules linking land and milk quota. From the outset, the Community rules envisaged that, in general, agricultural land used for milk production would be transferred only with the relevant milk quota attached. The original provision was Article 7(1) of Regulation 857/84, which provided:

> "*Where an undertaking is sold, leased or transferred by inheritance, all or part of the corresponding reference quantity shall be transferred to the purchaser, tenant or heir according to procedures to be determined.*"

348. There were differences between Formula A (where the milk quota is allocated to producers) and Formula B, adopted in Ireland, (where it is allocated to purchasers). However, rules were formulated to ensure that the same rules would apply where Formula B was adopted. (See Commission Regulation (EEC) No 1374/84, Article 5 and Murphy J in *Lawlor*, page 3640).

349. It may be noted that this provision was not founded on any explicit reasoning to be found in any of the recitals in the preamble to the regulation. The respondents' argument that there were significant exceptions from the beginning to the rule of transfer of land with milk quota is not convincing. Article 7(3) merely provided part of the reference quantities might be added to the national reserve. Article 4, which was also invoked, authorised Member States to compensate milk *"producers undertaking to discontinue milk production definitively"* and to add the amounts so freed to the national reserve. Ireland did not, in fact, exercise these options. I am similarly unconvinced by a number of other examples of special exceptions which were cited from the years 1985 to 1987. It seems clear that the Community, as of 1984, opted firmly for a policy that land could be transferred only with the milk quota attached.

350. Regulation 857/84 was repealed by Council Regulation (EEC) No 3950/92 of 28 December 1992 establishing an additional levy in the milk and milk products sector. The fourteenth introductory recital to that Regulation states:

> *"Whereas when the additional levy system was brought in in 1984, the principle was established that when an undertaking was sold, leased or transferred by inheritance, the corresponding reference quantity was transferred to the purchaser, tenant or heir;*
> *whereas this original decision should not be changed; whereas, however, national provisions to safeguard the legitimate interests of the parties should be implemented in all cases of transfer, where the parties are not in agreement;"*

351. In the event, Article 7 was re-enacted by Regulation 3950/92 with some changes which are immaterial to the present case. Article 8 of Regulation 3950/92 provide for some other limited exceptions such as transfer to the national reserve when land is transferred for improvement of the environment. It also authorised Member States, with a view to restructuring of milk production, to permit transfer of reference quantities without the corresponding land *"with the aim of improving the structure of milk production at the level of the holding."* Generally, however, the link between land and milk quota was maintained.

352. This prohibition on sale or transfer of land without milk quota, because it was effected by a regulation was, of course, directly applicable in Irish law and needed no further enactment to give it effect. It was, nonetheless, reinforced, as the applicants point out, by penal provisions in Regulation 12(1) of the European Communities (Milk Levy) Regulations, 1985 (S.I. No. 416 0f 1985) and by Regulation 4 of the European Communities (Milk Quota) Regulations, 1995 (S.I. No 266 of 1995)(the "1995 S.I.")

353. Council Regulation (EC) No 1256/99 of 17 May 1999 amending Regulation (EEC) No Regulation 3950/92....... authorised radical change in the rules regarding the maintenance of the link between land and milk quota on sale or transfer.

354. Article 8 of Regulation 1256/99 replaces Article 7(1) of Regulation 3950/92 as follows:

> *"Reference quantities available on a holding shall be transferred with the holding in the case of sale, lease or transfer by inheritance to the producers taking it over in accordance with detailed rules to be determined by the Member States...."*

355. At the same time, Article 1(10) of Regulation 1256/99 inserts a new Article 8a into Regulation 3950/92, which provides:

> *"Acting in compliance with the general principles of Community law, Member States may take the following measures, with the aim of ensuring that reference quantities are solely attributed to active milk producers:*
> *(a).....*
> *(b) Member States may decide not to apply the provisions on transfer of reference quantities in Article 7(1)."*

356. The changes in the rules made by the Minister, the 2000 Regulations, regarding attachment of land to milk quota commence with Regulation 5(1) which provides, in relevant part:

> *"(1) Subject to the exceptions provided for in Regulations 6, 7, 8, 9, 10, and 11, where any holding, or part thereof, is transferred the milk quota attached to that holding or part thereof shall not be transferred to the person to whom the transfer is made;*
> *"(2) Where there is a transfer of land to which milk quota attaches then, such milk quota shall be added to the national reserve unless Regulation 6, 7, 8, 9, 10, 11, 19, 20, 21, or 22 have been availed of..."*

357. This amounts to a clear and explicit decision by the State to avail of the power given by Community law to break the link between land and milk quota. There are a number of exceptions. The applicants say that both by deciding to exercise that option and in choosing the exceptions, the Minister was impermissibly legislating.

358. It is crucial to this issue to discern whether, in making this decision, the State is pursuing a Community objective or, recalling the applicants' contention that power has been returned to the Member States, a purely national one. The power not to apply the provisions of Article 7(1) is given by Article 8a, inserted by Article 1(10) of Regulation 1256/99. That Article permits Member States to take such action *"with the aim of ensuring that reference quantities are solely attributed to active milk producers..."* This reflects policy expressed in the fourth recital in the preamble:

> *"Whereas the experience with the additional levy has shown that the transfer of reference quantities through legal constructions such as leases which do not necessarily lead to a permanent allocation of the reference quantities concerned to the transferee, can be an additional cost factor for milk production hampering the improvement of production structures; whereas, in order to strengthen the reference quantities' character as a means of regulating the market of milk and milk products, the Member States should be authorised to allocate reference quantities, which have been transferred through leases or comparable legal means, to the national reserve for re-distribution, on the basis of objective criteria to active producers in particular to those who have used them before; whereas Member States should also have the right to organise the transfer of reference quantities in a different way than by the means of individual transactions between producers; whereas it should be explicitly provided, in particular with a view to taking account adequately of existing legal rights, that, when using these authorisations, Member States are to take the necessary measures to comply with the general principles of Community law;.."*

359. I believe that this recital and the general scheme of the milk quota regime demonstrate that the State is acting as a delegate of the Community in making the choice to separate land and milk quota. As is shown by the case-law, the fact that Community regulations authorise the Member States to exercise discretion does not take action of the latter kind outside the scope of the Community regime. Member State discretionary action is circumscribed by the objectives of the scheme authorising it. The milk quota is itself a creature entirely of Community law. Member States are bound, by virtue of Article 10EC (formerly Article 5 of the Treaty), to ensure that Community law is implemented; national rules must comply with the general principles of Community law and the particular rules which apply. In the instant circumstances, Member States are authorised to act only to achieve the aim of ensuring that reference quantities are attributed to producers. Any action by the State in pursuit of a an unauthorised objective would be susceptible of challenge, by means of an infringement action pursuant to Article 226EC in the Court of Justice as being contrary to the terms of Regulation 1256/99.

360. Thus, applying the principles and policies test on the basis that Regulation 1256/99 stands in the place of an act of the Oireachtas, I believe that the State, in adopting Regulation 5 of the 2000 Regulations was exercising a power expressly conferred and for the purpose for which it was given.

361. In the light of that conclusion, it is probably not necessary to give separate consideration to the exceptions. They consist of modifications to the departure from the link of land and milk quota. However, they were argued as constituting distinct legislative choices.

362. The principal exceptions which have been canvassed in argument before the Court are those in Regulations 6, 7, 9 and 10. It will be sufficient to refer to these for the purpose of evaluating the extent and the nature of the legislative power exercised by the Minister in making the 2000 Regulations.

363. Regulation 6 provides that the " *milk quota attached to a holding shall be transferred"* in the case of *"sale, lease, gift or inheritance by a person to a relative of that person...,"* a term defined in Regulation 6(2). It includes spouses, parents, children, brothers, sisters, grandparents, grandchildren, uncles and aunts. It is suggested that this also involves the making of a legislative choice not contemplated by Community law. It is not clear that the applicants have any independent interest in challenging this provision. It would not benefit them if it were annulled. Their claim is in reality that the Minister did not have the power, by regulation, to end the link of land to milk quota in the event of sale or transfer. For what it is worth, however, I believe that this exception would be held to fall comfortably within the power conferred on the Member States by the regulation. I have already referred to the inclusion of *"the social structure of agriculture"* among the considerations relevant to the common agricultural policy. If it is correct to say that Member States are authorised by Community law to restrict or end the rule that milk quota transfers with land, there is no basis – and none has been suggested – for saying that Community law would regard it as impermissible to make an exception for certain defined family transactions. The wording of Article 7(1) has at all times included *"transfer by inheritance"* among the cases where the link would apply. There is enough evidence in the case-law cited to the Court (Case C-313/89 *Rauh* [1991] ECR I- 1647; Case C-44/89 *von Deetzen v Hauptzollamt Oldenberg* [1991] ECR I-5119 "*von Deetzen*") to show, not surprisingly, that the Court of Justice interprets provisions of Community law so as to favour family transactions. As already noted, Article 33EC requires account to be taken of *"the social structure of agriculture,"* which unarguably includes the family basis of farm ownership. The relaxation of the new rule to favour family transactions accords with that aim.

364. By virtue of Regulation 7, where a producer (or his legal personal representative) can obtain a certificate from the Minister, inter alia, that he has produced milk on the holding for a period of three years prior to the milk quota year in which the transfer is proposed, he may continue to transfer land with quota. This patently favours the active milk producer and accords with the objective of Article 8a and the sixth recital. This provision also demonstrates that removal of the land/milk-quota link is by no means as draconian as has been suggested. It remains open to each of the applicants, as they acknowledge, to resume production of milk on their own land and by this means and to regain the right to sell their land with milk quota.

365. Regulation 9 permits the purchase of land by a lessee of land and quota to be made with or without milk quota on the expiry or earlier determination of a lease. The lessee must, himself be a producer. This also favours the active milk producer.

366. Regulation 10 permits the renewal of an existing lease on its expiry, in which case the milk quota is transferred to the lessee for the term of the renewal. This provision cannot be the subject of complaint. Apart form favouring milk production, it represents the sort of fine regulatory choice which fits easily within the scope of action which can be taken without infringing Article 15.2.1 of the Constitution.

367. For these reasons, I do not think that the 2000 Regulations infringe Article 15.2.1 of the Constitution, in respect of the changes regarding the transfer of land with milk quota.

368. I should explain the purpose of the detailed consideration I have given to the Community provisions. It has never been contested that the 2000 Regulations were, in Community law terms, within the scope of the discretion available to the State. Therefore, I am not considering an issue of Community law. If I were, the court might be obliged to refer to the Court of Justice. I am judging, rather, whether the scope of the discretion conferred by Community law in regulations which become part of national law was so independent of principles and policies laid down by those Community regulations, as to place the State in conflict with Article 15.2.1 of the Constitution.

369. At this point, it is also necessary to consider the Communit *y* rules regarding temporary transfer of milk quotas. They, to some extent, also involve separation of land and milk quota. Temporary transfers were first authorised by Council Regulation (EEC) No 2998/87 of 5 October 1987 amending Council Regulation 804/68... This recites that *"experience has shown that certain producers do not intend, over a 12-month period, using up all their individual reference quantities* [and that]... *Member States should be authorised to place at the disposal of other producers for the 12-month period in question, the quantities which are not going to be used by other producers who are entitled thereto;"* On this premise, Article 1 inserted a new Article 1a in Regulation 804/68 as follows:

> *"1a. Member States may authorise, at the beginning of each 12-month period and for the duration thereof temporary transfers of that part of the individual reference quantity which the producer who is entitled thereto does not intend to use.*
> *Member State* s *may limit the transfer operations to certain categories of producers and on the basis of the milk production structure in the regions or collecting areas concerned."*

Regulation 3950/92 recited that "....*the temporary transfer of parts of individual reference quantities in Member State* s *which authorised this ha* [d] *proven to be an improvement to the scheme* [and that] *this facility should therefore be extended to all producers* [though its] *implementation........... should not stand in the way of further structural change and adjustment, nor fail to take account of the resulting administrative difficulties;"*

370. Consequently, Article 6 of Regulation 3950/92 renewed the power to permit temporary transfer, transforming it, however, into an obligation, and adding that Member States might *"determine to what extent transfer operations may be renewed."* Furthermore, Article 6(2) provided:

> *"Any Member State may decide not to implement paragraph 1 on the basis of one or both of the following criteria:*
> - *the need to facilitate structural developments and adjustments,*
> - *overriding administrative needs."*

The temporary transfer provisions were implemented in the State by Regulation 16 of the 1995 S.I. This delegated to the Minister the power to determine the categories of producers who might benefit and, more relevant to the present case, *"the extent to which temporary transfers.........* [might] *be renewed."* The public were to be informed by notices in a National newspaper.

371. Regulation 1256/99 made no significant change in the temporary transfer rules. It did, however, restate Article 6(1) of Regulation 3950/92 as follows:

> *"Before a date that they shall determine and by 31 March at the latest, Member States shall authorise, for the 12-month period concerned, temporary transfers of individual reference quantities which producers who are entitled thereto do not intend to use."*

372. Important restrictions are imposed, by Regulation 27 of the 2000 Regulations, on the system of temporary transfers as it has hitherto operated in the State.

373. Paragraphs (1) and (2) ostensibly preserve the right of a milk quota holder to make a temporary transfer of *"such part of his or her milk quota as he or she does not intend to use during that milk quota year."* Paragraph (3), however, denies this right where the holder has *"neither made milk deliveries to a purchaser, or sold milk or milk products directly for consumption, during any three successive milk quota years since 1 April 1997 and who made a temporary transfer of his quota under Regulation 16 of the Regulations of 1995 or under paragraph (2) during each of the 3 milk quota years in question.."*

374. Paragraph (4), on the other hand permits a person who, likewise, has *"neither made milk deliveries to a purchaser, or sold milk or milk products directly for consumption,"* but has leased the land and milk quota for the same period to make a temporary transfer but for one year only.

375. Paragraph (5) enables the Minister, on application, to approve a temporary transfer for one further milk quota year only by a person affected by paragraph (3) or (4), where exceptional circumstances have caused the failure to deliver milk.

376. The respondents have made it clear that the State has not exercised the option granted by Article 6(2) of Regulation 3950/92 not to implement Article 6(1). Consequently, it is said, the State was obliged by Article 6(1) to *"authorise... temporary transfers of individual reference quantities which producers who are entitled thereto do not intend to use."* However, it is further argued that the applicants do not come within the definition of producer. That term is defined in Article 9 of Regulation 3950/92 as a *"natural or legal person...... farming a holding within the geographical territory of the Community*:

- *selling milk or milk products directly to the consumer,*
- *and/or supplying the purchaser."*

377. The respondents rely on the decision of the Court of Justice in Case C-152/95 *Macon v Préfet de l'Aisne* [1997] ECR I-5429. That case dealt with the identical definition in Article 12(c) of Regulation 857/84, where farmers, who had ceased milk production, (no explanation for this cessation appears in the report) sought compensation under a Community scheme for *producers* undertaking to discontinue production definitively. The Court of Justice held that the *"term had not been given an independent meaning for the purposes of the rules on discontinuation of milk production."* (Paragraph 21). It held (paragraph 23):

> *"Only farmers actually selling milk or other milk products can... be considered to be producers. By contrast farmers who have spontaneously ceased milk production are no longer producers for the purposes of Article 12(c) of Regulation 857/84."*

378. The Court, in that judgment recalled its judgment in Case C-341 *Ballmann* [1991] ECR I-25, where it had said: *"the status of producer is accorded to any person who manages a holding, that is to say a set of production units... and sells or delivers milk or milk products."*

379. Since consideration of this issue involves the interpretation of a provision of a Community regulation, the issue of the obligation of this Court to refer questions to the Court of Justice can arise. For the moment, I will say only that, in my view, the meaning of the term *"producer"* is quite clear. None of the applicants come within that definition. Therefore, they cannot rely on Article 6(1) of Regulation 3950/92 to claim the right to continue to make temporary transfers of their milk quotas. Accordingly, the Minister, in denying them that right by the terms of Regulation 27 was not making a choice between different options conferred by Regulation 3950/92. He was not entitled in Community law to grant the right to make temporary transfers to persons who were not producers. That is, of course, a conclusion of Community law which might have to be referred for preliminary ruling.

380. However, this Court, as a *"court.... against whose decisions there is no judicial remedy under national law"* is not obliged by Article 234EC to refer a question of interpretation to the Court of Justice, unless *"a decision on that question is necessary to enable it to give judgment."* That is the situation which pertains in the present case, as I will explain.

381. As has been seen, Article 6 of Regulation 3950/92 authorises Member States to *"determine to what extent transfer operations may be renewed."* The State was, on any view, entitled to determine that the right to make temporary transfers should be permitted for one further year only, unless exceptional circumstances were demonstrated. In making this decision, the Minister acting on behalf of the State was exercising a discretion conferred by Community regulations and for one of the policy reasons clearly stated by Community law. This is supported by the fourth recital in the preamble to Regulation 1256/99. It expresses the view that Member States *"should have the possibility to decide in accordance with the general principles of Community law that, in cases of substantial under use* [of milk quota] *over a significant period of time, the under used reference quantities will revert to the national reserve with a view to their reallocation to other producers;"*

382. In my view, the Minister was entitled to decide, in the light of the general policy of favouring active producers that persons entitled to milk quotas, not in active production, but having used the facility of temporary transfer for three years past should be entitled to renew such temporary transfer for one further year only. In so doing, he was acting in accordance with principles and policies set out in the Community regulations.

383. The result of the foregoing is that:

1. The changes made in the rules regarding the link of milk quota to land on transfer constitute an exercise of discretions so closely linked to principles and policies laid down in Community law as not to require legislation for the purposes of Article 15.2.1 of the Constitution.

2. Although the applicants' ability to make temporary transfers of their milk quotas is severely restricted by the 2000 Regulations, they have no right under Community law, from which such a right exclusively derives, to make such transfers. Although this involves a question of Community law, it is not necessary for this Court to decide the case on that basis, since, in this case also, the State was pursuing principles and policies laid down in Community law.

Property Rights

384. It is only in respect of the first of these issues that the applicants are in a position to maintain that their property rights have been infringed. It has been established since at least as early as the judgment of the Court of Justice in Case 11/70 *Internationale Handellsgesellaschaft* [1970] ECR 1125, that fundamental rights and in particular rights to property are protected in the Community legal order. In Case 44/79 *Hauer v Land Rheinland-Pfalz* [1979] ECR 3727, that court explained that such protection was inspired by the common constitutional traditions of the Member States and the European Convention for the Protection of Human Rights and Fundamental Freedoms. The court drew attention specifically to the German and Italian Constitutions and to Article 43 of the Constitution of Ireland. However, it is equally clear from this judgment that "the question of a possible infringement of fundamental rights by a measure of the Community institutions can only be judged in the light of Community law itself." (paragraph 14). The other named sources of fundamental-rights protection are integrated into the Community legal order. In *Bostock,* the Court of Justice said, citing its earlier decision to the same effect in Case C-44/89 *Von Deetzen*:

> *"The right to property safeguarded by the Community legal order does not include the right to dispose, for profit, of an advantage, such as the reference quantities allocated in the context of the common organisation of a market, which does not derive from the assets or occupational activity of the person concerned..."*

385. In its judgment in *Demand,* the Court of Justice used the expression, *"regardless of the legal nature to be attributed to an additional reference quantity,"* when assessing and then rejecting a claim that Community provisions had infringed rights of property. As Murray J. explains in his judgment, when Member States exercise discretions conferred on them by Community law, as in this case, it is for Community law to decide whether they have infringed fundamental rights. The Court of Justice stated in *Duff,* at paragraph 29 that *"the protection of fundamental rights in the Community legal order are also binding on the Member States when implementing Community rules."* (emphasis added). In that case, the Court of Justice considered both Community rules and the exercise of discretion at national level. It did not refer in its judgment to the point made by the Advocate General, in his Opinion, that national law might *"in appropriate cases... ensure greater protection... than that afforded by the general principles applicable in the Community legal order."*

386. In my opinion, the applicants' complaint that their fundamental rights, whether or not described as property rights, have been infringed by the 2000 Regulations is unsustainable as a matter clearly decided in the constant case-law of the Court of Justice. Specifically, I cannot accept that their said rights were infringed by the State in exercising the discretion conferred on it to cease to apply Article 7(1) of Regulation 3950/92 (as amended) as introduced by the insertion by Article 1(10) of Regulation 1256/99 of Article 8a(b). I agree with the judgments of Denham and Murray JJ. on the issue of protection of property rights in milk quotas in Community law. I think that the position of the Court of Justice regarding claims based on infringements of property rights in milk quotas is clear beyond argument to the extent of being *acte clair.* On that basis-which was not seriously contested on behalf of the applicants-I do not think the Court is under an obligation to refer any question for preliminary ruling to the Court of Justice of the European Communities pursuant to Article 234EC.

387. In the present case the alleged infringements flow from the exercise of Member States' discretion within the framework and in pursuit of Community policies. In my view, the principle enunciated in *Hauer* applies to such a situation. It is not a case of the exercise of an autonomous power to impose restrictions permitted by Community law but in furtherance of national policies. If this was such a case, of course, Article 15.2.1 of the Constitution would apply and it would also follow that any law so enacted would be amenable to scrutiny by reference to other articles of the Constitution, specifically Article 43.

388. It need not follow that in every case an exercise of a power delegated by Community law which is valid in the sense of being within principles and policies laid down by the latter will survive scrutiny *vis à vis* other articles of the Constitution. It is difficult to envisage circumstances in which the exercise of a discretion would violate a provision of the Constitution protecting, for example, property rights without at the same time involving the invasion of the exclusive legislative role of the Oireachtas, but in principle that must be possible. I agree with Murray J. in his treatment of the issue of property rights.

389. In any event, in the circumstances, I would dismiss this appeal.

Meagher v The Minister for Agriculture and Food, Ireland and the Attorney General

[1993] IESC 2

Author's note: *Meagher* considered the constitutionality of the practice of implementing EU law by means of delegated (secondary) legislation.

Finlay CJ:

This is an appeal by the respondents in an application for judicial review against an order made in the High Court by Johnson J on 1 Apri 1 1993, whereby he declared that such portion of s. 3(2) of the European Communities Act 1972, as entitles a minister by regulation to repeal or amend or apply with or without modification other law exclusive of that of the said Act is unconstitutional.

The application for judicial review in which this declaratory order was made had sought a declaration that the European Communities (Control of Oestrogenic, Androgenic, Gestagenic and Thyrostatic Substances) Regulations 1988, SI No.218 of 1988, and the European Communities (Control of Veterinary Medicinal Products and their Residues) Regulations, SI No.171 of 1990, are *ultra vires* and void.

The application also sought an order of *certiorari* quashing a search warrant purportedly granted by a judge of the District Court pursuant to those regulations, and in addition, sought an order of prohibition of the first named respondent from proceeding to prosecute the applicant in respect of summonses alleging offences against the regulations.

The learned trial judge, having reached a conclusion that the particular subsection of the European Communities Act 1972 (the 1972 Act) was invalid, having regard to the provisions of the Constitution, did not make any declaration with regard to the questions of *ultra vires*, nor did he make an order quashing the warrant or prohibiting the prosecution.

The respondents in appealing against the order of the learned trial judge declaring the subsection of the Act of 1972 invalid, having regard to the Constitution, maintained in the alternative that if the court were to conclude that the statutory instruments concerned were *ultra vires* or constituted an unconstitutional exercise of the power to legislate by regulation then the statutory instruments, alone, should be condemned but the subsection of the statute should not.

The applicant for judicial review who is the respondent on this appeal, had not served any notice to vary, but was permitted in the interests of justice by the court to make the case that even if his challenge to the constitutional validity of the subsection of the Act of 1972 were to fail he should be entitled to maintain a challenge which he submitted was correct, against the validity of the regulations made pursuant to that subsection and that, accordingly, the warrant of search provided under them and the summons for an offence against them would both be invalid.

This decision, which is the Decision of the Court, pronounced pursuant to Article 34.4.5° of the Constitution deals only with the challenge to the constitutional validity of the impugned subsection of the 1972 Act.

The impugned legislation

The relevant provisions of the European Communities Act 1972 are:

S. 2:

> From 1 January 1973, the treaties governing the European Communities and the existing and future Acts adopted by the institutions of those communities shall be binding on the State and shall be part of the domestic law thereof under the conditions laid down in those treaties.

S. 3:

> (1) A minister of state may make regulations for enabling s. 2 of this Act to have full effect.
> (2) Regulations under this section may contain such incidental, supplementary and consequential provisions as appear to the minister making the regulations to be necessary for the purposes of the regulations (including provisions repealing, amending or applying with or without modification, other law, exclusive of this Act).

The constitutional provisions involved

The constitutional provisions involved are the provisions contained in Article 29.4.3°, 4° and 5° of the Constitution, which are in the form consequent upon the Eleventh Amendment of the Constitution enacted by the Eleventh Amendment of the Constitution Act 1992, which came into force on 16 July 1992, and also Article 15.2.

Article 29.4

> 3° The State may become a member of the European Coal and Steel Community (established by treaty signed at Paris on 18 April 1951), the European Economic Community (established by treaties signed at Rome on 25 March 1957) and the European Atomic Energy Community (established by treaty signed at Rome on 25 March 1957. The State may ratify the Single European Act (signed on behalf of the member states of the communities at Luxembourg on 17 February 1986, and at the Hague on 28 February 1986.)
> 4° The State may ratify the Treaty on European Union signed at Maastricht on 7 February 1992, and may become a member of that union.
> 5° No provision of this Constitution invalidates laws enacted, acts done or measures adopted by the State which are necessitated by the obligations of membership of the European Union or of the communities, or prevents laws enacted, acts done or measures adopted by the European Union or by the communities, or by institutions thereof, or by bodies competent under the treaties establishing the communities, from having the force of law in the State.

Article 15.2.1°

> The sole and exclusive power of making laws for the State is hereby vested in the Oireachtas: no other legislative authority has power to make laws for the State...

The challenge to the validity of the statutes

The broad nature of the challenge made to the constitutional validity of s. 3(2) of the Act of 1972 may thus be summarised.

1. If Article 29.4.5° of the Constitution does not apply to this subsection, then it would be invalid having regard to the provisions of Article 15.2 of the Constitution because a power provided by statute to a minister to make laws by regulation or statutory instrument which included provisions either repealing, amending or modifying other law, including statute law enacted by the Oireachtas, would constitute an invasion of the sole and exclusive power of making laws vested in the Oireachtas. In support of this contention reliance was placed on the decision of this Court in *Harvey* *v. Minister for Social Welfare* [1990] ILRM 185; *Cooke v. Walsh* [1984] ILRM 208; and *Cityview Press Ltd v. An Comhairle Oiliúna* [1980] IR 381. In respect of the last two decisions reliance was placed in particular upon the fact that the Act of 1972 did not in any of its other provisions lay down principles or policy which could be said to restrict the discretion vested in the minister in the making of regulations pursuant to s. 3(2) to application and administration of given guidelines.

2. It is submitted that Article 29.4.5° of the Constitution cannot protect the impugned subsection from the invalidity arising by reason of its inconsistency with Article 15.2 because, whereas in general terms the obligations of membership of the union and communities imposes upon the State a duty to apply the laws enacted and to implement acts done or measures adopted by those bodies which then become acts on the part of the State, necessitated by those obligations of membership, the obligations of membership never entail mandatory direction to the State to carry out its duty of applying or implementing laws, acts or measures by any particular legal procedure applicable within the national law of the State. It is, therefore, submitted that the choice purporting to be vested in the minister by s. 3(2), for the purpose of enabling s. 2 of the Act to have full effect, to make regulations which include the repealing or amending or modifying of a statute of the Oireachtas, cannot be an act done or a measure adopted by the State which is necessitated by the obligations of membership. All that is necessitated, it is urged, is the implementation, the method of it is a choice to be made by the State within its own national law framework, and must be consistent with the Constitution.

The submissions of the respondents

The respondents made to the claim for a declaration of constitutional invalidity of s. 3(2) a number of submissions in the alternative. Some of those were directed to and interwoven with the issues which arose in this case with regard to the validity of the statutory instruments actually made.

The primary and fundamental response to the claim of invalidity may, however, be summarised as follows. It cannot be disputed that upon joining the communities and subsequently joining the union, the State took upon itself an obligation to apply and implement fully and efficiently and with expedition laws enacted, acts done or measures adopted by the communities or, subsequently, by the union. That obligation fell into a broad necessity for two separate actions. One was in the case where laws enacted or acts done by the communities or union were done according to community law, in such a fashion as to have direct application within the State. In those instances significant minor administrative regulations may be necessary to facilitate the entry of such legal provisions into the legal structure of the State, carrying with them, of course, a primacy over any conflicting or inconsistent national legal principles or provisions. In such instances, it is said, as one example at least, the repeal, amendment or modification of any existing law by a simple ministerial regulation would be a strict necessity arising from the obligations of the State as a member of the community and union. In other instances it is urged where directives implemented by the State the terms of such directives may be sufficiently specific and clear to require simple administrative application, something which would be again, appropriately done by regulation.

In these circumstances it is urged that the entire of the Act of 1972, which has subsequently been amended, is necessitated by the obligations of the State to the community, and now to the union. No provision of the Constitution, therefore, it is submitted, including in particular, Article 15.2, can be brought to bear on the provisions of that Act so as to invalidate any part of it.

The decision

The court has considered these submissions and has come to the following conclusions.

1. The power to make regulations contained in s. 3(1) of the Act of 1972 is exclusively confined to the making of regulations for one purpose, and one purpose only, that of enabling s. 2 of the Act to have full effect. S. 2 of the Act which provides for the application of the community law and acts as binding on the State and as part of the domestic law subject to conditions laid down in the treaty which, of course, include its primacy, is the major or fundamental obligation necessitated by membership of the community. The power of regulation-making, therefore, contained in s. 3 is *prima facie* a power which is part of the necessary machinery which became a duty of the State upon its joining the community and therefore necessitated by that membership.

The court is satisfied that, having regard to the number of community laws, acts done and measures adopted which either have to be facilitated in their direct application to the law of the State or have to be implemented by appropriate action into the law of the State, the obligation of membership would necessitate facilitating of these activities, in some instances, at least, and possibly in a great majority of instances, by the making of ministerial regulations rather thanlegislation of the Oireachtas.

The court is accordingly satisfied that the power to make regulations in the form in which it is contained in s. 3(2) of the Act of 1972 is necessitated by the obligations of membership by the State of the communities and now of the union and is therefore by virtue of. Article 29.4.3°, 4° and 5° immune from constitutional challenge.

In so far as it may be possible to point to hypothetical instances of certain types of laws, measures or acts of the community or union which in their implementation or application within the national law might not, as to the method of implementation or application, be necessarily carried out by ministerial regulation, but rather should have been carried out by enactment of law by the Oireachtas, the court is satisfied, without deciding that such instances do occur, that the principles laid down by this Court in the decision of the *East Donegal Co-Operative Livestock Marts Ltd. v. Attorney General* [1970] IR 317 must be applied to the construction of the impugned subsection in the manner in which it was applied by the decision of this Court in *Harvey v. Minister for Social Welfare* to the construction of the section of the statute impugned in that case, namely, s. 75 of the Social Welfare Act 1952. That principle is that it must be implied that the making of regulations by the minister, as is permitted by the section, is intended by the Oireachtas to be conducted in accordance with the principles of constitutional justice, and therefore that it is to be implied that the minister shall not in exercising the power of making regulations pursuant to the section, contravene any provisions of the Constitution.

If therefore in such an instance challenge were to be made to the validity of a ministerial regulation having regard to the absence of necessity for it to be carried out by regulation instead of legislation and having regard to the nature of the content of such regulation it would have to be a challenge made on the basis that the regulation was invalid as *ultra vires* being an unconstitutional exercise by the minister of the power constitutionally conferred upon him by the section.

Having reached the conclusion that the challenge to the constitutional validity of this subsection has not been established, and the court satisfied that the subsection is invalid, having regard to the Constitution, it is not appropriate for the court to deal with any of the alternative submissions in defence of the constitutional validity of the subsection which were put forward on behalf of the appellants, since those are involved in other aspects of this appeal, namely, the challenge to the validity of the statutory instruments which have been made by the minister in pursuance of s. 3 of the Act of 1972.

Such statutory instruments are not laws within the meaning of Article 34.4.5° of the Constitution and, therefore, may be the subject matter of separate judgments.

Blayney J (Finlay CJ, O'Flaherty and Egan JJ concurring):

On 24 August 1992 the respondent was served with 20 District Court summonses relating to offences under the European Communities (Control of Oestrogenic, Androgenic, Gestagenic and Thyrostatic Substances) Regulations 1988 (SI No. 218 of 1988) and the European Communities (Control of Veterinary Medicinal Products and their Residues) Regulations 1990 (SI No.171 of

1990). The offences were alleged to have been committed on 27 March 1991, being the date on which a number of officers of the Department of Agriculture, acting on the authority of a search warrant granted by the District Court pursuant to article 16 of the 1988 Regulations, had carried out a search of the respondent's Baptist Grange, Lisronagh, Clonmel in the County of Tipperary.

The respondent immediately applied for and was granted leave to seek by way of judicial review the following reliefs:

(1) A declaration that the 1988 and 1990 Regulations are *ultra vires* and void.
(2) A declaration that the provisions of s. 3(1) and s. 3(2) of the European Communities Act 1972 are contrary to the Constitution of Ireland and are void.
(3) An order of *certiorari* quashing the search warrant granted by the District Court pursuant to article 16 of the 1988 Regulations.
(4) An order of prohibition restraining the Minister for Agriculture from proceeding with the 20 summonses issued against the respondent.

The motion seeking these reliefs was heard by Johnson J and by order dated 1 April 1993 it was declared 'that such portion of s. 3(2) of the European Communities Act 1972 which entitles a minister by regulation to repeal or amend or apply, with or without modification, other law exclusive of that of the said Act is unconstitutional'. The minister appealed against that order and during the hearing the court accepted that it would deal not only with the constitutional issue but also with the other reliefs which had been sought in the High Court but in respect of which no order had been made.

The constitutional issue having been dealt with in the Decision of the Court which has just been pronounced by the Chief Justice, what remains to be considered is the other reliefs which are claimed and these were narrowed down in the course of the argument to a single issue: whether the 1988 and 1990 Regulations are *ultra vires* the Minister for Agriculture and Food under s. 3 of the European Communities Act 1972 in so far as they authorise the District Court to grant a search warrant and permit a summons to be brought in the District Court within two years of the commission of the offence notwithstanding s. 10(4) of the Petty Sessions (Ireland) Act 1851. Mr Hogan, on behalf of the respondent, stated that he did not take objection to any of the other provisions of the regulations. His sole claim, accordingly, is that article 16 of the 1988 Regulations, which is the article authorising the issue of search warrants by the District Court, and article 32(8) of the 1988 Regulations and article 11(4) the 1990 Regulations, both of which provide the two year time limit for issuing summonses, are *ultra vires.*

The law

The relevant law to be considered is the same as had to be considered on the constitutional issue but it would probably be helpful if I were to set it out again:

1. Article 189 of the Treaty of Rome:

> A directive shall be binding, as to the result to be achieved, upon each member state to which it is addressed, but shall leave to the national authorities the choice of form and methods.

2. Article 29.45° of the Constitution:

> No provision of this Constitution invalidates laws enacted, acts done or measures adopted by the State which are necessitated by the obligations of membership of the European Union or of the communities, or prevents laws enacted, acts done or measures adopted by the European Union or by the communities, or by institutions thereof, or by bodies competent under the treaties establishing the communities, from having the force of law in the State.

3. European Communities Act 1972:

S.2:

> From 1 January 1973, the treaties governing the European Communities and the existing and future acts adopted by the institutions of those communities shall be binding on the State and shall be part of the domestic law thereof under the conditions laid down in those treaties.

S.3:

> (1) A minister of state may make regulations for enabling s. 2 of this Act to have full effect.
> (2) Regulations under this section may contain such incidental, supplementary and consequential provisions as appear to the minister making the regulations to be necessary for the purposes of the regulations (including provisions repealing, amending or applying with or without modification, other law, exclusive of this Act).

The submissions made in the course of the hearing were directed both to the constitutionality of the impugned provision in s. 3(2) of the 1972 Act and to the issue with which this judgment is concerned and it would be rather difficult to segregate them. Rather than attempt to do so I propose to proceed directly to the question that has to be addressed and I will refer to the different submissions as occasion arises.

In considering whether the two statutory instruments are *ultra vires*, the first thing that has to be done is to see exactly what power the minister is given by s. 3 of the 1972 Act. The power is a very wide one. It is to enable s. 2 of the Act to have full effect and since that section provides that 'the treaties governing the European Communities and the existing and future acts adopted by institutions of those communities shall be binding on the State and shall be part of the domestic law thereof under the conditions laid down in those treaties' the relevant power of the minister in the context of the present case is to ensure that the EEC directives referred to in the two statutory instruments are part of our domestic law under the conditions laid down in the treaties. Furthermore, under s. 3(2), the minister has express power to include in the regulations incidental, supplementary and consequential provisions as appear to him to be necessary for the purposes of the regulations 'including provisions repealing, amending or applying, with or without modification, other law, exclusive of the 1972 Act'.

These being the powers of the minister, had he power to include in the regulations the provision authorising the District Court to grant a search warrant, and the provision allowing a period of two years for instituting prosecutions for offences? The answer in my opinion clearly is that he had such power provided that it was necessary for the purpose of giving effect to the directives. Accordingly the directives have to be looked at to see if these provisions are necessary for their implementation and when this is done it becomes quite clear that they are.

I start with the power given to the District Court to issue a search warrant. This is clearly required by some of the provisions of Council Directive 85/358/EEC of 16 July 1985 which is one of the directives implemented by the 1988 Regulations. Two of the recitals in the preamble to the directive are as follows:

> Whereas provisions should be made for the official taking of samples at the slaughter-house; whereas, furthermore, where there is a justified suspicion of infringement, provision should be made for the possibility [of] taking such samples at the farm of origin; whereas, where the presence of prohibited substances or of the residues of such substances is confirmed, an investigation should be made at the farm of origin in order to exclude the meat in question from human and animal consumption and to place the prohibited substances under official control.

The relevant articles of the directive provide as follows:

> *Article 1*:
> The member states shall ensure that official on-the-spot random controls are made on the substances referred to in Directive 81/602/EEC at the manufacturing, handling, storage, transport, distribution and sales stages for the presence of prohibited substances and veterinary pharmaceutical preparations containing prohibited substances which may be intended to be administered to animals for fattening purposes.
>
> *Article 3*:
> Member states shall ensure that:
> (1) Where there is justified suspicion of an infringement, the competent department make or arrange to have made:
> –random controls on animals on their farms of origin, particularly in order to detect traces of implants;
> –an official control for the presence of the substances the use of which is prohibited on farms where animals are reared, kept or fattened;
> such controls may include the official taking of samples;
> (2) Random samples are taken from animals from fattening farms.

Article 5 then provides for the samples referred to in article 3 to be analysed in a laboratory approved by the competent authorities.

Finally, article 6 provides as follows:

> (1) Where the analysis referred to in Article 5 confirms the presence of prohibited substances or of residues either exceeding the maximum natural physiologic levels for the authorised substances or proving that authorised substances hay been used abusively, the competent authority shall be informed immediately of:
> (a) All the particulars needed to identify the animal and its farm of origin. These particulars shall be determined in accordance with the procedure laid down in article 10.
> (b) The result of the analysis.
> (2) The competent authorities shall then ensure that
> (a) An investigation is made at the farm of origin to determine the reason for the presence of hormone residues;
> (b) An investigation of the source or sources of the substance concerned is made as necessary, at the manufacturing, handling, storage, transport, distribution or sales stage.

It is clear that these provisions could not be implemented without creating a power to enable a compulsory search to be made of farms where animals are kept. It follows that the minister had power to include in the 1988 Regulations clause 16 which gives the District Court power to issue search warrants.

As regards the two year period for instituting proceedings for an offence under the regulations, it is relevant to note firstly that no objection was taken to the fact that the regulations create a number of offences. It is accordingly accepted by counsel for the respondent that this was required for the implementation of the relevant directives. And it must follow logically that the implementation required in addition that the offences could be effectively prosecuted. So the regulations had to be in a form to enable this to be done and if it was necessary for this purpose to allow a period of two years the minister clearly had power to allow such a period.

The only evidence on this point, which is uncontested, is that of Ms Maureen Waters, an assistant principal of the Department of Agriculture and Food. In an affidavit sworn on 19

February 1993 she deals in detail with the unavoidable delays in the investigation of offences under the regulations by reason of the necessity for analyses to be carried out in the State Laboratory and says that experience 'had shown that in carrying out the type of investigation necessary having regard to the inquiries which would be required and the possible need to avail of the very sophisticated analytical procedures which had waiting lists for the service the six-month statutory period for instituting proceedings would not be met in many cases'.

She then goes on to deal with other possible causes of delay in the final paragraph of her affidavit:

> 4. In particular the directives require investigations to be carried out in more than one member state if it is suspected that the offence may have connections outside the State where initially detected and organising the necessary co-operation from another State may be time-consuming. For these reasons an opinion was formed that in order to fully implement the directives to the extent of exercising sanctions against offenders and to determining the source of the problem (where possible) that it was necessary to extend the period during which proceedings may be instituted. Accordingly recourse was made to the enabling power in s. 3(2) of the European Communities Act 1972 to provide that the time limit in s. 10(4) of the Petty Sessions (Ireland) Act 1851 would not apply and to substitute a two year period in its place.

It is quite clear from Ms Waters' affidavit that if the power of prosecution given in the regulation was to be effective, the six-month period was too short and so it was necessary to extend it. It follows that the minister had power to provide for a longer period and so had power to extend the six months to two years.

It was submitted by Mr Hogan that there was nothing in the directive which expressly required a two-year time limit and for that reason it was not justified. I reject that submission. The directive clearly required, as Mr Hogan accepted, that offences had to be created and obviously, as I said earlier, it had to be possible for these offences to be effectively prosecuted. Accordingly, the implementation of the directive required that the regulation should provide for an adequate time for the preparation of the prosecutions. It was not necessary that the directive should itself fix a time. It was a matter for the State to decide on the length of time required to enable the prosecution to be brought and that is what the minister has done in providing for a period of two years.

Mr Hogan also submitted that s. 10 of the 1851 Act could not be amended except by statute. The Decision of the Court already delivered has upheld the constitutional validity of the part of s. 3(2) of the 1972 Act which gives the minister express power to include in a regulation a provision amending other law. In so far therefore as this submission may be construed as meaning that the portion of the regulation amending s. 10 of the 1851 Act is invalid, it seems to me that it should be rejected rejected for the following reasons.

It is well established that community law takes precedence over our domestic law. Where they are in conflict, it is the community law that prevails. See *SA v. La Comercial Internacional de Alimentacion SA Case C-106/89* [1990] ECR 1- 4135 and *Francovich v. Italy Case C-6, C-9/90* [1991] ECR 1-5357. The relevant directives here were binding on the State, from the moment they were adopted, 'as to the result to be achieved'. One result to be achieved clearly was the creation of effective sanctions for the enforcement of the measures contained in the directives. So the State was bound to introduce effective sanctions, and if this necessitated adopting a measure which impliedly amended an existing statute, that measure would prevail over the statute because it was in substance a measure of community law. It is only in form that it is part of the domestic law. It derives its force from the directive which is binding on the State as to the results to be achieved. Such is my opinion of the character of article 31(8) of the 1988 regulations providing for the two-year period for instituting prosecutions.

Finally, I would not accept Mr Hogan's submission that merely because Article 189 of the Treaty of Rome leaves to the State the choice of the form and methods of implementing a directive, what is done by way of implementation is not necessitated by the State's obligations of membership and so may be subjected to constitutional challenge. The article obliges the State to implement the directive and equally obliges the State, in exercise of the discretion given to it, to choose an appropriate method of implementation. If the State were free not implement the directive, then clearly, if it were to do so, it would be a voluntary act not necessitated by the obligations of membership and would not be protected by Article 29.4.5° of the Constitution. But the State is not free. It is obliged to implement the directive and so is obliged to choose a method of implementation and, provided the method it chooses is appropriate for the purpose of satisfying the obligation of the State and the measures it incorporates do not go beyond what is required to implement the directive, it is correctly categorised as being necessitated by the directive. In any instance where the method was not appropriate, or its measures went beyond what was required, it would not be necessitated and would be open to constitutional challenge. This not such a case.

For all these reasons I would refuse all the relief sought by the respondent by way of judicial review.

Denham J (Finlay CJ, O'Flaherty and Egan JJ concurring):

The court in the decision which has just been pronounced by the Chief Justice having rejected the constitutional challenge to the validity of s. 3(2) of the European Communities Act 1972 this judgment deals with the remaining issue as to the validity of the regulations made by the minister pursuant to that section.

The issue for determination is whether regulations, European Communities (Control of Oestrogenic, Androgenic, Gestagenic and Thyrostatic Substances) Regulations 1988 (SI No. 218 of 1988) and European Communities (Control of Veterinary Medicinal Products and their Residues) Regulations 1990 (SI No. 218 of 1988) are *ultra vires* the powers of the Minister for Agriculture and Food under s. 3 European Communities Act 1972 insofar as they authorise procedure for the granting of a search warrant, and insofar as they extend the time within which a summons can be sought thereby amending s. 10(4) Petty Sessions Ireland Act 1851.

The facts and issues have been fully set out by the Chief Justice and Blayney J. The directives relevant to this case are Council Directive No. 81/602/EEC of 31 July 1981, Council Directive No. 81/851/EEC of28 September 1981 (insofar as it relates to substances with oestrogenic, androgenic, gestagenic or thyrostatic action), Council Directive No. 85/358/EEC of 16 July 1985, Council Directive No. 86/469/EEC of 16 September 1986, Council Directive No. 88/146/EEC of 7 March 1988 and Council Directive No. 88/299/EEC of 17 May 1988. S. 3 European Communities Act 1972 and the said directives are the basis upon which the minister made the regulations in issue in this case.

Law

The sources of the law in issue are both national, constitutional and statutory, and European, however all are part of the domestic law. The relevant sections have been set out previously but for analysis I re-state them.

(i) Bunreacht na hEireann. Article 15.2.1°:

> The sole and exclusive power of making laws for the State is hereby vested in the Oireachtas: no other legislative authority has power to make laws for the State. [Hereinafter referred to as Article 15.2.1°.]

(ii) Bunreacht na hEireann, Article 29.4:

> (3) The State may become a member of the European Coal and Steel Community (established by Treaty signed at Paris on 18 April 1951), the European Economic Community (established by treaty signed at Rome on 25 March 1957) and the European Atomic Energy Community (established by treaty signed at Rome on 25 March 1957).
> The State may ratify the Single European Act (signed on behalf of the member states of the communities at Luxembourg on 17 February 1986, and at the Hague on 28 February 1986).
> (4) The State may ratify the Treaty on European Union signed at Maastricht on 7 February 1992, and may become a member of that union.
> (5) No provision of this Constitution invalidates laws enacted, acts done or measures adopted by the State which are necessitated by the obligations of membership of the European Union or of the communities, or prevents laws enacted, acts done or measures adopted by the European Union or by the communities, or by institutions thereof, or by bodies competent under the treaties establishing the communities, from having the force of law in the State.

(iii) European Communities Act 1972.

> S. 2: From 1 January 1973, the treaties governing the European Communities and the existing and future acts adopted by the institutions of those communities shall be binding on the State and shall be part of the domestic law thereof under the conditions laid down in those treaties. [Hereinafter referred to as s. 2 of the 1972 Act].
> S. 3(1): A minister of state may make regulations for enabling s. 2 of this Act to have full effect.
> S. 3(2): Regulations under this section may contain such incidental, supplementary and consequential provisions as appear to the minister making the regulations to be necessary for the purposes of the regulations (including provisions repealing, amending or applying, with or without modification, other law, exclusive of this Act). [Hereinafter referred to as s. 3(1) or s. 3(2) of the 1972 Act].

(iv) Treaty of Rome, Article 5:

> Member States shall take all appropriate measures, whether general or particular, to ensure fulfilment of the obligations arising on this treaty or resulting from action taken by the institutions of the community. They shall facilitate the achievement of the community's tasks.
> They shall abstain from any measure which could jeopardise the attainment of the objectives of this treaty'. [Hereinafter referred to as Article 5].

(v) Treaty of Rome, Article 189:

> In order to carry out their task the council and the commission shall, in accordance with the provisions of this treaty, make regulations, issue directives, take decisions, make recommendations or deliver opinions.
> A regulation shall have general application, it shall be binding in its entirety and directly applicable in all member states.
> A directive shall be binding, as to the result to be achieved, upon each member state to which it is addressed, but shall leave to the national authorities the choice of form and methods.... [Hereinafter referred to as Article 189].

This case is not about a balance of power between community authorities and national authorities. It was accepted by the parties that community law has primacy.

The issue to be determined is the balance within the national forum of s. 2 and s. 3 of the 1972 Act, Article 15.2 and Article 29.4.5 of Bunreacht na hÉireann and Articles 5 and 189 of the Treaty of Rome. Thus the kernel is the word 'necessitated' in Article 29.4.5° and the 'choice' afforded in Article 189.

Facts

On the facts of the case there was no contest. There was no replying affidavit to either of the affidavits filed by the State.

The State set out facts which established that under the directive an extension of time within which to apply for a summons was necessary, as was a power to search.

I am satisfied that on the facts of the case, as set out by the State and not controverted by the applicant/respondent, it was necessary in view of the substance of the directive to both extend time within which a summons could be issued and to authorise search warrants.

Thus, while, in general, facts may be judicially reviewable they were not in contest in this case.

'Necessitated'

It is clear that on the facts of this case it was necessary (a) to amend Petty Sessions (Ireland) Act 1851 as to the time limits within which to apply for a summons and (b) to create a right of search.

There is no doubt that these two factors must be brought into Irish domestic law under its obligations under community law.

However, the fact that they were 'necessitated' under the directive to be incorporated into national law is not the end of the matter.

'Choice'

Article 189 leaves to the national authorities the choice of form and methods. In choosing the form and method the minister has to act in accordance with the law and the Constitution. Thus the minister must balance the relevant articles of the Constitution, which in this case are Article 15.2 and Article 29.4.5°. His choice, under Article 189, must be in accordance with national law, the Constitution and community law. His decision is judicially reviewable.

The fact that the substance of the directive is binding as to the result to be achieved, and that a minister must initiate an enabling national process, does not determine the issue of choice of method. Whereas the State is required to implement the substance of the directive into law, the State is not required by community law to choose any particular form or method.

'Form or Method'

In determining the form or method the State, minister, must have due regard to the Constitution, both Article 15.2 and Article 29.4.5°.

Under Bunreacht na hEireann as enacted in 1937 the sole and exclusive power of making law for the State was vested in the Oireachtas. This is a fundamental aspect of democratic government, based on the separation of powers.

That basic tenet has been qualified by membership of the European community which has established other law making authorities. *Inter alia* it has established law making in the form of directives, which are binding on the State, as to the result to be achieved, leaving to the national authorities the choice of form and methods.

Were the Constitution still in its 1937 form the State, minister, would have no choice- he would have to initiate a process of legislation through the Oireachtas. However, the Constitution has been amended, and community law has been introduced to the domestic law, and the situation is not now governed by Article 15.2 alone. Article 15.2 cannot be read in isolation.

The term 'necessitated' in Article 29.4.5° together with Article 189 of the treaty make it clear that in balancing the two the mere fact that the substance in laws enacted, acts done or measures adopted, is necessary to be incorporated into domestic Irish law, is not the end of the matter.

The term 'necessitated' is relevant to the choice of method, however membership has not itself obligated a special form and method of implementation. Article 15.2 and the choice of form and methods of Article 189 must then be read together with Article 29.4.5°.

Article 29.4.5° refers to 'laws enacted, acts done or measures adopted.' Clearly this refers to legislation through the Oireachtas and other methods of implementation, including the two sets of regulations herein.

The minister made the regulations under s. 3 of the 1972 Act. The directive is 'binding' on the State as to the result to be achieved. The principles and policies are set out in the directive. Under s. 3(2) the minister's regulations may contain such incidental, supplementary and consequential provisions as appear to the minister to be necessary for the purposes of the regulations, including amending an Act (exclusive of the 1972 Act). Clearly incidental, supplementary and consequential provisions are not foundation principles and policies.

If the directive left to the national authority matters of principle or policy to be determined then the 'choice' of the minister would require legislation by the Oireachtas. But where there is no case made that principles or policies have to be determined by the national authority, where the situation is that the principles and policies were determined in the directive, then legislation by a delegated form, by regulation, is a valid choice. The fact that an Act of the Oireachtas has been affected by the policy in a directive, is a 'result to be achieved' wherein there is now no choice between the policy and the national Act. The policy of the directive must succeed. Thus where there is in fact no choice on a policy or a principle it is a matter appropriate for delegated legislation. If the directive or the minister envisaged any choice of principle or policy then it would require legislation by the Oireachtas.

The appropriate test is as set out by O'Higgins CJ in *Cityview Press Ltd v. An Chomhairle Oiliúna* [1980] IR 381, 399, where he stated:

> In the view of this Court, the test is whether that which is challenged as an unauthorised delegation of parliamentary power is more than a mere giving effect to principles and policies which are contained in the statute itself. If it be, then it is not authorised; for such would constitute a purported exercise of legislative power by an authority which is not permitted to do so under the Constitution. On the other hand, if it be within the permitted limits -if the law is laid down in the statute and details only are filled in or completed by the designated minister or subordinate body -there is no unauthorised delegation of legislative power.

Applying the test to this situation the test is whether the ministerial regulations under s. 3 of the 1972 Act are more than the mere giving effect to principles and policies of the said Act and the directives which are part of domestic law as to the result to be achieved.

If the regulations contain material exceeding the policies and principles of the directives then they are not authorised by the directives and would not be valid under s. 3 unless the material was incidental, supplementary or consequential. In those circumstances if they were not incidental, supplementary or consequential the regulations would be an exercise of legislative power by an authority not so permitted under the Constitution. If it be within the permitted limits, if the policy is laid down in the directive and details only are filled in or completed by the regulations, there is no unauthorised delegation of legislative power.

Democracy

The separation of powers is a fundamental principle of Bunreacht na hÉireann. The power to legislate for the State is solely within the Oireachtas- save where that authority has been assigned under the Constitution to community authorities and organs of the State to act in accordance with community law as integrated into national law.

There was no question in this case that the principles and policies of the directives were not within the treaties.

In the directives herein the policies and principles have been determined. Thus there is no role of determining policies or principles for the Oireachtas. While the directive must be implemented there is no policy or principle which can be altered by the Oireachtas, it is already binding as to the result to be achieved.

That being the case the role of the Oireachtas in such a situation would be sterile. To require the Oireachtas to legislate would be artificial. It would be able solely to have a debate as to what has already been decided, which debate would act as a source of information. Such a sterile debate would take up Dáil and Senate time and act only as a window on community directives for the members of the Oireachtas and the nation. That is not a role envisaged for the Oireachtas in the Constitution.

Consequently, solely because the minister is making a regulation which repeals a statute, does not of itself invalidate the regulation which as a vehicle, as a choice, can be *intra vires* the Constitution under Article 29.4. To say that a regulation breaches Article 15.2.1° simply because it repeals or amends a statute is to hold the false premise that the minister is determining principles or policy.

The regulations in this case being within the policies and principles of the directives the substance of the regulation is within the directives. There are no policies and principles enunciated in the regulations that are not within the directives. There are no policies and principles in the regulation additional to the directive.

Consequently, to state that such an action- effectively an administrative implementation of policies and principles of a directive- is superior legislation as envisaged in Article 15.2.1° -is a misnomer. Superior legislation involves a decision on policies and principles by the legislature and an implementation thereof in the form of a statute. Here what is at issue in essence is subordinate legislation as delegated under community law.

No constitutional right, other than the process under Article 15.2, of Bunreacht na hÉireann was submitted as part of the argument, or as being in issue. Nor was any issue raised as to the validity of the directives and their principles and policies under the treaties.

I am satisfied that the regulations in issue in this case were not *ultra vires* the power of the Minister for Agriculture and Food under s. 3 European Communities Act 1972 insofar as they authorised the procedure for the granting of the search warrant, and insofar as they extended time thereby amending s. 10(4) Petty Sessions (Ireland) Act 1851 being as they were implementations of policies and principles in the relevant directives.

I am in agreement with the judgment of Blayney J and consequently I would allow the appeal.

Metock v Minister for Justice, Equality and Law Reform

[2008] IEHC 7

Author's note: This case is one of the most important references from Ireland on account of its impact on the interpretation of the Citizens Rights Directive. The Court of Justice responded positively, overturning its previous decision in *Akrich*

Interim Decision of Ms. Justice Finlay Geoghegan delivered on 14th day of March, 2008

1. This decision is given pursuant to Article 234 of the EC Treaty to seek a preliminary ruling from the Court of Justice on the interpretation of Directive 2004/38/EC of the European Parliament and of the Council of 29 April, 2004 on the rights of citizens of the Union and their family members to move and reside freely within the territory of Member States as set out in the questions in this decision. The preliminary ruling is necessary to enable me give judgment in each of the four judicial review applications listed in the title. All were heard simultaneously and, in each, I have reserved my judgment. These applications are regarded as test cases as there are other pending applications which raise similar issues.

2. In all four cases, the applicants include a married couple. In one case the infant children are included among the applicants but they are not directly relevant to the questions upon which preliminary rulings are sought. In each couple, one spouse is a Union citizen of a Member State other than Ireland who is residing and working in Ireland and the other spouse is a non-EU national. All four couples were married in Ireland. Each non-EU national spouse applied for a residence card from the Minister as the spouse of a Union citizen residing and working in Ireland.

3. The respondent, in each of the proceedings, is the Minister for Justice, Equality and Law Reform ("the Minister") on whose behalf the challenged decisions were taken.

4. Three applications were refused by reason of the failure of the non-EU national to provide evidence that he had been lawfully resident in another EU Member State prior to arrival in Ireland. Such a requirement is included in the regulations made by the Minister for the purpose of giving effect to Directive 2004/38/EC in Ireland.

5. The applicants in each case challenge the validity of the decision of the Minister to refuse the application for a residence card. They contend that Directive 2004/38/EC does not permit Ireland include, as it has done in its implementing regulations, a requirement that a spouse of a Union citizen provide evidence of lawful residence in another EU Member State prior to arrival in Ireland. The applicants contend that such provision in the Irish regulation is invalid.

6. If the applicants are successful in that contention then their applications for a residence card will have to be reconsidered by the Minister. There are also further legal issues in dispute between the Minister and the applicants as to the proper meaning and scope of Directive 2004/38/EC. Questions relevant to those disputes are also set out below.

7. I must determine each Judicial Review application on its own facts but there are certain common issues which require to be determined in a majority or all of the proceedings. It is convenient to give one interim decision to make a reference to the Court of Justice in all four proceedings.

Relevant background facts

8. There is no significant fact in dispute between the parties which is relevant to the questions on which I seek preliminary rulings from the Court of Justice. For clarity, I propose shortly setting out the family and immigration history of the applicants and the decisions taken. Not all such facts are necessarily relevant to the questions I am putting to the Court of Justice for the reasons set out below.

9. In proceedings [2007] No. 1324 J.R., Ms. Ngo Ikeng is now a citizen of the United Kingdom. She was a national of Cameroon and was granted a declaration of refugee status in the United Kingdom in 1999 and, subsequently, citizenship. Mr. Metock is a national of Cameroon. He arrived in Ireland on the 23rd June, 2006 and made an application for asylum. That application was ultimately refused on the 28th February, 2007.

10. Mr. Metock and Ms. Ngo Ikeng married in Ireland on the 12th October, 2006. They met in Cameroon in 1994 and have been in a relationship for thirteen years. They have two children, one born in 1998 and the other in 2006, who are also applicants.

11. On the 6th November, 2006, Mr. Metock applied for residence in Ireland as the spouse of a Union citizen working and residing in Ireland. That application was considered by the Minister pursuant to the European Communities (Free Movement of Persons)(No.2) Regulations 2006 (S.I. No. 656 of 2006) ("the 2006 Regulations") which were made to give effect to Directive 2004/38/EC in Ireland.

12. A decision to refuse Mr. Metock's application was sent by letter of the 28th June, 2007. The single reason given was:–

> "The provisions of Regulation 3(2) require that in order to avail of residency rights under the Regulations, applicants must submit evidence showing lawful residence in another EU Member State prior to arrival in Ireland. Following a thorough examination of your file, it was decided that no evidence was submitted to satisfy this requirement and that therefore, residence can not be granted".

13. By Order of the High Court of the 15th October, 2007, the applicants were given leave to apply *inter alia* for:–

(1) An order of *certiorari* quashing the decision of the Minister of the 28th June, 2007;

14. In these proceedings, the Minister does not dispute that Ms. Ngo Ikeng is a Union citizen who is working and is residing in Ireland since October or November 2006 (the precise date is unclear but not relevant).

15. Mr. Metock continues to reside in Ireland. Since 28th February 2008 (refusal of declaration of refugee status), he has no permission to be in Ireland. This means *inter alia* that he has no permission to take up employment in Ireland.

16. In proceeding [2007] No. 622 J.R., Mrs. Chinedu is a Union citizen and a national of Germany. Mr. Chinedu is a national of Nigeria. He arrived in Ireland in December, 2005 and applied for asylum in Ireland.

17. Mr. and Mrs. Chinedu married in Ireland on the 3rd July, 2006. Mr. Chinedu made an application for residence in Ireland as the spouse of a Union citizen which was received by the Minister on the 1st August, 2006. On the 8th August, 2006, the Minister refused Mr. Chinedu's application for a declaration of refugee status.

18. On the 17th April, 2007, the Minister refused Mr. Chinedu's application for residence as the spouse of an EU citizen pursuant to the 2006 Regulations. The single reason given in the letter of refusal was:–

> "The provisions of Regulation 3(2) require that in order to avail of residency rights under the Regulations, applicants must submit evidence showing lawful residence in another EU Member State prior to arrival in Ireland. Following a thorough examination of your file,

it was decided that no evidence was submitted to satisfy this requirement and that therefore residence can not be granted".

19. The Minister does not dispute that Mrs. Chinedu is a Union citizen and German national lawfully residing in Ireland. Mr. Chinedu remains in Ireland. Since 8th August 2006 (refusal of declaration of refugee status), he does not have permission to be in Ireland. Mr. Chinedu states that he is now unable to work in Ireland due to his having no permission to do so from the Minister. He makes complaint that he is at a loss by reason of this fact.

20. On the 30th May, 2007, the High Court granted the applicants leave to apply by way of Judicial Review for *inter alia*:–

(1) An order of *certiorari* quashing the decision of the 17th April, 2007, refusing to grant residency;
and
(2) An order of *mandamus* directing the Minister to reconsider the application of Mr. Chinedu seeking residency pursuant to the 2006 Regulations in accordance with the provisions of Directive 2004/38/EC;
and
(3) Damages.

The claim for damages is not being determined as part of the present hearing.

21. In proceeding [2007] No. 106 J.R., Mrs. Ikogho is a Union citizen and national of the United Kingdom. She has resided and worked in Ireland since October, 1996.

22. Mr. Ikogho arrived in Ireland in November, 2004, and claimed asylum. The Minister refused the declaration of asylum and made a deportation order in respect of Mr. Ikogho on the 15th September, 2005. A challenge to the deportation order was made in the High Court which was dismissed by order of the 19th June, 2007.

23. Mrs. Ikogho came to Ireland in 1996 with her then husband and two children, born in 1991 and 1993. They had a further child, who is a citizen of Ireland, in 1998. Unfortunately, irreconcilable differences arose between Mrs. Ikogho and her first husband and they separated in 2001 and subsequently divorced. In December, 2004 she met Mr. Ikogho with whom she commenced a relationship. In August, 2005 he moved in with her and her three children and they continue to reside together.

24. Mr. and Mrs. Ikogho married in Ireland on the 7th June, 2006. On the 6th July, 2006, Mr. Ikogho made an application for residence as the spouse of a Union citizen living and working in Ireland. By a letter which is dated the 12th January, 2006, but is believed to have issued on the 12th January, 2007, his application was refused. The letter of refusal refers to article 3(2) of the 2006 Regulations and the reason given for the refusal is that, by reason of the deportation order made by the Minister on the 15th September, 2005, Mr. Ikogho was illegally resident in Ireland at the time of his marriage to the EU citizen on the 7th June, 2006. It was stated that Mr. Ikogho is not a person who can avail of the relevant provisions of the 2006 Regulations by reason of that fact.

25. By Order of the High Court of 12th February, 2007, the applicants were given leave to seek *inter alia*:–

(1) An order of *certiorari* quashing the decision refusing residence of the 12th January, 2007;
and
(2) An order of *mandamus* directing the Minister to reconsider the application of Mr. Ikogho for residency pursuant to the 2006 Regulations in accordance with the provisions of Directive 2004/38/EC

26. Mrs. Ikogho had been in regular employment in Ireland until about March, 2007. At that time she suffered a miscarriage, having become pregnant by Mr. Ikogho. In an affidavit sworn on the 23rd January, 2008, she states that she is again pregnant with her husband's child and due to give birth on or about the 11th May, 2008. She alleges that the refusal of her husband's application for residency is detrimental to the exercise of her fundamental freedoms under Community law.

27. The Minister does not dispute that Mrs. Ikogho is a Union citizen and a national of the United Kingdom exercising her rights of free movement and residence under Community law and entitled to reside in Ireland.

28. In proceeding [2007] No. 1620 J.R., Ms. Batkowska is a Union and Polish citizen. She came to Ireland on holidays in February, 2006 and met Mr. Igbonanusi in Ireland. She states that they formed a loving relationship and remained in contact on her return to Poland. She then came back to Ireland in April, 2006 and set up home with Mr. Igbonanusi in Ireland and is employed in Ireland. They were married in Ireland on the 24th November, 2006.

29. Mr. Igbonanusi is a national of Nigeria who arrived in Ireland and claimed asylum on the 2nd April, 2004. The Minister refused Mr. Igbonanusi a declaration of refugee status on the 31st May, 2005. Following further immigration procedures, the Minister made a deportation order against Mr. Igbonanusi on the 15th September, 2005. There is a dispute between the parties as to Mr. Igbonanusi's knowledge of that order and the reason for his failure to present himself to the Garda National Immigration Bureau in September, 2005 as required. That dispute is not relevant to the questions upon which I am seeking a preliminary ruling.

30. Mr. Igbonanusi made an application on the 27th February, 2007, for residence as the spouse of an EU citizen. That application was considered by the Minister under the 2006 Regulations. It was refused by letter of the 27th August, 2007. The single reason given for the refusal was:–

> "The provision of Regulation 3(2) required that in order to avail of residency rights in the State under the above mentioned regulations applicants must submit evidence showing lawful residence in another EU Member State prior to arriving in Ireland. No evidence was submitted by you to satisfy this requirement and therefore residence under Regulation 3(2) can not be granted".

31. On the 16th November, 2007, Mr. Igbonanusi was arrested and placed in Cloverhill Prison. An application was made on his behalf for revocation of the deportation order which was refused by the Minister by letter of the 4th December, 2007.

32. By Order of the High Court of the 13th December, 2007, the applicant was granted leave to seek *inter alia*:–

> (1) "An order of *certiorari* quashing the decision to refuse Mr. Igbonanusi residency pursuant to Directive 2004/38/EC as notified by letter of the 27th August, 2007; and
> (2) A declaration that Mr. Igbonanusi has the right and entitlement to remain, reside and work in Ireland and to benefit from the provisions of Directive 2004/38/EC as the spouse of a citizen of the Union working and residing in Ireland pursuant to Directive 2004/38/EC or exercising free movement of workers rights under European Community law".

33. On the same day, the High Court refused to grant to the applicants an interlocutory injunction restraining the Minister from deporting Mr. Igbonanusi from Ireland to Nigeria pending the determination of these proceedings. Mr. Igbonanusi was deported from Ireland to Nigeria in December, 2007.

34. The Minister does not dispute, in the proceedings, that Ms. Batkowska is a Union and Polish citizen and living and working in Ireland.

Implementation of Directive 2004/38/EC in Ireland

35. The Minister initially gave effect to Directive 2004/38/EC in Ireland by the European Communities (Free Movement of Persons) Regulations 2006 (S.I. No. 226 of 2006). These were made on the 28th April, 2006.

36. On the 18th December, 2006, the Minister made the European Communities (Free Movement of Persons) (No.2) Regulations 2006 (S.I. No.656 of 2006) also to give effect to Directive 2004/38/EC in Ireland. Those Regulations came into operation on the 1st January, 2007 and repealed the earlier Regulations.

37. In this decision I only propose to refer to the European Communities (Free Movement of Persons) (No.2) Regulations 2006 ("the 2006 Regulations"). Whilst certain of the applications were made to the Minister when the earlier Regulations were in force, all of the applications were expressly stated to have been decided under the 2006 Regulations. No objection has been taken to this. Further, the relevant articles of each Regulation challenged in these proceedings are identical. Therefore nothing, in my view, turns on the existence of the two sets of Regulations.

38. The 2006 Regulations, for the most part, give effect to Directive 2004/38/EC using identical provisions to those of the Directive. Article 7 of the 2006 Regulations requires a family member of a Union citizen to apply to the Minister for a residence card as envisaged in articles 9 and 10 of the Directive. This was the application made by each non-EU national applicant in these proceedings.

39. Articles 3(1) and (2) of the 2006 Regulations expressly and exhaustively specify the persons to whom the 2006 Regulations apply. These provide:

3. (1) These Regulations shall apply to—

(a) Union citizens,
(b) Subject to paragraph (2), qualifying family members of Union citizens who are not themselves Union citizens, and
(c) Subject to paragraph (2), permitted family members of Union citizens.

(2) These Regulations shall not apply to a family member unless the family member is lawfully resident in another Member State and is –

(a) Seeking to enter the State in the company of a Union citizen in respect of whom he or she is a family member, or
(b) Seeking to join a Union citizen, in respect of whom he or she is a family member, who is lawfully present in the State.

40. The definition of "qualifying" family members in the 2006 Regulations includes a spouse.

41. As appears, from the above, the 2006 Regulations exclude *inter alia* from their application a family member of a Union citizen unless, as is expressly stated, "The family member is lawfully resident in another Member State".

42. In considering applications from a family member of a Union citizen already resident in Ireland, the Minister has applied this provision by imposing a requirement that the family member have been lawfully resident in another Member State prior to arriving in Ireland.

Issues of Irish Law

43. As appears from the facts set out above, in three of the applications the single reason given by the Minister for the refusal of the application of the spouse of the Union citizen for residence was that the applicant had not submitted evidence showing lawful residence in another EU Member State prior to arrival in Ireland, as required by article 3(2) of the 2006 Regulations.

44. As a matter of Irish law, I am satisfied that I must determine the applications for orders of *certiorari* in those proceedings by deciding whether or not the single reason given by the Minister was one which is permissible under Directive 2004/38/EC.

45. In each case, the Minister made the decision based upon the failure of the non-EU national to meet the lawful residence requirement in article 3(2) of the 2006 Regulations. Each of the applicants contend that this requirement is invalid as it is inconsistent with Directive 2004/38/EC and hence *ultra vires* the powers of the Minister in making a regulation to give effect to Directive 2004/38/EC in Ireland, and void. As a matter of Irish law, I am satisfied that if article 3(2) of the 2006 Regulations is inconsistent with Directive 2004/38/EC, then it is *ultra vires* the powers of the Minister in making regulations to give effect to Directive 2004/38/EC in Ireland and void.

46. Whilst the Minister has raised other objections to the entitlement of the non-EU national spouse of the EU citizen to benefit from the provisions of Directive 2004/38/EC in certain of the proceedings, those objections are not relevant to the determination of whether or not the applicants are entitled to an order of *certiorari*. That issue must be determined by reference to the single reason given by the Minister for the refusals. Hence, the individual facts of the applicants' immigration history are irrelevant to the determination of this issue, except for the fact that the non-EU national spouse of the EU citizen was not lawfully resident in another EU Member State before he arrived in Ireland.

47. In the remaining proceeding, [2007] No. 106 J.R., counsel for the Minister indicated, in the course of the hearing, that the Minister was now consenting to an order of *certiorari* being made by the Court quashing the decision given on the 12th January, 2007, refusing the application for residence of Mr. Ikogho. No reason was given for this consent, nor was any concession made as to the legal position contended for by the Minister on the statement of opposition in the proceedings. I am satisfied that the Court should not draw any conclusion from the Minister's consent to the order of *certiorari,* save that it is unnecessary for the Court now to consider the legality of the decision made, which was by reason of the alleged illegal residence of Mr. Ikogho in Ireland at the time of his marriage to the EU citizen.

48. The Minister is also consenting to the order of *mandamus* claimed "directing the Minister to reconsider the application of Mr. Ikogho for residency pursuant to the 2006 Regulations in accordance with the provisions of Directive 2004/38/EC" and a declaration to similar effect. There remains a dispute between the applicants and the Minister, on the pleadings and submissions, as to the proper meaning of Directive 2004/38/EC. That dispute includes whether or not the requirement of lawful residence prior to arrival in Ireland in article 3(2) of the 2006 Regulations (which Mr. Ikogho does not satisfy) is or is not a permissible requirement under Directive 2004/38/EC, I determined, for reasons given in a ruling in the course of the hearing, that I should not make the orders for *mandamus* and a declaration and remit this matter to the Minister without resolving that dispute. Accordingly, the determination of that issue is likewise relevant to my judgment in proceeding.

Prior High Court Decision

49. The validity of article 3(2) of the 2006 Regulations and its consistency with Directive 2004/38/EC is already the subject of a decision of the High Court. In *S.K. and Anor. v. The Minister for Justice, Equality and Law Reform and Ors.* [2007] I.E.H.C. 216, Hanna J. decided that the prior lawful residence requirement in article 3(2) of the 2006 Regulations is consistent with Directive 2004/38/EC and lawful. He determined that such provision gives effect to Directive 2004/38/EC and the decision of the Court of Justice in *Secretary of State for the Home Department v. Hacene Akrich (Case C-109/01)* [2003] ECR. I – 9607 ("*Akrich*"). Hanna J. concluded that Directive 2004/38/EC "is intended to apply to families which were established in a Member State prior to the move to the host Member State".

50. This is a decision of a court of equal jurisdiction by which I am not bound. Nevertheless, I should only depart from this decision if the applicants clearly establish that it was wrongly decided, in accordance with the principles set in *Irish Trust Bank v. Central Bank of Ireland* [1976 – 7] I.L.R.M. 50. *S.K. and Anor. v. The Minister for Justice, Equality and Law Reform and Ors.* is presently the subject of an appeal to the Supreme Court but has not been heard.

51. The applicants herein submit that the judgment in *S.K. and Anor. v. The Minister for Justice, Equality and Law Reform and Ors.* is in error in the conclusion reached on the interpretation of Directive 2004/38/EC and the validity of article 3(2) of the 2006 Regulations. They also contend that Hanna J. was in error in not taking into account the judgment of the Court of Justice in *Yunying Jia v. Migrationsverket (Case C-1/05)* [2007] ECR. I-1 ("*Jia*") in reaching his conclusions on the meaning of Directive 2004/38/EC and the validity of article 3(2) of the 2006 Regulations. They also submit that, in reaching a conclusion in these cases on the proper meaning of Directive 2004/38/EC, I must also take into consideration the judgment of the Court of Justice in case *Minister voor Vreemdelingenzaken en Integratie v. R.N.G. Eind (*C-291/05) (Unreported, European Court of Justice, 11th December, 2007) ("*Eind*") which post-dates the judgment in *S.K. and Anor. v. The Minister for Justice, Equality and Law Reform and Ors.*

52. In *S.K. and Anor. v. The Minister for Justice, Equality and Law Reform and Ors.,* Hanna J. refers extensively to the helpful analysis of the Advocate General in *Jia* and to relevant paragraphs from the judgment of the Court of Justice. However, he then decided that, as the facts in *S.K.* did not fit circumstances in *Jia,* "for the purposes of dealing with this application, the *Jia* decision should be left to one side". Undoubtedly, the facts relating to the applicants in *S.K.* differed greatly from *Jia*. However, also at issue in *S.K.* was the proper meaning of Directive 2004/38/EC and the validity of the lawful residence requirement in article 3(2) of the 2006 Regulations. Both of these provisions have general application. In determining their meaning or validity it does not appear to me that what was decided by the Court of Justice in *Jia*, in particular at paragraphs 25-33 in relation to the application of its decision in *Akrich*, can be left to one side.

53. Accordingly, I have determined that I should not now simply follow the decision in *S.K. and Anor. v. The Minister for Justice, Equality and Law Reform and Ors.* on the interpretation of Directive 2004/38/EC and validity of article 3(2) of the 2006 Regulations but rather seek a preliminary ruling from the Court of Justice on the interpretation of Directive 2004/38/EC. As observed by the Advocate General in his opinion in *Jia* (at para. 38), the Court of Justice case law on the Community instruments repealed or amended by Directive 2004/38/EC "is not entirely free from ambiguity". In the course of the hearing I sought the views of counsel for the parties as to whether I should exercise my discretion to make a reference. Counsel for all parties submitted that I should do so.

Submission of Minister on Prior Lawful Residence Requirement

54. The Minister submits that the prior lawful residence requirement in article 3(2) of the 2006 Regulations is permitted by Directive 2004/38/EC. In summary his submissions are as follows.

55. The Minister submits that the division of competences between the Community and Member States is such that Community law, and in particular Directive 2004/38/EC, is only concerned with the movement of Union citizens and their family members within the territory of the Member States and not with the entry of such persons into the territory of Member States from outside.

56. The Minister therefore submits that the Member States, including Ireland, retain competence in relation to the admission of non-EU nationals from outside of the territory of Member States into a Member State including, in this instance, Ireland. He submits that if Directive 2004/38/EC is interpreted as meaning that non-EU nationals who are not already lawfully resident in a Member State enjoy an automatic right to enter and reside within the host Member State on the basis of family relationship alone, it would undermine the Member States' powers to control immigration at their external border.

57. The Minister submits that this division of competences is confirmed by the judgment of the Court of Justice in *Akrich* and, in particular, paras. 49 and 50 of the judgment which provide:

> "49. However, Regulation No 1612/68 covers only freedom of movement within the Community. It is silent as to the rights of a national of a non-Member State, who is the spouse of a citizen of the Union, in regard to access to the territory of the Community.50. In order to benefit in a situation such as that at issue in the main proceedings from the rights provided for in Article 10 of Regulation No 1612/68, the national of a non-Member State, who is the spouse of a citizen of the Union, must be lawfully resident in a Member State when he moves to another Member State to which the citizen of the Union is migrating or has migrated."

58. The Minister contends that his entitlement to rely upon the decision of the Court of Justice in *Akrich* as permitting him to confine the scope of Directive 2004/38/EC to those family members who were lawfully resident in another Member State prior to coming to Ireland, is not diminished by the judgment in *Jia*.

59. The Minister submits that the judgment of the Court of Justice in *Jia* must be understood as not requiring Member States to make the grant of residence pursuant to Directive 2004/38/EC subject to prior lawful residence in another Member State but not preventing a Member State from doing so if it so wishes. The Minister submits that the question asked in *Jia* by the Swedish Court, as interpreted by the Court of Justice, was whether Community law requires a Member State to impose a condition of lawful residence and that the Court did not address the question as to whether Directive 73/148/E.EC (which was at issue in those proceedings) permits a Member State to impose a condition of lawful residence. The Minister does not consider that the judgment of the Court of Justice in *Eind* alters this position.

60. The Minister submits that Directive 2004/38/EC must be interpreted in accordance with the principles set out by the Court of Justice in *Akrich* and *Jia*. Further, he submits that Directive 2004/38/EC when so construed, whilst it does not require Member States to impose a condition of prior lawful residence in another Member State for family members of a Union citizen who seeks entry or residence pursuant to Directive 2004/38/EC, does leave to Member States a choice or discretion to impose such a condition if they so wish.

61. The Minister does not rely on articles 27 or 35 of Directive 2004/38/EC as authorising article 3(2) of the 2006 Regulations. He accepts that article 3(2) is a measure of general application which is not so authorised.

Submission of Applicants on Prior Lawful Residence Requirement

62. The applicants make varying submissions, in particular, in relation to the reasons for which the judgment of the Court of Justice in *Akrich* does not enable the Minister to impose by Regulation the disputed prior lawful residence requirement. However, counsel for each applicant adopted the submissions made by the other and, therefore, it is appropriate to summarise the submissions of the applicants without distinguishing between same.

63. The applicants submit that the Minister is incorrect in his submission on the division of competences between Community law and the Member States in relation to the immigration of family members of a Union citizen who exercises his or her right to move to or reside in another Member State. The applicants submit that Directive 2004/38/EC governs the entry into the territory of Member States of family members of a Union citizen who is residing in a host Member State. They submit that this follows from a consideration of the enabling EC Treaty provisions (in particular Article 18) and of Directive 2004/38/EC and, in particular, its articles 1,3,5,6,7(1)&(2), 10,27 and 35 when construed in a accordance with the Treaty and the recitals to the Directive, in particular recitals (1),(3),(5),(6),(11) and (22).

64. They submit that the fundamental right is that of the Union citizen which derives from the EC Treaty and not from Directive 2004/38/EC. The rights of the Union citizen include a right to move and a separate and distinct right to reside in another Member State. The right of the family member is consequential to and dependant on the right of the Union citizen and in the case of a spouse derives from the family relationship alone. The applicants rely on the judgments of the Court of Justice in *Movement Contre le Racisme, l'antisémitisme et la xénophobie ASBL (MRAX) v. Belgian State (Case C-459/99)* [2002] ECR. I-6591 ("*MRAX*") and *Commission of the European Communities v. Spain (Case C-157/03)* [2005] ECR. I-2911 ("*Commission v. Spain*").

65. The applicants submit that the requirement of lawful residence as stated by the Court of Justice in *Akrich* (at paras. 49 and 50) in relation to Council Regulation (EEC) No. 1612/68 does not now apply to the interpretation of Directive 2004/38/EC for a number of reasons:

(1) The statement of the Court of Justice in *Akrich* must be considered in the context of the facts and rights at issue in the main proceedings in that case. *Akrich* was concerned with an implied right to return to a home Member State derived from the express right of free movement in Regulation (E EC) No. 1612/68. This did not include the distinct right to reside in another Member State referred to in Directive 2004/38/EC and deriving from Article 18 of the Treaty.

(2) The Court of Justice in *Jia* (at paras. 25-33) confirms that what is stated in *Akrich* does not have general application. This limited application of the lawful residence requirement in *Akrich* has been confirmed by the opinion of the Advocate General (at para. 46) and the judgment of the Court of Justice (at paras. 36, 41 and 45) in *Eind*.

(3) Directive 2004/38/EC was adopted on the 29th April, 2004, after the judgment of the Court in *Akrich*. Recital (3) states that it is to "strengthen the right of free movement and residence of all Union citizens". The applicants submit that articles 5 and 7 of the Directive in particular, are inconsistent with an implied requirement of prior lawful residence for a non-EU family member.

(4) *Akrich* should properly be considered as an "abuse of rights" case. Article 35 of Directive 2004/38/EC now expressly enables Member States to take measures to prevent abuse of rights or fraud in accordance with the conditions set out therein. Article 3(2) of the 2006 Regulations is not such a provision.

66. The applicants submit that Directive 2004/38/EC cannot be interpreted as leaving Member States a discretion or choice to include a general requirement of prior lawful residence in another Member State for family members of Union citizens seeking either entry or residence in Ireland. They contend that the scheme of the Directive, as appears from article 1(a) and(c), is that it lays down the conditions governing the exercise of the right of free movement and residence within the territory of Member States by Union citizens and their family members and the limits which may be placed on those rights by Member States. Further, the applicants submit that articles 5, 7 and 10 set out exhaustively what Member States may require of a family member who seeks either entry or residence. They submit that there is nothing in those articles which permit individual Member States to introduce an additional substantive requirement, as Ireland seeks to do in article 3(2) of the 2006 Regulations.

67. The applicants submit that the limits which may be placed by Member States on entry and residence of family members of a Union citizen are those decisions and measures authorised by article 27 and article 35 of Directive 2004/38/EC. Article 3(2) of the 2006 Regulations is not a measure made pursuant to article 27 or article 35 of the Directive, as it is a Regulation with general application.

68. The applicants contend that Directive 2004/38/EC does not permit of differing substantive requirements in different Member States. The applicants referred to the Immigration (European Economic Area) Regulations 2006 made to implement Directive 2004/38/EC in the United

Kingdom which contains no prior lawful residence requirement similar to that in article 3(2) of the 2006 Regulations.

69. The applicants rely on the response given to Petition 0646/2006 by Hanna Sobczak (Polish) to the European Parliament (in which reliance is placed on on the Court of Justice's judgment in *Jia)* to the effect that article 3(2) of the 2006 Regulations:

> "Would appear to be contrary to Community law as the right of residence in Ireland cannot be made conditional upon having resided legally in another Member State before arriving in Ireland. The Commission services envisage drawing the attention of the Irish authorities to this judgment and require that the Irish legislation fully complies with Community law."

Question on Prior Lawful Residence Requirement

70. The single question upon which I need the preliminary ruling of the Court of Justice to enable me to determine the applications for *certiorari* and underlying challenge to the validity of article 3(2) of the 2006 Regulations is:

> Does Directive 2004/38/EC permit a Member State to have a general requirement that a non-EU national spouse of a Union citizen must have been lawfully resident in another Member State prior to coming to the host Member State in order that he or she be entitled to benefit from the provisions of Directive 2004/38/EC.

71. I must respectfully emphasise that, for the reasons set out at paragraphs 43 to 48 above, the question must be answered independently of the immigration history of the applicants except of the fact that the non-EU spouse was not lawfully resident in another Member State prior to arriving in Ireland if it is to be of assistance to me in determining the claims for *certiorari* in these proceedings. In refusing the three relevant applicants, the Minister only relied on their failure to provide evidence of prior lawful residence in another Member State and not on their personal immigration history in Ireland. Further, the prior lawful residence requirement in article 3(2) of the 2006 Regulations applies, irrespective of the immigration status of the non-EU applicant spouse. Other applications in which leave to seek Judicial Review has been granted by the High Court (some of which have been settled and others not yet heard) demonstrate reliance upon article 3(2) to refuse applications for residence from non-EU national spouses of Union citizens who had been permitted to enter Ireland on a "join EU spouse visa" and other types of visa.

72. In the context of the submissions made on behalf of the applicants during the hearing before this Court, the position of non-EU spouses of Irish citizens is not relevant to this Court's decision.. However, as the Court of Justice took into account in *Jia* the analogous position under Swedish law it may be relevant for the Court of Justice to be aware that the Minister, through his counsel, informed this Court that applications for residence for non- EU spouses of Irish citizens are considered and determined by the Minister as part of his executive functions. There are no statutory provisions applicable. The Minister has indicated that each application is decided on its own facts. There is no automatic entitlement to residence and there is no automatic exclusion even of non-EU nationals who may have entered or be in Ireland illegally.

Ancillary Questions

73. If, following the preliminary ruling of the Court of Justice on the question referred at paragraph 70 above, I determine that I should grant an order of *certiorari* of the decisions made on behalf of the Minister to refuse the applications of the non-EU nationals for a residence card, then those applications will be sent back to the Minister to be determined in accordance with Directive 2004/38/EC and the 2006 Regulations.

74. On the notice of opposition filed by the Minister and legal submissions made both in writing and orally, there is one further objection made by the Minister to the eligibility of at least certain of the non-EU applicants in these proceedings which raises the proper interpretation of article 3(1) of Directive 2004/38/EC. As this legal issue is crystallised in the submissions made and on the undisputed facts affects certain of the applicants, it appears appropriate that the Court determine this issue before remitting the matter to the Minister. If not, there would be uncertainty as to the meaning of any Order made by the Court that the application "be determined in accordance with Directive 2004/38/EC" which is undesirable. Also, on the undisputed facts it would appear to follow, inevitably, that if the Minister applies Directive 2004/38/EC in accordance with the legal meaning for which he contends, he will again refuse certain of the applications and, having regard to the legal submissions made on behalf of the applicants, there would be a further set of Judicial Review proceedings with consequent delay and cost to both parties.

75. I wish to emphasize that, in determining this legal issue in dispute between the parties as to the proper meaning of article 3(1) of Directive 2004/38/EC, I am not seeking to determine the applicants' entitlement to a residence card. In those cases in which leave was granted to claim an order of *mandamus* requiring the Minister to grant the residence card or a declaration to that effect, counsel for the applicants did not pursue those reliefs at the hearing.

76. Article 3(1) of Directive 2004/38/EC provides:

> "This Directive shall apply to all Union citizens who move to or reside in a Member State other than that of which they are a national, and to their family members as defined in point 2 of Article 2 who accompany or join them".

77. The dispute between the applicants and the Minister relates to the proper meaning of the requirement that the family member "accompany or join" the Union citizen. The dispute arises in the following way.

78. In three of the cases, the non-EU national arrived in Ireland independently of the EU citizen. The applicants in [2007] No. 1324 J.R. are not included in this description as, whilst they arrived separately in Ireland, they had met in the Cameroon and had been in a relationship for thirteen years. In two of the three cases, the non-EU national arrived in Ireland before the EU citizen.

79. In all three cases, the EU citizen and non-EU national married in Ireland, subsequent to the EU citizen moving to Ireland and taking up residence in Ireland.

80. In all three cases, at the date the non-EU national applied for a residence card, pursuant to article 10 of Directive 2004/38/EC as implemented by the 2006 Regulations, he was the spouse of the EU citizen who then had a right to reside in Ireland for a period in excess of three months pursuant to article 7(1) of the Directive and was stated to be residing with the EU citizen in Ireland.

81. The applicants contend that at the date of application for the residence card, the non-EU nationals were persons who came within the scope of article 3(1) by reason of the following:

(i) The Union citizen was residing in Ireland with a right of residence for a period longer than three months pursuant to article 7(1);
(ii) The non-EU national was a family member of the Union citizen, being her spouse;
(iii) The non-EU citizen was at that time accompanying the Union citizen in Ireland within the meaning of article 3(1).

82. The applicants refer to the application of the Directive, in article 3(1), to Union citizens who "move to or reside" in a Member State other than their own. They submit that the Directive applies to a Union citizen whilst residing in a Member State other than his or her own. Hence, if at any time whilst s/he is so residing, the Union citizen acquires a family member, by marriage or otherwise and that person is with them in the host Member State (regardless of how they came to be there), they are a family member who is then accompanying the Union citizen in the host Member State.

83. The applicants also rely upon the distinct right of residence of the Union citizen in the host Member State for a period longer than three months if he or she satisfies the conditions in article 7(1)(a), (b) or (c) of Directive 2004/38/EC.

84. The applicants, finally, rely upon the terms of article 7(2) in relation to the right of residence of the non-EU national spouse. This provides:

> "The right of residence provided for in paragraph 1 shall extend to family members who are not nationals of a Member State, accompanying or joining the Union citizen in the host Member State, provided that such Union citizen satisfies the conditions referred to in paragraph 1(a), (b) or (c)."

The applicants submit that the right of residence is conferred on the family member who is accompanying the Union citizen in the host Member State and is not in any way dependent upon the circumstances in which the non-EU family member came to enter the host Member State.

85. The applicants submit that, at the date of application for the residence card, the non-EU national spouse of the EU citizen was within the scope of article 3(1) and was then accompanying the Union citizen (who satisfied the conditions in article 7(1)(a), (b) or (c)) and, accordingly, had a right of residence pursuant to article 7(2). They submit that the Minister may only require presentation of the documents referred to in article 10(2) and may only refuse the application pursuant to measures or decisions authorised by articles 27 or 35 of Directive 2004/38/E.C.

86. The applicants submit that their contentions are supported in particular by the judgment of the Court of Justice in *MRAX*.

87. The essential submission made on behalf of the Minister is that the non-EU nationals do not come within the scope of the Directive in accordance with article 3(1) because at the time the non-EU national entered Ireland, he was not a family member of a Union citizen. The Minister submits that where a Union citizen is residing in a Member State other than his own, a family member may only be regarded as accompanying him in the host Member State if the family member enters the host Member State at a time when he is already a family member of a Union citizen who is either moving to the host Member State or already residing therein.

88. The Minister, in the oral submissions made in the course of the hearing, had initially submitted that the non-EU national spouses were excluded from the scope of Directive 2004/38/EC because they were not married to the Union citizen at the time the Union citizen moved to Ireland. However, in the course of the submissions, counsel for the Minister appears to have resiled from that submission and accepted that there were certain circumstances in which the spouse of a Union citizen who married subsequent to moving to and commencing to reside in a host Member State could come within the scope of article 3(1) of Directive 2004/38/EC. Counsel appeared to accept that if a Union citizen married outside of the host Member State subsequent to taking up residence therein and his non-EU national spouse then sought to join the Union citizen in the host Member State, that such person would then come within article 3(1) as the non-EU national spouse would then be joining the Union citizen in the host Member State as a family member. This acceptance was, of course, without prejudice to the Minister's position on prior lawful residence.

89. The submission persisted with on behalf of the Minister appears to be based upon the contention that a non-EU national spouse of a Union citizen cannot be considered to be accompanying the Union citizen in the host Member State within the meaning of article 3(1) (and article7 (2)) unless, at the time of the arrival of the non-EU national to the host Member State, he or she was already a family member of a Union citizen.

90. This submission of the Minister is made independently of the circumstances in which the non-EU national arrived in the host Member State or his or her status in the host Member State prior to asserting a right of residence under article 7(2) and applying for a residence card pursuant to article 10 of Directive 2004/38/EC.

91. The parties did not contend for any difference in the circumstances in which a non-EU national spouse would be considered to be "accompanying or joining the Union citizen "for the purposes of article 3(1) or 7(2). The focus of the submissions was on whether or not the applicants came within the scope of Directive 2004/38/EC and hence article 3 (1).

92. Whilst the Minister did not make express submissions relating to the date on which the family member of a Union citizen who asserts a right of residence pursuant to article 7(2) and applies for a residence card, must come within the scope of the Directive. However, it appears implicit from the submissions made by the Minister that he is contending that the family member of the Union citizen must have come within the scope of the Directive on the date he sought to enter Ireland. This is consistent with the provisions of article 3(2) of the 2006 Regulations made by the Minister set out at paragraph 39 above. As appears, article 3(2) confines the scope of the 2006 Regulations to family members who either seek to enter Ireland in the company of a Union citizen, or seek to join a Union citizen in Ireland in respect of which he or she is already a family member.

93. The questions upon which I seek a preliminary ruling from the Court of Justice to enable me give judgment on the dispute between the applicants and the Minister on the scope of Directive 2004/38/EC are:

(1) Does article 3(1) of Directive 2004/38/EC include within its scope of application a non-EU national who is:
   (i) A spouse of a Union citizen who resides in the host Member State and satisfies a condition in article 7(1)(a),(b) or(c)
   And
   (ii) Is then residing in the host Member State with the Union citizen as his/her spouse Irrespective of when or where their marriage took place or when or how the non-EU national entered the host Member State.
(2) If the answer to the preceding question is in the negative, does article 3(1) of Directive 2004/38/EC include within its scope of application a non-EU national spouse of a Union citizen who is:
   (i) A spouse of a Union citizen who resides in the host Member State and satisfies a condition in article 7(1)(a),(b) or (c); and
   (ii) Resides in the host Member State with the Union citizen as his/her spouse; and
   (iii) Has entered the host Member State independently of the Union citizen; and
   (iv) Subsequently married the Union citizen in the host Member State.

Accelerated Procedure

94. The parties (both applicants and the Minister) submitted to this Court that a ruling by the Court of Justice on the questions referred hereby is a matter of exceptional urgency. I am satisfied that it does appear a matter of exceptional urgency and hereby request the President to apply an accelerated procedure pursuant to article 104a of the Rules of Procedure. My reasons for this conclusion and request are as follows.

95. The ruling on the first question in particular will apply to many others as well as the applicants in these proceedings. Article 3(2) of the 2006 Regulations applies to all applications pursuant to Directive 2004/38/EC. The Minister has indicated that currently he receives approximately 180 such applications per month. He received 2,283 such applications in 2007. It appears probable from the analysis given to the Court on his behalf that a significant number of the non-EU national applicants cannot provide evidence of prior lawful residence in another Member State.

96. The four cases which are the subject of this reference form part of in excess of fifty cases commenced before the High Court in 2007 seeking orders of *certiorari* of decisions of the Minister refusing applications under Directive 2004/38/EC as implemented by the 2006 Regulations. These were case managed by the High Court and given priority by reason of the importance and general application of the issues raised. Initially, approximately ten such cases were listed for hearing in January 2008 as test cases. Prior to the hearing date, all except the four herein were settled by the Minister to the satisfaction of the applicants. With one exception, the terms of settlement were not disclosed to the Court, other than a consent order that the applicants recover their reasonable costs from the Minister. The settled cases appear primarily to have related to non-EU national spouses who had lawfully entered Ireland on a visa. In excess of 40 such cases were settled. There remain a number of applications commenced in 2007 and earlier where the non-EU nationals are in analogous situation to those in these applications or the applicants in *SK.*

97. The Minister is obliged by Directive 2004/38/EC to issue a Residence card to family members within six months of the date of application (article 10(1)). Hence, he continues to take decisions many of which are to refuse applications from non-EU national spouses who cannot provide evidence of prior lawful residence including from some who have been permitted to enter Ireland on a visa. These refusals give rise to continuing applications to the High Court. Since the hearing of these proceedings, the High Court has granted leave to challenge the Minister's refusal of residency in at least twenty applications. Three such applications which relate to applicants who were permitted to enter Ireland on a visa are listed for hearing in April 2008. The hearing date has been fixed as a matter of priority as the applicants contend they are in a different factual position to the non-EU applicants herein having been given express permission to enter Ireland. Further, they contend that the earlier settlements by the Minister of similar intended test cases have precluded the inclusion in this reference of cases with similar facts to theirs.

98. At present, it appears probable that the Minister's decisions to refuse in reliance on article 3(2) of the 2006 Regulations, followed by applications to the High Court, will continue until the preliminary ruling requested herein is determined. These involve significant costs and expenses for the Minister and applicants and court resources. The Minister seeks clarity as soon as feasible on the questions on which the ruling is sought.

99. Whilst I have formed the view that it is necessary to seek a preliminary ruling on the interpretation of Directive 2004/38/EC in relation to the prior lawful residence requirement in article 3(2) to enable me give judgment on the applications for *certiorari* I am also of the view that the applicants have adduced strong arguments in favour of the contention that Directive 2004/38/EC does not permit Member States to have a general requirement that a non-EU national spouse of a Union citizen must have been lawfully resident in another Member State prior to coming to the host Member State in order that he or she be entitled to benefit from the provisions of Directive 2004/38/EC. The Minister accepts that Directive 2004/38/EC does not so require. Subject to what may be determined by the Court of Justice in response to the requested preliminary ruling, the applicants' submission that the Directive sets out exhaustively the substantive conditions governing the exercise of the right of free movement and residence within the territory of the Member States of Union citizens and their family members and the limits which may be placed on those rights, appears persuasive as does the further submission that the limits which may be placed by Member States on the rights are those authorised by articles 27 or 35. The overall purpose and intention of the Directive appears to be that the general conditions set out therein apply throughout all the territory of the Member States. It is difficult to envisage that it permits of differing general conditions in the territory of different Member States as contended for by the Minister.

100. To take a simple example: a French national is employed initially in France by a French subsidiary of an American corporation. He is promoted to work at head office in New York. He spends ten years in New York and whilst there marries a US citizen who has never lived outside of the US. He is then offered a choice between becoming chief executive of the United Kingdom or Irish subsidiary and must live in the relevant country. If the Minister's contention is correct, he has no real choice. If the French national chooses the United Kingdom, his wife appears entitled to residence pursuant to the national provisions implementing Directive 2004/38/EC, whereas if he chooses Ireland, she is excluded by the prior lawful residence requirement in article 3(2) of the 2006 Regulations. This appears a real deterrent to exercising his Community right to move to and reside in Ireland. Subject to the ruling of the Court of Justice on the questions herein, it is difficult to envisage how this additional condition in Ireland is consistent with the overall purpose and effect of Directive 2004/38/EC.

101. The present personal circumstances of the four applicant couples are also relevant factors in the urgent need for the ruling. It is not in dispute that all are Union citizens exercising their right to reside and work in Ireland. There is no challenge to the *bona fides* of the marriages. The three non-EU national spouses who remain in Ireland are not permitted to work. In two families there are minor dependant children. The four Union citizens are women (one of whom is currently pregnant) who should be able to benefit from family life with a working spouse. If the non- EU national spouses are within the scope of Directive 2004/38/EC as they contend, then they have an express right to take up employment pursuant to article 23. The other Union citizen is also deprived of the company of her spouse in Ireland other than as a result of a procedure authorised by article 27 of Directive 2004/38/EC. Similar factual circumstances exist for others whose applications are dependant on the requested ruling.

102. Finally, the Minister is facing claims for damages in certain of the proceedings, principally relating to alleged loss of earnings. If there is a liability (which has not been determined), the amount will inevitably increase with the length of the period prior to final judgment.

Order

103. There will be an order requesting a preliminary ruling from the Court of Justice on the following questions.

(1) Does Directive 2004/38/EC permit a Member State to have a general requirement that a non-EU national spouse of a Union citizen must have been lawfully resident in another Member State prior to coming to the host Member State in order that he or she be entitled to benefit from the provisions of Directive 2004/38/EC.

(2) Does article 3(1) of Directive 2004/38/EC include within its scope of application a non-EU national who is:

(i) A spouse of a Union citizen who resides in the host Member State and satisfies a condition in article 7(1)(a),(b) or(c)

And

(ii) Is then residing in the host Member State with the Union citizen as his/her spouse Irrespective of when or where their marriage took place or when or how the non-EU national entered the host Member State.

(3) If the answer to the preceding question is in the negative, does article 3(1) of Directive 2004/38/EC include within its scope of application a non-EU national spouse of a Union citizen who is:

(i) A spouse of a Union citizen who resides in the host Member State and satisfies a condition in article 7(1)(a),(b) or (c); and

(ii) Resides in the host Member State with the Union citizen as his/her spouse; and

(iii) Has entered the host Member State independently of the Union citizen; and
(iv) Subsequently married the Union citizen in the host Member State
And a request that such ruling be the subject of accelerated procedures pursuant to article 104a of the Rules of Procedure of the Court of Justice.

Minister for Justice Equality and Law Reform v Slonski

[2010] IESC 19

Author's note: *Slonski* is one of the many important decisions on the definition of the "flight" or "fleeing" pursuant to the European Arrest Warrant Act 2003, as amended.

Judgment delivered on the 25th day of March, 2010 by Macken, J.

This is an appeal from the judgment of the High Court (Peart, J.) delivered on the 10th March, 2009 and the Order made thereon by which the High Court directed the surrender of the appellant to Poland, pursuant to s.16 of the European Arrest Warrant Act, 2003 ("the Act of 2003").

The warrant in question, dated the 17th March, 2008, issued from a judicial authority in Poland in respect of the appellant and was duly endorsed by the High Court. The appellant was thereafter arrested. In the usual way, when the person sought to be surrendered pursuant to a European arrest warrant does not consent to the same, as the appellant did not, a Notice of Objection was filed on his behalf, the revised version of which, dated the 11th November, 2008, contained three objections to surrender, namely:

(i) That the appellant did not come within the provisions of s.10 of the Act of 2003 on the basis that he had not "fled" Poland after the imposition of a sentence of imprisonment;
(ii) The surrender was prohibited by part 3 of the Act of 2003 because the description of the offence contained in the European arrest warrant was not one to which Article 2.2 of the Framework Decision applied and was not either an offence which corresponds to an offence within the State, as required by s.38, and is not "a corresponding offence" as defined by s.5, of the Act of 2003;
(iii) The appellant should not be surrendered to Poland because he had already served all the required penalty during the course of his imprisonment in the State, he having been arrested, pursuant to the provisions of the Act of 2003. It would, therefore, be futile to surrender him to Poland.

Affidavits were filed, both on behalf of the appellant and also on behalf of the Minister, and it is common case that additional information was sought on behalf of the Minister from the Polish judicial authority pursuant to s.20 of the Act of 2003, and certain additional information was thereupon made available. I will refer to these matters further in the course of my judgment, where necessary.

Decision

Having regard to the findings which I propose to make, it is appropriate to commence with the first issue raised on behalf of the appellant in this appeal, namely, whether the learned High Court judge was correct in law, and the appellant says he was not, to direct the surrender of the appellant pursuant to s.16 of the Act of 2003, having regard to the appellant's claim that he was not a person who comes within s.10 of the Act of 2003, he not having fled Poland, or more correctly, as it developed in the course of argument, on the basis that there was no evidence before the learned High Court judge upon which the judge could have properly found that the appellant had fled Poland within the meaning of the section.

Section 10 of the Act of 2003 provides as follows:

> *"Where a judicial authority in an issuing state duly issues a European arrest warrant in respect of a person—*
>
> *(a) ...*
>
> *(b) ...*

> *(c) ...*
> *(d) on whom a sentence of imprisonment or detention has been imposed in respect of an offence to which the European arrest warrant relates, and who fled from the issuing state before he or she—*
> *(i) commenced serving that sentence, or*
> *(ii) completed serving that sentence,*
> *that person shall, subject to and in accordance with the provisions of this Act and the Framework Decision, be arrested and surrendered to the issuing state."* (emphasis added)

In his affidavit, sworn on the 17th December, 2008, the appellant, in its material part, averred as follows:

> *"(3) I have been in Ireland since 2005 and I have been in custody here since March, 2005 when I was arrested for a drugs offence and subsequently sentenced to seven years imprisonment. Whereas I have been in different prisons, I have been in the Midlands prison since August, 2008. I was arrested on the extradition warrant on 25th December, 2008 and I have been in custody on that since then.*
> *...*
> *(5) I was not present in court in Poland on 4th November, 2005 when I was ordered to serve a period of imprisonment. I was in custody in Ireland. In the circumstances, I believe I cannot be regarded as having fled Poland before I commenced or completed serving that sentence.*
> *(6) I believe the details specified in the European Arrest Warrant are inadequate and incomplete."*

It is helpful to set this issue in context by indicating what it is the learned trial judge said in relation to the issue of s.10 of the Act before dealing further with the issue. He stated as follows:

> *"The surrender of the respondent is sought by a judicial authority in Poland on foot of a European arrest warrant dated 17th March 2008 so that he can serve a sentence of 12 months imprisonment which was imposed upon him there on the 21st November 2003. That sentence satisfies the minimum gravity requirement, being a sentence of more than four months.*
> *...*
> *The sentence of imprisonment was conditionally suspended, the condition being that described in the warrant as "a curator's supervision". It appears that by the 4th November 2005 it had become known by the Polish court that the respondent had left Poland, which was a breach of the supervision condition, and on that date the court lifted the suspension and ordered execution of the sentence. The warrant discloses also that on the 4th April 2005 the respondent had landed at Dublin Airport and was detained there "while smuggling 500g of cocaine". He was sentenced here in respect of that offence and sentenced to a term of seven years' imprisonment which he is currently serving here."*

Insofar as the learned High Court judge's finding is concerned, vis a vis fleeing, he stated as follows:

> *"I am satisfied firstly that the date on which this sentence was imposed was the 21st November 2003, and not the date on which the suspension was lifted on 4th November 2005. The wording of s. 10(d) is clear and unambiguous. If the respondent leaves the issuing state after that sentence was imposed and before he has served the sentence, it is clear that he must be considered as having fled the issuing state before serving the sentence, regardless of the fact that the suspension was lifted after he left. I reject this ground of objection."* (emphasis added)

That is the learned High Court judge's finding in respect of the point of objection raised under s.10 of the Act of 2003.

It was argued on behalf of the appellant that the word *"fled"* in s.10 of the Act of 2003 must mean a person who has fled justice in the sense of having consciously evaded prosecution or serving a sentence, and cannot apply to leaving the issuing state for an unrelated reason, even a reason which involves engaging in a criminal enterprise, such as in the present case. If it had been intended otherwise, it is suggested that the Oireachtas would have used a more neutral word, such as *"left"* the issuing state. In that regard, Mr. Kelly, counsel on behalf of the appellant, invokes dictionary meanings of the word *"flee"*, but for the purposes of my judgment it is not necessary to consider these definitions in detail. Counsel on behalf of the appellant also invokes the decisions of this Court in *MJELR v. Tobin* [2008] I.E.S.C. 3, and *MJELR v. Sliczynski* [2008] I.E.S.C. 73, in support of his argument. He submitted, in particular, that there was no information before the High Court of the type which permitted this Court in *MJELR v. Sliczynski*, supra. to find that the appellant in that case *"fled"* within the meaning of s.10 of the Act.

Counsel argues that while additional information was sought by the respondent, pursuant to the provisions of s.20 of the Act of 2003, the information furnished, which was received on the 16th June, 2008, did not mention any factors concerning the conditions attaching to the suspension, the meaning of a *"curator's supervision"*, the basis upon which the supervision or suspension was lifted, that is to say what particular terms were allegedly breached by the appellant, or the consequences of that breach which led apparently to the lifting of the suspension by the order made on the 4th November, 2005.

Mr. Farrell, counsel for the respondent, argues that it can be clearly implied from the terms of the warrant and from the lifting of the suspension, that there had been a breach of the curator's supervision. He also contends that the appellant breached the terms of his suspended sentence by leaving Poland, because the practical effect of leaving was that he would no longer be subject to the supervision of the curator. Finally, he submits that although the appellant swore an affidavit for the purposes of contending that he had not fled Poland, he did not deal in his affidavit with any reason for leaving Poland or with any of the other information or material concerning leaving of Poland or, indeed, the curator's supervision.

Mr. Farrell also submits that the learned High Court judge was likewise entitled to draw certain inferences from the information contained in the European arrest warrant and the additional information, that he did so correctly, and that having regard to the appropriate inferences which he drew, he was then entitled to conclude that the appellant had fled Poland within the meaning of s.10 of the Act of 2003, as the requirements for that section had been met, in accordance with the above cited case law, which he also invokes.

Apart from the submission made on behalf of the respondent by counsel, arising out of the above factors, there is one other piece of information that was before the learned High Court judge which is the content of paragraph 7 of the affidavit of Sergeant Jim Kirwan sworn on the 7th January, 2009 in the following terms, and arising out of his arrest of the appellant:

> *"I read over a praecipe of the offences contained in the warrant and asked "do you know what these are about" to which he (the appellant) replied "yes, I remember that I got a suspended sentence on this. ...".*

I mention again the contents of paragraph 5 of the affidavit of the appellant, sworn on the 17th December, 2008, which in my view is slightly disingenuous and ambiguous as to the consequences which the appellant is contending for. It is as well to set this out again:

> *"I was not present in Court in Poland on 4th November 2005 when I was ordered to serve a period of imprisonment. I was in custody in Ireland. In these circumstances I believe I cannot be regarded as having fled Poland before I commenced or completed serving that sentence."*

The sentence therein referred to is the sentence which was suspended, but as I read paragraph 6 of the affidavit it appears to suggest, wrongly in my view, that the sentence only commenced on the 4th November, 2005 when the suspension was lifted. This is incorrect, and in that regard I am satisfied that the learned High Court judge was correct when he found that the sentence of imprisonment in question was the sentence imposed on the 21st November, 2003 (suspended) and not the order requiring that the appellant be admitted to prison once the suspension was lifted on the 4th November, 2005.

In one sense, therefore, the appellant does not, in his grounding affidavit, challenge at all the imposition of the sentence of imprisonment, or the suspension order, or the effect of that suspension order. It is, therefore, appropriate to consider only the legal argument made on the basis that the respondent failed to bring to the attention of the learned High Court judge evidence upon which the learned High Court judge could properly conclude that the appellant fled Poland.

It is, of course, for the respondent, as applicant, to bring to the attention of the High Court factors upon which the respondent contends the learned High Court judge could properly find that the appellant fled, within the meaning of s.10 of the Act. The appellant's contention in this case, as mentioned above, is that there was no such material before the High Court upon which the learned High Court judge could have concluded that he did, in fact, flee.

This issue of what is meant by *"fled"* in s.10 of the Act of 2003 has been dealt with in several cases, but of relevance to this appeal is the case of *MJELR v. Sliczynski*, supra., in which I considered an appropriate approach to be adopted in assessing whether or not, where a sentence has been suspended, a person had *"fled"* an issuing state within the meaning of s.10 of the Act of 2003, with which analysis, Murray, C.J., in the same case, agreed.

In that case I set out all the factors which were before the learned High Court judge as furnished by the issuing judicial authority, as well as the subjective averments of the appellant as to the reasons why he left Poland. As to the material furnished either in the warrant, or pursuant to additional information sought, there was before the High Court judge in that case the following information:

(1) The number of sentences in issue;
(2) The fact that the appellant was sentenced in his presence in relation to the material sentences;
(3) The fact that those latter sentences were suspended in accordance with Polish law and that those suspensions were subject to conditions, the conditions specified including that he maintain contact with the Probation Officer and remain subject to their supervision, reside at a particular address, and inform the Probation Officer of each change of residence, and in particular of any plan to travel abroad.

The evidence before the High Court in that case was also to the effect that the person sought to be surrendered, who was subject to the above sentences, as suspended, had breached the terms of the suspension by failing to give any notification to the Probation Officer, or any other appropriate person, of his intention to leave Poland and failed to provide each change of address, no change of address in Ireland having been furnished.

As to the norms or requirements to be applied to the information available to the High Court judge in determining whether a person sought to be surrendered, pursuant to the Act of 2003, had fled the issuing state, I stated:

> *"All of the factors germane to whether a person can be said to have fled must be taken into account. That includes the motivation of the person sought to be returned to the requesting Member State, which is almost inevitably likely to be a subjective motivation. So also the court must take into account other material factors, such as whether the sentence was*

> *suspended, and where the suspension of the sentence was subject to terms, whether those terms were known to the convicted person and whether those terms were complied with.*
>
> ...
>
> *The court then must determine whether, objectively speaking, bearing in mind all of these factors, it can be reasonably concluded that the appellant "fled" within the meaning of the sub-section. If it were the case that the subjective motivation, as averred to on affidavit, had to be accepted as being conclusive of the question whether a person fled within the meaning of the section, it seems to me that this would always or almost always "trump" any information or material factor presented to the Court and upon which it could be objectively found that a person had fled the requesting state."*

In the present case, the information as to the sentence in question and the conditions of suspension were given in the following terms, as translated into English:

> "By virtue of a sentence of District Court in Ostroda, Act No. II K1507/02 dated 21/11/2002, Dominik Slonski was convicted to one year of imprisonment. The punishment was conditionally suspended and a curator's supervision was imposed on the convict. Then on 4/11/2005 the District Court in Pruszkow, Act No. D483/03, ordered execution of punishment of imprisonment against the convict. The convict did not appear at the custody to fulfil the penalty.
>
> It was established that the convict left Poland and on 4/4/2005 he was detained at Dublin Airport while smuggling 500g of cocaine. He was convicted to seven years of deprivation of freedom for this offence. Now he has been serving the term of imprisonment in Mountjoy Prison in Ireland."

On the basis of all the material presented, the following information was before the High Court:

(a) That on the 21st November, 2003 the appellant was convicted to one year imprisonment for the offence in question;
(b) That the punishment was suspended conditionally;
(c) That a *"curator's supervision"* was imposed on the appellant;
(d) That on 4th November, 2005 execution of the punishment of imprisonment was ordered against the appellant.

There was no information before the learned High Court judge as to the conditions imposed, as to what constituted a *"curator's supervision"*, as to what conditions attaching to his suspension were allegedly breached, or led to the lifting of that suspension, and in particular as to whether or not the fact that the appellant left Poland was a breach of the conditions attaching to the suspension, or if becoming involved in criminal activities, whether inside or outside Poland, constituted a breach of the same conditions or other conditions attaching to the suspension. It is unclear to me on what evidence the learned High Court judge based his finding of fact that the appellant's leaving of Poland, *"was a breach of the supervision condition"*. Unlike the position in *MJELR v Sliczynski*, there was no information before the High Court that the terms of the suspension had been imposed in the presence of the appellant, such that would have permitted the High Court to conclude that he knew them, had not denied them, and appreciated that any breach of them would naturally lead to the suspension being lifted.

It would not appear that the judgments of this Court in the *MJELR v. Sliczynski*, supra. were brought to the attention of the learned High Court judge, possibly because of the timescale of their delivery. The Court is satisfied that had the judgments been brought to the attention of the learned High Court judge, he would have approached the assessment of the material before him on the basis of those judgments.

I am satisfied in the foregoing circumstances that there was wholly inadequate material before the learned High Court judge upon which he could properly reach the conclusion that the appellant was a person who came within the ambit of s.10 of the Act of 2003, as a person who fled Poland.

In the circumstances, the appellant cannot be surrendered pursuant to the provisions of s.16 of the Act of 2003, on the basis of the information presented to the High Court on this particular European arrest warrant. Having regard to this finding, is both unnecessary and inappropriate to deal with either of the two additional grounds raised on behalf of the appellant in the present appeal.

I would allow the appeal and set aside the order of the High Court directing the surrender of the appellant pursuant to s.16 of the European Arrest Warrant Act, 2003.

Minister for Justice, Equality and Law Reform v Stapleton

[2007] IESC 30

Judgment of Mr Justice Fennelly delivered on the 26th day of July, 2007.

This appeal concerns the European Arrest Warrant. The Minister (hereinafter "the Applicant") appeals against the decision of the High Court (Peart J) refusing to order the surrender of the Respondent to the United Kingdom. The learned trial judge decided, pursuant to section 37 of the European Arrest Warrant Act, 2003 (hereinafter "the Act"), that the surrender of the Respondent would constitute an infringement of the constitutional rights of the Respondent, by reason of the lapse of time since the alleged commission of the offences for which the Respondent is to be tried.

The Proceedings

The Respondent is an Irish citizen, aged sixty three years. Prior to 1994, he had lived for a number of years in the United Kingdom and subsequently in Spain and, for a short time, in France. Since the end of 1994, he has lived in Ireland.

A European Arrest Warrant ("the EAW") was issued by on the 20th July 2005 at Bow Street Magistrates' Court, London. The warrant relates to a total of 30 offences involving fraud. The offences are alleged to have been committed over a period from 1978 to 1982. It is alleged that the Respondent obtained in excess of Stg£3 million through the commission of these offences.

The EAW was duly transmitted to the Central Authority in the State and endorsed by the High Court for execution pursuant to the provisions of the Act. The Respondent was arrested on 14th September 2005 at Redgap, Rathcoole, County Dublin, brought before the High Court and committed to prison pending the hearing of the application for an order for his surrender.

The Respondent filed a number of Points of Objection. The only one of present relevance is that based on section 37 of the Act, which is the ground upon which the Respondent succeeded before Peart J. He also filed a notice claiming that the Criminal Justice (Terrorist Offences) Act 2005 is repugnant to the Constitution in that it represents a disproportionate implementation of the objective of enforcement of the European Union Council Framework Decision of 13 June 2002 on the European Arrest Warrant and the Surrender Procedures Between Member States (the "Framework Decision"). The learned trial judge dismissed that claim. The Respondent has appealed to this Court. The constitutional matter was not argued at the hearing of the appeal and remains outstanding.

In the course of the proceedings before the High Court, the Respondent unsuccessfully applied for discovery of a wide range of documents from the authorities of the issuing Member State (the United Kingdom). Affidavits were exchanged, including one from each side concerning law and procedure in the English courts.

Following a hearing on 13th December 2005, the learned trial judge gave judgment on 21st February 2006 refusing the order for surrender of the Respondent.

Background: The Facts

Normally, it would be unnecessary to consider the nature of the offences in any detail. However, the Respondent states that he wishes to advance a very specific line of defence to the charges, involving allegations of collusion in his activities by the Export Credit Guarantee Department of the United Kingdom. This has become linked with his complaint about prejudice resulting from delay and makes it necessary to advert to the nature of the charges he faces.

The EAW contains the following account of the circumstances in which the offences are alleged to have been committed:

> *"In August 1985 an investigation was launched following allegations made by the Department of Trade and Industry that the Directors of two Lincoln-based companies, Lumiere Ltd. and Ultraleisure Ltd., had committed a large-scale fraud. Robert Francis Stapleton , the person sought, was the Chairman of both companies which manufactured and supplied fold-away squash courts. It is alleged that between 20th May 1978 and 31st December 1982, the period of time covered by the offences, Robert Francis Stapleton masterminded a fraud from which he obtained in excess of £3 million to support his companies and fund an extravagant lifestyle. The nature of the fraud was essentially very simple. Bogus invoices and supporting documents, for example shipping certificates, were typed up that purported to show that Ultraleisure had exported goods and services to foreign buyers. Two banks, Coutts and Co. and Lloyds Bank, then advanced funds to Ultraleisure in the belief that the transactions represented on the documents were genuine. When it became necessary for Ultraleisure to repay an advance on the maturity of the relevant promissory note, a larger advance was obtained on similarly false documents and part of that used to repay the earlier borrowing. Ultraleisure therefore had to borrow ever larger sums of money to hide the fraud."*

While there is much dispute about the facts surrounding the Respondent's departure from the United Kingdom and subsequent events, it is not so much the essential chronological history that is in dispute as the interpretation to be placed on events.

The Respondent says that he is entirely innocent of the charges and that he could not be prosecuted for similar offences under the law of the State, by reason of the lapse of time. The offences are alleged to have been committed on dates ranging now from 24 to 29 years ago.

The Respondent says that he wishes to mount a defence which is both complex and wide-ranging. He accepts that the company, Ultraleisure Ltd. went into liquidation on 13th June 1983. He says, however, that the events described in the EAW were not a fraud "masterminded" by him. In fact, he says that they were the creation of the Export Credit Guarantee Department of the United Kingdom, designed to circumvent the State Aid Rules of the European Community. The Banks were content to collude in supplying bridging finance because the borrowing was guaranteed by the ECGD. He says that a problem arose when a Danish journalist uncovered the existence of a Swiss Company which was the vehicle to provide security for the ECGD. The response of the ECGD was to leave that company unaided which resulted in its liquidation. At this stage, neither the ECGD nor the Banks are willing to assist the Respondent.

The Respondent says that he would require the evidence of a large number of witnesses to enable him to present his defence. He mentions at least seventeen such potential witnesses and says that three of them have died since the occurrence of the relevant events. In addition, he would require *"the retention and disclosure of all relevant documentation in the possession of the relevant companies' liquidators, the relevant companies' auditors and accountants, the relevant banks and ECGD and related government departments."* He says that much of the relevant documentation was in his wife's or his own possession and that it has been disposed of in the ordinary course of events or lost or destroyed. In particular, the files of his UK auditors have been destroyed.

He mentions one person, Mr John Taylor, manager of Lloyds Bank, Lincoln Branch, who has since died. He had tape-recorded an interview with Mr Taylor shortly before his death. Mr Taylor had told him that Lloyds Bank and the ECGD had worked closely together *"on the construction and/or management of the transactions which form the subject matter of these charges."* He says that the tape has been taken by the Lincolnshire Police and not returned to him.

The Respondent also says that his wife was tried in the United Kingdom in 1986 for participation in these or similar offences. She was convicted and received a suspended sentence. Her solicitors have destroyed their files. The Respondent would require transcripts in connection with her trial.

At this point, I will refer to the affidavit evidence of Mr Derek Canton, a retired member of the Lincolnshire Police Force. He was an Officer with that force from 1st September 1975 to 31st August 2005. On 30th September 1985, he became involved in an inquiry into allegations of fraud and conspiracy against the Respondent.

Mr Canton says that the Respondent was chairman of a group of companies in Lincolnshire between 1978 and 1984. His wife was a director of a number of the companies. A report from a liquidator of two of the companies, Lumiere Ltd. and Ultraleisure Ltd., of which the Respondent was Chairman, reported on 19th October 1984 that the directors of these companies had committed a large-scale fraud. These suspicions were reported to the Director of Public Prosecutions for England and Wales in 1985. That led to the establishment of a six-man investigation team within the Lincolnshire Police Force.

Mr Canton refers to a separate set of charges of fraudulent activity related to Value Added Tax which were preferred against the Respondent in 1985. He was committed to stand trial in respect of these matters and was to appear at Lincoln Crown Court on 28th October 1985. He had been granted unconditional bail by Magistrates in order to attend his trial at Lincoln Crown Court. Mr Canton refers to Court records (the Respondent objects to the use of these records) purporting to show that on 2nd October 1985, the Respondent was in Spain suffering from a nervous breakdown. The records also show that the Respondent did not appear for a Direction Hearing and was not represented, though his legal representatives later wrote to state that they had been unable to obtain instructions. A warrant was issued for the arrest of the Respondent on 28th October 1985. Mr Canton also alleges that the Respondent collected his son from school in Cumbria on 26th October 1985. Finally, the Crown Court records include a letter from the Respondent's wife dated 1st November 1985 explaining his non-appearance as being due to illness.

Clearly, Mr Canton is not in a position to verify, from his own knowledge, several of the matters mentioned in the preceding paragraph. Nonetheless, their main tenor is not seriously disputed by the Respondent.

The Respondent, in his first affidavit sworn on 18th October 2005, stated that his son had been diagnosed with a serious skin condition in 1983 and that, based on medical advice, the family moved to live in Spain in September 1985. They had been "openly" looking for accommodation in Spain since June 1984. He says he returned to England in October "shortly before the school midterm break" and made three visits and several telephone calls to the Lincolnshire Police.

He did not move to Spain to "avoid charges." On the other hand, the Respondent does not deny that he was aware of the VAT-related charges. He says that he was phoned in Spain by his solicitor to tell him that the police wished to search his house, that he flew back to England to be present, but that the search had been conducted in his absence.

On return to Spain, he contracted bronchitis which developed into pneumonia. He received a telephone call on 27th October 1985 informing him of the hearing in Lincoln Crown Court on 28th October. He was unable to attend due to his illness. He states: *"I now understand that the Court issued a warrant for my arrest."* This gives the impression that he had only recently learned of that fact. With regard to the criminal proceedings relating to alleged VAT fraud, he says:

> *"I had believed that those proceedings, which, as far as I was concerned, were entirely misconceived from the outset, had subsequently discontinued and that the warrant had simply lapsed."*

The Respondent does not give any basis for these beliefs or state when he arrived at them. It is of note that, on 14th August 1986 Spanish lawyers acting for the Respondent wrote to the Lincolnshire Police referring to the charges in respect of which he had been committed for trial and stating, *inter alia,* that the Respondent intended to return to the United Kingdom to face trial. That letter also referred to the issue of a warrant by the Judge at Lincoln Crown Court on 28th October 1985, whereas his affidavit of October 2005 gives the clear impression that he had only then learned of that fact. In a second affidavit, the Respondent complains bitterly about the behaviour of the requesting state and accuses it of introducing *"prejudicial hearsay of the grossest kind,"* of making scurrilous allegations, *"cheap shots"* and the like. He does not suggest that he was unaware of the proceedings or of the fact that he was returned for trial and was on bail. He explains that the warrant was issued by the Lincoln Crown Court when he was bed-bound in Spain. He appears to accept that he had visited Sedbergh school to collect his son, as alleged by Mr Canton, though he disputes the state of his health as then observed.

There is much dispute about peripheral matters, including the circumstances leading up to and during the trial of the Respondent's wife. The Respondent specifically alleged that he had a fear of being subjected to *"inhuman and degrading treatment."* That was based on the fact that his wife was, as is admitted, detained in custody pending her trial for almost three months before being granted bail and that during some or all of that time she was *"held as a 'category A' or high security prisoner."* He gave no details of the circumstances or conditions in which his wife was detained. In any event, the learned trial judge ruled that the Respondent's claim that he would be subjected to inhuman and degrading treatment was *"nowhere nearly made out."* There is no appeal on the point and it is unnecessary to consider it further.

He complains, in addition, that, at the outset of his wife's trial, the judge made a ruling excluding evidence from the ECGD and Lloyds Bank. This evidence would, he says, have shown how the ECGD used Swiss companies to circumvent EU state-aid rules. He believes that any similar ruling at his own trial, which he says is "probable," would constitute a breach of his rights pursuant to the European Convention on Human Rights.

The Respondent says that, at the request of his wife, he did not return to England after her arrest. He explains that, if he were charged and detained in custody, a substantial risk would arise that their children might be placed in care. Nonetheless, he claims that he was never a fugitive *"in relation to the charges at issue, since no charges were ever preferred against* [him] *prior to* [his] *family's move to Spain and no warrant ever issued for* [his] *arrest until......14th January 2004."* He moved to Spain for reasons connected with his son's health and was not motivated by any wish to avoid charges in the UK. He was not aware, at the time he moved to Spain, of the absence of any extradition arrangements between the two countries.

The Respondent continued to reside with his family in Spain. For reasons related to the health of their son, they moved to Montpelier in France (on an unnamed date apparently in the early 1990's) until they moved to Ireland in December 1994. The Respondent states that he and his family have always resided in the various places mentioned openly and under their own names. He has conducted business and established companies in Ireland.

In respect of his period in Spain, the Respondent complains that the Lincolnshire Police made no effort to visit or question him while he was there, though he did, he says, in fact receive a visit from Treasury Solicitors representing the ECGD in 1991.

Mr Canton says that there were no extradition arrangements between the United Kingdom and Spain at the time the Respondent was being sought. Furthermore, when such arrangements were subsequently made, they were not made retrospective under Spanish law. Thus, they did not cover the offences in question. While, the Respondent claims that he openly moved to and lived in Spain, it is clear that the police believed he had moved there in order to avoid prosecution in the UK.

Mr Canton does not deny that Mrs Stapleton was detained as a Category A prisoner and even refers to suggestions that, apart from the risk of escape, the police were motivated by some concerns regarding the use of firearms and other violent action. Mr Canton does not know the source of such information. He asserts that the Respondent was fully aware that the Lincolnshire Police wished to interview him and points out that the Respondent has not, over a period of more than twenty years returned to the United Kingdom to answer questions in respect of deficiencies in his group of companies, although he did cause his solicitors to write to the Lincolnshire Police in 1986 complaining about various police actions. Mr Canton says that the Police considered it inappropriate to visit the Respondent in Spain where the requirements of English law were not enforceable and in a country from which he could not be extradited or otherwise compelled to answer criminal charges. The visit by the Treasury Solicitors, of which the Lincolnshire Police learned after the event, related to a civil matter connected with the liquidation of the companies. Mr Canton adds that, in August 1996, following contact between these two bodies, the ECGD solicitors visited the Respondent at his solicitors' offices in Spain. Lincolnshire Police were not concerned in either meeting. Curiously, this 1996 meeting took place after the Respondent had been resident in this jurisdiction since the end of 1994.

Mr Canton says that the Lincolnshire Police received information in 2001 that the Respondent was living near Dublin, but they had no such prior information. Having confirmed his identity, the Police reported to the Crown Prosecution Service and instructions were given to reassess the case against the Respondent *"in order to determine viable witness evidence."* In June 2002, Mr Canton reported back to the Crown Prosecution Service and thereafter to junior and senior counsel. Following a number of enquiries a decision was made to apply for extradition of the Respondent in November 2003. Subsequently, the Director of Public Prosecutions for England and Wales gave instructions not to apply for extradition pending the coming into force of the European Arrest Warrant procedure on 1st January 2004. Subsequently again, a decision was made not to proceed in the Respondent's case until the determination of the appeal to this Court in the case of *Dundon v Governor of Cloverhill Prison* [2006] 1 IR 518.

So far as the line of defence outlined by the Respondent is concerned, Mr Canton says that he is unaware of any of the matters alleged concerning the ECGD and that, in any event, they are irrelevant to the criminal charges. He appears to accept that certain evidence of the type alleged by the Respondent was excluded at the trial of Mrs Stapleton , but says that this was because the judge held it not to be relevant in that the alleged avoidance or circumvention of EC State Aid Rules did not occur until after the date of all of the alleged offences. That evidence was, on the other hand, admitted at the later trial in England of a fellow director of the companies. Mr Canton says that the issue of admissibility of any such evidence or statements as is referred to will be determined by the Court that tries the Respondent.

The High Court Judgment

The learned High Court judge declined, essentially on the ground of delay, to make the order, sought by the Applicant, for the surrender of the Respondent.

He observed that the complaints of the Respondent were in large measure the kind of submissions which could have been made under section 50(2) (bbb) of the Extradition Act 1965, introduced by amendment by the Extradition (Amendment) Act, 1987. Since that provision was repealed by the 2003 Act, the Respondent could not rely upon it.

He assessed the Respondent's complaints of delay in the context of section 37 of the 2003 Act. His key conclusion on the law was that the Court should not order the surrender of a requested person if to do so would not be compatible with this State's obligations under the European Convention on Human Rights or its Protocols, or would constitute a breach of any provision of the Constitution. He believed that there was *"no meaningful distinction to be drawn between surrendering the respondent to the requesting state to face a trial which would be either unfair or not within a reasonable time, and him actually facing such a trial."* His view was that:

"... if the applicant enjoys a Convention and a constitutional right to a trial of offences with which he is charged within a reasonable time, that is a right which he is entitled to invoke and have protected on the first occasion on which it becomes relevant for argument, and that it is not a matter to be postponed so that it can be ventilated at some date in the future in another country, and after the respondent has been returned in custody to that place."

In addition, he believed that the High Court was *"in just as good a position to be satisfied as to whether the respondent would receive a trial on these offences within a reasonable time as a Court in the requesting state."*

The learned judge reviewed all of the evidence, much of it summarised above, in great detail. In particular, he reviewed the affidavit evidence sworn on behalf of the respective parties by two English barristers. Mr Peter Caldwell, on behalf of the issuing state, outlined in considerable detail the principles governing criminal trials in England, referring, *inter alia,* to the obligation of full disclosure of the prosecution case, to allow sufficient time to prepare a defence, and the opportunity to question and call witnesses. Most relevantly, he referred to the existence of the procedure for placing a stay on proceedings on the ground of abuse of the court's process where there has been unjustifiable delay in the proceedings. Mr Caldwell swore that there were sufficient remedies available in English law "to ensure that Mr Stapleton can have a fair trial." Mr Michael Mansfield QC, in an affidavit on behalf of the Respondent, accepted that *"a court may order a stay of a criminal prosecution where it considers that the prosecution is an abuse of court process."* He drew a distinction between the prosecution obligations of disclosure which applied at the time of the offences alleged against the Respondent and the more onerous obligations which have been applied under later case-law. He deduced from this that *"......the domestic courts are unlikely to stay the case on the grounds of abuse of process because although the prosecution would have breached current standards of disclosure, they did not breach standards applicable at that time."*

The learned trial judge was persuaded, having examined the affidavits of English law, to make the following observations:

- He was not assured by the affidavit of Mr Caldwell, sworn on behalf of the United Kingdom authorities, that there is the same probability as would in his view exist in this jurisdiction, that the respondent would be successful in his application to have his trial stayed on the grounds of lapse of time;
- He thought it was clear that under the English jurisprudence referred to by that deponent, there was not the same regard for what he described as a free-standing right to an expeditious trial, even in the absence of actual prejudice;
- He found that there was no contradiction of Mr Mansfield's opinion (on behalf of the Respondent) that given the date of the alleged offences the more recent disclosure rules would not be applicable to the prosecution's obligations as to disclosure of all material.

He could not, therefore, *"accept that the rights of the respondent under the Constitution would not be contravened by his being surrendered at this point in time to face trial on these charges..."* and continued: *"I do not believe that it would be appropriate to expose him to the hazard that his rights might not be vindicated there in the same manner in which they would in my view in this jurisdiction."*

The Appeal

The central issue in the appeal is the extent to which our courts, in dealing with surrender requests under the procedures for the European Arrest Warrant should seek to incorporate Irish case-law with regard to lapse of time or delay in criminal proceedings by grafting it on to surrender requests. The Applicant also referred to parts of the evidence to show that, in any event, the Respondent was himself a principal author of the delay which has occurred between the dates of the offences he is alleged to have committed and the initiation of the procedures leading to the request for his surrender.

Mr George Bermingham, Senior Counsel for the Applicant recalled a number of aspects of the evidence. First, a number of points are made relating to the Respondent's conduct in reference to the original VAT-related charges. He was aware that he was on bail to appear at Lincoln Crown Court on 28th October 1985, but did not appear. His explanations regarding his own illness and that of his child do not enable him to escape the undoubted fact that he was wanted for prosecution on criminal charges in England. Indeed, his wife wrote to the Clerk of the Lincoln Crown Court on 1st November 1985 explaining that her husband was unable to travel as he was suffering from pneumonia. The Respondent, on affidavit, explains his continued failure to answer these charges, as stated above, by stating his belief, without furnishing any basis for that understanding, that those charges *"had subsequently discontinued and that the warrant had simply lapsed."* Nonetheless, lawyers, wrote on his behalf from Madrid on 14th August 1986, acknowledging that a warrant had been issued for the arrest of their client on 28th October 1985 and stating, *inter alia,* that the Respondent wished to return to England to face trial.

There were no extradition arrangements between the United Kingdom and Spain at the time the Respondent moved to Spain. The Respondent has sworn that *"at the time of* [his] *family's move to Spain,* [he] *knew nothing..."* of these matters (my emphasis). However, it is clear that he was aware of the fact of his wife's prosecution in England on charges closely related to those in respect of which his surrender is sought. He did not, himself, return to England at that or any other time. On affidavit, he explains that his wife was adamant that he stay in Spain, *"at first to look after the children and later to avoid being subjected to the same ordeal that she was being forced to undergo."* He also claims to have received *"legal advice that* [he] *could better assist [his] wife's case by remaining at liberty in Spain, than by running the risk of arrest and detention – under Category A status – in the United Kingdom."*

The Respondent also makes a particular point of alleging that he lived openly in Spain and that the Lincolnshire police could have interviewed him in that country at any time. Mr Canton's response is that the police did not consider it appropriate to interview a suspect in circumstances where they had no police powers. This, it is submitted was a reasonable attitude to take.

The foregoing is rather secondary to the general question of the correct approach for the court to take to the question of delay. I would comment, nonetheless, that it has to be a material fact that the Respondent himself has been a significant, if not the major, contributor to the lapse of time of which he complains. On the facts, it seems to me to be quite obvious that the Respondent, while he may have had other motives, knowingly moved to reside in Spain at a time when he was fully aware that he was wanted by the police in the United Kingdom. His plea of having lived "openly" in Spain is unconvincing. It appears that he conducted vigorous correspondence with the Lincolnshire police, gave press interviews and caused questions to be asked in the House of Commons. He did not, however, return to the United Kingdom to face charges. While this matter was much debated at the hearing, I did not understand Mr Brian O'Moore, Senior Counsel for the Respondent to dispute that these matters can at least be taken into account.

I turn then to consider the general question of delay.

The parties were agreed that section 40 of the 2003 Act is not the governing provision, though it might, at first sight, appear to be relevant. That section provides:

> *"A person shall not be surrendered under this Act where—*
> *(a) the act or omission constituting the offence specified in the European arrest warrant issued in respect of him or her is an offence under the law of the State, and*
> *(b) the person could not, by reason of the passage of time, be proceeded against, in the State, in respect of the second-mentioned offence."*

Counsel agreed that this provision applies only to a situation where the actual offence in respect of which surrender is sought could be prosecuted in the State. The purpose of section 40 is to give effect to Article 4.4 of the Framework Decision. Article 4 lists *"Grounds for optional non-execution of the European arrest warrant."* It provides:

> *"The executing judicial authority may refuse to execute the European arrest warrant:*
>
> ....
> *4. where the criminal prosecution or punishment of the requested person is statute-barred according to the law of the executing Member State and the acts fall within the jurisdiction of that Member State under its own criminal law..."*

The effect of Article 4.4 and of section 40 is to permit refusal to surrender to an issuing Member State in a case where the actual offence could form the subject-matter of a prosecution in the executing Member State, but is statute-barred in the latter. It is accepted that this situation does not prevail here.The appeal, therefore, must be considered, as it was considered by the learned trial judge, in the context of section 37(1) of the Act, which provides:

> *37.—(1) A person shall not be surrendered under this Act if—*
> *(a) his or her surrender would be incompatible with the State's obligations under—*
> *(i) the Convention, or*
> *(ii) the Protocols to the Convention,*
> *(b) his or her surrender would constitute a contravention of any provision of the Constitution (other than for the reason that the offence specified in the European arrest warrant is an offence to which section 38 (1)(b) applies),*
> *(c) there are reasonable grounds for believing that—*
> *(i) the European arrest warrant was issued in respect of the person for the purposes of facilitating his or her prosecution or punishment in the issuing state for reasons connected with his or her sex, race, religion, ethnic origin, nationality, language, political opinion or sexual orientation, or*
> *(ii) in the prosecution or punishment of the person in the issuing state, he or she will be treated less favourably than a person who—*
> *(I) is not his or her sex, race, religion, nationality or ethnic origin,*
> *(II) does not hold the same political opinions as him or her,*
> *(III) speaks a different language than he or she does, or*
> *(IV) does not have the same sexual orientation as he or she does,*
> *or*
> *(iii) were the person to be surrendered to the issuing state—*
> *(I) he or she would be sentenced to death, or a death sentence imposed on him or her would be carried out, or*
> *(II) he or she would be tortured or subjected to other inhuman or degrading treatment."*

I have quoted sub-section (1) in its entirety, as it reflects provisions or recitals of the Framework Decision. Only paragraphs (a) and (b) have been invoked in this case. Paragraph (c) reflects recitals (12) and (13) of the Framework Decision. Thus, the legislature intentionally gave effect, in Irish law, to some of the parts of the preamble to the Framework Decision, which do not correspond to and have not been implemented by any substantive provisions in the body of that instrument. I have commented upon the problems of interpretation presented by this incongruity in the drafting of the Framework Decision in my concurring judgment in *Dundon v Governor of Cloverhill Prison,* cited above.

It is clearly established that this Court is obliged to interpret provisions of the 2003 Act, so far as possible, in the light of and so as not to be in conflict with provisions of the Framework Decision (see (Case C-105/03) *Criminal proceedings against Pupino* [2005] ECR I-5285.) The corner stone of the entire system is, of course, the principle of mutual recognition of the judicial decisions and mutual trust of the legal systems of the other Member States.

Paragraphs (a) and (b) of Section 37(1) concern respectively the State's obligations under the European Convention on Human Rights and Fundamental Freedoms and, though rights are not expressly mentioned, rights guaranteed by the Constitution. No relevant distinction, for the purposes of the case, between the two provisions emerged during argument. The Respondent's complaints are all referable, directly or indirectly, to the right to a fair trial.

Mr Bermingham argued, in the first instance, that issues of delay or lapse of time are covered expressly by Article 4.4 of the Framework Decision and section 40 of the Act in a manner which does not assist the Respondent. Mr Bermingham also cited a number of cases decided under the extradition regime which existed between some Member States prior to the entry into force of the European Arrest Warrant. He cited, in particular, *Hanlon v Fleming* [1981] I.R. 489, a case concerning the procedure for endorsement of warrants pursuant to Part III of the Extradition Act, 1965, where there had been a very long lapse of time between the alleged commission of the offence charged and the potential extradition. Henchy J, speaking for a unanimous Supreme Court ruled at page 494 of the judgment:

> *"As to the first point, the delay has been inordinate and it is in part unexplained; but I do not think it is in itself a good ground for refusing extradition. The failure to have the charge against the accused tried in due time in London has been the accused's own fault primarily. Such evasion of a trial is usually the reason for extradition proceedings. If the accused had not broken bail and fled to Ireland, the charge against him would have been tried and disposed of long since. If the superimposed delay, due to the extraordinary lapse of time between the hearing in the High Court and the delivery of the reserved judgment, could be said to imperil or render impossible a fair trial, that would be a matter which would have to be raised in the first instance in an English court. But the scheme of reciprocal extradition between Ireland and The United Kingdom, represented on the Irish side by the Extradition Act, 1965, does not recognise delay as a ground for refusing extradition. For the Courts in this State to recognise delay as such a ground, it would be necessary to read into the statute something that has been omitted, presumably, on purpose."*

That decision pre-dated the insertion, by section 2 of the Extradition (Amendment) Act, 1987, of section 50(2)(bbb) into the Extradition Act, 1965. That provision did allow the court to have regard to *"lapse of time...... and other exceptional circumstances"* such that it would, *"having regard to all the circumstances, be unjust, oppressive or invidious to deliver"* the person. As already mentioned, the learned trial judge ruled that the Respondent was not in a position to rely on that provision in the High Court, since it had been repealed by the Act of 2003.

Mr Bermingham also referred to *Harte v Fleming* [1988] I.L.R.M. 70, where Carroll J, in the High Court followed and applied the dictum of Henchy J, quoted above.

The nub of the issue and the core of the debate between counsel at the hearing of the appeal was whether the undisputed delay or lapse of time since the dates of the alleged offences is a matter to bne considered by these Courts, as the courts of the executing Member State, as the High Court decided, or rather is a matter to be considered by the courts of the issuing Member State.

Mr Bermingham submitted that, at least on the facts of this case, adjudication on lapse of time is a matter for the issuing Member State. He relied on the existence, as established in the evidence and as accepted by the learned trial judge, of procedures entitling the Respondent to a hearing on that issue. He acknowledged that it might be established in other cases that the procedures in the issuing Member State were so inadequate or so divergent from what is regarded as fair under our law as to demonstrate that the human rights of the person in question would be infringed on surrender. The Applicant, in his written submissions, drew attention to

the approach adopted by the Queen's Bench Division in England in *Woodcock v Government of New Zealand* [2004] 1 WLR 1979. That court was concerned with an extradition request in respect of sexual offences alleged to have been committed many years previously. Simon Brown LJ said that the question was not whether *"having regard to the passage of time, it would be unjust to try the accused, but rather whether it would be unjust to return him (albeit, of course, return him for trial)."* In answer to that question, as appears at page 1985 of the report, he said:

> *"To my mind that entitles, indeed requires, this court to have regard to whatever safeguards may exist in the domestic law of the requesting state to ensure that the accused would not be subjected to an unjust trial there. There are, it should be borne in mind, clear advantages in having the question whether or not a fair trial is now possible decided in the domestic court rather than by us. That court will have an altogether clearer picture than we have of precisely what evidence is available and the issues likely to arise. For example, the accused is likely to be interviewed on return (in New Zealand, we are told, under caution administered in terms similar to our own) so that more is likely to be known about his defence. If, of course, we were to conclude that the domestic court in the requesting state would be bound to hold that a fair trial of the accused is now impossible, then plainly we would regard it as unjust (and/or oppressive) to return him. Equally, we would have no alternative but to reach our own conclusion on whether a fair trial would now be possible in the requesting state if we were not persuaded that the courts of that state have what we would regard as satisfactory procedures of their own akin to our (and the New Zealand courts') abuse of process jurisdiction."*

He went on to say that it seemed plain that the New Zealand courts had satisfactory procedures for guarding against an unjust trial. The Applicant proposes that test to this Court as being consistent both with existing Irish authority and the principle of mutual recognition of and respect for judicial decisions of other Member States.

The Applicant also referred to a number of authorities to establish the proposition that a person whose extradition is sought will not succeed in relying on delay which is the result of his own actions: *Harte v Fleming,* (already cited, Per Carroll J at page 74); *Ellis v O'Dea* [1991] I.L.R.M. 346; *Sloan v Culligan* [1992] 1 I.R. 223; *Quinlivan v Conroy and Sreenan* [2000] 3 IR 154. In *Kwok Ming Wan v Conroy* [1998] 3 I.R. 527, Hamilton C.J. at page 533 cited with approval a passage from the judgment of Lord Diplock in *Kakis v. Republic of Cyprus* [1978] 1 W.L.R. 779 at p. 783 of the report:

> *"Delay in the commencement or conduct of extradition proceedings which is brought about by the accused himself by fleeing the country, concealing his whereabouts or evading arrest cannot, in my view, be relied upon as a ground for holding it to be either unjust or oppressive to return him. Any difficulties that he may encounter in the conduct of his defence in consequence of the delay due to such causes are of his own choice and making. Save in most*

> *exceptional circumstances it would be neither unjust nor oppressive that he should be required to accept them.*"

Both the House of Lords and the Supreme Court were concerned in the two cases last mentioned to apply specific but different statutory provisions permitting delay to be taken into account. Their precise terms do not matter. The interpretation of the cause of delay does.

Mr O'Moore, by contrast, maintained in argument that Recital 12 of the Framework Decision permits a Member State to include provision for national constitutional rights of due process and that section 37 of the 2003 Act permits an individual to claim that his constitutional rights will be infringed if he is surrendered. Thus, if a person can discharge the burden of showing that a fair trial is impossible, if he is surrendered, it is incumbent on this Court to vindicate his rights. He argued that it was irrelevant whether the Respondent had contributed to any delay. He relied on the part of the judgment of Simon Brown LJ, cited above, where he said that, if it were clear that *"the domestic court in the requesting state would be bound to hold that a fair trial of the accused is now impossible,"* it would be unjust or oppressive to return him. By extension, he argued that it is for this Court to determine whether a fair trial is possible in England. This Court should consider the fairness of trial procedures in the issuing Member State it should not surrender the Respondent if there is a risk that his trial will not be fair.

Mr O'Moore distinguished *Hanlon v Fleming* and *Harte v Fleming* as being based on particular statutory construction and not having considered the issue of fair trial or the constitutional right of due process.

Conclusion

Judicial decisions delivered under prior extradition arrangements can undoubtedly assist in analysing the sorts of problem that will necessarily continue to arise in practice under the Framework Decision and implementing legislation. The first recital to the Framework Decision declares that *"the formal extradition procedure should be abolished among the Member States."* The new system is, nonetheless, one whereby a person is to be surrendered, whether or not under the name of extradition, for trial on criminal charges in another jurisdiction. His rights are necessarily at issue. The Framework Decision, as it declares, in Article 1.3, is not to *"have the effect of modifying the obligation to respect fundamental rights and fundamental legal principles as enshrined in Article 6 of the Treaty on European Union."*

There is one central difference between the European Arrest Warrant and former extradition arrangements. Recital (6) of the Framework Decision refers to *"the principle of mutual recognition..."* as *"the 'cornerstone' of judicial cooperation."* Moreover, as is stated in Recital (10):

> *"The mechanism of the European arrest warrant is based on a high level of confidence between Member States. Its implementation may be suspended only in the event of a serious and persistent breach by one of the Member States of the principle set out in Article 6(1) of the Treaty on European Union, determined by the Council pursuant to Article 7(1) of the said Treaty with the consequences set out in Article 7(2) thereof......"*

It is true that the principle of mutual trust and confidence must also have been at the heart of former bilateral or multilateral extradition arrangements. Such arrangements were (and still are so far as extradition arrangements with states outside the European Union are concerned) an expression of the sovereign power of the respective states. They implied at least some level of mutual political trust and, at the judicial level, confidence in the legal systems of the cooperating states. McCarthy J, in his concurring judgment in *Ellis v O'Dea* [1991] I.R. 251 at 262 stated:

> *"The making of the extradition arrangement presupposes that the Government and the Oireachtas are satisfied, amongst other things, that, an Irish citizen being extradited either*

> *to the United Kingdom, as in this instance, or to any other State with which Ireland has such an arrangement, will not have his constitutional rights impaired."*

Murray C.J., in his judgment in *Altaravicius v Minister for Justice, Equality and Law Reform* (Supreme Court unreported 5th April 2006, [2006] IESC 23) cited the above passage before referring, in the context of the Arrest Warrant to *"...the principles and objects recited in the preamble to the Framework Decision when it refers to mutual recognition of judicial decisions, judicial cooperation and a high level of confidence between Member States."*

The principle of mutual recognition applies to the judicial decision of the judicial authority of the issuing Member State in issuing the Arrest Warrant. The principle of mutual confidence is broader. It encompasses the system of trial in the issuing Member State. The Court of Justice has ruled, in its recent decision in Case C-303/05 *Advocaten voor de Wereld v Leden van de Ministerrad,* delivered in 3rd May 2007 (since the hearing of this appeal) that the issuing Member State, as is *"stated in Article 1(3) of the Framework Decision, must respect fundamental rights and fundamental legal principles as enshrined in Article 6 EU....."*

It follows, in my view, that the courts of the executing Member State, when deciding whether to make an order for surrender must proceed on the assumption that the courts of the issuing Member State will, as is required by Article 6.1 of the Treaty on European Union, *"respect .. .human rights and fundamental freedoms."* Article 6.2 provides that the Union is itself to *"respect fundamental rights, as guaranteed by the European Convention on Human Rights and Fundamental Freedoms...........and as they result from the constitutional traditions common to the Member States, as general principles of Community law."*

Article 1.3 of the Framework Decision, read with the recitals to the Framework Decision and, as further explained by the Court of Justice in the decision in *Advocaten voor de Wereld,* imposes these obligations, which in turn impose the obligations found in Article 6 of the Convention on each issuing Member State when seeking the surrender of a person and, necessarily in any subsequent trial process. It follows that I am satisfied that the learned trial judge was mistaken in holding that there was "*no meaningful distinction to be drawn between surrendering the respondent to the requesting state to face a trial which would be either unfair or not within a reasonable time, and him actually facing such a trial."* Equally, he was, mistaken in holding that the Respondent was entitled to have his right to a speedy trial

> *"...protected on the first occasion on which it becomes relevant for argument, and that it is not a matter to be postponed so that it can be ventilated at some date in the future in another country, and after the respondent has been returned in custody to that place."*

The learned trial judge found that there were possible differences between the level of protection to which the Respondent would be entitled pending trial in England and what would be available to him in this jurisdiction. Firstly, he considered that there was not, in the other jurisdiction, *"the same regard for a free-standing right to an expeditious trial, even in the absence of actual prejudice."* In this respect, it seems that the learned trial judge may have been proceeding on the assumption that the Respondent would, if he were to be tried in this jurisdiction, be entitled to apply to have his trial prohibited on the ground of delay alone. His decision was, of course, pronounced prior to the decision of this Court in *P.M. v Director of Public Prosecutions* [2006] I.L.R.M. 361. In that case, Kearns J, speaking for a unanimous Court explained, at page 373, the need for a balancing exercise, where a person seeks to prohibit his trial on the ground of delay: *"......an applicant must put something more into the balance where prosecutorial delay arises to outweigh the public interest in having serious charges proceed to trial."* More generally, I do not believe it has ever been established, in spite of a number of *obiter dicta* raising that possibility, that a person is entitled to have his trial prohibited on the basis of mere delay, without more. Secondly, he accepted the opinion of Mr Mansfield, Q.C., to the effect that the more recent disclosure rules in criminal trials in England would not benefit the Respondent.

The learned trial judge was mistaken in seeking parity of criminal procedure in the issuing Member State. It is apparent that, even under the long-established extradition jurisprudence, as it applied between some Member States prior to 2004 and, as it still applies between this country and third countries, such a comparison was not required. Extradition does not demand that there be parity of criminal procedures between contracting states. It is notorious that criminal procedures vary enormously between states. Indeed, it is obvious that they approximate much more closely between this country and the United Kingdom than between either of those states and the great majority of Member States practising the civil law system, where, for example, there is no tradition of cross-examination of the sort practised in our courts, and which is here regarded as totally fundamental to the rights of the defence.

Since the hearing of this appeal, this Court has given judgment in the case of *Minister for Justice Equality and Law Reform v Brennan* [2007] IESC 21, where Murray C.J. considered the correct approach to the balancing of constitutional rights against the obligations of the state pursuant to the Framework Decision. The appellant there contended that, if a form of minimum sentence, without any residual judicial discretion would be applied in the issuing state, his surrender would be contrary to his constitutional rights and therefore contrary to s. 37(1)(b) of the Act of 2003. The Chief Justice, with whom the other members of the Court agreed, responded to that submission as follows:

> *"The effect of such an argument is that an order for surrender under the Act of 2003, and indeed any order for extradition, ought to be refused if the manner in which a trial in the requesting State including the manner in which a penal sanction is imposed, does not conform to the exigencies of our Constitution as if such a trial or sentence were to take place in this country. That can hardly have been the intention of the Oireachtas when it adopted s. 37(1) of the Act of 1973 since it would inevitably have the effect of ensuring that most requests for surrender or extradition would have to be refused. And indeed if that were the intent of the Framework Decision, which the Act of 1973 implements, and other countries applied such a test from their own perspective, few, if any, would extradite to this country.*
> *......I am not aware of any authority for the principle that the extradition or surrender of a person to a foreign country would contravene the Constitution simply because their legal system and system of trial differed from ours as envisaged by the Constitution.*
> *That is not by any means to say that a Court, in considering an application for surrender, has no jurisdiction to consider the circumstances where it is established that surrender would lead to a denial of fundamental or human rights. There may well be egregious circumstances such as a clearly established and fundamental defect in the system of justice of a requesting State where a refusal of an application for surrender may be necessary to protect such rights. ...*
> *...The sole matter which I wish to make clear here is that the mere fact that a trial or sentence may take place in a requesting State according to procedures or principles which differ from those which apply, even if constitutionally guaranteed, in relation to a criminal trial in this country does not of itself mean that an application for surrender should be refused pursuant to s. 37(2) of the Act."*

I cannot see that any of the differences discerned by the learned trial judge between the right to seek prohibition of trial in the English courts and our own could amount to the establishment of infringement of the right to fair trial, or fair procedures, whether by reference to the Convention or to the Constitution. They certainly do not amount, to repeat the words of Murray C.J., to *"a clearly established and fundamental defect in the system of justice of* [the] *requesting State."*

On the facts of this case, there is available to the Respondent a procedure which will enable him, on surrender to the issuing Member State to seek a remedy based on the very long period of time which has elapsed since the alleged commission of the offences. Moreover, on the facts of the case, it is demonstrably more efficient and more convenient that those matters be debated before the courts of the country where the Respondent is to be tried. The prosecuting and police authorities as well as other witnesses are available to and amenable to the jurisdiction of the courts of that country. Documentary evidence, of the type demanded by the Respondent, will be more readily available there. If not, its absence may be more readily explained. There may, in addition, be arguments or points of domestic law, whether based on precedents or otherwise, which the Respondent can advantageously argue or rely upon which may not be available to him in this jurisdiction and of which an Irish court might not necessarily be aware. I would echo and adapt the words of Simon Brown L.J. in the *Woodcock* case cited above and say that the English courts *"will have an altogether clearer picture than we have of precisely what evidence is available and the issues likely to arise..."*

Thus, I do not think the learned trial judge was right to refuse to make the order for surrender on the grounds of delay.

In these circumstances, it is not strictly necessary to rule on the effect of the Respondent's own very substantial contribution to the lapse of time which has occurred. On the evidence, the Respondent was responsible for all delay from 1985 to 2001, when the Lincolnshire police first became aware that he was residing in Ireland. He made a deliberate decision to reside in Spain in 1985, at a time when he knew that he was wanted in the United Kingdom for trial on charges, other than those relevant to the present application. He failed to answer for his bail. A bench warrant was issued, but he declined to return to the United Kingdom. Even if he swears that he was unaware of the absence of extradition arrangements between the United Kingdom and Spain at that time, it is quite clear that he became aware some time thereafter—at a time when he was aware that his wife was arrested in the United Kingdom for offences linked to the present offences—that he was safe in Spain. It is an obvious inference from his affidavit that he made a considered decision to remain in Spain.

His suggestion that he was living "openly" in Ireland from the end of 1994 does not impress. The Lincolnshire police did not know that he was here until September 2001. The only contact between the Respondent and the Lincolnshire police was in 1986, when the Respondent, via Spanish lawyers, made a series of allegations of wrongful behaviour against the police. There was undoubtedly some delay from 2001 until 2004 when the initial steps for the issue of the Arrest Warrant were taken. Mr Canton explained the need to establish that the evidence was still "viable." He reported back to the Crown Prosecution Service in June 2002. Advice from counsel was needed. This and other steps seem to have taken up to November 2003, when a decision was taken to seek extradition. The United Kingdom authorities decided to await the entry into force of the new European Arrest Warrant procedure and the outcome of one of the first legal cases concerning that new procedure. There is no doubt that the comparative slowness of all these procedures may well be open to criticism. However, each of the steps taken was in itself reasonable. A final decision as to the periods involved can best be made by the English courts in the context of any application that may be made to stay the trial. Taken in the overall context of lapse of time, any delay from 2001 is comparatively minor. The major delay was from 1985 to 2001. The Respondent must bear the entire responsibility for that period. The authorities already cited support the rather obvious proposition that a person will not be heard to claim that delay in the prosecution of extradition proceedings is unfair or oppressive, where he has himself been the author of the delay.

For this additional reason, therefore, I would reject the Respondent's reliance on delay or lapse of time. He was himself the principal culprit.

I would, therefore, allow the appeal and make an order for the surrender of the Respondent. Counsel should be heard with regard to the disposal of the outstanding question of the constitutionality of the Criminal Justice (Terrorist Offences) Act 2005.

Minister for Justice, Equality and Law Reform v Tobin

[2008] IESC 3

Author Note: This is a very controversial Supreme Court interpretation of the concept of "flight" or "fleeing" pursuant to the European Arrest Warrant Act 2003, as amended.

Judgment of Mr. Justice Fennelly delivered the 25th day of February, 2008 giving reasons for decision pronounced on 3rd July 2007.

1. This appeal concerns the meaning of the word "fled" in the European Arrest Warrant Act, 2003. The Court has already pronounced its decision on 3rd July 2007. I here give the reasons for that decision.

2. The warrant concerns a quite appalling tragedy which occurred in the year 2000. The respondent caused the death of two small children while driving a motor car in Hungary. While his prosecution was pending, he left that country lawfully and regularly. He was later convicted and sentenced in his absence. Peart J held that he had not "fled" that jurisdiction within the meaning of section 10 of the European Arrest Warrant Act, 2003 and, for that reason, declined to make the order for his surrender. The appellant (whom I will call "the Minister") has appealed against this decision.

3. Peart J decided a number of other points against the respondent, which he had raised by way of objection. There is a cross-appeal and a notice to vary. The Court decided to hear, in the first instance, the Minister's appeal, since that concerns the single issue of whether the respondent had fled. This judgment deals with that issue.

The facts

4. 12th October 2005 Pest County Court, Budapest in the Republic of Hungary issued a European Arrest Warrant seeking the surrender of the respondent in respect of a sentence imposed on him for an offence of negligence causing death arising out of a road traffic accident.

5. The respondent was born in 1964. He is an Irish citizen and a chartered accountant. He is married and has two children. At the time of the tragic events giving rise to his prosecution, he was living in Hungary as part of his employment with a large Irish financial institution.

6. The European Arrest Warrant arises out of a fatal road traffic accident, which occurred when the respondent was driving a motor car on 9th April 2000. Two very small children, a brother and sister, lost their lives. The respondent, in his affidavit, says that his car lurched onto the pavement, that he applied the brake but that the car would not stop. He accepts that the car struck the two children, who were killed. He accepts that this was a terrible tragedy and he has expressed deep and sincere sympathy to the bereaved family.

7. The respondent engaged the services of a Hungarian lawyer to advise and assist him during the police investigation of the accident. There were severe language difficulties. The lawyer's daughter acted as interpreter and translator at the police interviews. Those interviewed included the respondent, his wife and two Irish friends who had been in the car. It appears that their statements were translated into Hungarian by the daughter of the lawyer.

8. The respondent was permitted to return to Ireland with his family in August 2000, while the investigation was proceeding. His passport was returned to him at his request. The reasons given for the proposed visit to Ireland were that the respondent's wife had been asked to be a bridesmaid at her sister's wedding and that he wished his own parents, who were getting on in years, to have the opportunity to meet his children since they could not easily come to Hungary. Pursuant to a provision of the Hungarian Criminal Code, he made a deposit of 500,000 HUF by way of bail. On 9th October 2000, he returned to Hungary and duly notified the Hungarian court. On 30th November 2000, he left Hungary permanently, as his term of service there had come to an end. It is clear from the legal materials provided by the Hungarian Authorities that his second and final departure from Hungary came within the scope of the approved arrangements.

9. Criminal proceedings were commenced against the respondent in Hungary on 11th September 2000. He was charged with "*causing a fatal road traffic accident through negligence.*" He says the terms of the charge were not received by his lawyers until 7th June 2001. As will appear later, the applicable provisions of the Criminal Code, of which the respondent had availed, permitted service of documents on lawyers.

10. The respondent did not attend his trial. He says that he had understood that the statements made at police interviews (and translated into Hungarian) would be admitted at the trial. He learned in April 2002 that there was a doubt about the admissibility of these documents, by reason of the relationship of the translator to his lawyer. He made a declaration at the Hungarian Consulate in Dublin that this fact had had no influence on the nature or content of the statements.

11. The trial took place in Hungary on 7th May 2002, in the voluntary and duly authorised absence of the respondent. The statements of the Irish witnesses were ruled inadmissible in their entirety pursuant to a provision of the Hungarian Code of Criminal Procedure. This was by reason of the lack of independence of the translator, as she was a daughter of the lawyer. The respondent was convicted and sentenced to three years imprisonment, banned from driving and fined.

12. It should be said that the judgment of the Hungarian court, insofar as it is available, is detailed and meticulous. The respondent has not suggested that the excluded evidence would have assisted his defence in any particular way. Furthermore, the arrangements into which the respondent entered permitted his trial to take place in his absence, with the further consequence that the judgment could not be set aside so as to enable a retrial to take place.

13. The respondent appealed unsuccessfully against his conviction, but the sentence was altered to one where he would be required to serve only half of the three years and then to be released on what is described in the translation of that decision as "*ticket of leave.*"

The High Court judgment

14. Section 10 of the Act of 2003, as amended by the Criminal Justice (Terrorism Offences) Act, 2005 provides that, "*[w]here a judicial authority in an issuing state duly issues a European arrest warrant in respect of a person,*" who falls within one of the prescribed categories, subject to the Act and to the Council Framework Decision of 13th June 2002 on the European Arrest Warrant and the surrender between Member States, he is to be arrested and surrendered to the issuing state.

15. It was common case, in the High Court, as it remains, that the only provision capable of applying to the respondent is paragraph (d), according to the lettering of the amended version of section 10. To be brought within the scope of that provision, the respondent must be shown to be a person:

> "*on whom a sentence of imprisonment or detention has been imposed and who fled from the issuing state before he or she—*
> *(i) commenced serving that sentence, or*
> *(ii) completed serving that sentence,...*"

16. Peart J considered the facts and the terms of the judgment of the Hungarian court before concluding that the respondent had been permitted to leave Hungary lawfully once the procedures of the Hungarian Criminal Code had been observed. He considered that, by leaving Hungary, in those circumstances, the respondent was not acting in breach of any law. Peart J was satisfied that "*by the plain and ordinary meaning of these words, the fleeing must occur following the imposition of sentence, and not as in this case, where the respondent left before his trial.*" He held that paragraph (d) covered "*a situation where both conviction and sentencing has taken place and the person has "fled" before that sentence was served.*"

17. He then turned to the meaning of the word, "*fled*," and held:

> "*In my view the plain and ordinary meaning of 'fled' cannot be regarded as the same as the plain and ordinary meaning of 'left'. The former has within it an intention to escape from or to evade something, such as in this case, justice. It is not so neutral as the word "left". One can leave for any or no reason whatsoever, but in ordinary usage, the word "fled" is used when there is a particular purpose in leaving, namely to avoid some consequence not desired.*"

18. He then reviewed the various language versions of the Framework Decision, including the Irish one before declaring:

> "*It seems to me to do obvious and serious violence to the stated objective, as given effect to by section 10 of the 2003 Act as amended, if the section giving effect to this objective is extended to cover persons such as the respondent who did not "flee" within the meaning normally attributed to that word, and who left legitimately having availed of a procedure in place to deal with just such a departure, and on the basis that he could be represented by his lawyers and that his statements and those of his witnesses could be available to the Court.*"

Submissions on appeal

19. There are two threads to the submissions of the parties to the appeal. The first concerns the general principles of interpretation of the Act of 2003, in the light of the wording and purpose of the Framework Decision. Both parties cite the principle of "conforming interpretation," obliging the courts of the Member States to interpret national law in the light of the instrument of European law which that law implements. The second concerns the ordinary and natural meaning of the word, "flee" or "fled."

20. The Minister submits that the Framework decision, and hence the Act of 2003, were intended to replace existing extradition arrangements between Member States of the European Union. Peart J interpreted the word, "fled," so that it would have the effect of creating a new exception. He also submits that the word "flee" is capable of a number of different meanings and that it does not exclude a person who left a country in the manner in which the respondent left Hungary. It can apply to a person who left or went away from the issuing Member State, thereby evading the sentence which was imposed upon him. The Minister contests the view of Peart J that it necessarily has any connotation of escape or evasion.

21. The respondent fully supports the reasoning of Peart J. He submits that he left the issuing state in a perfectly legal fashion, as permitted by a specified provision of the Hungarian Criminal Procedure, and then failed to return to Hungary after he had been convicted and sentenced in his absence. If the word is used in its natural and ordinary meaning, the respondent did not "flee" from the issuing state.

Conclusion

22. S. 10 of the Act of 2003 gives effect, in Irish law, to the general obligation to surrender made incumbent on Member States, by the Framework Decision. That section, as amended by the Criminal Justice (Terrorist Offences) Act, 2005, provides:

> *10.—Where a judicial authority in an issuing state duly issues a European arrest warrant in respect of a person—*
>
> *(a) against whom that state intends to bring proceedings for an offence to which the European arrest warrant relates,*
>
> *(b) who is the subject of proceedings in that state for an offence to which the European arrest warrant relates,*
>
> *(c) who has been convicted of, but not yet sentenced in respect of, an offence to which the European arrest warrant relates, or*
>
> *(d) on whom a sentence of imprisonment or detention has been imposed in respect of an offence to which the European arrest warrant relates, and who fled from the issuing state before he or she—*
>
> *(i) commenced serving that sentence, or*
>
> *(ii) completed serving that sentence,*
>
> *that person shall, subject to and in accordance with the provisions of this Act and the Framework Decision, be arrested and surrendered to the issuing state.*

23. Clearly, sub-paragraph (d) is the only provision capable of applying to the respondent.

There are two components to this provision:

- That a sentence of imprisonment has been imposed;
- That the person in question "fled" the jurisdiction which imposed the sentence.

24. This Court has to ask itself, firstly, whether the respondent "fled" Hungary. If he did, then he should be surrendered. If he did not, the further question arises as to whether the principle of "conforming interpretation," nonetheless, obliges the Irish courts to order his surrender. As already noted, Peart J considered that the sentence imposed, in order to come within paragraph (d), must have been imposed prior to the flight. I am not convinced that this is necessarily so. That paragraph may equally apply where the sentence has been imposed at the time the European Arrest Warrant is issued. However, I prefer not to express a concluded opinion. I will confine this part of the analysis to the meaning of the word, "fled."

25. The respondent left Hungary, to use a neutral verb, before the sentence was imposed. The question is whether he "fled."

26. The Court is asked to interpret a word used in an Irish statute. Peart J noted that the first recital to the Framework Decision cited the Tampere conclusions of the European Council of October 1999 as advocating, inter alia, that "*the formal extradition procedure should be abolished among the Member States in respect of persons who are fleeing from justice after having been finally sentenced...*" (emphasis added) . This led to him to conduct a careful linguistic comparison of the French, German and Italian texts of the same recital.

27. It seems to me, however, that the Court should confine itself to a consideration of the word, "fled" as it appears in the Act of 2003, as amended. I will explain my reasons later when discussing the obligation of "conforming interpretation." Thus, the question is whether the respondent "fled" Hungary. Peart J thought that it would do "violence" to the language of the legislative text to extend it "*to cover persons such as the respondent who did not "flee" within the meaning normally attributed to that word, and who left legitimately having availed of a procedure in place to deal with just such a departure.........*"

28. The regularity of the procedure whereby the respondent left Hungary is confirmed in several documents, notably the Arrest Warrant itself, which contains the following:

> *"Pursuant to Section 586, subsection (1) of Act XIX of 1998 on the Hungarian Criminal Code, "In cases where the accused lives abroad bail may be deposited upon his request, with*

> *permission of the prosecutor prior to submission of the indictment, and after it, with the permission of the court. In such a case the proceedings may take place in absentia."*

29. The document continues by referring to provisions, where the accused person has followed this procedure, for serving documents on the legal representatives of the accused. The Hungarian Ministry of Justice informed the Minister, in a letter, that "the reason why Mr **Tobin** was not present during the trial was because he laid a deposit of 500,000 HUF at the court." The principal consequence for the respondent of his having availed of this procedure was that, although he had been tried in absentia, there could be no retrial if he returned to Hungary. For present purposes, however, the pursuit of this procedure mainly demonstrates that the respondent left Hungary with the full authority and approval of the Hungarian prosecutor and of the court.

30. At the level of first impression, using the word as it is commonly understood, I am satisfied that the respondent did not "flee" Hungary when he sought permission to leave Hungary, secured the return of his passport for that purpose and put up a financial bond.

31. "Fleeing" necessarily implies escape, haste, evasion, the notion of movement away from a pursuer. Nothing in citations from the Oxford Dictionary suggests otherwise. The Shorter Oxford Dictionary on Historical Principles (Third Ed.) provides the following four meanings:

(1) To run away from or as from danger; to take flight;
(2) To withdraw hastily, take oneself off, go away….
(3) To make one's escape…;
(4) To disappear, vanish……

32. Peart J also considered the Irish version, not of the Act, but of the Framework Decision. Since the word is the same, it is of some interest to note his citation from Dineen's Irish – English Dictionary of 1927 to show that the phrase, "ar a teicheadh" means "on the run "and "avoiding arrest".

33. The respondent's leaving of Hungary could not reasonably be described as "fleeing" or "flight," in accordance with any generally understood meaning of the word. I agree with Peart J that to apply the term to the actions of the respondent in the present case would do violence to language.

34. It follows that the High Court was neither entitled nor bound, on the basis of a correct interpretation of the relevant section to order the surrender of the respondent.

The question then arises as to whether an over-riding obligation, arising from the principle of conforming interpretation, leads to a different result.

35. The provenance of the principle of "conforming interpretation" can be traced, in Community law, to 1984 (Case 14/83 *Von Colson and Kamann* [1984] ECR 1891). In Case C-105/03, *Pupino*, the Court of Justice adapted that principle to framework decisions adopted pursuant to the Treaty on European Union. The Court ruled that the principle was "*binding in relation to framework decision's adopted in the context of Title VI of the Treaty on European Union.*" Thus, it stated:

> *"When applying national law, the national court that is called upon to interpret it must do so as far as possible in the light of the wording and purpose of the framework decision in order to attain the result which it pursues and thus comply with Article 34(2)(b) EU."*

36. Before proceeding, I should mention that first recital to the Framework Decision, recalls the Tampere Conclusions of the European Council of 1999, which represent the political origin of the proposal for the Framework Decision. The reference to "persons who are fleeing from justice after having been finally sentenced" quoted in the first recital to the Framework Decision was the subject of debate in the High Court and led Peart J to compare the French German and Italian and Irish versions of the expression. I do not think this exercise is necessary in this particular case. It is undoubtedly the case that the Court of Justice may have regard to the Tampere conclusions, together with other relevant preparatory material, when it is required to interpret the Framework Decision. It is also the case that the recitals to a legislative act frequently provide valuable guidance when interpreting it. The Tampere conclusions, other than the part cited, do not themselves form part of the Framework Decision. From the point of view of this Court, they are at one remove from the Framework Decision. The principle of conforming interpretation focuses on the objective of the Framework Decision. The Tampere conclusions, as cited in the first recital, certainly recite the principle of mutual recognition, which is central to the entire system, but they are not directly linked to the substantive legislative content of the Framework Decision which contains no other reference to "fleeing." That phrase is not reflected in any operative provision of the Framework Decision. Thus, I believe it suffices to approach the principle of conforming interpretation without reference to the first recital or the Tampere conclusions.

37. The Court of Justice qualified the principle of conforming interpretation by stating that:

> *"The obligation on the national court to refer to the content of a framework decision when interpreting the relevant rules of its national law ceases when the latter cannot receive an application which would lead to a result compatible with that envisaged by that framework decision. In other words, the principle of conforming interpretation cannot serve as the basis for an interpretation of national law contra legem. That principle does, however, require that, where necessary, the national court consider the whole of national law in order to assess how far it can be applied in such a way as not to produce a result contrary to that envisaged by the framework decision."*

38. This Court has restated and applied these principles in cases concerning the European Arrest Warrant, notably *Minister for Justice, Equality and Law Reform v Dundon* [2005] I.R. 261; *Minister for Justice, Equality and Law Reform v Altravicicus* [2006] 2 ILRM 241.

39. The object of the Framework Decision is simply stated in Article 1.2 of that instrument:

> *Member States shall execute any European arrest warrant on the basis of the principle of mutual recognition and in accordance with the provisions of this Framework Decision."*

40. That Article, in a nutshell, states the objective of the entire system. It imposes an obligation on Member States to implement it in their law. The courts of the Member States are under a corresponding obligation to give effect to those laws. When performing that obligation, courts must interpret those laws in a way which will best achieve that objective, i.e., in the light of the Framework Decision. They are not, on the other hand, required to set aside or rewrite national laws for the stated purpose. The Court of Justice does not demand an interpretation contrary to the law: *contra legem*. Murray C.J. explained the obligation and its limits in his judgment in *Minister for Justice, Equality and Law Reform v Altravicicus*:

> *"The principle of conforming interpretation is limited, as the Court of Justice has pointed out in Pupino and other cases, to the extent that it is possible to give such an interpretation. It does not require a national court to interpret national legislation contra legem. If national legislation, having been interpreted as far as possible in conformity with community legislation to which it purports to give effect, but still falls short of what is required by the latter, a national Court must, as a general principle, apply that legislation as interpreted although there may be other consequences for a Member State which has failed to fully implement a Directive or Framework Decision."*

41. If it is to order the surrender of the respondent to Hungary to serve the sentence of imprisonment which has been imposed on him by the Hungarian Court, this Court must be satisfied that he falls within one of the headings of s. 10 of the Act of 2003, as amended. Only paragraph (d) is capable of applying. It is a condition of the application of that provision that the respondent have "fled." For reasons already given, I am satisfied that he did not "flee." If the court were to hold otherwise, it would be acting contrary to the clear meaning of the Act of 2003, i.e., *contra legem*.

42. It follows that his surrender cannot be ordered. For these reasons, the appeal should be dismissed.

Rimsa v Governor of Cloverhill Prison

[2010] IESC 47

Author's note: *Rimsa* is another recent example of the mis-implementation of the European arrest warrant into Irish law.

Judgment of Murray C.J. delivered on the 28th day of July 2010

This judgment sets out the reason why at the hearing of the appeal in this matter, the Court ordered the release of the appellant pursuant to Article 40.4.2 on the grounds that it was not satisfied that his then detention in custody was in accordance with law.

By order of the High Court dated 13th December 2007 it was ordered, pursuant to s. 16 of the European Arrest Warrant Act 2003, as amended, that the appellant be surrendered to the authorities of the Republic of Latvia in respect of a criminal offence specified in European Arrest Warrants seeking such surrender.

That order of the High Court which was addressed, inter alia, to the respondent, the Governor of Cloverhill Prison directed that the appellant be lodged in Cloverhill Prison and there to be detained in custody for a period of not less than fifteen days from the date of the order "until the date of his delivery as aforesaid and for any further period as may be necessary under the law".

Section 16 of the Act of 2003

Section 16 of the European Arrest Warrant act 2003 as amended by s. 76 of the Criminal Justice (Terrorist Offences) Act 2005 provides as follows:

> 16.— (1) Where a person does not consent to his or her surrender to the issuing state or has withdrawn his or her consent under section 15(9) the High Court may, upon such date as is fixed under section 13 or such later date as it considers appropriate, make an order directing that the person be surrendered to such other person as is duly authorised by the issuing state to receive him or her, provided that—
> (a) the High Court is satisfied that the person before it is the person in respect of whom the European arrest warrant was issued,
> (b) the European arrest warrant, or a facsimile or true copy thereof, has been endorsed in accordance with section 13 for execution of the warrant,
> (c) where appropriate, an undertaking under section 45 or a facsimile or true copy thereof is provided to the court,
> (d) the High Court is not required, under section 21A, 22, 23 or 24 (inserted by sections 79, 80, 81 and 82 of the Criminal Justice (Terrorist Offences) Act 2005), to refuse to surrender the person under this Act, and
> (e) the surrender of the person is not prohibited by Part 3 or the Framework Decision (including the recitals thereto).
>
> (2) Where a person does not consent to his or her surrender to the issuing state or has withdrawn his or her consent under section 15(9), the High Court may, upon such date as is fixed under section 14 or such later date as it considers appropriate, make an order directing that the person be surrendered to such other person as is duly authorised by the issuing state to receive him or her, provided that—
> (a) the European arrest warrant and, where appropriate, an undertaking under section 45, or facsimile or true copies thereof are provided to the court,
> (b) the High Court is satisfied that the person before it is the person in respect of whom the European arrest warrant was issued,

(c) the High Court is not required, under section 21A, 22, 23 or 24 (inserted by sections 79, 80, 81 and 82 of the Criminal Justice (Terrorist Offences) Act 2005), to refuse to surrender the person under this Act, and

(d) the surrender of the person is not prohibited by Part 3 or the Framework Decision (including the recitals thereto).

(2A) Where the High Court does not—

(a) make an order under subsection (1) on the date fixed under section 13, or

(b) make an order under subsection (2) on the date fixed under section 14, it may remand the person before it in custody or on bail and, for those purposes, the High Court shall have the same powers in relation to remand as it would have if the person were brought before it charged with an indictable offence.

(3) An order under this section shall take effect upon the expiration of 15 days beginning on the date of the making of the order or such earlier date as the High Court, upon the request of the person to whom the order applies, directs.

(4) When making an order under this section the High Court shall also make an order committing the person to a prison (or if he or she is not more than 21 years of age, to a remand institution) there to remain pending his or her surrender in accordance with the order under this section, and shall inform the person—

(a) that he or she will not, without his or her consent, be surrendered to the issuing state, before the expiration of the period of 15 days specified in subsection (3), and

(b) of his or her right to make a complaint under Article 40.4.2° of the Constitution at any time before his or her surrender to the issuing state.

(5) Subject to subsection (6) and section 18, a person to whom an order for the time being in force under this section applies shall be surrendered to the issuing state not later than 10 days after—

(a) the order takes effect in accordance with subsection (3) (inserted by section 76 (d) of the Criminal Justice (Terrorist Offences) Act 2005),

or,

(b) such date (being a date that falls after the expiration of that period) as may be agreed by the Central Authority in the State and the issuing state.

(6) Where a person makes a complaint under Article 40.4.2° of the Constitution, he or she shall not be surrendered to the issuing state while proceedings relating to the complaint are pending.

(7) A person (to whom an order for the time being in force under this section applies) who is not surrendered to the issuing state in accordance with subsection (5) shall be released from custody immediately upon the expiration of the 10 days referred to in that subsection unless, upon such expiration, proceedings referred to in subsection (6) are pending.

(8) Where the High Court decides not to make an order under this section—

(a) it shall give reasons for its decision, and

(b) the person shall, subject to subsection (9), be released from custody.

(9) Subsections (7) and (8) shall not apply if—

(a) (i) the person has been sentenced to a term of imprisonment for an offence of which he or she was convicted in the State,

(ii) on the date on which he or she would, but for this subsection, be entitled to be released under subsection (7) or (8), all or part of the term of imprisonment remains unexpired, and

(iii) the person is required to serve all or part of the remainder of that term of imprisonment,

(b) (i) the person has been charged with or convicted of an offence in the State, and

(ii) on the date on which he or she would, but for this paragraph, be entitled to be released from custody under subsection (7) or (8), he or she is required to be in custody by virtue of having been remanded in custody pending his or her being tried, or the imposition of sentence, in respect of that offence.

(10) If the High Court has not, after the expiration of 60 days from the arrest of the person concerned under section 13 or 14, made an order under this section or section 15, or has decided not to make an order under this section, it shall direct the Central Authority in the State to inform the issuing judicial authority and, where appropriate, Eurojust in relation thereto and of the reasons therefor specified in the direction, and the Central Authority in the State shall comply with such direction.
(11) If the High Court has not, after the expiration of 90 days from the arrest of the person concerned under section 13 or 14, made an order under this section or section 15, or has decided not to make an order under this section, it shall direct the Central Authority in the State to inform the issuing judicial authority and, where appropriate, Eurojust in relation thereto and of the reason therefor specified in the direction, and the Central Authority in the State shall comply with such direction.
(12) An appeal against an order under this section or a decision not to make such an order may be brought in the Supreme Court on a point of law only.

Background Circumstances

In accordance with s. 16(3) of the Act the order of the High Court for the appellant's surrender was not to take effect before the expiration of a period of 15 days after the making of the order. This is intended to facilitate, inter alia, an appeal from the High Court Order. No appeal was lodged or other application made to a Court during that period.

Accordingly the High Court Order of 13th December directing the appellant's surrender to Latvia took effect 15 days after that. The Irish and Latvian Central Authority proceeded on the basis that, having regard to s. 16(5), this meant that his surrender to the issuing state, Latvia, was required to take place not later than ten days after December 28th namely not later than the 7th January 2008 unless paragraph (b) of s. 16(5) applied. No issue arises as to the relevant dates. As can be seen from that section (cited above) paragraph (b) means that surrender may be postponed by agreement to a date not later than ten days after "such date (being a date that falls after the expiration of that period) as may be agreed by the Central Authority in the State and the issuing state." In the event of such later date being duly agreed in accordance with the section, the section requires the surrender to be made not later than ten days after the newly agreed date.

In this case if no agreement on a later date had been entered into pursuant to s. 16(5)(b) and surrender had not taken place before or on January 7th, s. 16(7) required the immediate release of the appellant, that date being the tenth day following the date on which the order for surrender was considered to take effect.

In this particular case the Latvian Central Authority was notified on 13th December 2007 of the making of the Order and of the period of 15 days before which it would take effect. This was done by an official in the Department of Justice, Equality and Law Reform, acting as the Central Authority in the State.

By fax dated 28th December 2007 the Department, again as the Central Authority in the State, reminded the Latvian Central Authority that the surrender of the appellant should take place within ten days of December 28th.

Again by fax dated the 2nd January 2008 the Department reminded the Latvian Central Authority that they should contact An Garda Siochana to make the necessary arrangements for the surrender of the appellant.

In spite of the three communications between December 13th 2007 and 2nd January 2008 no response was received by the Central Authority in the State from the Latvian Central Authority.

On 3rd January 2008 the Department eventually sent an e-mail, marked urgent, to the Latvian Central Authority pointing out that the appellant, the subject of the order for surrender, "must now be collected by your Police Authorities by 07/01/2008".

On the same date a response was received from the Latvian Central Authority which asserted, inter alia, that "due to national holidays (before New Year's Eve and the following days), respective notification on granted surrender was received at this office only on 02.01.2008". They went on to state that they would not be able "to collect the subject (with 7th January 2008 being the deadline) since there were tickets available for flights to Dublin only for 08, 09 and 10.01.2008". The Latvian Central Authority indicated that for practical reasons including the question of flight availability that they were not in a position to collect the appellant by 7th January 2008. The communication went on to state that a precise proposal for an alternative date would be communicated when they had exact flight details for arrival and departure. By e-mail dated 4th January 2008 the Department responded indicated that they had no objection to the extension of the deadline for the surrender of the appellant.

By e-mail dated the same date the Latvian Central Authority responded by stating that surrender could take place on January 9th 2008 based on the availability of flights to and from Riga and Dublin.

The Department responded on the same date stating that the revised surrender date of January 9th was acceptable "to the Central Authority and An Garda Siochana".

Before the surrender on the re-arranged date could take place the appellant obtained an order of the High Court directing an inquiry into the lawfulness of his detention pursuant to Article 40.4.2 he having contended that his then detention was unlawful because of the failure of the State to release him from custody on the expiry of ten days from December 28th 2007 the date on which the High Court Order for his surrender took effect. It was also contended that the purported agreement between the two Central Authorities for surrender to take place at a later date was not a valid or lawful postponement of the surrender within the meaning of s. 16(5)(b).

The hearing of the appellant's application on the merits was held promptly and a judgment delivered on the 11th January 2008. The Court dismissed the appellant's application concluding that he was detained in accordance with law. The appellant appealed against that decision to this Court.

While that particular appeal was pending the appellant made a new and distinct application to the High Court for his release pursuant to Article 40.4.2 essentially on the grounds that s. 16(5)(b) of the Act of 2003 was unconstitutional. The High Court ruled that the said subsection was not invalid having regard to the provisions of the Constitution and that the appellant's then detention was in accordance with law. The appellant also appealed against the decision of the High Court in that case but that appeal, which was not heard, would now appear to be moot.

High Court Judgment of 11th January 2008

For the purposes of the issues in this appeal there were two relevant issues decided by the High Court in its judgment of 11th January 2008.

In contending that the purported postponement was invalid as not complying with the provisions of s. 16(5)(b) the appellant had submitted that such postponement could only be agreed where it was "necessary" to do so and that in any event there were no reasonable grounds for such a postponement because there were seats available on the flights from Riga to Dublin on dates preceding the deadline date of January 7th. In those circumstances the Latvian Authorities could, it was contended, readily have made arrangements for the surrender to be effected within the initial ten days envisaged by the Act. The appellant contended that paragraph (b) should be interpreted in the light of that portion of Article 23 of the Framework Decision which only envisaged the postponement of a surrender beyond the initial period of ten days where surrender is "prevented by circumstances beyond the control of any of the member states". So interpreted s. 16(5)(b) means that an agreement between the two authorities on a later date could only be entered into if it was necessitated by circumstances beyond the control of the two States concerned.

Having reviewed the evidence before him the learned trial judge concluded:

> "It seems reasonable to accept that during the New Year holiday season seat availability might well be limited. I do accept this and, therefore, I accept there were grounds of necessity requiring the arranging of a later date.
>
> Notwithstanding my finding in this regard, I do not think that s. 16(5)(b) makes any requirement of necessity in order to ground an extension although it is clear that the surrender should be effected as soon as possible. I do accept that the Framework Decision may be looked to in order to interpret the national legislation. To that extent paragraph (3) of Article 23 does provide that where the surrender of the requested person is prevented by circumstances beyond the control of any the Member States, there may be agreement on a new date and the surrender should take place within ten days of the new date. Nonetheless the national legislation does not make such a requirement of necessity. In any event, in the light of my finding above re availability of airline seats; there appears to have been an existence of such circumstances and, therefore, a necessity to postpone."

The second issue relevant to this appeal and decided by the High Court relates to the argument made by the appellant, and referred to at page 6 of the judgment of the learned High Court judge, to the effect that the Framework Decision has direct effect in certain circumstances which are present here. The basis on which that appellant had argued for direct effect in the High Court is not entirely clear. On those grounds, it was submitted that any agreement to postpone surrender to a later date must, as required by Article 23 of the Framework Decision, be made between the Judicial Authorities of both the issuing state and the executing states and not, as provided in the European Arrest Warrant Act, by the Central Authority in the State.

At page 5 of his judgment the learned trial judge had noted that s. 16(5)(b) of the Act provides for a later date to be "agreed by the Central Authority in the State and the issuing state". He added: "Thus, whilst that person in Ireland is the Minister for Justice, Equality and Law Reform, in relation to the issuing state no particular persons are specified." He went on to note that it is clear from the documents before the Court that as a matter of fact it was the Central Authority of Latvia which entered into the agreement for the postponement of surrender with the Central Authority in Ireland.

In addressing the second issue referred to above the learned trial judge stated: "In the first case, it seems clear to me that whereas the Framework Decision may well be referred to in order to clarify an ambiguity or assist in interpretation, it cannot be held to overrule the national legislation enacted to implement it. Article 34(2)(b) of the Treaty on European Union explicitly states that Framework Decisions shall not have direct effect." In this respect he cited from Denham J's judgment in *Dundon v. Governor of Cloverhill Prison* [2006] 1 I.R. 518 where she stated: "Thus, the Council Framework Decision does not have direct effect and is not part of the domestic law of this State. It is binding on the State as to the result to be achieved. It promotes common action by the States of the European Union to advance approximation of the laws in the States on specific issues. It is left to the national authorities to choose the form and method of implementation." He also cited Fennelly J. (in the same case) where he stated: "These Courts are bound to apply the provisions of Acts of the Oireachtas the Framework Decision does not have direct effect. Where a provision of an Act of the Oireachtas conflicts directly with the provision of a Framework Decision this Court must give preference to the former. To do otherwise would, to cite the language of the Court of Justice [in the Pupino case], be contra legem."

The learned trial judge then concluded: "In this case s. 16(5)(b) explicitly specifies that the agreement on a different date is made by the Central Authority in the State and the issuing state. To hold that the agreement had to be made between the judicial authorities of the two States would be contra legem."

Having regard to the foregoing conclusions and his findings on other points not pursued in the appeal before this Court, the learned High Court judge refused the appellant's application.

The Appeal

The appellant's appeal to this Court against the findings of the High Court was confined to two essential grounds. The first ground which I propose to refer to is the submission of the appellant that his detention was unlawful because the State had not entered into a valid or lawful agreement for the postponement of his surrender because the agreement in question was made between the Central Authorities of the two States in breach of Article 23 of the Framework Decision which requires that it be entered into between the judicial authorities of the two States concerned. During the course of the argument counsel relied on s. 10 of the Act as requiring the State to comply with Article 23 of the Framework Decision.

The State in its submissions acknowledges that the Act of 2003 may be interpreted in the light of the Framework Decision but that the Act cannot be given a meaning contra legem. The State also acknowledged that once the ten day period provided for in s. 16(5) expired there was a mandatory requirement that the person concerned be released. The issue was however, it was submitted, the date from which the ten day period ran. In this case it was submitted that there had been an agreement duly entered into between the relevant authorities pursuant to s. 16(5)(b) of the Act postponing the date for surrender to a later date and the ten day period ran from that date. In this case the agreed postponed date was the 9th January 2008 and the ten days ran from that date. Accordingly the High Court was correct in determining that the appellant was then in lawful detention. It was submitted that the Framework Decision, unlike a Directive, does not have a direct effect and even if a statute is in conflict with the Framework Decision effect must be given to the statute. It was submitted that s. 10 itself is a provision that is entirely general in nature and a harmonious interpretation of that section with the remaining sections of the Act "does not override the general presumption that an issuing state is complying with a Framework Decision." It was further submitted that on the facts as found by Hedigan J., that the Framework Decision does not prohibit the surrender of the appellant. In this case it was submitted that s. 16(5)(b), so far as Ireland was concerned, required the Central Authority in the State to agree on the postponed date. It also provided for that agreement to be entered into with the issuing state and it was a matter for the issuing state to determine the authority which could enter into the agreement. Accordingly, it was submitted that the agreement to postpone the surrender of the appellant was entered into in accordance with s. 16(5)(b) and that was sufficient. Moreover, it was submitted that so far as Article 23 is concerned the Oireachtas is entitled to allow some discretion to the issuing state as to what constituted a "judicial authority" so this phrase in the Framework Decision cannot be regarded as imposing a requirement that only a court or judge must discharge a particular function.

The other ground raised by the appellant in the appeal concerned his submissions that the learned trial judge erred in law in determining, on the basis of the evidence before him that there were reasonable grounds justifying the authorities in question entering into an agreement to postpone the surrender. It was also submitted that s. 16 interpreted in the light of Article 23 meant that there must be grounds which necessitated such an agreement for postponement being entered into and the learned trial judge was also incorrect, on the evidence, in concluding that there were such grounds.

In the light of the conclusions which I have reached in relation to the ground first mentioned above I do not think it is necessary to deal with this latter ground.

Decision

The Act of 2003 (as amended)

I think it is convenient at this point to cite again the most relevant subsection of s. 16 of the Act of 2003, as amended:

> "(5) Subject to subsection (6) and section 18, a person to whom an order for the time being in force under this section applies shall be surrendered to the issuing state not later than 10 days after—
>
> (a) the expiration of the period specified in subsection (3), or
>
> (b) such date (being a date that falls after the expiration of that period) as may be agreed by the Central Authority in the State and the issuing state."

Neither subsection (6) nor s. 18 are relevant to the issue in this appeal.

Subsection (7) then goes on to provide that "a person . . . who is not surrendered to the issuing state in accordance with subsection (5) shall be released from custody immediately upon the expiration of the ten days referred to in that subsection unless, upon such expiration, proceedings referred to in subsection (6) are pending."

The reference to subsection (6) is not relevant to the issue in this appeal.

Accordingly, once the period of ten days after the order for surrender taking effect has expired it is mandatory that the person the subject of the Order for surrender be released from custody unless a later date for surrender, has, in the terms of paragraph (b) been "agreed by the Central Authority in the State and the issuing state."

This section is clearly intended to give effect to Article 23 of the Framework Decision although it departs from it in a fundamental respect.

The Framework Decision

The relevant provisions of Article 23 of the Framework Decision provide as follows:

> The person requested shall be surrendered as soon as possible on a date agreed between the authorities concerned.
>
> He or she shall be surrendered no later than ten days after the final decision on the execution of the European Arrest Warrant.
>
> If the surrender of the requested person within the period laid down on paragraph 2. is prevented by circumstances beyond the control of any of the member states, the executing and issuing judicial authorities shall immediately contact each other and agree on a new surrender date. In that event the surrender shall take place within ten days of the new date thus agreed." (*emphasis added)*

It will be noted that the Framework Decision requires that any agreement to postpone a surrender after the initial ten days provided for must be one which is agreed upon by the judicial authorities of *both* the executing state and the issuing state.

Thus there is a clear and manifest conflict between Article 23.3 of the Decision and s. 16(5)(b) of the Act of 2003 in that the latter expressly permits and requires any agreement, by an authority in the State, on a new surrender date to be agreed by the Minister, as the Central Authority in the State and not the executing judicial authority.

Section 9 of the Act specifies that the High Court is the executing judicial authority in the State. That authority was at no stage involved in agreeing the postponed date.

At this point I think it is appropriate to refer briefly to the role conferred on the Central Authority of the Member States by the Framework Decision.

Recital 9 of the Preamble to the Framework Decision states "The role of central authorities in the execution of a European arrest warrant must be limited to practical and administrative assistance." *(emphasis added)*

In giving substantive effect to that recital, Article 7 of the Decision provides that each member state "may designate a central authority or, when its legal system so provides, more than one central authority to assist the competent judicial authorities." Paragraph (2) of Article 7 then goes on to provide that "A member state may, if it is necessary as a result of the organisation of its internal judicial system, make its central authority (ies) responsible for the administrative transmission and reception for European arrest warrants as well as for all other official correspondence relating thereto."

It may be seen therefore that the Framework Decision intends that the role of any Central Authority, which, in contrast to a Judicial Authority referred to in the Framework Decision, belongs to the executive arm of a state, is confined to assisting the competent judicial authority and may also, if necessary, have responsibility for the administrative transmission and reception of European arrest warrants and related official correspondence.

This limitation placed on the role of the central authorities of the member states, in contrast to that of a judicial authority, is of importance when one considers an objective of the Framework Decision, as set out at Recital (5) of the Preamble, is the establishment of an area, within the Union, of freedom, security and justice which would lead to the abolition of extradition between member states and replace it "by a system of surrender between judicial authorities." *(emphasis added)*.

Recital (6) of the Decision speaks of the measure being "...the first concrete measure in the field of criminal law implementing the principle of mutual recognition which the European Council referred to as the 'cornerstone' of judicial co-operation."

Recital (8) states: "Decisions on the execution of the European arrest warrant must be subject to sufficient controls, which means that the judicial authority of the member state where the requested person has been arrested will have to take the decision on his or her surrender".

Thus, as has been pointed out in several judgments of this Court concerning the application of the Act of 2003, mutual co-operation and recognition of judicial decisions between judicial authorities of the member states are fundamental to the operation of the new system of "surrender" on foot of the European arrest warrant.

As Fennelly J., stated in *Dundon v. Governor of Cloverhill Prison* [2006] 1 I.L.R.M. 321 at 346: "The European arrest warrant is designed to operate fundamentally within a judicial process. This essential aspect of the procedure is not merely a recognition that its execution "must be subject to sufficient controls" as is stated in the Eighth Recital but of the principle of legality. Persons cannot be surrendered compulsorily from one member state to another except in accordance with an open and transparent judicial procedure which guarantees respect for human rights."

No doubt it was for the above considerations and with a view to achieving those objectives that any decision by agreement to delay the surrender of a requested person pursuant to judicial order beyond that ten day period, must, according to Article 23, be made by the judicial authorities of the two states concerned and not by any administrative authority. By this means the Framework Decision ensures that any postponement of the date on which the surrender is due to take place on foot of a judicial order already made remains under judicial control. It also avoids any extension of a period of custody pending surrender being decided by the executive authorities as a form of administrative detention.

Interpretation of s. 16(5)(b) of the Act of 2003

The Act of 2003, as amended, is intended to give effect at national level to the Framework Decision. As this Court has frequently pointed out (see for example *Minister for Justice v. Altaravicious* [2006] 3 I.R. 148) when applying and interpreting the Act the Court must do so in the light of the wording and purpose of the Framework Decision in accordance with the principles stated in C-105/03 Criminal Proceedings against Maria Pupino [2005] ECR I-5285. Like a Directive, a Framework Decision is a legislative act of the European Union but, unlike a Directive, it cannot, by virtue of community law, have direct effect since Article 34.2(b) of the Treaty on the European Union expressly excludes such effect.

In the Pupino case the Court of Justice stated, at paragraph 43, "When applying national law, the national court that is called on to interpret it must do so so far as possible in the light of the wording and purpose of the Framework Decision in order to attain the result which it pursues and thus comply with Article 34(2)(b)(EU)."

That is a reference to that part of Article 34(2)(b) of the Treaty which provides that Framework Decisions "shall be binding on member states as to the result to be achieved ..."

Moreover, in a reference to the principle of interpreting national law in conformity with a Framework Decision the Court of Justice stated, at paragraph 47:

> "That principle does, however, require that, where necessary, the national court consider the whole of national law in order to assess how far it can be applied in such a way as not to produce a result contrary to that envisaged by the Framework Decision."

That interpretive principle only applies to the extent to which it is reasonably possible to interpret national legislation in conformity with the Framework Decision and does not require national legislation to be interpreted contra legem as the learned trial judge stated.

As pointed out earlier, it is manifest from the plain and express terms of Article 23.3 that an agreement for postponement of the surrender to a later date must be agreed between (a) the executing Judicial Authority (which in this case is the High Court) and (b) the issuing Judicial Authority (which here is the "First Instance Riga Vidzeme Suburb Court of the Republic of Latvia" as identified in the European arrest warrant in this case).

On the other hand, as has been seen, s. 16(5)(b) of the Act excludes the High Court and permits a postponement of the date for surrender beyond the initial ten day period where that is agreed "(b) by the Central Authority in the State and the issuing State". While that clearly requires the Central Authority in this State to enter into the agreement the section does not specify what authority in the issuing State must agree to the postponement. It certainly does not specify that it be the Central Authority of the issuing State. The section does not, for example say 'be agreed by the Central Authority in the State and in the issuing State'.

As the learned trial judge correctly pointed out at page 5 of his judgment in relation to this phrase "Thus, whilst that person in Ireland is the Minister for Justice, Equality and Law Reform, in relation to the issuing State no particular persons are specified."

Any such agreement obviously cannot be entered into in the abstract with the issuing state but must be with some authority of that state.

In this regard the State had argued that paragraph (b), so far as Ireland was concerned, clearly authorises the Central Authority in the State to agree the new date for the surrender taking place and that to hold otherwise would be to interpret the section contra legem. I have no doubt that that is correct as concerns the Act.

The State went further and argued, that as concerns the authority in the issuing state with which the agreement may be entered into that the Oireachtas intended in s. 16(5)(b) that it would be a matter for the issuing state to decide which authority could enter into such an agreement. As a matter of fact the Latvian Central Authority decided to do so.

I do not consider that this attribution or presumption as to the intention of the Oireachtas is well founded. On the contrary in my view the presumption must be that the section was intended to do what the Act expressly purports to do, namely to give effect to the terms of the Framework Decision.

The Act was adopted by the Oireachtas in order "to give effect to Council Framework Decision ... on the European arrest warrant and the surrender procedures between Member States" as is stated in the long title to the Act. That was the obligation of the State so as to ensure that surrender on foot of the European arrest warrant takes place in accordance with the Framework Decision.

The subsection in question falls to be interpreted as a matter of Irish law, in the light of the Decision, and not as a matter of Latvian law. Its provisions involve the requirements of national law by which the State is bound.

Subsection (b) of s. 5 certainly does not specify the Central Authority or any authority in the issuing state as the authority with which an agreement for a postponed surrender date may be made. Faced with the silence of the subsection on that point the Central Authority here would have to ask itself whom does it contact in the issuing State where the question of agreeing a postponed surrender date arises? As a consequence of these proceedings the Court is required to answer that question. A reference to Article 23 which s. 16 seeks to implement points to the judicial authority of the issuing state as being the only answer to that question. At the very least there is an ambiguity in the Act as to whether the reference to the "issuing state" permits the Central Authority in the State to enter into such an agreement with any authority in that State.

Any such an ambiguity, can, in my view, only be resolved by looking at the provisions of the Framework Decision in order to avoid, to the extent to which the language of the provision permits, "a result contrary to that envisaged by the Framework Decision" as stated in the *Pupino* case. Of course once one looks at the provisions of the Framework Decision the manner in which that ambiguity should be resolved is obvious and permissible because of the express requirement in Article 23.3 that any such agreement should be reached with the issuing judicial authority which in this case is the Latvian Court referred to above. Such an interpretation also accords with the objectives of the Framework Decision namely a system of surrender, in lieu of extradition, designed to operate fundamentally within a judicial process, as Fennelly J., so aptly described it in the citation above from his judgment in the *Dundon* case.

Accordingly, even though paragraph (b) of s. 16(5) of the Act of 2003 expressly authorised the Central Authority in the State to reach an agreement on a new date for surrender, the agreement to do so could only be made by that Authority with the judicial authority of the issuing state, Latvia, as the subsection properly construed, requires.

Since this was not done there was no valid or effective agreement to postpone the date of surrender within the meaning of s. 16(5)(b).

It will be recalled that subsections (7) provides "A person ... who is not surrendered to the issuing State in accordance with subs. (5) shall be released from custody immediately upon the expiration of the ten days referred to in that subsection unless, upon such expiration, proceedings referred to in subs. (6) are pending." There were no such proceedings pending.

In reference to the time limit specified in s. 16 Fennelly J., in the *Dundon* case cited with approval the following statement in the judgment of O'Sullivan J., in the latter's High Court judgment in that case, where he stated "The time limits specified for surrender *after* the final decision are in a different category, namely, they are mandatory in principle with the result that the requested person is intended to be released if they are not complied with."

That dictum was obiter in that case but it is clearly a correct statement as to the meaning and effect of s. 16(7).

There having been no valid agreement for the surrender of the appellant on a date after the expiry of the ten day period referred to then he should have been released immediately on its expiry on January 8th 2008.

Compliance by the State with the Framework Decision

There is however another argument advanced in relation to this issue. Section 10 of the Act of 2003, as amended, provides:

> "10. – Where a judicial authority in an issuing state duly issues a European arrest warrant in respect of a person –
>
> . . .
>
> that person shall, subject to and in accordance with the provisions of this Act and the Framework Decision, be arrested and surrendered to the issuing state." (*emphasis added).*

In this appeal the appellant submitted, relying on the case-law of this Court, that s. 10 rendered the Framework Decision directly applicably to arrest and surrender on foot of a European Arrest Warrant.

The words adopted by the Oireachtas in this section are very explicit. The Oireachtas expressly requires any arrest or surrender on foot of a European arrest warrant to be done not only in accordance with the Act but in accordance with the Framework Decision. It is of course entirely correct, as I have pointed out above, and this Court has pointed out many times, a Framework Decision, unlike a Directive in certain circumstances, is incapable, by virtue of community law, of having direct effect. That does not prevent the terms of the Directive having an application at national level by virtue of an Act of the Oireachtas which the Act of 2003 does in a number of provisions of which s. 10 is one. Then its application is a consequence of national law not community law.

In *Minister for Justice v. Altaravicious* (cited above), I concluded that the section of the Act of 2003 relevant in that case was clear and did not require that a copy of the underlying domestic warrant be incorporated in the European arrest warrant or be attached to it, as the appellant in that case had contended. I then went on to state:

> "If that was the only provision governing what a European Arrest Warrant should specify the issues in this matter might have been more readily resolved. Although the Framework Decision cannot, in terms of community law, have direct effect (since Article 34.2(b) of the Treaty on European Union expressly excludes such effect) the Oireachtas has chosen to give it, at least as regards a significant number of its provisions, such effect and make it directly applicable within the State. This is achieved, inter alia, by s. 10 of the Act of 2003 which provides that where a European Arrest Warrant has been duly issued in respect of a person "that person shall, subject to and in accordance with the provisions of this Act and the Framework Decision, be arrested and surrendered to the issuing State". The Act does not confine itself to including the Framework Decision in a schedule for reference purposes. There are other provisions of the Act of 2003 which require the Courts to interpret and apply the Framework Decision directly but it is sufficient for present purposes to note that s. 10 means that in deciding on an application for a surrender pursuant to the terms of the Act of 2003 the Court must apply both the provisions of the

> Act and the Framework Decision. It is, to say the least, an idiosyncratic method of legislating and likely to create ambiguity."

Later in that judgment I observed: "Thus this Court is in the unusual position of having to interpret and apply Article 8 of the Framework Decision directly because of the effect given to it in national law by the Oireachtas and not by community law".

In *Dundon v. Governor of Cloverhill Prison* (cited above) Fenelly J., also alluded to the direct application of the Framework Decision as provided for, not by community law, but by the Act of 2003, as amended. At page 348 of his judgment in that case he stated "Insofar as the statutory permitted grounds of refusal to surrender go beyond the terms of Article 1(3) of the Framework Decision, but are covered by its Recitals, they are, nonetheless, expressly invoked by s.16(1)(e) of the Act. Section 16(1)(e) permits surrender provided, inter alia, that "the surrender of the person is not prohibited by Part III or the Framework Decision (including the Recitals thereto)."

Fennelly J., then went on to point out that the Courts are bound to apply the provisions of Acts of the Oireachtas and that where the provision of an Act of the Oireachtas conflicts directly with a provision of the Framework Decision the Court must give preference to the former which could not be interpreted contra legem. He then however added "The precise contours and limits of the rights that can be invoked under the Act will have to be explored as cases arise. I am merely concerned to show that, while the 60 day period does not confer protection on individuals, there are other features of the Framework Decision, at least as that measure is implemented in Irish law, upon which reliance may be placed by individuals in appropriate cases."

So far as this case is concerned s. 10 expressly requires that the surrender of the appellant in this case be done not only and in accordance with the Act but, additionally, in accordance with the Framework Decision. An individual must be able to rely on such provisions of the Framework Decision at least so far as that measure is made applicable in Irish law by the Act itself. If it were otherwise it would render the express reference to the Framework Decision in s. 10 meaningless.

Accordingly the appellant was entitled to place reliance, pursuant to s. 10, on the provisions of the Framework Decision which applied to his surrender to the issuing State, Latvia.

In my view Article 23.3 is clearly an article which governs the surrender of a person on foot of a European arrest warrant. Accordingly by virtue of s. 10 of the Act of 2003 the Central Authority, in assisting and giving effect to the Order of the Court for surrender, was under a duty to do so in accordance with the provisions of the Framework Decision as s. 10 expressly provides.

While the entering into an agreement with the Latvian authorities by the Central Authority in the State was in conformity with sections 16(5)(b) it was in direct conflict with the provision of Article 23.3 and therefore not in accordance with s. 10 of the Act of 2003.

It was rather belatedly accepted, during the course of the hearing, on behalf of the Central Authority, that there was a direct conflict between the provisions of Article 23.3 and those of sections 16(5)(b) which failed to properly give effect to the Framework Decision. If the Central Authority had acknowledged from the outset that obvious conflict, this litigation would probably have been resolved at a much earlier stage or indeed rendered unnecessary.

It is also somewhat disconcerting that the Central Authority, even if it was of the view that it complied with the provisions of the statute, would nonetheless persist with the surrender pursuant to purely administrative arrangements which were manifestly in conflict with the legal obligations imposed on the State by virtue of Article 23 of the Framework Decision.

The issues in this case have been complicated by the fact that the Act has been drafted in such a way as to apply two legal norms to the same matter. In this instance s. 16(5)(b) of the Act and Article 23(3) of the Framework Decision are both applicable to the matter of agreeing a postponed surrender date. In *Altaravicius* the two applicable norms were s. 11 of the Act and Article 8 of the Framework Decision. In the latter case I referred to this manner of legislating, in restrained language, as "idiosyncratic". It is a most unsatisfactory way of legislating and I still consider that I am expressing myself in restrained terms. Framework Decisions, as their name suggests, are legislative measures drafted in terms which range from the general to the specific intended to be effectively implemented in each Member State through its own national legislative measures as Article 34(2((b) of the Treaty makes clear. In principle therefore it is national legislation which must give effect to the Framework Decision and achieve its objectives. That will usually mean that the provisions of the Acts of the Oireachtas themselves contain all the elements necessary to give effect to a Framework Decision. That would not preclude, however, an Act expressly requiring something to be done in accordance with a specific provision of a Framework Decision particularly, where such a provision is sufficiently clear and defined so as to be capable of being enforced or applied by a Court.

That might be done provided a section of the Act itself does not at the same time, and in parallel with the particular provision of the Framework Decision, purport to give effect to the latter provision so as to ensure that there is only one legal norm or provision applying to a particular matter.

What is unsatisfactory and which has given rise to litigation, and likely to do so in the future, is to have a provision of a Framework Decision made applicable to a particular matter at the same time or in parallel with a specific section or part of an Act governing the same matter.

Even where that is done so as to ensure that the provision in an Act is, at least on its face, in harmony with the applicable provision of the Framework Decision it means nonetheless that the Court has to interpret and apply two legal norms as happened in the *Altaravicius* case.

Such a situation is then exacerbated of course when there is a manifest divergence between the express terms of an Act and the express terms of a Framework Decision, as has happened in this case.

For the reasons set out above the Central Authority in the State in entering into the agreement to postpone the date for surrender rather than taking steps to ensure that there was agreement between the two respective judicial authorities as Article 23(3) requires failed to act in accordance with the requirements of s. 10 of the Act. This is in addition to the earlier conclusion that the agreement was also contrary to s. 16(5)(b) insofar as it was made with the Central Authority of Latvia rather than the Latvian judicial authority as identified in the arrest warrant.

It is for the reasons set out in this judgment that I concluded that there was no valid agreement to postpone the date of surrender pursuant to s. 16(5)(b) of the Act and that therefore his continued detention was unlawful.

Scaife v Falcon Leisure Group

[2007] IESC 57

Judgment delivered on the 4th day of December 2007 by Macken, J.

This is an appeal from a judgment of the High Court of the 23rd February 2005, and from the Order made thereon by which the High Court found in favour of the Plaintiff against the Defendant in respect of personal injuries sustained by the plaintiff in the course of a holiday in Spain contracted for with the Defendant in the State.

The Background Facts

The plaintiff/respondent entered into an agreement ("the agreement") with the defendant/ appellant, a company registered in the United Kingdom and having a place of business in the State, and who is a provider of, inter alia, package holidays. The agreement in writing was made through a travelling companion of the plaintiff on 29th January 1998. By the terms of the same the defendant agreed, in consideration of the payment of an appropriate sum, to supply to the plaintiff/ respondent and others in a small group travelling with her, a "package holiday", including flights and hotel accommodation, the latter in the present case comprising what is known as "half board", that is, breakfasts and evening meals, at Cambrils Princess Hotel in Salou, Spain. The High Court judge found, as a fact, that the hotel itself was of a good standard, since the plaintiff and others in her group had previously stayed there and had chosen to return to that particular hotel.

On the 21st May 1998 during the course of an evening meal, taken towards the end of the serving period, the plaintiff was injured. The injury occurred when the plaintiff, while walking past a pillar on her way to the buffet table to serve herself, fell on liquid foodstuff which had fallen on the floor behind a pillar in circumstances where, it was found by the High Court, she could not have seen the spillage and had no warning of its existence until she fell in it. She suffered physical injuries as a result, and these are not disputed by the defendant.

Although in the course of the High Court proceedings the defendant alleged that the Plaintiff had caused or contributed to her injuries, this defence was rejected by the High Court judge as being without foundation, and the defendant does not seek to maintain that defence in this appeal. In the High Court evidence was tendered by and on behalf of the Plaintiff. The Defendant did not go into evidence, relying instead on legal submissions as to liability.

The High Court proceedings, the argument and the legal findings

In the High Court the plaintiff relied on the provisions of the Package Holidays and Travel Trade Act of 1995 ("the Act of 1995"), an Act which transposed into Irish law Council Directive 91/314/EEC of 13 June 1990 on package travel, package holidays and package tours (OJ 190 L 158) ("the Directive"). The defendant/appellant has accepted that it is an "organiser" that the plaintiff/respondent is a "consumer" the hotel proprietor in Spain a "service supplier", and that the holiday was a "package holiday" all within the meaning of S.20 of the Act of 1995, which Section corresponds to Article 5 of the Directive.

By an ex-tempore judgment of the High Court (Herbert, J.) delivered after an oral hearing, it was held that the plaintiff was entitled to succeed against the Defendant under S. 20 of the Act of 1995. The High Court judge found that there was a legal duty on a hotel proprietor to take reasonable care to ensure that his hotel was reasonably safe and was maintained in a reasonably safe condition for visitors to the hotel. He determined that S.20 of the Act was not to be given a restrictive meaning, but that the hotel proprietor was not, under the Act of 1995 and contrary to the argument of counsel for the defendants, an insurer to the plaintiff, or bound to foresee or forefend against every possible event. It was only obliged to take reasonable care in respect of an event which was reasonably foreseeable, such as the event which befell the plaintiff. He found that even if the hotel ordinarily operated to a satisfactory standard, there was no evidence to suggest that any appropriate system for avoiding the accident or for warning of the existence of the liquid was in place on the evening in question. Rather on the contrary, it had not acted with reasonable skill and care on the evening in question.

As concerns the Act of 1995, the learned High Court judge held that the clear intention of the legislature, on the plain meaning of the words used, was to give effect to the intention behind the Directive. This intention was to:

> *"facilitate citizens of Member States who have accidents while on a package holiday abroad by allowing them to sue, so to speak, a central person, [so] that they do not have to sue the supplier of the particular service, in this case the hotel in the country of domicile of the hotel which in this case would have been Spain. They can sue the organiser. And the Section says that the remedy or right of action the organiser may have against the retailer or other supplier of services is not in any way affected".*

He found that the Directive was sufficiently clear on its wording so as not to require him to embark on a purposive interpretation of it. He continued:

> *"So although in this case Falcon Leisure Group (Overseas) Ltd could be said to have done nothing wrong whatsoever [nevertheless] because of the business which they are in, that is organising and selling package tours, they have to accept as one of the downsides of that, that they will be responsible if somebody providing a [service] does not properly perform the contract. In this case it would have been clearly an implied term of the contract, if not an express term, that the place provided where the ladies were to stay under the package holiday would be safe and would be kept safe"*

The High Court judge found that the legislative scheme has as its consequence that the organiser *"though not in any way to blame himself, must shoulder the position of defendant to the plaintiff and then recoup their losses from the actual tortfeasor or the person who is the contract breaker, in this case the provider of the service".*

The High Court judge determined that according to the Act of 1995, the defendant was liable for the wrongful acts of the hotel owner, being the latter's improper performance of one of the obligations under the package holiday agreement and that the plaintiff was entitled to recover from the defendant, by virtue of Section 20 of the Act of 1995, damages in respect of the injuries sustained by her. From that judgment the defendant has appealed to this court.

The Appeal

Senior counsel Mr Counihan, on behalf of the appellant argues that Article 5 of the Directive, and therefore S. 20 of the Act of 1995, and was never intended to harmonise the law of torts relating to accidents causing injury, but only the law relating to obligations arising under a "package holiday" contract itself, so as to ensure the proper performance of the obligations undertaken. Section 20 of the Act of 1995 does not equate the proper performance of those obligations with their perfect performance. He submits that the learned High Court judge misdirected himself in law in holding the appellant was liable, because Section 20 of the Act of 1995 does not cover what he calls an event of "casual" negligence, such as occurred in the present case and about which the appellant could have no knowledge and over which it could have no control, within the meaning of S.20(2)(C)(ii) of the Act of 1995. Although he accepts that, according to the scheme provided for in the Directive and the Act of 1995, in which there is an organiser, a consumer, and other suppliers of services which the organiser has undertaken contractually to provide to the consumer, the correct interpretation of Section 20 of the Act of 1995, he argues, is to make the appellant liable to the respondent only where the supplier of the service, that is to say, the hotel owner in Spain, would have been liable to the respondent were it not for the existence of the scheme established by the Directive and the Act of 1995. It follows that the Act of 1995 cannot be understood as providing that the appellant is to be made liable to the respondent merely because the former's right of action over against a non performing service supplier, such as the hotel, is enshrined in the Act of 1995.

Further, counsel submits that none of the recitals to, nor Article 5 of, the Directive provides that the protection afforded to a consumer is to constitute a form of insurance or guarantee on the part of an organiser. Therefore the principle of strict or absolute liability which he argues the High Court judge adopted, cannot apply to the appellant in respect of every injury howsoever caused to a consumer such as the respondent who undertakes a package holiday. The Act of 1995 must be understood as providing for liability on the part of the appellant only if there has been fault on the part of the hotel owner in Spain leading to the improper performance of the particular obligation in the contract. The respondent must first therefore establish that there was such a failure on the part of the hotel owner or operator in this case to perform an obligation under the contract. The mere fact that there was a spillage of food upon which the respondent then fell does not, ipso facto, establish that either the hotel failed properly to perform obligations arising under the contract. Counsel for the appellant argues that, for the purposes of determining the liability imposed on him for wrongful acts of a service supplier such as the hotel pursuant to Section 20 of the Act of 1995, it is not possible to discern whether the standard to be imposed on the hotel owner or proprietor for whose acts the appellant is being sought to be made liable, is the Irish legal standard or the Spanish legal standard, but that it must be the latter, being the standard governing the place where the accident occurred.

Senior Counsel Mr McGovern for the respondent, clarifies that he does not contend that S.20 of the Act of 1995, and by implication, Article 5 of the Directive, imposes strict liability on an organiser such as the appellant for the breach of obligations by a service supplier, in all circumstances. He submits that the effect of Section 20 of the Act of 1995 implementing the Directive is to place primary liability on the appellant for the proper performance of the obligations comprised in the contract "package", whether the obligations are to be performed by him or by others, such as the hotel owner in Spain. The appellant can escape liability only in the limited circumstances identified in Section 20(2) of the Act of 1995, that is to say, only if the events in question could not have been foreseen or forestalled by the appellant or the hotel owner. He submits that the intention to protect the consumer in circumstances such as the present is reinforced by the provisions of Section 20(2) of the Act of 1995.

Finally, he argues that, since the contract provided for travel, accommodation, and the provision of meals on a half board basis, it was an implied term of the contract between the appellant and the respondent that all services and facilities would be provided with reasonable skill and care and to a reasonable standard, and they were not. He reminded this Court that the High Court judge had found that, on the evidence, the hotel had been very satisfactory in all respects on an earlier occasion when the respondent had stayed there, but not on the occasion in question, in that any system which might ordinarily have operated in the hotel to avoid or minimize accidents, had not operated appropriately or properly on the occasion in question, for which the appellant, as organiser, was liable under the Act of 1995.

Each of the parties to the proceedings has invoked Irish and United Kingdom case law in support of their respective submissions. This case law is considered further below.

Conclusion

For the purposes of this judgment, it is essential first to set out the provisions of Section 20 of the Act of 1995 which transposed into Irish law the relevant corresponding provisions of the Directive.

The Act of 1995 has as its long title, the following:

> *"An Act to enable effect to be given to Council Directive No. 90/314/EEC of 13 June 1990 of the European Communities on package travel, package holidays and package tours, to amend the Transport (Tour Operators and Travel Agents) Act 1982, and to provide for connected matters".*

Article 5 of the Directive is transposed by the provisions of S.20 of the above Act which in its relevant part reads as follows:

> *"20.—(1) The organiser shall be liable to the consumer for the proper performance of the obligations under the contract, irrespective of whether such obligations are to be performed by the organiser, the retailer, or other suppliers of services but this shall not affect any remedy or right of action which the organiser may have against the retailer or those other suppliers of services.*
>
> *(2) The organiser shall be liable to the consumer for any damage caused by the failure to perform the contract or the improper performance of the contract unless the failure or the improper performance is due neither to any fault of the organiser or the retailer nor to that of another supplier of services, because—*
>
> *(a) the failures which occur in the performance of the contract are attributable to the consumer,*
>
> *(b) such failures are attributable to a third party unconnected with the provision of the services contracted for, and are unforeseeable or unavoidable, or*
>
> *(c) such failures are due to—*
>
> *(i) force majeure, that is to say, unusual and unforeseeable circumstances beyond the control of the organiser, the retailer or other supplier of services, the consequences of which could not have been avoided even if all due care had been exercised, or*
>
> *(ii) an event which the organiser, the retailer or the supplier of services, even with all due care, could not foresee or forestall.*

...

> *(8) The provisions of this section are without prejudice to the provisions of the Hotel Proprietors Act, 1963."* (emphasis added)

The Hotel Proprietors Act 1963, referred to in S.20(8) is an Act which legislates for certain rights and obligations concerning hotel proprietors and guests of a hotel. The relevant provision of this Act is the following:

> *"4(1) Where a person is received as a guest at a hotel, whether or not under special contract, the proprietor of the hotel is under a duty to take reasonable care of the person of the guest and to ensure that, for the purpose of personal use by the guest, the premises are as safe as reasonable care and skill can make them".*

The Occupiers Liability Act 1995 is an Act which legislates for certain rights and obligations concerning occupiers of premises and visitors to those premises. Section 3 of that Act provides as follows:

> *(1) An occupier of premises owes a duty of care ("the common duty of care") towards a visitor thereto except in so far as the occupier extends, restricts, modifies or excludes that duty in accordance with section 5.*

> *(2) In this section "the common duty of care" means a duty to take such care as is reasonable in all the circumstances (having regard to the care which a visitor may reasonably be expected to take for his or her own safety and, if the visitor is on the premises in the company of another person, the extent of the supervision and control the latter person may reasonably be expected to exercise over the visitor's activities) to ensure that a visitor to the premises does not suffer injury or damage by reason of any danger existing thereon."*

As concerns the Directive itself, since Section 20 of the Act of 1995 faithfully transposes the provisions of Article 5 of the Directive, it is not necessary to set out the terms of that Article separately. It is, however, relevant to cite Article 8 of the Directive which reads:

> *"Member States may adopt or retain more stringent provisions in the field covered by this Directive to protect the consumer."*

It seems to me that the provisions of the Hotel Proprietors Act 1963 are within the ambit of Article 8 of the Directive since the obligation concerning the state of hotel or other premises, as well as the safety of guests, are provisions protecting the consumer which are or may be, more stringent than the provisions of the Directive. Similarly, apart from the statutory protection given to hotel guests as set forth above, and as specifically retained by the Act of 1995, an occupier's common law liability to visitors, now enshrined in S.3 of the Occupiers Liability Act 1995, may well also fall within Article 8 of the Directive, even if not specifically referred to in the Act of 1995. Having regard to Mr. Counihan's argument for the appellant, that the appropriate standard for the High Court to have applied is the standard operating in Spain and not the standard in Ireland, the question arises as to whether the High Court judge was entitled to invoke the standard operating by virtue, inter alia, of the above sections of the above Acts or the established common law tests.

Section 20 of the Act of 1995

Section 20(1) of the Act of 1995 expressly makes the organiser primarily liable to the consumer, and maintains a right of action over in favour of the organiser against the service supplier, in the present case a supplier with whom the appellant entered into arrangements for the provision to the respondent of hotel accommodation in Spain on a half board basis. What requires to be determined is what is meant by "improper performance" of an obligation, and the consequent extent or scope of the liability of the appellant, as organiser, to the respondent, as consumer.

First, it is appropriate to have regard to the wording of the legislation. On a plain reading of this, it seems to me that the correct meaning to be attached to the combination of subsections 20(1) and (2) of the Act of 1995 is that when contractual obligations are assumed by an organiser-the appellant in this case-as part of a "package holiday" contract entered into with a consumer, such as the respondent in the present case, those obligations to the consumer remain the organiser's obligations, and do not become the independent obligations of the service supplier, such as the hotel in Spain, to the consumer. The Section speaks of (a) the obligations under the contract; (b) irrespective of whether those obligations i.e. the organiser's obligations, are to be performed by the organiser himself, or (whether such obligations) are to be performed by other suppliers of services; and (c) a right of action over is maintained by the organiser against such other supplier(s) for the latter's failure to perform the organiser's contracted for obligations. Thus, when the consumer – the respondent in this appeal – enters into the agreement, it may well be that some of the organiser's contractual obligations will be performed by other persons, such as hotel proprietors, even in another Member State. That, however, does not change the relationship between the organiser and the consumer, who frequently will not even know the name of the supplier of the services not being performed by the organiser himself.

This is why, when considering the meaning of Section 20(2) of the Act of 1995 (Article 5.2 of the Directive), that organiser's liability continues to exist "unless" there is to be no fault on his part "because" the failure was due to an event which "the organiser or the supplier of service, even with all due care, could not foresee or forestall." Apart from such excusing circumstances, it seems to me that the organiser remains at all times liable to the consumer for the wrongful acts in question. If it be the case that the organiser wishes to invoke the defence available in subsection 20(2)(c)(ii) of the Act of 1995, it is for him to establish that there was no such fault either on his own part or on the part of a supplier of the service which he has engaged, once a failure to perform is established by the consumer.

On the questions raised by Mr. Counihan as to the standard to be applied and as to whether the respondent discharged the burden of proof in this case, it is useful first to consider the Irish and United Kingdom cases on the appropriate test or standard to be applied, and which have been invoked by both parties. In Ireland, prior to the passing of the Act of 1995, the case law establishes that the standard of reasonable skill and care is appropriate in assessing the performance of services for the purpose of establishing whether there has been a breach of contract or that a party is liable to another in tort. In *McKenna v Best Travel Ltd.* [1998] I.R. 57, a case whose events predated the transposition of the Directive, an appeal was taken to the Supreme Court on a limited point of law as to whether the defendant tour organiser was liable in tort for failure to give a warning in respect of conditions in Israel which the customer was visiting as part of a holiday. The claim was originally founded both in contract and in tort. The High Court judge had found that there had been no breach of contract but a breach of duty in tort to the customer. In the course of his judgment on the appeal to this court, Barron, J. stated:

> *"The duty of care in tort arises from the proximity creased by the contractual relationship. The duty extends to all matters concerning the safety, well being and comfort of the tourists which by the nature of the relationship between the tourists and those providing the service would or should be known to the latter but not to the former. ... The defendants in this case were not insurers that nothing would happen to injure the plaintiff. Their obligation stops at taking all reasonable steps to ensure the safety and well being of their customers. ... The test is what a reasonably prudent tour operator exercising reasonable care would consider necessary to inform those travelling with it."*

The first of the English cases cited to this court is *Hone v Going Places Leisure Travel,* unreported, 13 June 2001, [2001], a decision of the English Court of Appeal. There the plaintiff, in the course of an emergency crash landing in which passengers had to disembark from the aeroplane by emergency chute, being unable to avoid colliding into another passenger who was stationery at the bottom of the chute, was in turn struck by the next passenger exiting the aeroplane, and suffered damage to his spine. He sued the defendant under United Kingdom legislation corresponding to the Act of 1995. He alleged there was a failure to perform, or an improper performance, of the contract because, inter alia, there was no trained personnel at the top or bottom of the emergency chute and no instructions to passenger to remove footwear or to use the chute only when it was clear of other passengers. He also claimed that the United Kingdom Regulations, which transposed the Directive more or less verbatim, imposed a strict liability test on the organiser, subject only to the defences found in the Regulations, which mirror those in Section 20(2) of the Act of 1995.

The High Court judge held there that it was for the plaintiff to show that there was improper performance, and in the context of that case, this meant he had to show that his injuries were attributable to the fault of someone supplying services in relation to the package tour. Liability was thus not absolute or strict, subject to certain exceptions. The judge also held that the plaintiff had, in that case, wholly failed to establish that the accident was anyone's fault. The plaintiff was given leave to appeal to the Court of Appeal on the single question whether the English Regulations transposing the Directive imposed strict liability.

In the Court of Appeal, Longmore, L.J. found that it is necessary frequently to imply a term as to the standard of performance, since the requirement will not normally be set out in any detail in a contract, and that the normal implication will be that the service contracted for will be rendered with reasonable skill and care, unless absolute obligations are assumed (for example the provision of a hotel specifically with a swimming pool). Whereas previously at common law it was controversial as to whether a travel agent himself assumed the relevant contractual responsibility, or only agreed to put the customer into contractual relations with the actual provider of the service, this situation is now resolved by the Regulations. The United Kingdom Regulations do not give any guidance as to the extent of the obligation. However the judge found that the case of *Wong Wee Wan v Kwan Kin Travel Services Ltd* [1996] *1 WLR* 38 was a good example of the approach of the common law on both questions. In that case it was held that a term was to be implied into the contract that reasonable skill and care would be used in the rendering of the services which the travel agent had contracted to provide, whether carried out by him or by someone else.

Longmore, L.J. stated that it was not possible to determine whether a particular complaint founds improper performance, by reference to the Regulations themselves. He stated:

> *"To my mind Regulation 15(2) does not give the answer to the question "What is improper performance?" Rather it is a requirement of the application of Regulation 15(2) that there should be improper performance. That can only be determined by reference to the terms of the contract. There may be absolute obligations ..., but in the absence of the assumption of an absolute obligation, the implication will be that reasonable skill and care will be used in the rendering of the relevant service. There will thus be no improper performance of the air carriage unless there is an absence of reasonable skill and care in the provision of that service. If, as here, it is the claimant who seeks to rely on regulation 15(2), then he has to show that there has been improper performance.*
> *Mr. Dean submits that there was improper performance because the parties expected that the air carriage would be safely executed. That would only be the position if there were a term of the contract that the air carriage would be safely executed. For my part, I do not consider that there was any such absolute term. In the absence of an express agreement, the implication was that the air carriage would be performed with skill and care."* (emphasis added)

The above case of *Wong Mee Wan v Kwan Kin Travel Services Limited & Ors, supra.*, also cited by both parties before this court, was a case which came on appeal from the Hong Kong Court of Appeal to the Privy Council, and concerned the appropriate standard to be applied in a contract of service, being a package tour of part of mainland China offered by a Hong Kong travel company at an all inclusive price. The main purpose of the tour was to visit a lake in China, and part of the tour consisted of a lake crossing, during which crossing the plaintiff was injured. The Privy Council held that there was an implied term of the contract that the services would be carried out with reasonable skill and care. This term did not mean that the defendant undertook to ensure the safety of the plaintiff or of the component parts of the package, or that the plaintiff's daughter would be reasonably safe. It was a term that reasonable skill and care would be used in rendering the services to be provided. The trip had not been carried out with reasonable skill and care in that no steps had been taken to see that the driver of the speedboat was of reasonable competence and experience and the first defendant was liable for such breach of contract.

On the question that such a term would impose an intolerable burden on package tour operators, Lord Slynn of Hadley. stated:

> *"It must be borne in mind that the tour operator has the opportunity to seek to protect himself against claims made against him in respect of services performed by others by negotiating suitable contractual terms with those who are to perform those services. He may also provide for insurance cover. ... It also has to be borne in mind, in considering what is 'tolerable' or reasonable between the parties, that the traveller in the position of Miss Ho Shui Yee could have no influence on the terms negotiated by the tour operator with third*

parties, and if injured by their lack of care would, if having no right against the package tour operator, be obliged to pursue a claim in a foreign country. The difficulty involved in doing so does not need to be elaborated. In considering what is or is not tolerable as between traveller and tour operator it is of some relevance to note the Package Travel, Package Holiday and Package Tours Regulation 1992 ... made pursuant to Council Directive 90/314 (EC). The organiser or retailer of the package tour –

'15(1) ... is liable to the consumer for the proper performance of the obligations under the contract, irrespective of whether such obligations are to be performed by that other party or by other suppliers of services but this shall not affect any remedy or right of action which that other party may have against those other suppliers of services.

(2) The other party to the contract is liable to the consumer for any damage caused to him by the failure to perform the contract or the improper performance of the contract ...'

...

These terms do not of course apply to the present contract but they do throw some light on the contention that an unreasonable burden would be imposed if the contract were held to contain a term that reasonable skill and care would be used. ..."

The case of *Healy v Cosmoair Plc* [2005] All E.R. 432*),* invoked by Mr. Counihan on behalf of the Appellant, also proceeded on the basis that the standard was that of reasonable skill and care. The technical issue in that case, which depended on Spanish standards applicable to them, concerned only the question of slippiness of tiles. There is no true comparison between the position in the present case and the facts in that latter case. The Respondent invokes that case apparently on the hypothesis firstly that there may be a difference between Irish and Spanish law on the appropriate legal standards governing the safety of hotels for visitors or guests, and on the further hypothesis that it may be the case that the Spanish standard governing the safety of hotel premises is lower than that which is applicable in Irish law, and more easily met by the hotel owner, for there would be no point in the appellant raising such an issue unless that were the case. Apart from the fact that this does not appear to have been an issue in the High Court, there was no evidence to support either hypothesis. Further, the application of a lower standard, if such exists in respect of the safety of hotels in Spain, might not necessarily comply with the provisions of the Directive. In that regard, the following extract from the Opinion of Advocat General Tizzano in the case of *Leitner v TUI Deutschland GmbH & Co. KG,* a case invoked by both parties, is telling:

"More specifically, I note that, in the event of any doubt, the provisions of the Directive in question must be interpreted in the manner most favourable to the person whom they are intended to protect, namely the consumer of the tourism service. That may be inferred not only from the systematic analysis of the text and aims of the Directive, but also from the abovementioned fact that it was adopted pursuant to Article 100a, paragraph 3 of which requires that harmonisation measures in respect of consumer protection should be based on a high level of protection."

The conclusions to be drawn from all of the above cited cases are that, both before and after the coming into force of the Directive and its transposition in national law, the established principle is that the organiser is not an insurer to the customer. The learned High Court judge correctly found that the hotel proprietor was not such an insurer under the legislation. The above cases also establish the principle that the test is not one of strict liability, and in that regard I am satisfied also that the High Court judge's finding, when correctly read, was not that strict liability applied. The final principle clearly established by those cases is that the standard by which the acts in question are to be judged is that of reasonable skill and care, which standard, if not expressed in a contract will be readily implied into it. In the circumstances, I am satisfied that the reasonable skill and care test generally applicable according to the above case law and by statute, and applied by the learned High Court judge, was the correct test in law.

There remains only the question as to whether the plaintiff established that there was a failure to perform an obligation under the contract on the part of the hotel proprietor in Spain by reference to that test of reasonable skill and care. I reject the appellant's argument that the extent of the liability on the organiser under a contract of this nature is confined, so far as hotel premises are concerned, to ensuring that the structure itself is safe. The contract here was for travel and hotel accommodation on a half board basis, and the latter clearly included the provision of an evening meal as a necessary ancillary part of the accommodation service provided. An implied term that the same would be furnished with reasonable skill and care follows from my earlier findings. The learned High Court judge heard and accepted the evidence of the plaintiff and others as to the following facts: (b) there was evidence of a liquid substance being on the hard marble floor measuring about 30 inches in diameter which, from its description, could properly be found by him to be a soup or a sauce which had fallen on the floor and on which the plaintiff slipped; (c) the nature of the spillage was such that it must have been caused by staff clearing away foodstuffs, it being evident that they were doing just that when the accident occurred; (d) it was not possible for the plaintiff, while navigating past a pillar where the spillage had occurred, to have seen it or to have had any opportunity to avoid it, (a fact now accepted by the defendant); (e) the spillage had not been removed when the respondent went towards it; (a) there was no warning or other indication by means of any crash of utensils, for example, such that might have put the plaintiff on notice that something untoward had occurred; and (f) there was no barrier or tape or other item placed around the area, if there had been insufficient time for the hotel staff to remove the spillage before the Plaintiff suffered the accident . Moreover, when the accident did occur, it is unchallenged that there was an immediate direction to the staff to bring buckets of sawdust or some such absorption material, to where the spillage took place to cover it and sweep away the debris. It is telling that this was done on the instructions of the Manager of the hotel, for it clearly follows that the spillage could have been readily taken care of, and that the hotel had a system in place for dealing with just such an event, and was able to do in the normal course of events, but had not done so on the occasion in question, prior to the respondent falling.

Having regard to the foregoing, the learned trial judge had before him evidence that the accident was a wholly foreseeable event on the part of the service supplier, the hotel in Spain, that they had in place a system which could have warned of the hazard and/or prevented the accident, but had not operated that system on the evening in question. In the circumstances, the learned High Court judge was entitled to find that the service in question was not supplied with reasonable skill and care. He was therefore correct to find for the Plaintiff.

I would dismiss the appeal and affirm the order of the High Court.

Smith v Meade

[2009] IEHC 99

Author's note: *Smith v Meade* concerns the use of the doctrine of indirect effect to affect a contract. It forms part of the Motor Insurance Directives saga.

Judgment delivered by Mr. Justice Michael Peart delivered on the 5th day of February 2009

The plaintiff was injured on the 19th June 1999 when the car in which he was a passenger, which was owned by the second defendant, and being driven by the first defendant, was in collision with another vehicle due, it is alleged, to the negligence of the first named defendant.

The part of this vehicle where the plaintiff was when this accident occurred had not been designed and constructed with seating accommodation for passengers.

There was in existence a compulsory insurance policy in respect of this vehicle which the second named defendant had taken out with the third named defendant "FBD", whereby that body was required to provide an indemnity in respect of loss and damage sustained by third parties as a consequence of any negligence, breach of duty and breach of statutory duty by the second named defendant and any persons driving the vehicle with his consent and authority.

FBD has declined to provide an indemnity to the second named defendant in respect of the plaintiff's injuries, on the basis that the policy in question does not cover liability in respect of personal injuries to persons being carried as a passenger in a part of the vehicle which was not designed and constructed with seating accommodation for passengers.

In its Defence FBD has pleaded that the policy of insurance taken out by the second named defendant does not cover the plaintiff's loss because the vehicle in question was a van and that the plaintiff was travelling as a passenger in the rear of the van where there were no seats for passengers. It pleads also that at all material times FBD complied with its obligations under the Road Traffic Acts and under S.I. 346 and 347 of 1992. It relies upon the provisions of s.65 (1) (a) of the Road Traffic Act, 1961, as amended by Article 7 of S.I. 347of 1992. Section 65 of the Act provides a definition of "excepted person" i.e. persons whose injuries are not required to be covered in a policy of insurance. That amended section provides:

> *"65. – (1) (a) Any person claiming injury to himself sustained while he was in or on a mechanically propelled vehicle (or a vehicle drawn thereby) to which the relevant document relates, other than a mechanically propelled vehicle, or a drawn vehicle, or vehicles forming a combination of vehicles, of a class specified for the purposes of this paragraph by regulations made by the Minister, provided that such regulations shall not extend compulsory insurance in respect of civil liability to passengers to –*
>
> *(i) any part of a mechanically propelled vehicle, other than a large public service vehicle, unless that part is designed and constructed with seating accommodation for passengers, or*
>
> *(ii) a passenger seated in a caravan attached to a mechanically propelled vehicle while such a combination of vehicles is moving in a public place."*

FBD submits that the plaintiff is therefore an excepted person, and one in respect of whose injury while a passenger it was not required by law to cover the liability of the first and second named defendants.

The policy of insurance taken out by the second named defendant provided, inter alia, that "passenger cover only operates for one passenger seated on a fixed seat in the front of the vehicle".

The preliminary issue for decision at this point ahead of the hearing of the plaintiff's claim for damages for his injuries is whether or not the clause in the policy upon which FBD seek to rely in order to decline an indemnity to the first and second defendants in respect of any liability they may be found to have to the plaintiff is in fact void, having regard to certain EU Directives and certain judgments of the European Court of Justice. I will come to those in due course. In the event that the Court concludes that this clause is not void, certain other issues arise such as whether the plaintiff has a claim against the fourth named defendant arising from what is submitted would have been a failure, neglect or refusal to transpose these Directives into Irish law as of the date of the collision in which the plaintiff was injured, the 31st December 1998 being the date by which the fourth named defendant was required to have transposed same into Irish law.

...

Article 1 of Council Directive of 14th May 1990 (90/232/EEC) (hereinafter referred to as "the Third Directive")

"Without prejudice to the second subparagraph of Article 2 (1) of Directive 84/5/EEC, the insurance referred to in Article 3 (1) of Directive 72/166/EEC shall cover liability for personal injuries to all passengers, other than the driver, arising out of the use of a vehicle." (my emphasis)

In addition to Article 1 thereof, Mr Collins has referred to certain recitals in the Third Directive which state that motor accident victims should be guaranteed comparable treatment irrespective of where in the European Community accidents occur, and note that there are gaps in the compulsory insurance cover of motor vehicle passengers in certain Member States and that, in order to protect "this particularly vulnerable category of potential victims" such gaps should be filled. Other recitals therein state that the first and second directives should be supplemented in a uniform manner, and that such an addition which leads to greater protection for the parties insured and for the victims of accidents, will facilitate still further the crossing of internal Community frontiers and hence the establishment and functioning of the internal market.

Mr Collins has referred to the fact that in its judgment in *Ruiz Bernáldez* [1996] E.C.R.I-1829 at paragraphs 16 and 18 the Court of Justice has observed:

> "16. *In order to reduce the disparities which continued to exist between the laws of the Member States with respect to the extent of the obligation of insurance cover (third recital in the preamble to the Second Directive), Article 1 of the Second Directive required compulsory cover, as regards civil liability, for both damage to property and personal injuries, up to specified sums. Article 1 of the third Directive extended that obligation to cover for personal injuries to passengers other than the driver.*
> 18. *In view of the aim of ensuring protection, stated repeatedly in the directives, Article 3 (1) of the First Directive, as developed and supplemented by the Second and Third Directives, must be interpreted as meaning that compulsory motor insurance must enable third party victims of accidents caused by vehicles to be compensated for all the damage to property and personal injuries sustained by them, up to amounts fixed in Article 1 (2) of the Second Directive."*

Mr Collins has referred to the fact that the Road Traffic (Compulsory Insurance) (Amendment) Regulations 1992 (S.I. No. 346 of 1992) and the European Communities (Road Traffic) (Compulsory Insurance) (Amendment) Regulations 1992 (S.I. 347 of 1992), which purported to transpose the Third Directive into Irish law, expressly excluded passengers in the rear of vehicles not generally designed or constructed to carry passengers from the scope of compulsory third party motor insurance.

By way of submission that the Third Directive has not been properly transposed into Irish law, and also that the exclusion clause at issue in these proceedings is void, has referred to the judgment of the Court of Justice in *Farrell v. Whitty* [2007] E.C.R. I-3067 arising from a reference for a preliminary ruling under Article 234 EC by the High Court here concerning the interpretation of Article 1 of the Third Directive. The plaintiff in that case had been travelling in a van which was not designed and constructed for the carriage of passengers in the rear of the vehicle. She had been seated on the floor of the van behind the front seats thereof. The driver was not insured, but the MIBI had refused to compensate her since she was travelling in that way, and that her injuries were not therefore a liability for which insurance was compulsory under the Road Traffic Act, 1961. Firstly it was pointed out that Article 1 provides that compulsory insurance is to cover liability for personal injuries to "all passengers, other than the driver". Secondly it was stated that it would be contrary to the objectives of the Community legislation to exclude from the concept of 'passenger' and thus from insurance persons such as the plaintiff in that case, and therefore the plaintiff in the present proceedings, and that such an interpretation had been confirmed by the case-law of the Court. The Court stated that "*Article 1 of the Third Directive is to be interpreted as precluding national legislation whereby compulsory motor vehicle liability insurance does not cover liability in respect of personal injuries to persons travelling in a part of a motor vehicle which has not been designed and constructed with seating accommodation for passengers*". The Court went on to state that Article 1 of the Third Directive has direct effect, the criteria of unconditionality and sufficient precision being satisfied.

Mr Collins submits that FBD cannot rely on the exclusion clause in the policy of insurance in this case, and thereby refuse to indemnify the first and second named defendants in respect of the plaintiff's injuries, and in support refers to the judgment of the Court of Justice in *Ruiz Bernáldez* [supra]. That case is factually different to the present case in so far as the exclusion clause sought to be relied upon so as to absolve the insurance company in question was one that excluded damage to property caused where the driver of the vehicle was intoxicated. Nevertheless, the questions asked by the national court and the Court's judgment speak to the issue in the present proceedings. The judgment of the Court states:

> "*By Questions 1 to 4, which may be considered together, the national court seeks to ascertain whether Article 3 (1) of the First Directive is to be interpreted as meaning that, without prejudice to the provisions of Article 2 (1) of the Second Directive, a compulsory insurance contract may provide that in certain cases, in particular where the driver of the vehicle was intoxicated, the insurer is not obliged to pay compensation for the personal injuries and damage to property caused to third parties by the insured vehicle, or whether in such cases the compulsory insurance contract may provide only that the insurer is to have a right of recovery against the insured.*"

I have already set out what the Court stated at paragraphs 16 and 18 of its judgment, and at paragraph 24 of its judgment, the Court concluded as follows:

> "*The answer to Questions 1 to 4 must therefore be that Article 3 (1) of the First Directive is to be interpreted as meaning that, without prejudice to the provisions of Article 2 (1) of the Second Directive, a compulsory insurance contract may not provide that in certain cases, in particular where the driver of the vehicle was intoxicated, the insurer is not obliged to pay compensation for the damage to property and personal injuries caused to third parties by the insured vehicle. It may on the other hand provide that in such cases the insurer is to have the right of recover against the insured.*"

Mr Collins in addition has referred to passages from the Opinion of Advocate General Lenz in the same case delivered on the 25th January 1996. I do not feel it necessary to set these out in my judgment.

FBD's legal submissions

The Court has received very helpful submissions on behalf of the Third named defendant from both Patrick Connolly SC and Anthony Kidney SC. They have highlighted the fact that the Third Directive was not transposed into Irish law by the date limited for such transposition, namely 31st December 1995, and that FBD in issuing the policy of insurance to the second named defendant, it did so in accordance with the statutory regime in place here as of the date of issue, and in compliance therefore with S.I. 346 of 1992 and S.I. 347 of 1992. In such circumstances, it is submitted, FBD was not required to provide insurance cover in respect of injuries caused to any passenger travelling "*in any part of a mechanically propelled vehicle . . . unless that part is designed and constructed with seating accommodation for passengers*", and in these proceedings are entitled to rely upon that exclusion clause in order to decline an indemnity to the first and second named defendants in respect of the plaintiff's injuries.

It is submitted on behalf of FBD that since it had operated in accordance with the statutory regime in place when it issued this policy to the second named defendant, the plaintiff's remedy is against the fourth named defendant on the basis of a failure to transpose the Third Directive into Irish law by the required date, in accordance with so-called Frankovich principles. It is submitted also that in so far as this Third Directive may have direct effect, it does so against the State and any emanation of the State only, and not against FBD which, it is accepted, is not an emanation of the State. Having referred to judgments of the Court of Justice in cases *Marshall v. Southampton & South-West Hampshire Area Health Authority* (Case 152/84) [1986] ECR 723, and *Faccini Dori v. Receb Srl* (Case C-91/92) [1994] ECR I-3325, Mr Connolly has referred to the judgment of the Court of Justice in *Whitty v. Farrell* [supra] and to what is stated at paragraph thereof in relation to Question 2 in the preliminary reference submitted to the Court by the High Court as to whether individuals may rely directly upon Article 1 of the Third Directive before the national courts. In that regard the Court of Justice stated at paras. 37 – 40 of its judgment:

> "*37. . . . . it should be pointed out that it has consistently been held that a provision in a directive has direct effect if it appears, as far as its subject-matter is concerned, to be unconditional and sufficiently precise . . . .*
>
> *38. It must be held in the present case that, as the Commission argues, those criteria are satisfied by Article 1 of the Third Directive. That article allows both the obligation of the Member State and the beneficiaries to be identified, and its provisions are unconditional and precise. Article 1 of the Third Directive may accordingly be relied upon in order to set aside provisions of national law which exclude from the benefit of the guarantee provided by compulsory insurance cove persons travelling in any part of a vehicle which is not designed and constructed with seating accommodation for passengers.*
>
> 39. *The question remains whether that provision may be relied on against a body such as the MIBI.*
>
> 40. *A directive cannot be relied on against individuals, whereas it may be relied upon as against the State, regardless of the capacity in which the latter is acting, that is to say, whether as employer or as public authority. The entities against which the provisions of a directive that are capable of having direct effect may be relied upon include a body, whatever its legal form, which has been made responsible, pursuant to a measure adopted by the State, for providing a public service under the control of the State and has for that purpose special powers beyond those which result from the normal rules applicable in relations between individuals. . . . . . ." (my emphasis)*

It is paragraph 40 above upon which Mr Connolly has placed particular reliance.

In these circumstances Mr Connolly has submitted that the consequence of the State's failure to transpose the Third Directive is not one which can be visited upon FBD, that entity not being an emanation of the State, and that the appropriate remedy, given the direct effect nature of the

Directive, is one against the State only, since all FBD has done is issue a policy of insurance permitted under the laws of the State at the time that the policy issued to the second named defendant.

In further submissions on behalf of FBD, Anthony Kidney SC referred the Court to a judgment of the Court of Justice delivered on 24th July 2003 in *Viegas v. Companhia de Seguras Zurich SA* (Case C-166/02) where at paragraph 23 the Court stated:

> "*The Court has consistently held that the obligation of national courts to disapply national legislation contrary to a directive does not have the effect of enabling it to impose on an individual an obligation laid down by a directive which has not been transposed* ...".

Mr Kidney relies on this passage in support of the submission by FBD that where the State has failed to transpose the Third Directive by the time limited for so doing, any consequence resulting to the plaintiff by reason of the first and second named defendants being denied an indemnity by FBD in respect of the plaintiff's injuries, cannot be visited upon FBD, but must result in a claim against the State for failure to so transpose the Directive.

In response to these submissions, Mr Collins has submitted that the question of direct effect is not the real issue in this case. He accepts that if direct effect was the beginning and end of the question to be determined, the plaintiff would have no case to make against FBD. He submits that quite apart from any question of direct effect, it is a principle of community law that individuals are entitled to rely upon community law rights in national courts in certain circumstances against private individuals on the basis of the principle of the primacy of community law.

...

Mr Collins submits that accordingly this Court must, on the basis of primacy of community law, and the case-law of the Court of Justice to which he has referred, give to the plaintiff the benefit of the Directives in play in this case as against FBD, even though they do not enjoy direct effect, by holding that the clause sought to be relied upon as excluding an indemnity is void in the light of the wording and purpose of the Directives, and particularly the Third Directive.

...

Hugh Mohan SC also supports the plaintiff's submissions in addition to making other submissions relating, inter alia, the entitlement of the plaintiff to seek redress against the State in the event that he cannot recover against FBD, and whether FBD are entitled to any indemnity from the State in the event of it being found liable to the plaintiff. I do not need to set out these submissions in detail, and I intend no disrespect to any of these submissions by not doing so. Eileen Barrington BL has also made submissions on behalf of the fourth and fifth submissions which largely support the submissions of Mr Collins in relation to harmonious interpretation and the judgment of the Court of Justice in Marleasing.

Conclusions

The relevant facts in this case are not in dispute. There is no doubt that the policy of insurance taken out by the second named defendant with FBD excluded any indemnity in respect of this plaintiff's injuries as he was seated in the rear part of this vehicle which was not fitted with a seat. FBD has by letter dated 13th August 2001 invoked that clause and has denied to provide such indemnity.

There is no dispute either that at the date of this accident, 19th June 1999, the Third Directive had not been transposed into Irish law, and that the time by which such transposition was to have taken place had by then passed.

It is also clear from the case-law of the Court of Justice to which I have been referred that the Third Directive has direct effect, but in that regard direct effect does not provide a remedy as against an individual such as FBD, but rather against the State or any emanation of the State. That is accepted by the plaintiff. Some submissions have been made as to the possibility that the plaintiff could pursue a remedy against FBD on the basis of a horizontal direct effect or indirect effect, but it is in my view unnecessary to reach a conclusion in that regard.

In my view the conclusion to the issue for determination in this case is reached by the route of harmonious interpretation and the primacy of community law, as submitted by Mr Collins and Ms. Barrington, and in that regard the position seems clear. When one reads the three directives, including the recitals thereto, which are in play in this case, the objectives sought to be achieved is very clear. Those objectives have been explained in the cases to which the Court has also been referred and I have set out certain of the passages to which I have been referred.

All passengers being carried in vehicles and who are injured as a result are intended to be guaranteed equal treatment throughout the European Community regardless of in which Member State the injury is caused. The Second Directive required each member state to take necessary measures to ensure that any statutory provision or any contractual clause contained in an insurance policy which excludes from insurance persons, inter alia, such as this plaintiff shall for the purpose of Article 3 (1) of the First Directive be void. I should perhaps note that this obligation is one imposed upon Member States i.e. to put measures in place to so ensure. The Directive does not itself state that such a clause is void. Nevertheless the objective is clear. The amendment to s. 65 of the Road Traffic Act, 1961 which I have set forth above is clearly in conflict with these objectives, and the failure to transpose the Third Directive by the date required has meant that on the date of the accident in which the plaintiff received his injuries, the law of this State was out of line with what was required by community law.

I have set out the relevant passage from the Court of Justice's judgment in Marleasing. It requires a national court, when applying national law, to do so as far as possible in the light of the wording and purpose of the directive in order to pursue the result sought to be pursued by the directive. It seems inescapable that in the present case this Court is required to read s. 65 of the Act as amended by S.I. 346 and 347 of 1992 by overlooking or ignoring the exclusion permitted therein in respect of liability for injuries caused to persons such as the plaintiff in this case. It seems to follow inevitably from this that the Court must conclude that the clause to that effect contained in the policy of insurance by the second named defendant must be regarded as void, therefore disentitling FBD from relying upon it in order to refuse to indemnify the first and second named defendants in respect of the plaintiff's claim for damages for his injuries and loss, in the event that he is found at hearing to have so suffered as a result of the negligence of the first named defendant. I so find.

INDEX